## DATE DUE

| | |
|---|---|
| APR 18 1995 | |
| DEC 0 8 1995 | |
| MAY 18 1996 | |
| MAR 23 1998 | |
| | |
| MAY 20 1998 | |
| MAY 10 1999 | |
| NOV 24 1999 | |
| DEC 8 2000 | |
| DEC 21 2001 OCT 29 2002 | |
| NOV 25 2003 | |
| | |
| | |
| | |

# ALCOHOL

## SECOND EDITION

## BRENT Q. HAFEN

Department of Health Sciences
Brigham Young University

**with**

**Molly J. Brog**

WEST PUBLISHING COMPANY
St. Paul • New York • Los Angeles • San Francisco

## Photo Credits

Strix Pix; xii, 62, 82, 252
Jeff Grosscup; 28, 42, 194,
228, and 264
Dennis Tasa; 100

COPYRIGHT © 1983 By WEST PUBLISHING CO.
                     50 West Kellogg Boulevard
                     P.O. Box 3526
                     St. Paul, Minnesota 55165

Library of Congress Cataloging in Publication Data

Hafen, Brent Q.
    Alcohol.
    Rev. ed. of: Alcohol, the crutch that cripples.
© 1977.
    Bibliography: p.
    Includes index.
1. Alcoholism—United States. 2. Alcohol—Physiological effect. 3. Alcoholism—Treatment. 4. Alcoholism—
Prevention. I. Brog, Molly J. II. Title.
HV5282.H27 1983    362.2'92    82-20270
ISBN 0-314-69652-0

to sylvia, cory, kenneth, jennifer, mark, christy, john, and brad, whose love makes life worthwhile and this work possible.

# Contents

# Preface

"Alcohol has been appreciated, craved, respected, abhorred, and feared, but it has never been thoroughly understood."[1] Alcohol is America's most destructive drug. By whatever standard we assess a drug problem—extent of use and abuse; availability; cost in dollars, disease, crime, and death—alcohol is number one. "In terms of combined physical, mental, social, and economic damages to the body drugs should be ranked in the following order: 1) *alcohol,* 2) barbiturates, 3) amphetamines, 4) heroin and narcotics, 5) cocaine, 6) hallucinogens, 7) marijuana and hashish, 8) solvents, and 9) tobacco."[2]

Alcohol abuse is a national health problem. None other has been so seriously neglected. Facts recently gathered by the National Institute on Alcohol Abuse and Alcoholism are both impressive and depressing. Some of the NIAAA findings are:

1. Alcoholism and alcohol abuse continue to occur at high incident rates in American society.
2. The proportion of American teenagers who drink has been increasing so that currently it is almost universal. The highest scores on an index of probable problem drinking behaviors were recorded in the youngest age group for which data are available—the 18- to 20-year olds.
3. After heart disease and cancer, alcoholism is the country's biggest health problem. An alcoholic's life span is shortened by ten to twelve years, and recently medical researchers have found evidence suggesting that excessive use of alcohol may also quietly contribute to certain kinds of heart disease and that it eventually damages the brain.
4. Excessive use of alcohol, especially when combined with tobacco, has been implicated in the development of certain cancers.
5. Heavy drinking during pregnancy can adversely affect the offspring of alcoholic mothers.
6. The U.S. system of alcoholic controls is a chaotic relic. It provides little support in mitigating alcohol problems and may induce a counterproductive ambivalence in the minds of the public.
7. The economic cost associated with the misuse of alcohol is estimated at $61 billion a year.

[1]Morris E. Chafetz, "Alcohol and Alcoholism," *American Scientist* (May–June 1979): 293.

[2]California Medical Association, "Where We Stand on Drug Abuse," *California Medicine* 118 (June 1973): 58.

8. The public suffers from much ignorance concerning alcohol and from ambivalent feelings toward it. Worse yet, heavier drinkers know less about alcohol than do lighter drinkers or abstainers. In general, American attitudes about drinking are marked by confusion.
9. In half of all the murders in the United States, either the killer or victim or both have been drinking. One-fourth of all suicides are found to have significant amounts of alcohol in their bloodstreams.
10. People who abuse alcohol are seven times as likely to be separated or divorced than the general population.

A recent national public opinion survey by the NIAAA shows that almost two-thirds of adult Americans know someone who "drinks too much." Over one-third of those polled said that this drinker is "close to me" (a relative or friend), and that the problem has existed for at least ten years. The respondents were also shown a list of sixteen leading personal problems and asked whether they knew anyone with these problems. "Excessive drinking" was the fourth most common on the list. Only "excessive smoking," "overeating," and "having trouble making ends meet" were mentioned more frequently. Drinking problems were listed more often than family quarrels, trouble with children, chronic physical and mental illness, loneliness, and job troubles.

Each year over 50,000 Americans die in traffic accidents. About half of those deaths (an estimated 25,000) involve drunk drivers or pedestrians.

About 16 million Americans share alcoholism secondhand because of alcohol problems in their families.

Problem drinking is increasing dramatically among the young. Thousands of problem drinkers are under 21.

Of the approximately 95 to 100 million Americans who drink, one in ten is now either a serious problem drinker or a full-fledged alcoholic.

These are shocking facts, especially in a culture inclined to accept the use of alcohol with little question. Many people have made alcohol a part of their lifestyle in such a way that it has become detrimental to their well-being. But effects of excessive drinking on one individual, tragic as they are, indicate only one aspect of the problem. It is compounded by the effects of that person's behavior on family, friends, fellow workers, and neighbors. In the aggregate, excessive drinking concerns our entire society.

The price we pay for alcohol problems must be counted in terms of the impact on the quality of our lives, not just in terms of the diminished health for those Americans directly affected. Without question, alcoholism seriously and significantly diminishes the quality of life in this country—resulting in wasted resources, the anguish of a family when a spouse with a drinking problem loses status and employment, the misery of the alcoholic, and the painful torment of a battered spouse or abused child. Statistics alone cannot measure the cost in human misery endured by millions of Americans every day and every year.

A nation increasingly concerned with improving the quality of life cannot tolerate a health and social problem of this magnitude that, with increased understanding and commitment, could be controlled. Polio has succumbed to control; heart disease and certain cancers are yielding to concerted efforts. Alcohol abuse and alcoholism—our largest untreated, treatable disease—can also be controlled if we can generate the necessary national commitment.(9)

What can we do? First, existing rehabilitation programs, aimed at both the alcoholic and those around the alcoholic, need improvement. Compassion for the problem drinker must replace disgust and indifference if we are to treat him/her successfully. Even more urgently needed is an understanding of alcohol problems so that we can prevent them. The key to prevention is to help people develop a lifestyle in which chemical intervention is unnecessary. Based on responsibility to self and to society, that lifestyle includes an entire range of responsible alcohol use options, including exclusion of alcohol completely.

The purpose of this book is to help the reader develop an understanding of (1) the use of alcoholic beverages in American society; (2) the physical, emotional and social effects of alcoholic beverages; (3) problem drinking and alcoholism; (4) prevention and treatment of alcohol problems; (5) how to deal with alcohol-induced emergencies; and (6) the laws and regulations concerning alcohol use.

This book draws heavily on research reports published by the National Institute of Mental Health and the NIAAA. The chapter on treatment of alcoholism is almost entirely reprinted from the *Fourth Special Report to the United States Congress on Alcohol and Health* from the Secretary of Health, Education, and Welfare, and is the chapter entitled "Laws, Regulations, and Drinking Patterns." This latter chapter is presented as an overview of the concepts expressed by concerning the control of alcohol-related problems.

Several governmental agencies have prepared materials that are available to the general public and that can be useful in helping us understand alcohol-related problems. In general, these materials are of excellent quality. Most suggest that the answer to the alcohol problem in the United States is to teach responsible drinking. This is important for those who choose to drink. But one alternative, often overlooked because of our desire to be inoffensive and to allow everyone freedom in making decisions, is abstinence. If presented properly with scientific data and without moralizing, this might be seen more often as the best approach to the development of healthy individuals, families, and communities.

This book represents a gleaning from the research and writings of prominent experts in the field of alcohol and alcoholism. It can be used as a text for courses in the social and health sciences, or it may serve to help those affected by an alcohol problem to understand the nature of the problem and the courses of action that might alleviate it.

Where we feel further reading on a topic would be helpful, we have referred to a book, article, or pamphlet in the bibliography (numbers in parentheses). These works are the source of much of the material in this book.

# Tables

# Figures

# 1

# Introduction:
# Alcohol and Its Use

## The History of Alcohol Use

Whenever and wherever people have been, so, usually, has alcohol—man's oldest social "beverage-drug."[1] Although it is not known exactly when man discovered alcohol and its properties, paleontologists say that prehistoric man had the four basic ingredients needed to produce it—sugar, water, yeast, and mild warmth—as long ago as 200 million years. We have ample testimony from ancient Egyptians, Hebrews, Greeks, and Romans that intoxicating beverages— both wines and stronger drinks—were well known within their cultures. Alcohol may be the most popular drug in recorded history. We know humans have been drinking alcoholic beverages since 6400 B.C., when beer and berry wine were discovered. The drinking custom is probably even older than that. Some experts believe that mead, an alcoholic beverage made from honey, was used about 3000 B.C.

The destruction of individuals and families by excessive, irresponsible drinking has been recorded as well. Many moral, religious, political, and social leaders scorned drinking, favoring abstinence or at least moderation. An eighteenth-century Frenchman, Francois de Salignac de la Mothe Fenelon, summed up the tragedy of drunkenness: "Some of the most dreadful mischiefs that afflict mankind proceed from wine. It is the cause of disease, quarrels,

[1]Morris E. Chafetz, "Alcohol and Alcoholism," *American Scientist* (May–June 1979): 293.

sedition, idleness, aversion to labor, and every species of domestic disorder."[2]

One of the oldest temperance tracts on record was written in Egypt, about 3,000 years ago, under the title of "Wisdom of Ani," and reads as follows: "Take not upon thyself to drink a jug of beer. Thou speakest and an unintelligible utterance issueth from thy mouth. If thou fallest down and thy limbs break there is none to hold out a hand to thee. Thy companions in drink stand up and say 'away with this sot,' and thou art like a little child."[3]

Similar sentiments are found in Greek, Roman, Indian, and Japanese literature, and in both the Old and New Testaments, denouncing drunkenness. Leaders throughout history have encouraged moderation. King Solomon warned the ancient Hebrews to beware of alcohol, as did Plato and other Greek philosophers. In ancient times, an intoxicated person was often shunned and condemned.

Laws to prevent people from using alcohol have been tried in many countries. In China, wine-drinking prohibitions were enacted and repealed forty times between 1100 B.C. and 1400 A.D. In the United States, an amendment to the Constitution in 1919 made it illegal to manufacture or sell any alcoholic beverage. This amendment remained in effect until 1933 and had significant impact on the nation's social patterns, economy, and underground life during those years and after. Even now, fifty years later, prohibition remains a controversial subject. Its defenders claim that it caused substantial reduction in drinking, a decrease in drunkenness, and a marked economic improvement in the country. Its opponents say that the experiment deterred only the moderate drinker and brought new and dangerous glamour to intoxication. They claim that it destroyed public respect for law enforcement officers and bred crime, violence, and general corruption through liquor bootlegging.

By the beginning of World War II, total per-capita sales returned to their pre-1900 levels, where they remained for nearly twenty years. Total per-capita sales began to rise significantly in about 1960, due at least in part, it is believed, to liberalization of alcohol control laws at a time when increasing numbers of teenagers and women started drinking.(9)

Today, adults in our country who wish to drink have a legal right to do so.(5) But legal rights are not the only factors involved. Social rights and social pressures are also important, and these may vary widely in different groups and regions. There is no national attitude toward drinking that is acceptable to everyone, and perhaps there never will be. But there is a growing feeling that the right to drink must carry with it certain responsibilities.

The use of beer, wine, or liquor for sealing friendships, toasting good

[2]As quoted in National Institute of Mental Health, National Institute on Alcohol Abuse and Alcoholism, *Alcohol and Alcoholism: Problems, Programs, and Progress*, PHS Publication No. (HSM) 72-9127, p. 1.

[3]As quoted in *ibid.*

fortune, and celebrating events such as births and weddings has become an established social ritual in America and many other countries. Alcohol (usually wine) is also an integral part of many religious rituals; in Judaism, for example, the Passover Seder requires it, as does Communion in many Christian sects.

Alcoholic beverages were secularized for common use in some of the early civilizations, including the Sumarian, Acadian, Babylonian, Chaldean, and Egyptian civilizations. Part of the reason for secularization may have been the desire to use a "sacred" drink on nonreligious but important occasions, such as weddings; another reason may have been the simple pleasure and satisfaction people got from alcohol.

Alcoholic beverages became mandatory in many early cultures, not only in worship and in the practice of magic and medicine, but also to solemnify formal councils, to ratify compacts and crownings, to commemorate festivals, to display hospitality, to stimulate war-making, and to celebrate peace. It was used, as well, to confirm all rites of passage through life, including birth, initiations, marriages, and funerals.

## Is Alcohol a Drug?

The Commission on Marijuana and Drug Abuse uses the term *drug* to include "psychoactive drugs which have the capacity to influence behavior by altering feeling, mood, perception, or other mental states." Alcohol clearly fits this definition. Alcohol *is* a drug; in fact, it is the most commonly used—and misused—drug in the United States. It may be classified as a sedative, tranquilizer, hypnotic or anesthetic drug, depending on the quantity consumed.

The commission offers some compelling statistics on alcohol and other drugs. It estimates that at least 100 million Americans are using alcoholic beverages and that at any given time 10 percent of these demonstrate "intensified and compulsive use" with a "serious decrement in social functioning noticeable in half of this group." The alcohol industry annually produces over 1 billion gallons of spirits, wine, and beer, for which consumers pay $24 billion. Prescribed psychoactive drugs, by contrast, involve only 214 million prescriptions, with an annual retail value of $1 billion.(143)

But most of the public does not see alcohol as a drug. The commission notes that most people "do not think about the alcohol experience as an altered state of consciousness, but rather as a means to some other end such as promoting conviviality, or stimulating conversation." The commission also suggests that the misconceptions that exclude alcohol from substances usually thought of as drugs can seriously compromise the national effort to cope with drug abuse.(61)

While there are many similarities between alcohol and other drugs, one significant difference is noteworthy. It has legal acceptance and most other drugs do not, unless prescribed by a physician.

## What Alcohol Is

Ethyl alcohol ($C_2H_5OH$), or ethanol, is the main alcohol used in beverages. It is one of many alcohols produced in nature and in industry by the process of fermentation. Alcohols also occur naturally in the human body, where enzyme systems produce and dispose of them.

All alcohols are intoxicating. Ethyl alcohol is less toxic than others, such as methyl alcohol and butyl alcohol, because the body changes it into harmless substances—carbon dioxide and water. When, for example, methyl alcohol, or wood alcohol, is oxidized in the body, it is converted into formic acid and formaldehyde. Formaldehyde has a special affinity for the optic nerve and can produce blindness.

The forming of alcohol through fermentation takes place when certain fruit, juices, or cereals are left in a warm place. Living yeast cells, either manually placed in the liquid or deposited from the air, convert the sugar in the fermenting matter into alcohol. This conversion continues until there is no more sugar or there is so much alcohol that it kills the yeast. In the manufacture of alcoholic beverages, fermentation is carefully controlled to ensure that the alcohol produced is ethyl alcohol.

Yeast, a microscopic plant, is widely distributed in nature. It floats in the air as dust, ready to drop into any suitable material and begin fermentation. As Leon Greenberg explains, the fermentation process is the same as that of raising bread with yeast in baking. Carbon dioxide gas is caught and held as bubbles in the dough, making the bread porous. Most of the alcohol formed in baking is driven out by the heat. In making beverage alcohol, however, the carbon dioxide is allowed to escape into the air.(67)

# Types of Alcoholic Beverages

Three types of alcoholic beverages are commonly used—beer, wine, and distilled liquor (see Table 1).

## Beer

The brewing of beer and ale is an ancient process. A broth made from cereal grains is heated and allowed to ferment. Then malt, yeast, and mold are added to it. Malt (sprouted barley which has been dried and ground up) changes the starch in the broth to sugar so the yeast can work on it. The yeast converts the sugar into alcohol and carbon dioxide gas—hence the bubbles in the beer. Finally, hops are included in the mixture to give the beer a bitter flavor.

The alcohol content of beer is usually 3 to 7 percent. Beer retains some of the water, minerals, solids, and vitamins from the original broth. Most American beers are about 4.5 percent alcohol by volume.

With beer consumption on a steady increase in the United States, the U.S. Department of Agriculture says that beer consumption has now surpassed that of milk—with an annual per-capita consumption of 24.3 gallons of beer as compared to 21.6 gallons of milk.

Some manufacturers have slightly altered the brewing process to result in what are called "light" beers—beers with lower caloric content than their regular

### Table 1
### Some common alcoholic beverages

| Beverage | Source | Average % of alcohol by volume |
|---|---|---|
| Fermented Beverages* | | |
| Beer | Malted barley | 3—6 |
| Ale | Malted barley | 6—8 |
| Wines | | |
| Dry (dinner) | Grape juice | 12-14 |
| Sweet (dessert) | Grape juice † | 18-20 |
| Distilled spirits ‡ | | |
| Whiskey | Fermented cereals | 40-50 |
| Brandy | Fermented grape juice | 40-50 |
| Rum | Fermented molasses | |
| Vodka | Fermented potatoes and other sources | 40-50 |
| Gin | Various sources | 40-50 |

*The action of yeast cells converts the sugar in grains and grape juice into alcohol.
†The sweet wines are fortified with additional alcohol and have sugar added after fermentation.
‡These beverages are produced by distilling an already fermented brew.

counterparts. Most of the light beers are manufactured as an addition to the regular beer—for example, Anheuser Busch, which manufactures Budweiser beer, also manufactures Natural Light.

Statistics show that not all "light" beers are the same, however—in fact, there's quite a broad range in terms of both calorie and alcohol content. Among the top brands of light beer, calories per 12 ounces range all the way from 97 (Natural Light) to 139 (Michelob Light). And variations in alcohol content occur from brand to brand, too—with the percentages ranging all the way from 2.65% (natural Light) to 3.37% (Miller Lite).

## Wine

To make wine, all that one needs to do is leave fruit juice which contains sugar in a warm place, exposed to air. As Greenberg points out, prehistoric people may have discovered this. The yeast needed for fermentation may be present on the fruit, or settle in the juice from the air. Fermentation stops when the alcohol content reaches about 14 percent—high enough to kill the yeast. At this point, unless the process is controlled, airborne bacteria will land in the wine, changing it to vinegar. This is why wine, left exposed to air for any length of time, "sours."(67)

The wine retains the water, minerals, and some of the vitamins from the original fruit (wines can be made from many plants, but most are made from grapes). All or part of the sugar has been changed to alcohol. Dry wines are those in which no sugar remains. In "sparkling" wines, such as champagne, some of the carbon dioxide gas is retained to give a soda-like effect. Most ordinary wines contain 12 to 14 percent alcohol. Fortified wines, such as sherry and port, have an alcohol solution added to raise the alcohol content to between 18 and 20 percent.

### Distilled liquor

The distillation process came along after the discovery of fermentation. It was known to the Greeks and possibly to the scientists of Egypt as early as the beginning of the Christian era but was not introduced into Europe until the 18th century.

Alcohol boils at a lower temperature than water. When fermented liquid is heated, the alcohol vapors are given off first. These can be condensed back to liquid in a cooling coil and collected. The result is a water and alcohol solution containing no solids, minerals, or vitamins. This distilling process can be repeated until the solution is almost pure alcohol. But because of the affinity alcohol has for water, a 100 percent alcohol solution cannot be maintained; most commercial alcohol called "pure" alcohol contains about 5 percent water.

Distilled liquors are essentially flavored alcohol and water. Whiskey, rum, and brandy are flavored by the fermented brews used in their distillation. Whiskey is distilled from fermented grains such as rye, corn, or barley; rum, from fermented molasses; brandy, from wine. Gin is alcohol distilled from various sources, flavored with berries. Vodka, usually distilled from potatoes, is essentially unflavored. Distilled liquors contain 40 to 50 percent alcohol, usually expressed as "proof."

## Alcohol Proof and Percent

Proof is twice the alcoholic content. A 90-proof beverage contains 45 percent alcohol; 80 proof, 40 percent; 100 proof, 50 percent.

During the first half of this century, the whiskey trade flourished to the extent that a barrel of whiskey became a medium of barter. Whiskey offered for barter was expected to be 50 percent alcohol. To make sure he was not getting diluted whiskey, the buyer devised a simple test—he moistened some gunpowder with whiskey. If the gunpowder burned, it was considered proof that the whiskey was at least 50 percent alcohol. Whiskey passing the test was called "100 proof." This term has persisted.

## Congeners

In the process of fermentation and distillation, small amounts of many substances besides alcohol and carbon dioxide are formed. Some of them are ketones, aldehydes, acids, and alcohols other than ethyl alcohol. These substances are called congeners.

Alcoholic beverages vary in congener content. Vodka contains approximately 3.3mg/100ml; bourbon, 2.85mg/100ml. The amount of congeners in an alcoholic beverage depends partly on the material used for fermentation and especially on the sanitary conditions prevailing during the beverage-making process. Modern sanitary distillation methods attempt to reduce the presence of these toxic compounds. They affect the odor and taste of the beverage and, in crudely prepared spirits, may be found in sufficient quantity to cause physical injury.

Congeners produce gastrointestinal irritation when swallowed; effects on EEG, respiration, and cardiovascular activity are also common with larger doses. The presence of various amounts of congeners in different distilled spirits is thought to account for their dissimilar physiological effects. Congeners may act separately or synergistically with alcohol.(10) A headache after drinking may be partly an allergic reaction to them. One study noted that human subjects given high-congener beverages showed a greater incidence of risk-taking than those given low-congener beverages. Both groups received the same amount of alcohol.(10)

## Why People Drink

Obviously, the reasons for drinking vary from individual to individual, but there are some societal and motivational factors that influence drinkers of all ages to seek refuge in drugs, including alcohol:[4]

1. The use of many drugs simply has become an integral part of everyday life—a fact that especially holds true in the case of alcohol.
2. Alcohol use helps counterbalance the frustrations that tend to make life more complex and difficult; drinkers turn to alcohol in order to banish frustrations and make life easier to deal with. For these, drinking may provide a psychological escape from the realities of life.
3. Society seems to emphasize the importance of interpersonal relationships and the fact that individual members of society should like, tolerate, be affectionate toward, and want to be with others—something that is too painful or difficult for some. Alcohol use enables these people to reduce the intimacy of interpersonal relationships, allowing for involvement without conscious effort and without fear or pain.
4. Alcohol promotes a sense of well-being in the user.
5. Teenagers may use alcohol as a way to rebel against society and parental restraints; alcohol may also become their means of rejecting parental values or their way of striking out against emotional neglect by parents. In another sense, rebellion may imply a love of danger and risk; for many young people, the thrill comes in violating societal mores.
6. Some alcohol use is based on the notion that the drug helps the user know himself/herself and the world better, thereby finding answers to life's problems.
7. Alcohol provides a sense of belonging, a sense of conforming, and a sense of increased sociability with the peer group.
8. Parents may view a teenager's drinking as mere rebellion when, in reality, the teenager is mimicking the parent's chosen method for escaping and solving

[4]Brent, Hafen, and Brenda Peterson, Medicines and Drugs: Problems and Risks, Use and Abuse (Philadelphia: Lea and Febiger, 1978), p. 120.

problems. Such imitation is generally unconscious, preventing examination and correction of the real, underlying problems.[5]

9. Many use alcohol to enhance creativity and to more fully appreciate the arts, music, and nature.
10. Curiosity plays a significant role with the young, who often have their first experience with alcohol simply to find out how alcohol affects the mind and body.
11. Having a drink with friends is the basis for many social gatherings, where it is used to relax the group, to create an atmosphere, and to encourage sociability and openness.
12. Alcohol is often used by rigid individuals in an attempt to gain relaxation. Many who live with daily stress, tension, and pressures use the drug to unwind "after a hard day at the office."
13. It has often been inaccurately believed that alcohol heightens and increases sexual desire and performance.(72)
14. Some people drink because they simply have nothing else to do—and drinking provides a sense of adventure.

Table 2 shows the relationship among levels of experience, motives, and alcohol-abuse patterns.(72)

### Table 2
### Motivations of drug/alcohol use

| Level of Experience | Type of Gratification | Motives, Needs, Aspirations |
|---|---|---|
| Physical | The general feeling of physical well-being and experience of the body | Physical relaxation |
| Sensory | The enhancement, exaggeration, or intensification of the physical senses | Enhancement of sexual experience |
| Emotional | Psychological and emotional experience, especially that which occurs within a personality; includes those internal feelings set off by the environment | Psychological escape or release from emotional agony Reduction of normal tension, anxiety, conflict Emotional relaxation Mood alteration Avoidance of decision- |

[5]Ibid., p. 125.

| Level of Experience | Type of Gratification | Motives, Needs, Aspirations |
| --- | --- | --- |
| | | making, pressure Desire for privacy, aloness Rebellion; assertion of independence or defiance of authority Intensification of personal courage Increase in self-esteem |
| Interpersonal | Interpersonal relations, acceptance in groups, feelings of communication among individuals, opposite sex relation-ships, etc. | Gain in peer recogni-tion, as in "showing off." Gain in peer accep-tance, as in behaving according to "peer pressure" Relaxation of inter-personal inhibition; facilitation of social interaction Escape/release from family/difficulties Escape/release from feelings of loneliness, alienation Establishment of feeling of "community" or belonging with actual or reference group |
| Mental-intellectual | The experience of mental and intellectual processes, such as thoughts, ideas, problem-solving, etc. | Reduction of boredom Curiosity |
| Creative-aesthetic | Artistic creativity; the performance or aesthetic appreciation or experience of creative works or artistic phenomena | Increase in enjoy-ment of artistic productions |
| Experiential | Pertaining to gener-alized personal expe-rience of new, unusual, | Desire for "pure pleasure," fun, recreation |

| Level of Experience | Type of Gratification | Motives, Needs, Aspirations |
| --- | --- | --- |
| | or intensified states of experience or consciousness (usually somewhat difficult to label) | Nonspecific changes in consciousness or awareness; e.g., any "high," intoxication for its own sake; desire for a change, any change, in experience Unusual distortion Engagment—the need to be personally and totally involved in the moment, whatever the experience; counteracting apathy and ennui |
| Stylistic | Styles of behaviors and attitudes, especially cognitive styles, cultural styles, and lifestyles | Need for identification through imitation, by youth of adults, by adults of youth, from media and subcultural "hero" figures; peer imitation Automatic chemical reliance—i.e., the culturally infused style of substance ingestion for any perceived deficiency Desire for immediacy of achievement; impatience; intolerance of delay of gratification |
| Social-political | Experiences generated by identification or involvement with social causes or political movements; also, reaction to social and political inertia or change | Overcoming discouragement or desperation with social-political future |
| Philosophical (general and personal) | The experience of a guiding philosophy of life, an explanation of the universe; also, personal identity, includ- | Search for personal identity Creation or change in values and philosophical lifestyle |

| Level of Experience | Type of Gratification | Motives, Needs, Aspirations |
|---|---|---|
| | ing goals, purpose, and values. | Overcoming frustration from lack of meaningful vocation and work |
| Miscellaneous: | Combinations of above levels; factors difficult to categorize in one schema | Need for risk-taking, danger |
| | | Need for adventure, exploration |
| | | "Vacuum phenomenon," or "What else is there to do?" |
| | | Combination of motives, needs, aspirations—none of which individually would produce drug abuse |
| | | Need to react to extreme mental or physical discomfort; e.g., as in the maintenance of narcotic addiction, or in extreme psychological pain and/or confusion |

Motivations for drinking can also be explained through Maslow's five levels of human needs. A person's most basic physiological drives are to meet physical needs of food, shelter, water, and survival. When any of these basic needs is missing or is threatened, the individual becomes preoccupied with meeting that need, and other needs are, for the moment, unimportant.

Once a person's basic physical needs are met, other needs assert themselves. The person is no longer satisfied with food and water for a day at a time, or shelter for a single night; he/she wants some assurance that those basic needs will be predictably met on a regular basis. He/she needs to feel personally safe and secure.

As the individual moves up the heirarchy, he/she begins to focus on others. People need other people, who in turn need them; everyone needs to belong, to be accepted for what he or she is. Each person needs friends and close relationships.

With an outward focus, a person feels a need to do something important and worthwhile, a need to achieve and experience esteem, whether it be in an occupation, child-raising, artistic endeavors, or some other aspect of life. One needs to be respected for what one does and to be recognized, praised, and rewarded for doing things well. The need for self-respect which comes from recognition of achievement is keen.

The most elusive of human needs is the need to be one's best self, sometimes called the need for self-actualization. Everyone needs to attain his or her potential—to have an opportunity to develop talents and reach personal goals. Unmet, this need frustrates workers in unfulfilling jobs and irritates some women who feel imprisoned by diapers and housework.

When basic needs have been met and gratified, the person is free to seek higher levels of need gratification. For example, a person who needs a job worries first about securing the job—then about social needs with regard to fellow employees.

Further, a person whose basic needs have been met is better able to deal with situations in which a need is not met. A person who has frequently been recognized for accomplishments, in other words, has enough self-confidence to deal with occasionally being overlooked.

Most of our efforts are directed toward our frustrated or unmet needs, not toward those needs that are already satisfied. For example, a person who works his or her way out of poverty is more interested in further personal fulfillment than in reflection on the past. He/she may then find fulfillment in helping others, or he/she may wish to attain public recognition in a field for a special talent or interest.

Each individual defines personal needs at every level in a unique way, and he/she personally decides how those needs will be satisfied. The problem begins when a person tries faulty ways of meeting needs, such as reliance on alcohol or other drugs.

## Drinking Patterns in the United States

In the years since prohibition, the percentage of abstainers in the United States has decreased, and the percentage of drinkers has increased correspondingly. Before World War II, about 40 percent of adult women and 60 percent of adult men drank. Recent data shows that about 60 percent of women and 80 percent of men now drink.

The 1980 Gallup Poll indicated that 70 percent of the adult American population class themselves as at least occasional users of alcohol. During that year, Americans spent a record $50.8 billion for alcoholic beverages (beer, wine, and distilled spirits)—which translates to $5.8 million per hour. The average drinker consumed 52 gallons of alcohol, with an average bar tab of $423.61.

A later Gallup Poll shows the approximate breakdown by sex, age, geographic location, profession, education, and religion of drinkers in the United States: (See Table 3)

Interestingly enough, per-capita consumption of coffee and milk is down, while consumption of alcohol has risen in America, a trend that is due in part to the relatively stable prices of alcoholic beverages.

The total number of drinkers in the United States, including the 14- to

**Table 3**
***Drinking patterns in the United States: Gallup Poll, 1981***

| Group | Drinkers | Abstainers |
|---|---|---|
| Men | 75% | 25% |
| Women | 66 | 34 |
| Under 30 years | 76 | 24 |
| 30–49 years | 74 | 26 |
| 50 years and older | 63 | 37 |
| East | 77 | 23 |
| Midwest | 75 | 25 |
| South | 58 | 42 |
| West | 72 | 28 |
| Professional/business | 85 | 15 |
| Clerical/sales | 78 | 22 |
| Manual/laborers | 71 | 29 |
| College trained | 81 | 19 |
| High school only | 70 | 30 |
| Grade school only | 52 | 48 |
| Protestants | 62 | 38 |
| Catholics | 82 | 18 |

SOURCE: Alcohol Research Information Service. *The Bottom Line,* Vol. 4, No. 4:29.

21-year-olds, is currently estimated at 96 million. They drink an average of about 4 gallons of absolute alcohol per year—the highest per-capita consumption in history (in pre-prohibition days, it was about 2.63 gallons). This represents a 24 percent increase in the last decade.

Heavier drinking increased significantly for males between 1971 and 1976. In all surveys, men showed three to six times the amount of heavy drinking as women, although women as a group have shown the largest recent increase in consumption, with women between the ages of 35 and 49 increasing the amount moderate drinking. This trend may be related to changing lifestyles, since women in this age group often re-enter the labor force, and moderate drinking is more likely among employed women than among housewives. Younger women drink more on a regular basis than do their older counterparts.

More drinkers are consistently found among young adults 18 to 24 years old, and more abstainers are found among older people. The number of 21- to 24-year-olds who drink once a month or more has increased dramatically, but heavy drinking is more common among 18- to 20-year-olds than in the 20 to 24 years old.(9)

Alcoholics of either sex drink eleven times more than other drinkers.

It is estimated that, overall, the percentages and types of drinkers in the United States are presently as shown in Tables 4 and 5.

**Table 4**
***Trends in alcohol consumption by type of drinker,
1971-1979 (in percentages)***

| Type of Drinker | Harris 1971 | Harris 1972 | Harris Spring 1973 | Harris Fall 1973 | Harris 1974 | Opinion Research Corp. 1975 | Response Analysis Corp. 1976 | National 1979 |
|---|---|---|---|---|---|---|---|---|
| Abstainer | 36 | 36 | 34 | 37 | 36 | 36 | 33 | 33 |
| Light | 34 | 32 | 29 | 30 | 28 | 31 | 38 | 34 |
| Moderate | 20 | 23 | 23 | 21 | 28 | 21 | 19 | 24 |
| Heavier | 10 | 10 | 14 | 11 | 11 | 12 | 10 | 9 |
| (N) | (2,195) | (1,544) | (1,588) | (1,603) | (1,578) | (1,071) | (2,510) | (1,772) |

NOTE: The percentages are weighted figures and may not total to 100 percent due to rounding; totals shown are the actual number of cases. Slight variations in these totals occur because of nonresponse, etc.

Alcohol consumed per day: Light drinker — .01-.21 oz.; Moderate .22-.99 oz.; Heavier — 1.0 oz. or more.

**Table 5**
***Trends in alcohol consumption for males and females
by type of drinker, 1971-1979 (in percentages)***

| | Harris 1971 | Harris Spring 1972 | Harris Fall 1973 | Harris 1973 | Harris Corp. 1974 | Opinion Research Corp. 1975 | Response Analysis 1976 | National 1979 |
|---|---|---|---|---|---|---|---|---|
| Males | | | | | | | | |
| Abstainer | 30 | 28 | 25 | 26 | 24 | 27 | 26 | 25 |
| Light | 29 | 29 | 24 | 29 | 24 | 27 | 33 | 29 |
| Moderate | 26 | 28 | 29 | 26 | 34 | 26 | 24 | 31 |
| Heavier | 15 | 15 | 22 | 19 | 18 | 20 | 18 | 14 |
| Females | | | | | | | | |
| Abstainer | 42 | 44 | 42 | 47 | 42 | 45 | 39 | 40 |
| Light | 40 | 34 | 35 | 32 | 32 | 35 | 44 | 38 |
| Moderate | 13 | 18 | 17 | 17 | 21 | 15 | 15 | 18 |
| Heavier | 5 | 4 | 6 | 4 | 5 | 4 | 3 | 4 |

SOURCE: Alcohol & Health, National Institute-on Alcohol Abuse and Alcoholism Fourth Special Report to the U.S. Congress, January, 1981.

# Patterns of Alcohol Use

Drinking practices are influenced by demographics, availability of alcoholic beverages, drinking context, geographical location, and historical trends.

## Demographics

Age, sex, ethnic background, religious affiliation, socioeconomic level, education, occupation, degree of urbanization, and behavioral factors such as childhood experience with drinkers all bear upon drinking experiences—relating to both beverage preference and amount consumed. For example, more than twice as many (22 percent) of those who said in a recent survey they never went to church were heavy drinkers as those who said they went to church every week (10 percent). Personality traits, neurotic tendencies, alienation, and impulsivity are also used in studying and classifying drinkers.

## Alcohol Availability

Although availability of alcoholic beverages is a function of supply and demand, both private enterprise and government affect the marketplace. Aggressive advertising and marketing may even increase demand, and, consequently, may increase the supply of alcoholic beverages.

The government controls distribution of alcohol through age requirements, number and location of sales outlets, and hours and days of sale. An increase in the number of stores selling alcohol and a lowering of age requirements may make alcohol more accessible to a wider segment of the population.

## Drinking Context

Americans generally drink in their own and their friends' homes. An analysis of survey data show that slightly more than 40 percent of all drinkers usually drank at home, slightly less than 40 percent drank most frequently at parties, and approximately 10 percent drank most often in restaurants, bars, or taverns.

The drinking context can influence the choice of beverage, the effect of the alcohol, and the amount consumed. For example, distilled spirits are thought of as a party drink and are consumed more often with friends than with family.

## Geographic Variation in Alcohol Consumption

Since population characteristics and alcohol availability vary considerably among the states, the apparent consumption and types of beverages sold also vary. Nevada, Wisconsin, and the District of Columbia have the highest apparent per-capita consumption; West Virginia, Arkansas, and Utah have the lowest.

Analysis of these variations is a complicated matter. In places such as Nevada and the District of Columbia, high apparent consumption rates are explained at least partly by tourism. Residents of nearby states often purchase their alcoholic beverages in New Hampshire and Vermont because prices are generally lower in those places. Consumption is relatively high in tourist states because people on vacation are likely to drink more. Finally, high wine consumption in California may be a reflection of the wine industry's importance to that state.(9)

Table 6 shows a state-by-state breakdown of the apparent consumption of alcoholic beverages in the United States.

### Table 6
### Consumption of Alcoholic Beverages in the U.S. 1970 & 1978

| State | Distilled Spirits 1970 | Distilled Spirits 1978 | Wine 1970 | Wine 1978 | Beer 1970 | Beer 1978 | Total Ethanol 1970 | Total Ethanol 1978 | Rank 1978 | Percent Change In Total Ethanol from 1970 to 1978 |
|---|---|---|---|---|---|---|---|---|---|---|
| Alabama | 0.70 | 0.87 | 0.09 | 0.12 | 0.60 | 0.98 | 1.39 | 1.97 | 46 | 42 |
| Alaska | 2.07 | 1.71 | 0.37 | 0.46 | 1.18 | 1.42 | 3.62 | 3.59 | 4 | -1 |
| Arizona | 1.05 | 1.14 | 0.32 | 0.39 | 1.37 | 1.78 | 2.74 | 3.31 | 10 | 21 |
| Arkansas | 0.59 | 0.72 | 0.13 | 0.11 | 0.71 | 0.97 | 1.43 | 1.80 | 50 | 26 |
| California | 1.37 | 1.32 | 0.63 | 0.68 | 1.10 | 1.42 | 3.10 | 3.42 | 6 | 10 |
| Colorado | 1.26 | 1.44 | 0.31 | 0.47 | 1.18 | 1.50 | 2.75 | 3.41 | 7 | 24 |
| Connecticut | 1.46 | 1.20 | 0.34 | 0.38 | 1.00 | 1.08 | 2.80 | 2.66 | 30 | -5 |
| Delaware | 1.74 | 1.36 | 0.21 | 0.23 | 1.17 | 1.34 | 3.12 | 2.93 | 19 | -6 |
| District of Columbia | 4.44 | 3.09 | 0.82 | 0.95 | 1.39 | 1.43 | 6.65 | 5.47 | 2 | -18 |
| Florida | 1.52 | 1.43 | 0.30 | 0.34 | 1.09 | 1.52 | 2.91 | 3.29 | 11 | 13 |
| Georgia | 1.02 | 1.15 | 0.14 | 0.18 | 0.79 | 1.12 | 1.95 | 2.45 | 34 | 26 |
| Hawaii | 1.13 | 1.31 | 0.25 | 0.47 | 1.11 | 1.39 | 2.49 | 3.17 | 12 | 27 |
| Idaho | 0.75 | 0.83 | 0.10 | 0.28 | 1.20 | 1.51 | 2.05 | 2.62 | 31 | 28 |
| Illinois | 1.34 | 1.18 | 0.27 | 0.31 | 1.21 | 1.38 | 2.82 | 2.87 | 20 | 2 |
| Indiana | 0.69 | 0.77 | 0.12 | 0.16 | 1.00 | 1.20 | 1.81 | 2.13 | 44 | 18 |
| Iowa | 0.68 | 0.74 | 0.06 | 0.11 | 1.09 | 1.52 | 1.83 | 2.37 | 36 | 30 |
| Kansas | 0.65 | 0.66 | 0.09 | 0.11 | 0.85 | 1.14 | 1.59 | 1.91 | 47 | 20 |
| Kentucky | 0.84 | 0.77 | 0.08 | 0.09 | 0.93 | 0.99 | 1.85 | 1.85 | 48 | 0 |
| Louisiana | 0.91 | 1.07 | 0.29 | 0.25 | 1.20 | 1.35 | 2.40 | 2.67 | 28 | 11 |
| Maine | 1.03 | 1.09 | 0.10 | 0.27 | 1.24 | 1.31 | 2.37 | 2.67 | 28 | 13 |
| Maryland | 1.39 | 1.37 | 0.25 | 0.31 | 1.31 | 1.37 | 2.95 | 3.05 | 15 | 3 |
| Massachusetts | 1.35 | 1.25 | 0.30 | 0.40 | 1.15 | 1.39 | 2.80 | 3.04 | 16 | 9 |
| Michigan | 1.07 | 1.05 | 0.24 | 0.27 | 1.37 | 1.43 | 2.68 | 2.75 | 23 | 3 |
| Minnesota | 1.23 | 1.16 | 0.16 | 0.23 | 1.14 | 1.31 | 2.53 | 2.70 | 26 | 7 |
| Mississippi | 0.71 | 0.92 | 0.08 | 0.10 | 0.82 | 1.16 | 1.61 | 2.18 | 42 | 35 |
| Missouri | 1.00 | 0.80 | 0.20 | 0.20 | 1.12 | 1.32 | 2.32 | 2.32 | 38 | 0 |
| Montana | 1.03 | 1.09 | 0.13 | 0.20 | 1.54 | 1.83 | 2.70 | 3.12 | 14 | 16 |
| Nebraska | 1.01 | 0.90 | 0.13 | 0.18 | 1.28 | 1.50 | 2.42 | 2.58 | 33 | 7 |

Apparent U.S. consumption of alcoholic beverages in gallons of ethanol per capita of the drinking age population

Notes: Drinking-age population is assumed to be 14 years and older. Ethanol = 4.5 percent for beer; 16 percent for wine in 1970; 12.9 percent for wine in 1978; 45 percent for spirits in 1970; 41.1 percent for spirits in 1978.

For comparative purposes only, amounts are calculated according to "tax-paid withdrawals" and do not show illegally produced alcohol that is consumed or certain other sales, such as military sales.

| | | | | | | | | | | |
|---|---|---|---|---|---|---|---|---|---|---|
| Nevada | 3.18 | 3.69 | 0.67 | 0.85 | 1.73 | 2.24 | 5.58 | 6.78 | 1 | 22 |
| New Hampshire | 2.83 | 2.93 | 0.32 | 0.54 | 1.68 | 1.98 | 4.83 | 5.45 | 3 | 13 |
| New Jersey | 1.38 | 1.10 | 0.38 | 0.42 | 1.17 | 1.17 | 2.93 | 2.69 | 27 | –8 |
| New Mexico | 0.98 | 0.98 | 0.36 | 0.32 | 1.20 | 1.65 | 2.54 | 2.95 | 18 | 16 |
| New York | 1.43 | 1.15 | 0.40 | 0.42 | 1.17 | 1.18 | 3.00 | 2.75 | 23 | –8 |
| North Carolina | 0.91 | 0.86 | 0.16 | 0.21 | 0.72 | 1.09 | 1.79 | 2.16 | 43 | 21 |
| North Dakota | 1.02 | 1.15 | 0.11 | 0.16 | 1.21 | 1.41 | 2.34 | 2.72 | 25 | 16 |
| Ohio | 0.81 | 0.73 | 0.19 | 0.20 | 1.22 | 1.30 | 2.22 | 2.23 | 40 | 0 |
| Oklahoma | 0.84 | 0.83 | 0.15 | 0.14 | 0.78 | 1.08 | 1.77 | 2.05 | 45 | 16 |
| Oregon | 0.90 | 0.98 | 0.39 | 0.47 | 1.17 | 1.35 | 2.46 | 2.80 | 21 | 14 |
| Pennsylvania | 0.82 | 0.74 | 0.19 | 0.21 | 1.26 | 1.36 | 2.27 | 2.31 | 39 | 2 |
| Rhode Island | 1.17 | 1.15 | 0.38 | 0.49 | 1.28 | 1.53 | 2.83 | 3.17 | 12 | 12 |
| South Carolina | 1.08 | 1.20 | 0.16 | 0.17 | 0.80 | 1.23 | 2.04 | 2.60 | 32 | 27 |
| South Dakota | 0.90 | 1.05 | 0.13 | 0.17 | 0.93 | 1.20 | 1.96 | 2.42 | 35 | 23 |
| Tennessee | 0.59 | 0.80 | 0.06 | 0.12 | 0.87 | 1.27 | 1.52 | 2.19 | 41 | 44 |
| Texas | 0.74 | 0.85 | 0.17 | 0.20 | 1.31 | 1.71 | 2.22 | 2.76 | 22 | 24 |
| Utah | 0.57 | 0.62 | 0.12 | 0.14 | 0.75 | 0.97 | 1.44 | 1.73 | 51 | 20 |
| Vermont | 1.73 | 1.59 | 0.39 | 0.47 | 1.38 | 1.51 | 3.50 | 3.57 | 5 | 2 |
| Virginia | 1.02 | 0.91 | 0.20 | 0.21 | 1.11 | 1.22 | 2.33 | 2.34 | 37 | 0 |
| Washington | 1.08 | 1.14 | 0.39 | 0.48 | 1.19 | 1.39 | 2.66 | 3.01 | 17 | 13 |
| West Virginia | 0.69 | 0.79 | 0.09 | 0.09 | 0.87 | 0.96 | 1.65 | 1.84 | 49 | 12 |
| Wisconsin | 1.25 | 1.26 | 0.22 | 0.28 | 1.71 | 1.80 | 3.18 | 3.34 | 9 | 5 |
| Wyoming | 1.15 | 1.36 | 0.16 | 0.22 | 1.28 | 1.53 | 2.59 | 3.41 | 7 | 32 |
| Total U.S. | 1.12 | 1.07 | 0.27 | 0.32 | 1.14 | 1.34 | 2.53 | 2.73 | — | 8 |

Source: Alcohol and Health. Fourth Report to the U.S. Congress, Jan., 1981, p. 25

### Characteristics of Drinkers

A recent survey by the National Institute of Mental Health suggests these typical characteristics of abstainers, light drinkers, and heavy drinkers:[6]

*Abstainers* are older people; belong to lower-than-average socioeconomic levels; live in the South and in rural areas: have native-born parents; belong to conservative or fundamentalist Protestant denominations; and have taken part in religious activities frequently.

*Heavy drinkers* observed more drinking by parents and friends; find drinking helpful to relieve depression.

*Light drinkers* are less alienated from society than other groups; are generally happier with ''lot in life'' than other groups.

The lowest incidence of alcohol-related problems for respondents in a recent national survey was found among: women, people over 50, widowed and married people, Jews, rural area residents, southerners, people with postgraduate education, people who are mostly wine drinkers.

The highest incidence of alcohol-related problems occurred among: men; separated, single, and divorced people (in that order); people who are mostly beer drinkers; people who agreed with the statements (in the survey) ''Drunkenness is usually *not* a sign of social irresponsibility'' and ''Drunkenness is usually a sign of just having fun.''

## Drinking Among Teenagers

An analysis of 120 surveys of American teenage drinking practices from 1941 to 1975 indicates that the proportion of teenage drinkers rose steadily from World War II until approximately 1965. That proportion has remained relatively constant since then, and more than 87 percent of today's teenagers have had a drink (see Figure 1). Teenagers typically have their first drink at age 13, and 7 percent more males than females in the teen years have had a drink.(10)

The proportion of high school students who reported ever having been intoxicated increased dramatically from 19 percent before 1966 to 45 percent between 1966 and the present (see Figure 2). The proportion reported being intoxicated at least once a month rose from 10 percent before 1966 to 19 percent between 1966 and the present.

A recent national survey of students in grades seven through twelve examined teenage drinking and problem drinking. The survey found that 74 percent of the teenagers were drinkers; 79 percent of the boys and 70 percent of the girls reported drinking. Problem drinking was defined as either drunkenness at least six times in the past year or the presence of negative consequences from

---

[6]Abstainers and infrequent drinkers drink less than once a month or not at all. Light drinkers drink at most 0.22 ounces absolute alcohol per day. Moderate drinkers drink 0.22 to 1.0 ounces absolute alcohol per day. Heavy drinkers drink 1.0 or more ounces absolute alcohol per day.

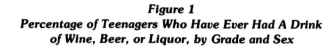

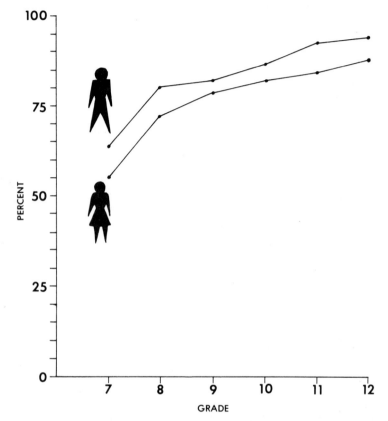

**Figure 1**
**Percentage of Teenagers Who Have Ever Had A Drink**
**of Wine, Beer, or Liquor, by Grade and Sex**

SOURCE: National Institute on Alcohol Abuse and Alcoholism, *Alcohol and Health,* Second Special Report to the U.S. Congress from the Secretary of Health, Education, and Welfare, June 1974, p. 9.
*These figures have remained relatively constant since 1974.

drinking two or more times in at least three of five specified situations in the past year, or both. By this definition, nearly 19 percent of the students were problem drinkers—23 percent of the boys and 15 percent of the girls. The negative consequences of problem drinking that students acknowledged were: (1) trouble with the teachers or the principal, (2) difficulties with friends, (3) driving under the influence, (4) criticism from others, especially dates, and (5) trouble with the police.

Drinking among college students has been rising steadily since 1936. Today's collegians drink more frequently and become intoxicated more often than today's high school students.

Young people drink less regularly than older people but tend to consume a

**Figure 2**
**Percentage of Teenage Drinkers Who Report Getting**
**Drunk, by Frequency and School Grade**

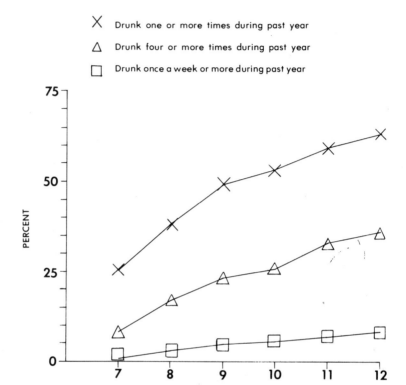

X   Drunk one or more times during past year

△   Drunk four or more times during past year

☐   Drunk once a week or more during past year

SOURCE: NIAAA, *Alcohol and Health,* Second Special Report to the U.S. Congress from the Secretary of Health, Education, and Welfare, June, 1974, p. 10.
*These figures have remained relatively constant since 1974.

larger amount on a single drinking occasion.

The NIAAA published a study in 1975 that gave the following national statistics on teenage drinking patterns:

        79.7 percent have had at least one alcoholic drink;

        73.8 percent have had at least two or three drinks;

        9.3 percent drink less than once a year;

        17.3 percent drink about once a year;

        14.9 percent drink once a month;

        15.0 percent drink one or two days a week;

        5.9 percent drink three to four days a week;

        2.4 percent drink every day.(85)

Table 7 gives the results of a 1978 national survey of teenage drinking patterns.

---

**Table 7**
**Distribution of 10th–12th graders by classes of drinkers:**
**1978 national survey**

| Drinking Group | Percentage |
|---|---|
| **Abstainers**—don't drink or drink less often than once a year.* | 25.0 |
| **Infrequent drinkers**—drink once a month at most and drink small amounts per typical drinking occasion.** | 7.6 |
| **Light drinkers**—drink once a month at most and drink medium amounts per typical drinking occasion or drink no more than three to four times a month and drink small amounts per typical drinking occasion | 18.8 |
| **Moderate drinkers**—drink at least once a week and small amounts per typical drinking occasion or three to four times a month and medium amounts per typical drinking occasion or no more than once a month and large amounts per typical drinking occasion. | 16.6 |
| **Moderate/heavier drinkers**—drink at least once a week and medium amounts per typical drinking occasion or three to four times a month and large amounts per typical drinking occasion. | 17.3 |
| Heavier drinkers—drink at least once a week and large amounts per typical drinking occasion | 14.8 |
| (N) | (4,918) |

SOURCE:

NOTE: Percentages are based on "weighted" observations.

*Those who drank less than once a year were classified as abstainers because the absolute alcohol consumed per day was essentially "0." Of those classified as abstainers above, 4.5 percent in 1974 and 4.0 percent in 1978 were "former drinkers"; i.e., they had had at least two or three drinks at some time in the past but not in the preceding year.

**Small, medium, and large amounts refer to one drink or less per drinking occasion, two to four drinks per drinking occasion, and five or more drinks per drinking occasion, respectively. A drink is equivalent to the following: 12 fluid oz. of beer, 4 fluid oz. of wine, or 1 fluid oz. of distilled spirits.

Source: Alcohol & Health, Fourth Report to the U.S. Congress, Jan., 1981, p. 25.

---

The occasions on which teenagers drink vary with age. Many youngsters begin to drink at home. As they grow older, more drinking tends to take place outside the home with less adult supervision. In grades ten through twelve, the most likely places for teenage drinking are parties where no adults are present. The preliminary survey data, shown in Figure 3, highlights these trends.

# Factors Influencing Teenage Drinking

Why do teenagers drink? They equate drinking with being grown up. Like adults, they use alcohol to increase their sociability. They drink to be part of the crowd or to celebrate special occasions. Very few use alcohol to escape reality, although they feel many adults use it for this purpose.

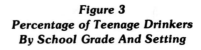

**Figure 3**
**Percentage of Teenage Drinkers**
**By School Grade And Setting**

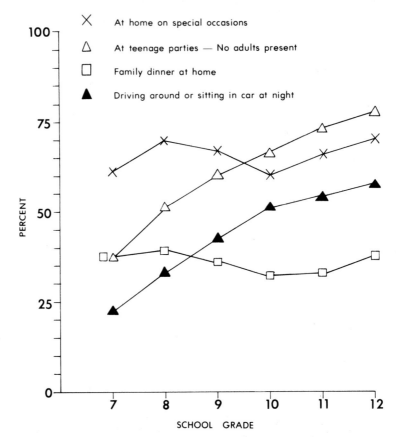

SOURCE: NIAAA, *Alcohol and Health,* Second Special Report to the U.S. Congress from the Secretary of Health Education, and Welfare, June, 1974, p. 21.

*These figures have remained relatively constant since 1974.

Researchers have concluded that high school drinking is influenced by factors in six major areas: (1) the peer group, family and parents, the sociocultural background, the environmental and contextual situation, personality, and the individual behavioral pattern. Peer and parental influences are considered the most critical because of the high correspondence between the drinking practices of adolescents and those of their parents and peers.

Direct relationships between parental attitudes and behaviors toward alcohol and adolescent drinking behavior can be demonstrated. Heavier drinking by the parents often forebodes problem drinking by their children. Regular drinking by the parents, especially if at home with meals, sets an example that their children typically begin to imitate during the high school years. Teenagers consume smaller amounts of alcohol when adults are present than when they are absent, which only serves to mask possible problems.

Apparently, the close to $5 million per year spent on alcohol advertising has a significant impact on not only a teenager's decision to drink, but on the *type* of alcohol the teenager drinks. According to a group of researchers from Michigan State University,[7] the 12- to 22-year-old group is bombarded by advertising on television and radio, in newspapers and magazines, and on billboards.

The scope of alcohol advertising can be vast indeed. Mostly during evening prime-time and weekend sports programs, television networks run more than 5,000 ads for beer during the course of a year. Almost 3,500 ads for alcohol (most of it liquor) appear in general and specialized magazines in each year, with the highest number being run in *Newsweek, People, Time, Sports Illustrated,* and *Playboy.*

Teenagers *are* paying attention to the alcohol advertising—reportedly, the average adolescent notices at least two billboards a week (a fourth of the teenagers notice ten or more a week) and 11 magazine ads. And a significant proportion of the teenager populations say they "watch or read the ads closely"—more than half of the teenagers questioned pay close attention to television beer ads.

The impact of alcohol advertising, say researchers, is varied. A third of the teenagers say they learned how to mix drinks and learned which brands are best from advertising. The alcohol ads helped a fourth of the teenagers determine which brands of alcohol were cheapest (and, therefore, most affordable to them), and a sixth of them learned information about how various brands and types of alcohol taste. Two-fifths of the teenagers say the ads taught them which alcohol famous people drink—and, therefore, which brands of alcohol would be most impressive to others.

Teenagers get from advertising a specific impression of alcohol, too—according to researchers, alcohol drinking is portrayed as elegant, romantic, relaxing, refreshing, and a means to social approval, escape, and social camaraderie.

What can be learned from research about the effect of family drinking patterns and practices?[8] Those who have studied the characteristics of families in which drinking problems are rare have found the following practices:

1. Parents who drink present a consistent, responsible example of moderation, without lecturing or preaching.

---

[7]Study results reported in "The Impact of Alcoholic Beverage Advertising," *The Bottom Line on Alcohol in Society,* Vol. 4, No. 4 (Fall 1981), pp. 2-17.

[8]Adapted from U.S. Department of Health, Education, and Welfare, *A Chip Off the Old Block: Parents as Models for Their Children's Behavior,* DHEW Publication No. (ADM) 77-454A, 1977.

2. Standards for using or not using alcohol are well established, understood, and agreed upon by all in the family.
3. Excessive drinking is not acceptable to the family.
4. Overindulgence or drunkenness is not looked upon as comical, even though family members recognize that people do some bizarre, funny things when under the influence.
5. Drinking is considered by parents to be morally neutral; it is neither virtuous nor evil.
6. Drinking is not viewed as an excape, a proof of adult status, or as representing anything else, for example, manliness, "chicness," etc.
7. Drinking is not carried on for its own sake, but it is a part of other activities.
8. No pressure is placed on a family member or a guest to drink.
9. No social significance is attached to a person's choosing not to drink.
10. In families where it is customary to drink moderately, children may be introduced to alcoholic beverages at an early age, in the home, as a natural part of life, and in a relatively unemotional way. (Here, the researchers say the important factor is *not* the physical act of sharing an alcoholic beverage with the child, but the importance and meaning which the child sees that the parent attaches to the practice of drinking. For example, if the parent gives the child a taste of wine but is not comfortable about doing it, the child will be quick to pick up the message and will be confused by the act. If, however, allowing children to taste small quantities of diluted alcoholic beverages has been a long-standing family custom, there seems to be no advice from the research to alter this practice.)
11. In nondrinking families, negative references are not made about others in the community who choose to drink. (Scare tactics and dire warnings only increase the guilt of a family member who decides to drink, and set the stage for ambivalence and internal conflict which may increase the probability of problem drinking.)

Researchers have frequently identified the following characteristics in families where problem drinking does occur:

1. Family standards about acceptable and unacceptable drinking practices are vague and inconsistent.
2. One parent favors drinking while the other parent is strongly opposed to drinking. (Thus the child can receive mixed messages about the appropriateness of drinking.)
3. Standards for acceptable drinking practices are different from men and for women (more mixed messages).(1)

## Attitudes About Drinking

The rising popularity of alcohol in the United States has caused more and more people to call for "responsible" drinking on the part of those who choose to drink.

But our society provides few, if any, guidelines distinguishing between responsible and irresponsible drinking.

One common American attitude is that social drinking is harmless and may even be helpful. Of course, some people drink alcohol in amounts and ways that cause no problems for themselves or others. But there are other "social drinkers" who have, as Max Hayman points out, hurt others with hostile criticism; and made unwelcome passes at other peoples' spouses; had unreasonable fights; given their children a model of drunkenness; wasted time needed for constructive activities; driven while drunk; had accidents coming home from cocktail parties; impatiently punished their children; spent the evening sitting in a semi-stupor in front of the television and detached from their families, because of several "social" drinks before dinner.(78) We cannot say that all social drinkers are responsible drinkers any more than we can say that all who drink are alcoholics.

Today there is agreement among many scientists, educators, physicians, religious leaders, and other professionals that an *understanding* of drinking and its physiological, psychological, and social implications is basic to solving alcohol problems. Science is beginning to seek ways to encourage personal and social control over drinking as well as ways to improve rehabilitation services for those whose drinking is already out of control. The ideal result of such understanding is a new attitude toward alcohol—a climate in which everyone who chooses to drink knows what alcohol can do and assumes responsibility for its intelligent, considerate use.

## International Comparisons

The most recent available data collected from 38 nations around the world[9] shows that the United States ranks thirty-first in per-capita consumption of wine, twelfth in per-capita consumption of beer, and tenth in per-capita consumption of distilled spirits. The United States average consumption of absolute alcohol is estimated at 2.20 gallons per capita — well under the 38-nation average of 3.01 gallons per capita — and placed the United States in tenth place for consumption of absolute alcohol, just behind Soviet Russia.

France leads the world in consumption of wine per capita at 24.46 gallons per capita; France is followed by Italy at 23.78 gallons and Portugal at 22.72 gallons per capita consumption. Lowest of all nations reporting, with less than half a gallon per capita consumption of wine each, were Morocco, Algeria, Peru, Turkey, Japan, Mexico, and Cuba.

West Germany holds its decades-old lead in per-capita consumption of beer, with 38.33 gallons; interestingly, that figure represents a slight drop from previous years. Following West Germany are Czechoslovakia, East Germany, Australia, and Belgium, with the United States ranking at number 12. Lowest of the nations

[9]"Alcohol Consumption Around the World," *The Bottom Line on Alcohol in Society*, Vol. 5, No. 1 (Winter 1982), pp. 28-32.

reporting, with less than one-tenth of a gallon per capita each, are Argentina, Tunisia, Paraguay, Turkey, Algeria, and Morocco.

Luxembourg now leads the world in highest per-capita consumption of distilled spirits, tallying in at 3.83 gallons to bump Poland from her traditional first-place slot. Following Luxembourg and Poland are Hungary, East Germany, Canada, and Czechoslovakia; the United States is tenth. Lowest of the reporting nations, with less than one-third of a gallon each, were Israel, Portugal, Cuba, Mexico, and Turkey.

### ABSOLUTE ALCOHOL PER CAPITA CONSUMPTION BASED ON TOTAL POPULATION FOR SELECTED NATIONS OF THE WORLD 1978-1979 (IN U.S. GALLONS)

| 1979 Rank | 1979 | 1978 | Change |
|---|---|---|---|
| France | 4.36 | 4.54 | − 4.0% |
| Luxembourg | 4.20 | 4.37 | − 3.9% |
| Spain | 3.82 | 3.80 | + 5% |
| Italy | 3.80 | 3.81 | − .3% |
| Portugal | 3.59 | 3.74 | − 4.0% |
| Hungary | 3.40 | 3.40 | — |
| West Germany | 3.33 | 3.15 | + 5.7% |
| Argentina | 3.16 | 3.24 | − 2.5% |
| Czechoslovakia | 3.12 | 3.08 | + 1.3% |
| Belgium | 2.99 | 2.91 | + 2.7% |
| East Germany | 2.94 | 2.81 | + 4.6% |
| Switzerland | 2.91 | 2.91 | — |
| Austria | 2.88 | 2.76 | + 4.3% |
| Australia | 2.45 | 2.47 | − .8% |
| New Zealand | 2.41 | 2.37 | + 1.7% |
| Netherlands | 2.32 | 2.22 | + 4.5% |
| Denmark | 2.30 | 2.18 | + 5.5% |
| Romania | 2.24 | 2.11 | + 6.2% |
| Republic of Ireland | 2.23 | 2.35 | − 5.1% |
| Canada | 2.20 | 2.19 | + .5% |
| U.S.A. | 2.20 | 2.15 | + 2.3% |
| United Kingdom | 2.19 | 2.11 | + 3.8% |
| Poland | 2.15 | 2.18 | − 1.4% |
| Yugoslavia | 2.08 | 2.12 | − 1.9% |
| Bulgaria | 1.98 | 1.82 | + 8.8% |
| Finland | 1.69 | 1.67 | + 1.2% |
| Sweden | 1.68 | 1.68 | — |
| Norway | 1.66 | 1.07 | +55.1% |
| U.S.S.R. | 1.64 | 1.64 | — |
| Cyprus | 1.18 | 1.13 | + 4.4% |
| Iceland | 1.01 | .95 | + 6.3% |
| Republic of S. Africa | .87 | .80 | + 8.8% |
| Japan | .80 | .75 | + 6.7% |

| 1979 Rank | 1979 | 1978 | Change |
|---|---|---|---|
| Peru | .70 | 68 | + 2.9% |
| Mexico | .63 | .55 | +14.5% |
| Israel | .50 | .50 | — |
| Cuba | .45 | .61 | −26.2% |
| Turkey | .20 | .21 | − 4.8% |
| Nation Average | 3.01 | 2.91 | + 1.3% |

Source: *The Bottom Line,* Alcohol Research Information Service, Vol. 5, Winter 1982, pg. 32

Four of the five top nations in per-capita consumption of absolute alcohol—France, Italy, Spain, and Portugal—consume their alcohol primarily as wine; only Luxembourg does not (consuming chiefly distilled spirits). Lowest per-capita consumption of absolute alcohol among all nations reporting occurs in Japan, Peru, Mexico, Israel, Cuba, and Turkey.

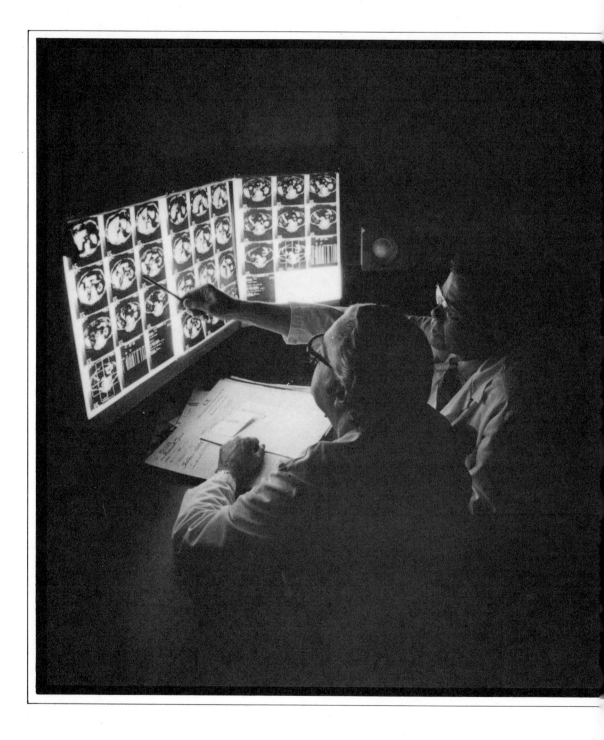

# Effects of Alcoholic Beverages on the Body

A first step in learning is the assessment of current knowledge: a person who determines how much he/she knows about alcohol can choose specific areas of study to expand his/her current information base, dealing briefly with familiar topics and spending valuable time on less familiar areas.

The quiz that follows can help in assessment. Place a check in the box to the right of each question you can answer correctly, and allow yourself one point for each correct answer. When you have finished, glance over the questions you could not answer. You will find the information pertaining to those areas in this text, and you will have the chance to broaden your information base about alcohol use and abuse.[1]

### Questions
(Answers follow the test)                                              *correct*

1. What is the chemical substance that makes all alcoholic beverages intoxicating?  ☐

2. Ethanol and ether have similar effects. Are they classified as depressants or stimulants?  ☐

[1]Adapted from *To Your Health: The Effects of Alcohol on Body Functions,* U.S. Dept. of Health, Education, and Welfare, DHEW Publication No. (ADM) 77-45A.

# EFFECTS OF ALCOHOLIC BEVERAGES ON THE BODY

3. True or false: All distilled spirits are 100 percent ethanol. ☐

4. The proof stated on the bottle is equal to twice the amount of ethanol it contains. What percentage of ethanol is contained in 90-proof whiskey? ☐

5. About how much ethanol does 1 ounce of distilled spirits contain? ☐

6. An average serving of most alcoholic beverages contains about the same amount of ethanol. About how much ethanol is contained in a 4-ounce glass of table wine? ☐

7. About how much ethanol is contained in a 12-ounce can of beer? ☐

8. True or false: Alcohol is not digested like other foods. ☐

9. About 20 percent of the alcohol you consume is absorbed through your stomach. From where is the other 80 percent absorbed? ☐

10. Alcohol affects behavior through which part of the body? ☐

11. How does alcohol get to the brain? ☐

12. Ninety percent of the ethanol in one's body is oxidized. This means the body produces heat and energy by combining alcohol with oxygen and ultimately converts the mixture to water and carbon dioxide. Will taking a cold shower or drinking hot coffee speed up oxidation? ☐

13. It is by means of oxidation that the body gets rid of most of the ethanol. Name a way, besides oxidation and urination, through which ethanol is eliminated from the body. ☐

14. Name one way to *measure* the amount of ethanol in a person's body. ☐

15. What results when a person drinks alcohol at a faster rate than his or her body can oxidize it? ☐

16. Name three factors that affect the absorption rate of alcohol in the body. ☐

17. How do the nonalcoholic substances (such as water, sugar, salts, and other carbohydrates found in beer) affect the rate of alcohol absorption in the body? ☐

18. Does food in the stomach increase or decrease the speed of alcohol absorption? □

19. A 4-ounce glass of table wine and a 12-ounce can of beer each contain about 1/2 ounce of ethanol. Which beverage contains the higher *concentration* of ethanol? □

20. Are champagne and other sparkling wines absorbed faster or slower than noncarbonated wines? □

21. True or false: There is approximately the same amount of ethanol in a 1-ounce shot of 100-proof distilled spirits, a 4-ounce glass of table wine, and a 12-ounce can of beer. □

22. Generally speaking, a larger person must drink more alcohol than a smaller person to become intoxicated. What factor influences intoxication once the alcohol has been absorbed in the bloodstream? □

23. An average person needs an hour to oxidize 1/2 ounce of ethanol. The average drink usually contains 1/2 ounce of ethanol. If you wish to drink but avoid intoxication, how far apart should you space your drinks? □

24. Which of the following are impaired by intoxication: judgment, memory, coordination, or auditory and visual perception? □

25. True or false: Two people of the same weight and physical condition will have the same physical and psychological reactions to an equal amount of alcohol. □

26. True or false: One person will have the same physical and psychological reactions to alcohol every time he or she drinks the same amount. □

27. Ethanol provides heat and energy through oxidation. Because of this chemical property, ethanol may be classified as both a drug and a
   ——————————————————————— . □

28. What is the condition in which a person requires increasing amounts of alcohol in order to achieve the same effect as formerly was achieved by much smaller quantities of alcohol? □

29. Frequent and heavy alcohol use can lead to what condition other than organic or mental disease? □

30. What is the name of the disease most frequently associated with prolonged drinking that causes scar tissue to replace functioning liver cells? ☐

31. True or false: In order to induce labor, physicians often administer small amounts of alcohol intravenously to pregnant women. ☐

32. True or false: A person's mood can influence the way alcohol affects him or her.

33. Name three beneficial changes in feeling caused by having alcohol in the bloodstream. ☐

34. True or false: Simple drunkenness comes from drinking simple drinks of straight liquor. ☐

35. True or false: Chronic drunkenness only affects the drinker. ☐

36. Name two illnesses which frequently are contracted by the chronic drinker. ☐

37. Which of the following may be considered a warning sign that a drinking problem may exist? ☐

    • preoccupation with alcohol; ☐
    • constantly feeling uncomfortable when no alcoholic beverages are available; ☐
    • drinking to deal with problems created by drinking; ☐
    • all of the above. ☐

## Answers

1. *Ethanol, ethyl alcohol.* Distilled spirits, wine, beer—all alcoholic beverages—contain ethanol. The concentration of ethanol is the primary intoxicant variable in alcoholic beverages.

2. *Depressants* (anesthetics/hypnotic-sedatives). Even though a little alcohol can release inhibitions and make a person forget his fatigue, alcohol is *not* a stimulant. Increasing amounts progressively depress the central nervous system.

3. *False.* Distilled spirits can contain up to nearly 100 percent ethanol but most American spirits contain 40 to 50 percent. The proof stated on the bottle is equal to twice the amount of ethanol it contains. For example, 100-proof whiskey contains 50 percent ethanol.

4. *45 percent.* The next time you buy a bottle of whiskey or other distilled spirits, keep in mind that a shot of 80-proof vodka doesn't "kick" the unwary drinker as hard as a shot of 100-proof bourbon.

5. *1/2 ounce.* Remember, distilled spirits and ethanol are not the same. The amount or percentage of ethanol is equal to half the proof indicated on the bottle.

6. *1/2 ounce.* Wine may be a connoisseur's drink, but it packs more of a wallop than a lot of people think. Wine punch can be particularly deceiving if you drink enough of it.

7. *1/2 ounce.* Despite its relatively mild alcoholic reputation, if you drink a lot of beer, you drink a lot.

8. *True.* That is why it acts on you so fast and why it seems to "go to your head."

9. *From the small intestine.* Alcohol is absorbed faster from the small intestine than from the stomach.

10. *The brain.* Different behaviors are affected by the action of alcohol on different parts of the brain.

11. *It is carried to the brain through the bloodstream.* The higher the concentration of alcohol in the blood, the greater the effect on the functioning of the brain and nervous system.

12. *No.* Oxidation proceeds at a constant rate. That is why time is the important factor in eliminating alcohol from the body. Taking a cold shower or drinking coffee merely allows the passage of time; it does not create sobriety by increasing the rate of oxidation.

13. *Exhaling.* Since 90 percent of the alcohol one drinks is oxidized or burned up at a constant rate, breathing faster or running around the block will not significantly speed up the time it takes to get rid of the alcohol consumed.

14. *Blood, urine, breath samples* can reveal the concentration of ethanol in a person's system. Each of these procedures, particularly blood sampling, is quite accurate. Police usually use a breath-testing device on suspected intoxicated drivers because of the test's convenience.

15. *Intoxication if enough alcohol is accumulated.* Remember, drinking does not have to go hand in hand with intoxication. People can drink alcoholic beverages at rates or in amounts that do not necessarily cause drunkenness or intoxication.

16. *Concentration of alcohol in beverage consumed; amount of alcohol consumed; rate of consumption; amount of food in stomach; nonalcoholic substances in beverage; emotions (i.e., stress, fear, anger); carbonation in beverage.* Any of these answers is correct. The next questions will further elaborate these points.

17. *Slow, decrease.* Any food substance blocks absorption to some extent. However, this does not mean the tomato juice in a Bloody Mary will offer a lot of protection.

18. *Decrease.* Food both dilutes the alcohol and cushions the wall of the stomach against absorption. Oily foods and proteins such as milk are especially effective in slowing down absorption.

19. *Wine.* As we said, a 12-ounce can of beer and a 4-ounce glass of table wine contain comparable amounts of ethanol. So, we may assume the wine is roughly three times as strong as beer. However, since few people stop at only 4 ounces of beer, an "average" serving of beer is as potent as an "average" glass of wine.

20. *Faster.* The carbon dioxide in carbonated beverages can cause the valve between the stomach and the small intestine to open. With the entrance to the small intestine open, one's alcohol absorption rate is increased.

21. *True.* An average serving of each has about the same alcohol content and is almost equally intoxicating.

22. *Body weight.* Large people have more blood. Alcohol is diluted in proportion to the amount of blood a person has. This is not to say a larger person can drink more than a smaller person without feeling the effects of alcohol; other physical and psychological factors are involved. However, body weight and size are large factors in one's rate of intoxication.

23. *About one hour.* In addition, you should "nurse" your drinks.

24. *Any of the above.* Different skills and behavior are affected as intoxication anesthetizes different parts of the brain. Most people show visible signs of intoxication at 0.10 percent to 0.15 percent blood-alcohol concentration. Most people's judgment and coordination, however, are impaired to some degree before they drink four or five drinks.

25. *False.* An individual's reaction to alcohol involves too many different physical, adaptational, and psychological factors to assume that any two people's reaction will be the same.

26. *False*. The same person may react differently on different occasions. Each individual's physical and psychological makeup, drinking experience, and condition and mood on any one occasion can affect the rate and intensity of reactions to an ounce of alcohol.

27. *Food*. Ethanol is classified as a simple, incomplete food with limited nutritional value: It lacks vitamins, amino acids, and minerals, yet is very high in calories. Those who make a habit of "drinking their meals" rather than maintaining a balanced diet may develop serious nutritional deficiencies.

28. *Tolerance* is the condition in which the body responds less and less to repeated use of the same drug—in this case the drug is alcohol—so that a greater dose is required to achieve the former effect.

29. *Addiction or dependence*. A person may become an alcohol addict just as one may become a heroin or nicotine addict. Addiction means that the body reacts markedly when deprived of the drug.

30. *Cirrhosis*. A heavy drinker may be likely to develop cirrhosis, rarely otherwise contracted. Less commonly related to drinking, but a real danger for heavy drinkers, are heart disease, ulcers, and other physical, mental, and nervous disorders.

31. *False*. In recent studies pregnant women were given small amounts of alcohol to successfully curb or reduce premature labor contractions. Precious growing time was gained for the premature infants, who were born free of ill symptoms.

32. *True*. Although alcohol may not affect an individual in the same way every time it is consumed, its effect is influenced by a person's mood.

33. *Lessened feelings of tiredness and fatigue; lessened feelings of tension, anxiety, and pressure; lessened feelings of self-consciousness and increased feeling of "I'm a pretty good person after all"; social relations may seem less difficult, more honest, healthy and open; release of inhibitions*. Any of these feelings may occur.

34. *False*. Simple drunkenness refers to intoxication which occurs occasionally or unpredictably, but not as part of any regular pattern.

35. *False*. Chronic and patterned drunkenness not only affects the drinker but also those around him or her. Marital and family problems are likely to occur. Excessive drinking may affect an individual's job performance. Even the general public may be affected because this type of drunkenness leads to a

much higher risk of accidents, particularly auto accidents.

36. *Alcohol hepatitis; cirrhosis.*

37. *All of the above.*

## Scoring

| | |
|---|---|
| *26–37 correct:* | Put out a shingle; you're guru material. |
| *21–25 correct:* | You're a budding genius; don't let it go to your head. |
| *16–20 correct:* | Better than most. |
| *11–15 correct:* | Average. |
| *6–10 correct* | Below average. |
| *0–5 correct* | Poor. |

# Alcohol Absorption

Under ordinary conditions, beverage alcohol is absorbed relatively quickly through the stomach and the small intestine, and then carried throughout the body. The absorption can be markedly influenced by a number of factors, including:

*Alcohol concentration in the beverage.* The greater the alcohol content of the beverage—up to a maximum of about 40 percent (80 proof)—the more rapidly the alcohol is absorbed and the higher the peak blood-alcohol concentration.

*Other chemicals in the beverage.* The greater the amount of nonalcoholic chemicals in the beverage, the more slowly the alcohol is absorbed. For example, vodka is absorbed very rapidly, and wines and beers more slowly.

*Presence of food in the stomach.* Eating with drinking affects the absorption of alcohol, especially if the alcohol consumed is in distilled spirits or wine. When alcoholic beverages are taken with a substantial meal, peak blood-alcohol concentration may be reduced by as much as 50 percent.

*Speed of drinking.* The more rapidly the beverage is ingested, the higher the peak blood-alcohol concentration. Thus, the amount of alcohol in the blood will be lower if the beverage is sipped than if it is gulped.

*Emptying time of the stomach.* The amount of time alcohol is in the stomach can affect the influence of alcohol on the body. Emptying time of the stomach may be either slowed or speeded by fear, anger, stress, nausea, condition of the stomach tissues, and type of food consumed.

*Body weight.* The blood-alcohol level in a 180-pound person who consumes 4 ounces of alcohol is usually substantially lower than that of a 130-pound person taking the same amount in the same length of time. The larger person has more blood and requires greater amounts of alcohol to reach a given blood-alcohol level.

*Drinking history.* Tolerance may be built up from a long history of drinking; increasing amounts of alcohol are needed to result in the physical and behavioral reactions formerly produced at lesser concentrations.

*Body chemistry.* Each individual has a pattern of physiological functioning that affects his/her reaction to alcohol. For example, some people experience the "dumping syndrome," in which the stomach empties more rapidly and alcohol is absorbed more quickly.

*Environment.* Where one drinks may determine how quickly the effects of alcohol are felt. There may be distinct differences in rapidity of effect depending upon whether drinking is done at the local tavern, a social gathering at a friend's home, a hostile environment, or an unfamiliar place.

*The Drinker's expectations.* The preconceived notions of the effects of alcohol will influence the actual effects produced by drinking. Many become intoxicated on less alcohol merely because they have that expectation before they begin drinking.

*General state of emotional and physical health.* Many people seem more susceptible to the effects of alcohol when they are extremely fatigued, have been recently ill, or are under emotional stress and strain. The usual amount of alcohol results in uncomfortable effects.

*Other drugs.* (Chapter Four discusses interactions of alcohol and other drugs.)

Reactions to alcohol, then, are determined less by the amount of alcohol drunk than by its concentration in the blood (see Table 8). Alcohol does not have to be digested before reaching the bloodstream, as food does. Instead, it is immediately absorbed into the blood, which passes directly through the walls of the stomach and small intestine. Absorption takes place by simple diffusion from higher to lower concentrations of alcohol. Within two or three minutes after a few sips of an alcoholic beverage have been swallowed, alcohol can be detected in the blood. Somewhat less than 20 percent of a drink goes into the bloodstream from the stomach. Most of the remainder is absorbed from the small intestine. The maximum blood-alcohol concentration is usually reached about one hour after consumption.

Once in the bloodstream, alcohol begins to affect the interrelated central and autonomic nervous systems.

The central nervous system includes the brain and spinal cord. The 31 pairs of spinal nerves handle impulses to and from muscles, skin, and sensory organs. Ingested alcohol depresses the central nervous system, causing, among other things, impairments in judgment, perception, self-control, and dilating blood

## Table 8
### Estimated blood-alcohol concentrations

Estimated potential blood-alcohol concentration in one hour*

| Alcoholic beverages | Alcohol content % | Normal measures dispensed | One drink (Body weight) | | | | Two drinks (Body weight) | | | | Three drinks (Body weight) | | | |
|---|---|---|---|---|---|---|---|---|---|---|---|---|---|---|
| | | | 100 | 140 | 180 | 220 | 100 | 140 | 180 | 220 | 100 | 140 | 180 | 220 |
| a) Ale | 5 | 12 oz. | 0.05 | 0.04 | 0.03 | 0.02 | 0.08 | 0.06 | 0.05 | 0.05 | 0.11 | 0.09 | 0.08 | 0.07 |
| b) Malt beverage | 7 | 12 oz. | 0.06 | 0.05 | 0.04 | 0.03 | 0.09 | 0.07 | 0.06 | 0.05 | 0.15 | 0.12 | 0.09 | 0.08 |
| c) Regular beer | 4 | 12 oz. | 0.04 | 0.03 | 0.02 | 0.02 | 0.07 | 0.05 | 0.04 | 0.04 | 0.10 | 0.08 | 0.06 | 0.05 |
| Wines — | | | | | | | | | | | | | | |
| a) Fortified: (port, muscatel, etc.) | 18 | 3 oz. | 0.04 | 0.03 | 0.02 | 0.02 | 0.07 | 0.05 | 0.04 | 0.03 | 0.10 | 0.08 | 0.06 | 0.05 |
| b) Natural: red, white, champagne | 12 | 3 oz. | 0.03 | 0.03 | 0.02 | 0.02 | 0.06 | 0.05 | 0.04 | 0.04 | 0.08 | 0.06 | 0.04 | 0.04 |
| Cider (hard) | 10 | 6 oz. | 0.05 | 0.04 | 0.03 | 0.02 | 0.08 | 0.06 | 0.05 | 0.05 | 0.11 | 0.09 | 0.08 | 0.07 |
| Liqueurs — | | | | | | | | | | | | | | |
| a) Strong: sweet, Syrupy | 40 | 1 oz. | 0.03 | 0.03 | 0.02 | 0.02 | 0.07 | 0.05 | 0.04 | 0.03 | 0.08 | 0.06 | 0.05 | 0.05 |
| b) Medium: fruit brandies | 25 | 2 oz. | 0.04 | 0.03 | 0.02 | 0.02 | 0.08 | 0.06 | 0.04 | 0.04 | 0.10 | 0.08 | 0.06 | 0.06 |
| Distilled spirits — brandy; cognac; rum; scotch; vodka; whiskey | 45 | 1 oz. | 0.04 | 0.03 | 0.02 | 0.02 | 0.07 | 0.05 | 0.04 | 0.03 | 0.09 | 0.07 | 0.06 | 0.05 |
| Mixed drinks & cocktails — | | | | | | | | | | | | | | |
| a) Strong: Martini; Manhattan | 30 | 3½ oz. | 0.08 | 0.06 | 0.04 | 0.04 | 0.15 | 0.12 | 0.09 | 0.08 | 0.22 | 0.16 | 0.12 | 0.10 |
| b) Medium: Old Fashioned; Alexander | 15 | 4 oz. | 0.05 | 0.04 | 0.03 | 0.02 | 0.08 | 0.06 | 0.05 | 0.05 | 0.11 | 0.09 | 0.08 | 0.07 |
| c) Light: High Ball sweet & sour mixes; tonics | 7 | 8 oz. | 0.05 | 0.04 | 0.03 | 0.02 | 0.08 | 0.06 | 0.05 | 0.04 | 0.12 | 0.09 | 0.07 | 0.06 |

SOURCE: U. S. Department of Transportation, "First Aid for the Drunken Driver Begins in Your Office," GPO 717-793, pp. 3-4.
*For each hour additional subtract 0.15% w/v from the number shown.

vessels beneath the skin. Initially, the resulting sensations are those of relaxation and well-being.(10)

The autonomic nervous system is a motor system, automatic in nature. It is involved in the functioning of blood vessels, sweat glands, skin, heart, lungs, gastrointestinal and genitourinary tracts, and hormone-secreting glands. Within the autonomic system are sympathetic and parasympathetic nerves, which balance bodily functions. The sympathetic nerves *mobilize* bodily resources that allow for vigorous physical activity or emotional response—for example, increased heart rate, raised blood pressure, enlarged pupils. The parasympathetic nerves *conserve* bodily resources—for example, slowed heart rate, lowered blood pressure, constricted pupils. Alcohol and other drugs simulate these responses in the body. They are called *adrenergic* drugs when they create the sympathetic effect, and *cholinergic* when they create the parasympathetic effect. Drugs can also inhibit or stop sympathetic and parasympathetic action, or even inhibit an inhibitor. Alcohol can, for instance, depress respiratory functioning, inhibit secretion of certain hormones, and slow down the absorption of some nutrients. The effects of alcohol on the nervous system and the bodily processes it controls are highly complex and important.(10)

The speed of alcohol absorption affects the rate at which one becomes intoxicated. Recent research reported in *Science Digest* indicates that there may be still another factor—the secretion of a group of prostaglandins, a class of compounds located in almost all body fluids and human tissue. While the prostaglandins affect virtually every biological activity, researchers now think that one of them, PGE1, is linked to intoxication and the resulting hangover. Dr. David F. Horrobin, a Montreal biologist, claims that drinking too much causes oversecreation of PGE1, which is what actually causes the alcohol "high" and feelings of euphoria and intoxication. In other words, it is the secretion of the PGE1—not the alcohol itself—that results in intoxication. When the balance shifts in the opposite direction as the alcohol consumption slacks off, not enough PGE1 is secreted, and the result is the hangover.[2]

While speed of alcohol consumption affects the rate of intoxication, the speed of alcohol *metabolism* affects the rate at which one becomes sober again.

## Metabolism

Once absorbed into the bloodstream and carried throughout the body, alcohol undergoes metabolic (or oxidative) changes. Most of these processes occur in the liver. Alcohol is changed first into *acetaldehyde,* a highly irritating toxic chemical. This conversion takes place as a liver enzyme—dehydrogenase—acts on the alcohol. Acetaldehyde rarely accumulates, since it is oxidized quickly into *acetate* by another enzyme, aldehyde dehrogenase. Acetate is transformed into a variety

[2]"RX: Alcohol and Health," *The Bottom Line on Alcohol in Society,* Vol. 5, No. 1 (Winter 1982), p. 20.

of other compounds, which are eventually oxidized completely into carbon dioxide and water. So the major changes involved in alcohol metabolism are:

$$\underset{(C_2H_5OH)}{\text{Ethanol}} + \underset{(O_2)}{\text{Oxygen}} \xrightarrow{\text{ADH}} \underset{(C_2H_4O)}{\text{acetaldehyde}} \xrightarrow{\text{ALDH}} \underset{(C_2H_4O_2)}{\text{acetate}} \longrightarrow \underset{(CO_2)}{\text{carbon dioxide}} \text{ and } \underset{(H_2O)}{\text{water}}$$

(ADH=alcohol dehydrogenase; ALDH=aldehyde dehydrogenase). The total metabolic process yields about seven calories for each gram of alcohol. All but 2 to 5 percent of the ingested alcohol is metabolized by the liver. The remainder is excreted chemically unchanged, mostly in urine, breath, and sweat.

The liver can metabolize approximately one-third of an ounce of absolute alcohol every hour. In terms of beverage alcohol, the rate of oxidation is estimated at two-thirds to three-fourths of an ounce of 50 percent (100 proof) whiskey, or an equivalent amount of any other alcoholic beverage, an hour. Individual differences do exist due to liver size, enzyme activity, disease, and so on, but the rate of alcohol oxidation is fairly constant for each person; there is little that can be done to increase the metabolism rate significantly.

If more than one-third of an ounce of alcohol is in the bloodstream, some of it escapes immediate destruction and is distributed throughout the body tissues at the same speed as water. The alcohol can also gain access to the fetal circulation in a pregnant woman. It is believed that the fetal circulation takes in as much alcohol as the general circulation, and the fetus becomes just as intoxicated as the mother.

## Nutritional Value of Alcohol

With the exception of small amounts of B vitamins and traces of minerals in wine and beer, alcoholic beverages contain no nutrients. These beverages are the prototype of "empty calories." The idea that alcohol calories are not fattening has no basis in fact. Each gram of alcohol metabolized in the body yields 7 calories. This adds up to approximately 200 calories per fluid ounce of alcohol. In beer, some additional calories—about 4 per ounce—remain from the surviving cereal content of the original fermented grain (see Table 9).

## The Sobering-Up Process

As a general rule, it takes as many hours as the number of drinks consumed for the drinker to sober up completely. Speeding up the process would require some method of speeding up the rate of alcohol metabolism, and this method has not been found. All one can do is wait and let the liver do its work.

The hangover—that morning-after misery of fatigue, headache, nausea, and vomiting—is a common aftereffect of overindulgence in alcohol. Several causes, such as drinking more than one type of beverage in an evening, have been assigned to the hangover, but it is produced by simply drinking too much. Any single alcoholic beverage, or pure ethyl alcohol, will do. Hangovers can be prevented only by drinking slowly, with food in the stomach, under relaxed social

**Table 9**
**Nutritional content of alcoholic beverages**

| Food nutrient** | Type of beverage and quantity† | | | | | |
|---|---|---|---|---|---|---|
| | Beer 12 oz. | Rum 1.5 oz. | Whiskey 1.5 oz. | Martini 2 oz. | Manhattan‡ 2 oz. | Wine§ 4 oz. |
| Calories | 175.0 | 150.0 | 110.0 | 160.0 | 160.0 | 160.0 |
| Calories from alcohol | 125.0 | 150.0 | 110.0 | 110.0 | 110.0 | 145.0 |
| Protein (g) | 2.0 | 0.0 | 0.0 | 0.0 | 0.0 | 0.0 |
| Fat (g) | 0.0 | 0.0 | 0.0 | 0.0 | 0.0 | 0.0 |
| Carbohydrate (g) | 12.0 | 0.0 | 0.0 | 0.0 | 0.0 | 4.2 |
| Thiamine (mg) | 0.1 | 0.0 | 0.0 | 0.0 | 0.0 | 0.0 |
| Nicotinic acid (mg) | 0.75 | 0.0 | 0.0 | 0.0 | 0.0 | 0.0 |
| Riboflavin (mg) | 10.0 | 0.0 | 0.0 | 0.0 | 0.0 | 0.0 |
| Ascorbic acid (mg) | 0.0 | 0.0 | 0.0 | 0.0 | 0.0 | 0.0 |
| Folic acid (mg) | 0.0 | 0.0 | 0.0 | 0.0 | 0.0 | 0.0 |

SOURCE: Adapted from Kenneth L. Jones, Louis Shainberg, and Curtis O. Byer, *Drugs and Alcohol,* 2nd ed. (San Francisco: Harper and Row, 1973), p. 125.

**Approximate amounts only.

†Quantities—as most often consumed.

‡Only accounts for caloric content of mixer.

§Dry wine—20% alcoholic content

conditions, with sufficient self-discipline to avoid intoxication, or not at all.

Hangovers, while rarely dangerous, are unpleasant. No satisfactory, specific treatment is known. There are numerous folk remedies—raw egg, oysters, chili peppers, ice cream, steak sauce, vitamins, and other drugs—but none are supported by scientific evidence. Since the hangover headache is usually caused by the pressure that distended arteries in the head put on cranial nerves (or it may be partly caused by allergic reaction to congeners), coffee may be helpful. The caffeine in it makes the distended arteries contract. Alkalizers, too, may give some relief by soothing the irritated digestive tract. But these do not "cure" the hangover; they only relieve symptoms and do not speed the sobering-up process.(10)

It has been hypothesized that there are ethnic differences in the rate of metabolism. Studies have shown that Eskimos and some Native Americans take longer than Caucasians to sober up, a difference that is attributed to variances in metabolism rates. A study of Caucasian twins revealed that ethanol elimination rates were under a significant degree of genetic control (approximately 80 to 90 percent).(56)

# The Effects of Alcohol on the Central Nervous System

Most people drink alcoholic beverages for pleasure as well as for relief from fears and tensions—which probably explains the widespread popularity of alcohol as a social beverage. Not everyone responds to alcohol in the same way, however. For some, the same small amounts of alcohol result not in relaxation, but in increased anxiety; not in happiness, but in suspicion and distrust. These atypical responses may lead to belligerent feelings or actions or to episodes of confusion and disorientation. Even the first few sips of alcohol may cause changes in mood and behavior, either because of a conditioned or a learned response based on previous drinking experiences.(10) Larger amounts of alcohol, however, lead to fewer individual differences in behavior as the depressant effect of alcohol begins to dominate. As this occurs, a typical sequence of tiredness, sleepiness, and, ultimately, stupor occurs. Depending on the individual and the circumstances, fatigue may be accompanied by either irritability or by mellowness and warmth.

These varied and complex effects of alcohol are due partly to the changes in central nervous system function—the effect of alcohol on the brain. Ingested alcohol is absorbed from the alimentary tract and carried by the circulating blood to the brain and other organs. The functioning of the brain is affected by a much lower concentration of alcohol in the blood than that needed to significantly affect the other tissues. The observable effects of alcohol intoxication (such as slurred speech and an unsteady gait) are not due to the direct action of alcohol on the tongue or legs, but are caused by its effect on the parts of the brain that integrate and control the activities of the tongue and legs.

Changes in the nervous system are due mainly to the fact that alcohol impedes electrical impulses in the nerves and inhibits the flow of sodium ions across the cell membrane. The resulting condition causes nerve refiring difficulty.

The most notable and dramatic effects of alcohol are the behavior patterns attributed to its action on the central nervous system. Low blood-alcohol levels usually produce mild sedation, relaxation, or tranquility. Slightly higher levels, in some people, produce behavioral changes that seem to suggest stimulation of the brain—talkativeness, aggressiveness, and excessive activity. But these symptoms are caused by *depression* of the brain centers that normally inhibit such behavior. At still higher levels, greater brain depression produces uncoordination, confusion, disorientation, stupor, anesthesia, coma, or death. Due to variations in body weight, rapidity of drinking, and so on, it is not possible to give the exact blood-alcohol level at which these changes occur. Table 10 provides a general guide.

Long-term excessive use of alcohol can result in premature aging of the brain; this alcohol-related organic brain syndrome (OBS) is permanent and irreversible. Whereas some difficulties with cognitive function clear up after a period of abstinence, residual problems may remain, usually due to a combination of nutritional deficiencies, repeated alcohol-related convulsions, head injuries, and degeneration of nerve and tissue cells. The clinical picture of an alcohol-related OBS is the same as that of a nonalcoholic-related OBS.(150).

The brain damage that occurs with chronic alcohol abuse is a result of the neurotoxicity of alcohol in long-term use. When nerves die, they are not replaced, since nervous tissue is not regenerative. Chronic alcohol abuse hastens brain aging, which can cause reduction of sensory acuity, loss of reasoning power, and

**Table 10**
**Blood-alcohol concentrations and depressant effects**
**on the central nervous system**

| Blood-alcohol concentration | Number of drinks consumed* | Effects that often occur** |
|---|---|---|
| .04% | 1–2 | Lowered efficiency of the cortex, or brain covering, in the uppermost part of the brain<br>Some impairment of judgment<br>Release of restraints and inhibitions<br>Feelings of warmth, relaxation, and buoyancy<br>Slight change in existing mood<br>Increased heart rate |
| .06 | 3–4 | Continued depression of the cortex<br>Disruption of judgment<br>Some loss of coordination<br>Less concern about environment<br>Feelings of warmth<br>Mental relaxation<br>Relaxation of inhibitions |
| .10 | 5–6 | Reduced operation of those parts of the brain controlling movement<br>Impairment of fine coordination skills<br>Delayed reaction time<br>Exaggerated emotions<br>Noticeable clumsiness<br>Talkativeness<br>Impairment of peripheral vision<br>Presumptive evidence of "impaired ability" to operate motor vehicle in all states |
| .16 | 6–8 | Progressive deterioration of higher cortical functions and some motor activities<br>Staggering<br>Slurred speech<br>Blurred vision<br>Serious loss of judgment and coordination<br>Unmistakable abnormality of gross bodily and mental functions |
| .20 | 8–10 | Lowered midbrain functioning<br>Feeling of need to lie down<br>Inability to walk or dress without help<br>Tears or rage with little provocation<br>Double vision |
| .30 | 10–15 | Reduced functioning of lower portion of brain—marked intoxication marked by increasing difficulty in maintaining motor function<br>High degree of uninhibited behavior |

| Blood-alcohol concentration | Number of drinks consumed* | Effect that often occur** |
|---|---|---|
| .40—.50 | 15—25 | Stupor and confusion<br>Boisterousness and belligerence<br>Involvement in violent incidents or accidents<br>Poor comprehension of what is seen or heard<br>Depression of function of the entire area of perception in the base of the brain—severe intoxication from which arousal is difficult<br>Loss of feeling<br>Unconsciousness<br>Shock (skin clammy, pupils dilated) |
| .60 and above | 25+ | Reduced operation of the medulla in the lowermost portion of the brain, which controls the involuntary processes such as digestion, heartbeat, breathing, and blood pressure<br>Coma and death from respiratory or cardiovascular failure |

*One drink would equal one 12-oz. bottle of 4.5 percent beer or one 4-oz. glass of 14 percent wine or 1 to 1.5 oz. of 50 percent alcohol.

**Corrections of blood-alcohol concentrations with changes in behavior or functions controlled by the central nervous system are relatively clear at higher blood-alcohol levels. However, at lower blood-alcohol levels, there may be considerable individual differences in behavior.

failure of memory. Things learned while under the influence of alcohol or afterward are distrubed. The effect on memory is greatest when the blood-alcohol concentration is rising. Under toxic conditions, a state may be reached where the drinker neither learns nor remembers.

Excessive alcohol use may also cause seizures. Alcohol-related seizures may be linked to several factors, such as withdrawal, increase of epileptic seizures, reactions to toxicity, fever, brain infections, head injuries, and chemical deficiencies.

## Effects of Alcohol on Motor Performance[3]

Tests of motor control or coordination show greater detrimental effects than sensory capabilities. Intoxicating doses of alcohol impair most types of performance, partly depending on familiarity with the task. Motor impairments (such as unsteady balance, a staggering walk, and slurred speech) are probably the most obvious behavioral characteristics of intoxicated people. Alcohol increases swaying, especially if the eyes are closed and the stabilizing effect of

[3]The following five sections are reprinted in part from Alcohol, Drug Abuse and Mental Health Administration, *Facts About Alcohol and Alcoholism*, DHEW Publication No. (ADM) 74-31.

visual cues is blocked. Sensory motor coordination is also adversely affected by alcohol, especially if the task, as in tracking a moving object, requires attention to multiple concurrent events.

People differ in their susceptibility to the effects of alcohol on motor performance, especially at blood-alcohol levels of 0.10 percent and below. Although sufficient alcohol impairs anyone's performance, anxious or determined people are better able to bring their performance up to its normal level.

# Effects of Alcohol on Sensation and Perception

Sharpness of vision seems relatively unaffected by alcohol. At high doses of alcohol, however, there is a decrease in ability to discriminate between lights of different intensities, and a narrowing of the visual field. The latter effect ("tunnel vision") may be particularly dangerous in automobile driving. Resistance to glare is impaired so that the eye requires longer to readjust after exposure to bright lights. Sensitivity to certain colors, especially red, appears to decrease.

For some people, alcoholic beverages such as wine may enhance the flavor of some foods. For others, alcohol reduces sensitivity to taste and odors, making food less appealing. Tactile response is not affected, but sensitivity to pain is decreased, resulting in an increased incidence of burns, cuts, scrapes, and bruises among problem drinkers.(150)

In general, the senses are resistant to alcohol, but the changes that do occur are detrimental.

## Attention, Memory, and Conceptual Processes

Although alcohol usually does not affect concentrated attention when only one source of incoming information is involved, alcohol has detrimental effects on the capacity to absorb information from more than one source simultaneously. Research findings suggest that alcohol may also impede the capacity of the brain to switch from one source of information to another.

After taking acute doses of alcohol, both alcoholic and nonalcoholic individuals suffer significant loss of memory functioning. These losses occur in nonalcoholic drinkers after the consumption of considerably smaller amounts of alcohol than those that produce the alcoholic blackout. These blackouts involve amnesia without loss of consciousness and are related directly to memory loss during intoxication.

Memory storage processes are particularly vulnerable to disruption by alcohol. When intoxicated, people have considerable difficulty processing new information and recalling that information later.

Sober alcoholics often display serious impairment in cognitive functioning, but the deterioration may not be pervasive. On full-scale IQ test scores, losses occur in visual, spatial, and abstracting abilities, in conceptual shifting, in perception, and in motor performance.

### Emotions

Empirical investigations have shown that drinking increases during some stressful situations, especially those perceived as threatening to self-esteem. Drinking also increases in intense situations over which individuals feel they have little or no control.

Studies have yielded conflicting results on whether drinking reduces feelings of tension and anxiety in social drinkers. However, male alcoholics have been found to become more anxious, depressed, and angry when drinking heavily—effects that were not found among female alcoholics.

Research indicates that alcohol increases aggression in certain circumstances but not in others. When male social drinkers drink in competitive group situations, interpersonal aggression increases significantly. In contrast, when male-female couples interact in an unstructured way, neither aggression nor hostility increases systematically in the drinking subjects. Research has also indicated that subjects' expectations about alcohol are highly relevant. Those who believe they have drunk alcohol act more aggressively than those who think they have consumed a nonalcoholic beverage, regardless of the actual contents of the drink.(10)

## Effects of Alcohol on Reaction Time

The direct action of alcohol on the body, coupled with its ability to relax feelings of self-criticism and inhibition, produce the "high" associated with alcohol use. Some studies show that alcohol tends to decrease fear and increase likelihood that an individual will accept risks. For example, when a group of bus drivers were given several drinks, they were more likely to drive their buses through spaces that were too narrow—and seemingly more willing to risk failure—than when they were sober. The judgment and skill impairment was not predictable on the basis of amount consumed: some drivers were more affected by two whiskeys than others were by six.

Reaction time is measured by the rapidity with which a subject makes a simple movement, such as pressing a button in response to a sound or visual signal. Below a blood-alcohol level of 0.07 percent, reaction time varies little. Between 0.08 and 0.10 percent, reaction time slows measurably. Higher levels consistently produce larger performance failures. A much greater effect of alcohol on reaction time is found when attention is divided, as when the subject is at the same time engaged in another task.

Other tests measuring both speed and accuracy suggest that alcohol has a greater effect on accuracy and consistency than on speed. A person who has had several drinks tends to "breeze through" a complex test but makes more errors than he normally would and is more erratic in his responses. Many subjects, however, feel their performance has improved and refuse to believe when shown the poor results.

## Effects of Alcohol on Sexuality

The capacity of alcohol to release inhibitions is connected in the public mind with the observation that after drinking, some people tend to show an increased amorousness. This has given rise to an assumption that alcohol promotes or improves sexual activity.

Tests have revealed consistently that large doses of alcohol frustrate sexual performance. Studies of alcoholic persons have revealed that their sex life was disturbed, deficient, and ineffectual. Impotence may result; it is usually reversible with the return of sobriety.

It appears that in nonalcoholic persons, a few drinks dull the sense of restraint and, by helping to overcome lack of confidence or feelings of guilt about sex, facilitate sexual activity. A subtle truth, however, was expressed by Shakespeare: Drink "provokes the desire, but it takes away the performance." Some studies have shown alcohol to cause nervous system damage which, if prolonged, may be irreversible, causing permanent sexual impotence.[10]

In addition, it is now well documented that prolonged administration of alcohol in humans causes their estrogen levels to rise and their androgen and testosterone levels to decrease. The increased estrogen correlates with an increase in the level of a liver enzyme called hepatic aromatase, which is involved in the conversion of androgens to estrogens. Because of the increase in estrogen and the subsequent decrease in androgen, male chronic alcoholics develop signs of feminization, including loss of hair, breast development, and more feminine patterns of fat deposition.(10)

# Effects of Alcohol on Sleep

The effects of alcohol on sleep are known to anyone who has gone to bed after having had too much to drink, only to toss and turn and awaken the following morning feeling headachy and fatigued. Taking several drinks before bedtime has been found to decrease the amount of REM (rapid eye movement) or dreaming sleep. The consequences of being deprived of REM sleep are impaired concentration and memory, as well as anxiety, tiredness, and irritability.

# Alcohol Related Disorders[4]

Common neurological and nutritional disorders that often accompany excessive drinking are described by Dr. Maurice Victor in the following classifications:

### Disorders Due to Alcohol Intoxication

*Simple (usual) intoxication.* Symptoms: exhilaration, slurred speech, staggering gait, loss of inhibitions, drowsiness, etc., progressing through stupor and alcoholic coma.

*"Pathologic" (unusual) intoxication.* Symptoms: agitation, combative and destructive behavior, not accompanied by the usual symptoms of

---

[4]Adapted from Maurice Victor, "Managing Alcoholism," *Drug Therapy* Vol. 00 (July 1973): 57–68.

intoxication, followed by sleep and loss of memory for the combative episode.

## Disorders Due to Withdrawal of Alcohol Following a Period of Chronic Intoxication

Withdrawal symptoms are important not only because they aid in establishing the presence of alcohol, but also because they encourage further drinking to get rid of the symptoms. Once withdrawal states have been established, alcoholism is definitely present.

*Minor (early) withdrawal syndrome.* Onset 8 to 9 hours after withdrawal; tremulousness, flushed face, insomnia, anorexia, weakness, hallucinations (25 percent of hospitalized patients), major generalized seizures ("rum fits"), mild or no disorientation, usually benign, affective disturbances (this feeling has been described as "frightening, ready to jump out of my skin, afraid of a knock on the door, unable to face anyone"), nausea and retching, and sweating (particularly night sweating).

*Major (late) syndrome: delirium tremens.* Onset between 48 to 96 hours after withdrawal; agitation, psychomotor and autonomic nervous system overactivity (rapid heartbeat, fever, profuse sweating, etc.), vivid hallucinations and delusions, profound mental confusion; fatal in 5 to 16 percent of cases.

## Neurological Disorders Caused by Nutritional Deficiency

*Wernicke's disease.* Symptoms: ophthalmoplegia, paralysis of the eyeballs, nystagmus, internal strabismus, squinting of the eyes, weakness or paralysis of conjugate gaze, inability to control muscles, mental confusion.

*Korsakoff's psychosis.* (Appears in most patients after acute signs of Wernicke's disease have subsided, and both conditions may be facets of one disease.) Symptoms: defect in retentive memory, confabulation, apathy, and inertia. Upon examination, the patient seems totally without spontaneity, mentally dull, listless, disoriented to time and place, and unable to correctly identify people and objects.

*Alcoholic polyneuropathy (neuritic beriberi).* Symptons may vary greatly but most patients complain of weakness, paresthesia (burning or prickling sensation), pain, muscle wasting, reflex loss, and changes in skin, hair, and nails. Legs are usually involved earlier and more severely than the arms. The disease responds slowly—usually over a period of one to two years—to balanced diet and multiple vitamin therapy. Recovery is generally incomplete because of peripheral nerve damage.

*Alcohol (tobacco-alcohol) amblyopia.* (Characteristic vision disorder in alcoholics.) Symptoms: blurred near and distant vision, central or centrocecal scotomatia (dark or blind spots in field of vision), mild papillitis (inflammation of tiny capillaries feeding the eye), (occasionally), retinal hemorrhages (occasionally), and red/green color blindness. (These changes are always bilateral and more or less symmetrical). Recovery may occur with nutritional and/or B-vitamin therapy.

*Alcoholic pellagra.* (Now practically confined to alcoholics.) Symptoms: mental and nervous symptoms (which may be attributed to psychoneurosis), diarrhea, dermatitis, and polyneuropathy (degeneration of the peripheral nerve tissue).

### Disorders Probably Caused by Nutritional Deficiency

The link between alcoholism and malnutrition has been definitely established; many evidences of malnutrition exist, usually because of undernutrition that results from dietary deficiencies. Those who subsist solely on alcohol often develop low-grade hypoglycemia, which stimulates the appetite-regulating center in the hypothalamus of the brain. As alcohol intake increases, food intake decreases, leading to weight loss and eventual malnutrition. Detection is difficult, even with laboratory tests, because a broad range of deficiencies may be present. Nutrients most commonly missing are protein and the B-complex vitamins.

Although alcohol is high in calories, overnutrition due to excess calories in addition to a nutritionally balanced diet is much less common than malnutrition among heavy drinkers.

*Alcoholic cerebellar degeneration.* (Usually found in long-term, heavy drinkers under the age of 50 who have neglected their nutrition). Symptoms: lack of muscle coordination in legs (disease usually evolves over short period of time, followed by years of stability) (stability means disease condition remains the same despite rapid onset), trunk instability, and involuntary finger movements (may be significant enough to cause handwriting problems).

*Central pontine myelinosis.* Symptoms: pseudobulbar palsy, quadriplegia (usually lesion is too small to produce symptoms and is only found at autopsy).

*Primary degeneration of the corpus callosum.* (Rare.) Symptoms: diverse cerebral symptoms referable mainly to frontal lobes: agitation, confusion, hallucinations, poor memory and judgment, abnormality of language, loss of bladder and bowel control, drooling, tremulous hands, psychic and emotional disorders, delirium and intellectual deterioration, convulsive seizures, rigidity, paralysis, loss of the ability to speak, and impaired sucking and grasping reflexes.

## Effects on the Liver

The largest and metabolically most complex organ in the body, the liver is functionally involved in circulation, excretion, immunity, metabolism, and detoxification. All of the liver's functions are affected by the presence of alcohol in the body. As the first recipient of digestive products and other substances absorbed from the gastrointestinal tract, the liver also receives substances from general circulation through the hepatic artery. Although it is the primary site for detoxification of alcohol, the liver can be damaged by alcohol and its metabolic products.

Alcohol has a number of metabolic effects on the liver. It inhibits the conversion of amino acids to glucose, the major energy-producing fuel in the body, when the liver store of glucose is low, as is often the case in poorly nourished alcoholics. The resulting hypoglycemia is similar to the condition of reduced blood sugar seen in diabetics who have taken too much insulin.

Another metabolic consequence of heavy alcohol ingestion is alcoholic ketoacidosis, which resembles diabetes by producing excessive blood acidity. The excessive breakdown of fatty acids in both conditions causes a buildup of intermediate breakdown products that back up into the bloodstream, causing toxic effects.

Still another consequence is the inhibition of the conversion of amino acids into certain important proteins manufactured by the liver. Included are albumin, transferin, complement, and several others involved in blood coagulation.(9)

Alcoholic liver disease is one of the most serious consequences of alcohol abuse. Its progressively serious manifestations take the form of fatty liver, alcoholic hepatitis, and cirrhosis. Concerning alcohol and the liver, Dr. Lieber states:[5]

Hardly any tissue in the body escapes physical damage from alcoholism, but liver disease is foremost as a major cause of incapacitating illness and premature death in the alcoholic person. In its milder form, alcoholic liver disease is characterized by accumulation of excess fat in the liver, so-called fatty liver. This is a very common complication of alcoholism, usually benign and fully reversible, though recently, increasing numbers of unexplained deaths have been described in alcoholic persons whose sole finding upon autopsy was a massive fatty liver. When a number of liver cells die and this necrosis causes inflammation, one is dealing with alcoholic hepatitis, a more severe form of alcoholic liver injury associated with a mortality ranging from 10 to 30 percent . . . . Eventually, scarring by fibrous tissue occurs, its excess distorts the normal architecture of the liver, and fibrous bands disect the liver and alter its function. The term cirrhosis characterizes this more severe, irreversible form of alcoholic liver injury.

Cirrhosis is a serious disease which afflicts the patient with numerous complications, especially those derived from the obstruction of blood flow by the scarred liver and the resulting portal hypertension with formation of ascites, collateral circulation (esophageal varices) and gastrointestinal bleeding. Bleeding and other complications such as hepatic coma often lead to a fatal outcome. With the steadily increasing incidence of alcoholism in our population, death rates have had a parallel rise.

After prolonged heavy drinking, the liver is likely to become swollen and tender (acute hepatitis). Hepatitis develops in one-third of all excessive drinkers,

[5]Charles Lieber, "Alcohol and the Liver—A National Problem," *Gastroenterology Medical World News* Vol. 13 (1972): 28.

and it can interfere with the functions of the liver. In severe cases it may lead to cirrhosis of the liver, a major cause of premature death among alcoholics. The amount and duration of alcohol consumption generally determines how serious a case of cirrhosis will be. A steady, daily drinker is more inclined to develop cirrhosis than a spree drinker. If they continue to drink heavily, people with alcoholic cirrhosis often die of portal hypertension or hepatic (liver) failure.

In large urban areas, cirrhosis is the fourth most common cause of death among people aged 25 to 45. In New York City it ranks third among people aged 25 to 65. Cirrhosis mortality is nearly twice as high for Blacks as for whites; for urban Black males aged 25 to 34, the rates are ten times higher than for white males of the same age.

The incidence of cirrhosis is increasing. Presently, about 10 to 20 percent of alcoholic people have it. Of course, not all people with cirrhosis are alcoholics, nor do all alcoholics develop cirrhosis. But most cases of cirrhosis used in these statistics are presumed to originate from alcoholism; in fact, up to 95 percent of all cirrhosis cases are estimated to be alcohol-related.(8)

It has been suggested that a combination of alcohol abuse and nutritional deficiency creates a predisposition to cirrhosis among heavy drinkers. But one long-standing debate appears to have been settled by recent research: adequate diet alone does not prevent alcohol from causing liver disease.(107) Development of cancer of the liver is a risk which accompanies late stages of cirrhosis. The latter occurs even in alcoholics who have not drunk for many years.(107)

## Effects on the Esophagus

It is clear that alcohol can damage the esophagus by direct chemical irritation to its mucosa, by inducing severe vomiting that tears the mucosa, or by interfering with normal motor functions, thereby causing an upward movement of the eroding stomach acid into the esophagus. The major complication in these processes is hemorrhage accompanied or preceded by local pain and difficulty in swallowing.(10)

## Effects on the Stomach

Alcohol may be said to act as an appetizer. A small amount, about 10 percent in the gastric juice of the stomach (one or two drinks' worth) stimulates mild stomach activity by increasing the gastric juice secretion. The brain interprets this as hunger. Some say that because of this, a little alcohol before a meal will improve digestion. But unfortunately, not everyone recognizes or acknowledges the 10 percent level.

If the premeal drink is taken as a strong alcohol solution—say, 20 percent or more—the contact of the alcohol with the throat, gullet, and stomach lining may cause irritation, resulting in a stinging or burning sensation. Without food, the irritation of the tissues actually inhibits gastric secretion. The "heartburn" felt by some who, without eating, drink a large amount of alcohol at one time may be a result of this irritation. Food in the stomach helps neutralize the action of the gastric juices.

Normally, alcohol is quickly diluted by gastric juices, stopping the irritation, but if the alcohol concentration is high enough to inhibit secretion, gastritis can result. Gastritis (chronic inflammation of the stomach lining) and gastric ulcers are common findings among alcoholics. Other organs, such as the liver and brain, cannot be irritated this way because the alcohol is diluted to far less than 1 percent before it gets to them. Alcohol-induced inflammation and irritation of the stomach and other digestive organs and the malabsorption that may occur can enhance the occurrence of malnutrition, which is common in alcoholics.

A large amount of alcohol dumped suddenly into an empty stomach, especially one not used to it, may be irritating enough to cause vomiting. This reflex sometimes saves a drinker from severe intoxication.(10)

## Effects on the Small Intestine

Digestive disturbances in the small intestine are common in alcoholics. Heavy drinking leads to changes in involuntary intestinal motions. In the jejunum (the division of the small intestine below the duodenum), impeding peristalic waves are decreased by alcohol and propulsive waves are unchanged, resulting in an increased rate of propulsion through the small intestine—a possible contributing factor to the diarrhea common among binge-drinking alcoholics.

Intestinal malabsorption may also result from alcohol ingestion, but the degree is determined by the compound to be absorbed, the amount of alcohol, and the method of alcohol administration.

Depending on the level of alcohol ingested or administered, alcohol can also damage cells and derange cellular metabolism in the small intestine. Enzyme systems involved in carbohydrate metabolism are impaired, and the activity of enzymes involved in the uptake and metabolism of lipids is increased. Enzymes involved in cholesterol synthesis are also affected.

## Effects on the Pancreas

Alcoholism (or chronic ingestion of alcohol over a prolonged period of time), is associated with significant increase in the incidence of pancreatitis, a chronic inflammation of the pancreas. Most researchers believe that the disease-causing mechanism is the alcohol-induced increase in protein concentration in pancreatic juice; the protein is thought to precipitate and form obstructive plugs in the pancreatic ducts. While acute alcohol ingestion does not appear to be associated with pancreatitis, it can interfere with pancreatic secretion of digestive enzymes, a change which might account for some of the abnormalities in the intestinal absorption associated with alcoholism.(10)

## Effects on the Kidneys and Other Glands

In spite of all old notions, alcohol is not particularly damaging to the kidneys. It does increase their urinary activity. Recent studies indicate that this is not caused by direct action of alcohol on the kidneys, but by its effect on the pituitary gland. This gland is a small extension of the lower part of the brain. Alcohol inhibits the secretion of an antidiuretic hormone produced in the pituitary gland. As alcohol reduces the activity of this gland, the kidney forms more urine. Normally the hormone acts as a brake on the production of urine. This leads the drinker to urinate frequently.

Alcohol suppresses the secretion of another pituitary hormone, oxytocin, which is normally involved in the onset of labor in pregnant women. In addition to the danger it poses when it crosses the placenta and affects the fetus, alcohol may also delay labor and make childbirth more difficult.

# Effects on Muscle

Although muscle weakness in alcoholic persons has been recognized for almost 150 years, a well-defined syndrome of muscle disease associated with chronic alcohol abuse was described in Russia only in 1928 and was not confirmed there until 1962. In the United States, the syndrome was first recognized in 1957 and since then has been increasingly accepted as a complication of alcoholism. Chronic heavy alcohol ingestion is associated with an acute and chronic muscle tissue disease; it may be independent of nutritional factors, but in some clinical cases the condition has been connected with water and electrolyte imbalance. This muscle disease is reflected primarily in an increase of blood serum creatine phosphokinase and in a diminished rise in blood lactic acid after exercise.[7]

# Effects on the Skin

The response of the skin parallels the progression of alcoholism, so certain skin marks accompany certain patterns of alcohol behavior. A variety of skin problems called *cutaneous stigmata* are associated with different patterns of alcoholism.

*Acute intoxication (the recurring bender).* This type of alcoholism is characterized by the development of any of the following skin problems: cigarette burns (especially on the fingers), tar stains on the fingers, a red face and acne rosacea, bruises in unusual places, ulcers on the backs of the thighs and on the back (from parts of the body being subjected to prolonged pressure), fire ant stings (from sleeping out-of-doors), skin erosions, varicose veins and skin ulcers, and frostbite.

*Chronic intoxication (long-term alcohol use).* This type of alcoholism is characterized by such skin conditions as scabies, pediculosis: (infestation with lice), septic hands and feet, folliculitis: (inflammation of hair follicles on skin), seborrhea: (increased secretion of sebrum (fatty lubricant), sun-exposure melanosis: (abnormal pigmentation (patches of color), in this case resulting from exposure to sun), purpura: (patches of purplish-colored skin caused by bleeding under the skin), flat opaque fingernails: (characteristic of cirrhosis), psoriasis: (chronic skin disease characterized by red patches covered with white scales), and erthematous: (abnormally reddened skin caused by inflammation), skin nodules.

*Dermatosis and alcohol.* Characteristically, these dermatoses are in the following forms: seborrhea, acne rosacea, dermatophytosis: (infestation of a fungus on the skin, hair, or nails), psoriasis, acne vulgaris, black hairy tongue, eczema, leukoplakia: (patches of white inside the mouth), and neurodermatitis: (inflammation of the skin involving nerve tissue).(91,158)

## Effects on Infectious Diseases

Infectious diseases are common complications of chronic alcohol abuse. Bacterial pneumonia, tuberculosis, bacterial peritonitis, and bacteremia are the most prevalent alcohol-related infectious diseases. Two mechanisms are believed responsible for this phenomenon. First, alcohol ingestion decreases glottis closure, which may especially contribute to an increase in respiratory infections. Second, alcohol seems to suppress immune response. There is a decrease in the number and activity of cell-mediated responses, so white blood cells may not adequately circulate to a site of infection. All in all, the breakdown in the primary mechanical barriers of the defense system of the body accounts for an increasing amount of bacterial infections among problem drinkers.

## Effects on Water Balance

Mark Keller's postulation that "alcohol has a drying effect—that it can draw water out of certain materials"—can easily be proven. But this is true only of pure alcohol. Some people believe that the alcohol in beverages does the same thing in the body, drying out the cells. This notion has been used to explain the thirst often felt after drinking heavily.

Laboratory experiments have shown that what actually takes place in the body after drinking is not a withdrawal of water, but a shift in its position. The body is about two-thirds water, and about two-thirds of this water is inside the cells. The amount of water outside the cells, including that in the blood, ordinarily changes little. Inside the cells, the amount changes with intake of fluids or output of urine and sweat. When the water in the cells is depleted, thirst is felt. After a person drinks a large amount of alcohol, water moves from inside the cells to the spaces around them. This causes the feeling of thirst, even though the body has not actually lost water. Whether this temporary shift in the distribution of body water has any effect other than causing thirst is not known.

Research done since Keller's has shown that in the acutely intoxicated patient, one who needs emergency care, there is actually overhydration. Initially, alcohol causes dehydration because it suppresses the antidiuretic hormone from the pituitary gland. This initial, brief diuresis (increased urine flow) is followed by activation of the antidiuretic hormone. So, prolonged drinking ultimately leads to sodium retention and overhydration. Recent evidence, moreover, indicates a link between marked sodium retention and severe depression. Therefore, it is possible that alcohol's pharmacological effects aggravate pre-existing anxiety and depression. This possibility is ironic because so much drinking is done in an attempt to relieve anxiety and depression.

## Effects on the Respiratory Tract

Alcohol dulls the three major mechanisms protecting the lung: (1) the cough reflex, (2) mucous transport, and (3) phagocytosis of the macrophages, consequences that lead to higher pulmonary infection. Pneumonia occurs frequently in alcoholics, with death rates that are three times higher for alcoholic men and seven times higher for alcoholic women than for the general public. There is a higher incidence of pus discharge from the bronchi in alcoholics, due to depressed cough reflex and aspiration. In addition, more cases of tuberculosis are found among alcoholics.(10)

## Effects on the Heart and Circulation

Alcohol and its metabolic product, acetaldehyde, have special effects on the heart muscle that can result in disease. In these alcohol-related diseases, changes occur in the electrocardiogram, heart rhythm, heart muscle contractility, and blood pressure, as well as at the cellular and biochemical levels.

A drink of whiskey may make the heart beat faster and give a sensation of warmth to the skin. This is caused by momentary irritation of the nerve endings in the mouth, throat, and gullet by the alcohol. The faster heartbeat increases the blood flow and the peripheral blood vessels (those near the surface of the skin) become dilated, producing the feeling of warmth. The widening of these blood vessels causes a slight loss of heat from the body. At the same time, the visceral blood vessels (those that surround the gastrointestinal tract) constrict, forcing blood to peripheral vessels and contributing to the heat loss.

These immediate reflexes may raise the blood pressure a bit for a very brief time. But the overall effect of a moderate amount of alcohol is to cause many of the blood vessels to relax and dilate. This results in a slight fall in blood pressure. The increase warmth of the skin is sometimes accompanied by flushing and sweating. If a considerable amount of alcohol is consumed, the increased flow of blood to the surface vessels may become visible as "bloodshot" eyes.(10) These short-term effects of a drink or two do not seem to cause any lasting changes in the heart, but they may cause short-term effects known as "holiday heart syndrome," temporary heart irregularities caused by the effects of acetaldehyde on the circulatory system.

There is no concrete evidence that moderate amounts of alcohol cause heart disease, high blood pressure, or hardening of the arteries, but recent research has shown that even in mildly intoxicating doses, alcohol can adversely affect ventricle function in the heart. In severe cases of continued intoxication, heart failure, irregularities, or clotting—separately or in combination—can result from the cumulative effects of numerous factors such as intensified drinking episodes, exposure to excessive amounts of trace metals, and nutritional deficiency or superimposed infection.(126) Some reports indicate that heavy chronic drinking predisposes an individual to coronary artery disease. Additionally, there is evidence that alcohol can produce angina pectoris (pains in the chest).

Government researchers, doing clinical and experimental studies on cardiomyopathy, a disease of the heart muscle, have indicated that "even moderate amounts of alcohol can stress tissue of the cardium, or the main heart muscle."[6] Alcoholic cardiomyopathy usually occurs in men with a long history of alcohol abuse. Its common characteristics include congestive heart failure, enlarged heart, distended veins, elevated disastolic blood pressure, and swelling in the arms and legs.(7) Cardiomyopathy also manifests itself in abnormalities of the left ventricle, which burdens the heart muscle. Numerous medical reports have verified that death can be caused by cardiomyopathy in alcoholic persons, even if malnutrition, which was formerly considered a main cause of heart disease in alcoholic people, is not involved. Whether a direct effect of ethyl alcohol on the heart cells plays a role in the causal mechanism leading to cardiomyopathy or whether a metabolic product such as acetaldehyde does, is not known at this time.

Irregularities in the heartbeat occur both in patients with alcohol-related diseases and in other individuals during alcohol intoxication. Ventricular fibrillation and palpitations caused by alcohol intoxication are common.

The view still persists that ethyl alcohol benefits the heart. For a long time some clinicians have been advocating the use of alcohol in the treatment of angina pectoris, on the basis that alcohol dilates the coronary arteries. However, careful studies fail to reveal that this is really beneficial. Getting drunk taxes the heart and would be dangerous for a person with heart disease.

Recent research by Dr. Melvin Knisely suggests that alcohol may produce an agglutination effect known as "blood sludging." Knisely's work showed that as blood alcohol increased, the following progression of events took place in the capillaries. First, red blood cells began to clump together. Second, there was a slower forward flow of blood in the capillaries. Third, there was actually plugging of the vessels, stopping the flow. Due to the resultant anoxia (lack of oxygen), there were then breaks in the capillary wall and microscopic hemorrhages, resulting in tissue damage. Actual sludging began at 25 mgs (.025 percent) alcohol in the blood.

Knisely was able to observe the sludging effect in conjunctival capillaries of the human eye by using high-powered ophthalmoscopes with attached cameras. Similar studies in monkeys have indicated that vascular changes in the brain of the monkey are even more marked than in the conjunctiva because the conjunctiva gets some oxygen from the surrounding area, whereas the brain is in a closed system.

Knisely concludes:[7]

[6]National Institute on Alcohol Abuse and Alcoholism, *Alcohol and Health,* Second Special Report to the U.S. Congress from the Secretary of Health, Education, and Welfare, June 1974, pp. 91–92.

[7]H. A. Moskow, R. C. Pennington, and Melvin Knisely, "Alcohol Sludge and Hypoxic Areas of the Nervous System, Liver, and Heart," *Microvascular Research* 1 (1968): 174–178.

The current data may be summarized as follows. With increasing concentrations of alcohol in the blood, an increase in the sizes of the blood-cell masses is correlated with a progressive reduction in the forward-flow rates, there was an increase in the numbers of vessels in stasis, with no flow through them. . . . When agglutinated blood is seen in the conjunctival vessels of intoxicated subjects, it is almost certain that agglutinated blood is present throughout the entire vascular system. Mechanisms whereby the ingestion of ethyl alcohol damages the tissues of the drinker have been largely speculative. These observations demonstrate a major mechanism of tissue damage, namely, severe local hypoxia or anoxia which, in a chronic alcoholic, are repeated at longer or shorter intervals over and over again, ad infinitum.

Knisely indicates that this information is also of significance to the social drinker in that the effects of alcohol are on a continuum. The red blood cells respond to the level of blood alcohol, not to a diagnostic label. The first evidence of sludging was found at levels as low as 25 mgs (.025 percent). This level is attained with one drink. Many social drinkers on many occasions have blood levels much higher than this. The brain, being the organ in the body most sensitive to anoxia, is the most likely to be damaged, even in social drinkers. (135) Thus, the evidence is mounting for both the fact and the mechanism of tissue damage from alcohol in nonalcoholics.

Alcohol, then, may make the red blood cells stick together in clumps. As these bits of sludge reach the capillaries, they pile into a wad that may entirely plug the capillary. When sludging is extensive, many capillaries become plugged and cells in extensive areas of an organ starve for oxygen. Since the researchers observed this sludging effect in the capillaries of the eye, they felt justified in concluding that they had discovered the mechanism by which alcohol injures and destroys cells, by depriving them of the oxygen they need to survive. This theory has not been accepted throughout the medical profession, but it may explain the measurable brain damage often seen in alcoholics.

## Effects on the Blood

Anemia is by far the most common blood system complication of chronic alcoholism, and folic-acid deficiency seems to be the most common cause of anemia. It has been shown that consumption of ethyl alcohol in large quantities over a period of a few months can cause such a folic-acid deficiency.

Three other types of anemias are also related to alcoholism. *Iron deficiency anemia* is common among chronic drinkers because of the prevalence of gastrointestinal erosions and resultant hemorrhage. *Zieve syndrome* is a type of hemolytic anemia associated with alcoholic fatty liver and hyperlipidemia. *Spur cell anemia* is characterized by spur-shaped red blood cells with increased membrane cholesterol.

Alcohol can cause thrombopathy (or abnormal platelet function) and derangement in bone marrow cell production, leading to decreased bone marrow proliferation. Alcohol consumption indirectly leads to production of smaller and fewer platelets.

EFFECTS OF ALCOHOLIC BEVERAGES ON THE BODY

## Alcohol, Decreased Immunity, and Complications of Other Conditions

Alcohol-dependent people frequently have a lower resistance to infections of all types because of the depressant effect of alcohol on the immunological system, especially the white blood cells. Upper respiratory infections and pneumonia are common. An increased incidence of emphysema and tuberculosis among alcoholics is related largely to the heavy cigarette use common among problem drinkers. Injuries, including surgical wounds, take longer to heal. Such pre-existing physical disorders as diabetes and epilepsy are aggravated and worsened by alcohol ingestion; for example, the high caloric value of alcohol elevates the blood-sugar level. In the withdrawal reaction, the blood-sugar level drops, producing a hypoglycemic condition. Ingestion of alcohol lowers the seizure threshold in the presence of epilepsy; the obvious dangers are compounded when the person forgets to take anticonvulsant medicine while drinking.(150)

## Alcohol and Cancer[8]

By 1950 the relationship between cigarette smoking and lung cancer was recognized, and this led investigators to take a closer look at the whole spectrum of personal habits in relation to the development of cancer. The drinking of alcoholic beverages also came under scrutiny, and during the following decade several epidemiological studies seeking to explore a link between alcohol and cancer were carried out.

Since then, clinical and epidemiological studies have implicated the excessive use of alcohol, especially when combined with smoking, in the development of certain cancers. Cancers of the mouth, pharynx, larynx, and esophagus and primary cancer of the liver appear to be definitely related to heavy alcohol intake in the United States and parts of the world where these occur with high frequency in men. Heavy smoking and heavy drinking seem particularly to be implicated (perhaps exerting a co-carcinogenic effect) in mouth, pharnyx, and larynx cancer, where heavy intake of both has not only an additive but apparently a potentiating effect in increasing risk. Cancer of the esophagus is associated with heavy consumption of distilled spirits in the western countries. Primary liver cell cancer, while not a common cancer in the United States, is more often seen in persons with a history of chronic heavy alcohol consumption. Cancer of the pancreas may also be associated with alcoholism.

Recent research has indicated a possible—though still tentative—link between alcohol consumption and breast cancer.[9] According to investigators from six universities and the Memorial-Sloan Kettering Cancer Center, women who

[8]Excerpted from NIAAA, *Alcohol and Health*, p. 83.
[9]"Alcohol Linked to Breast Cancer," *Science Digest*, August 1982, p. 93.

drink hard liquor, wine, or beer may be 40-90 percent more likely to develop breast cancer than are women who abstain from alcohol entirely. The study, reported in the British medical journal *Lancet* and involving more than 4,300 hospitals in the United States, Canada, and Israel, was conducted under the auspices of researchers at the Drug Epidemiology Unit of Boston University Medical School. While there does seem to be a link between breast cancer and alcohol ingestion, researchers stress that they have not yet established a definite cause-and-effect relationship between the two.

There is a rising incidence in the United States of cancer of the mouth, pharynx, larynx, esophagus, and pancreas in nonwhite men, and the relationship of this increase to alcohol use as well as smoking requires further investigation. On the other hand, it remains to be clarified why there has been a decline in the rate of cancer of the stomach in the United States in recent years while the consumption of alcohol has apparently increased.

There are wide geographic and sex variations in the incidence of cancers thought to be linked to alcohol, particularly cancer of the esophagus, and these variations must be borne in mind in any study of the causes of those cancers. Research to determine whether certain alcoholic beverages may contain carcinogens and further study of the possible association of alcohol consumption to cancer of certain sites is of vital importance in assessing the role of alcohol as one additional environmental factor in the spectrum of exogenous agents in cancer.

The frequent coexistence of alcohol and tobacco has made it difficult to identify the influence of each habit independently in relation to cancer, yet this question is critical in determining to what extent and how each may contribute to the development of cancer.

The means by which alcohol may exert a carcinogenic effect in many, and thereby increase the risks of cancer in specific body sites, are unknown, but the following mechanisms have been suggested and are being studied:

1. Alcohol may act by augmenting the cancer-inducing effect of other agents, such as smoking. The combined effect of alcohol and tobacco may be more than the sum of the two—it may be synergistic. Thus, either heavy smoking or heavy drinking increases a person's risk of developing oral cancer, but the risk resulting from both together is greater than the sum of the risk of either one alone.

2. Ethanol itself, especially in strong solutions, may act as a direct irritant to mucosal cells, making them more vulnerable to the other carcinogens, or it may serve as a solvent or vehicle for carcinogenic trace substances. Nitrosamines, aflatoxin, and other congeners present in the alcoholic beverages used in various parts of the world have been implicated as possible carcinogens.

3. Malnutrition associated with alcoholism, specifically as it affects the integrity of the mucosa, is a possible carcinogenic mechanism. Specific protein, iron, and vitamin deficiencies have also been suggested as perhaps important

carcinogenic factors in the malnutrition of alcoholism.

4. By producing cirrhosis, alcohol may lead to an altered metabolism of carcinogens in the liver so as to enhance their carcinogenic effect. Some factor related to regeneration of liver cells during the healing process of cirrhosis has been suggested as a possible pathogenic mechanism by which hepatoma may develop in alcoholic patients with cirrhosis.

5. In cancer of the upper aerodigestive tract, increased local exposure of tissues through a decrease in saliva volume and local pooling of saliva-containing carcinogens (such as tobacco tars) during intoxication—which would prolong exposure to a concentrated carcinogen—is a mechanism that is being hypothesized.

## Alcohol-related Mortality

Although epidemiologic data on alcohol use and morbidity are scarce, the relationship between alcohol use and mortality has been demonstrated by several kinds of data. Clinical research shows that alcoholics and those admitted for treatment of alcohol problems have a mortality rate 2.5 times higher than do people in the general population. Vital statistics also show a substantial number of deaths each year from alcoholism, alcoholic psychosis, and alcohol-related cirrhosis. Alcoholism and problem drinking also play a major role in accidents, homicides, suicides, cardiovascular and gastrointestinal diseases, cancer, and other life-threatening illnesses.

One examination of the alcohol-related mortality literature revealed that in 1980 alcohol was a direct cause of up to 35,295 deaths and an indirect cause of up to 59,708 deaths—that is, deaths from accidents, homicides, suicides, and so on. Alcohol, then, was either a direct or an indirect cause of a total of 95,000 deaths that year.

Although research has shown that there is a strong relationship between excessive alcohol use and certain cancers, heart disease, pancreatitis, stillbirths, the fetal alcohol syndrome, and other problems, sound morbidity and mortality statistics are severely limited.(9)

# 3

Alcohol-
Related Problems

Interaction between alcohol and other drugs may contribute to fatal automobile accidents and accidental or suicidal deaths in individuals who have consumed narcotics, barbiturates, tranquilizers, or other hypnotic-sedative drugs with alcohol. For example, a combination of alcohol and barbiturates may produce what is often referred to as synergism or *potentiation*. That is, $1 + 1$, one drug plus another drug, potentiate the effects of one another so that $1 + 1 = 3, 4, 5,$ or 6 instead of the normal additive effect of 2. The depressant action of each drug potentiates or increases the depressant action of the other, grossly exaggerating the usual response expected from alcohol or barbiturates alone, resulting in increasing depression of the central nervous system. The use of any drug that has a depressant effect on the central nervous system in combination with alcohol represents an extra hazard to health and safety, and, in some cases, to life itself.

## Drinking and Driving

Traffic accidents are the greatest cause of violent death in the United States and approximately one-third of the ensuing injuries and one-half of the fatalities are alcohol related. It is estimated that of the approximately 50,000 annual automobile deaths on our highways, alcohol is responsible for more than 25,000 (see Figure 4). One study reported that between 35 and 64 percent of drivers in fatal traffic accidents had been drinking, and research has consistently shown that between 45 and 60 percent of all fatal crashes involving a young driver are alcohol related. Interestingly, between 6 and 25 percent of the drivers in nonfatal

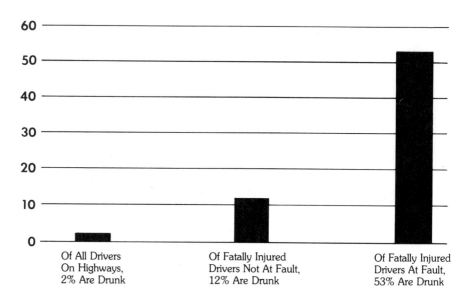

**FIGURE 4**

*Percentage "at fault" drivers in fatal crashes Who Are drunk*

accidents had been drinking prior to the accident. Motor vehicle crashes caused by alcohol abuse cost American society $7.33 billion a year.(11)(10)

In the U.S. annually, 8,000 or more pedestrians are killed and another 100,000 are injured in traffic accidents; post-mortem blood alcohol test results indicated that 44% of those tested had been drinking and 35% had a B.A.C. of .10 percent or greater.

Alcohol may be involved in over half of the estimated 15 million crashes and 1 million major injuries which occur in the United States each year. Many of the deaths or injuries are caused by the under-21 age group, and arrests of young people for drunken driving have rapidly increased since states began lowering the drinking age from 21. In the year following its lowering of the drinking age, Michigan, for example, reported a 14-percent increase in such arrests.(16) The trend now in many states is return to the 21 year-old drinking age.

Regardless of the legal drinking age for young people, alcohol is likely to affect driving performance of young drivers more than adults for the following reasons:

1. The young person who drinks lacks experience in compensating for the effects of alcohol.
2. The young driver is an inexperienced driver; skills are less automatic and more inclined to deteriorate because of the effect of alcohol.
3. The inclination to take risks, especially strong in young people, may be accentuated by alcohol.

4. On the average, young people weigh less than adults and are therefore more susceptible to the effects of smaller amounts of alcohol.

Study results suggest that almost 25 percent of all drivers on the road have recently consumed alcohol and 4−7 percent have a blood-alcohol level of 0.10 percent or more. The individual most likely to drive while intoxicated has been found to be male, under the age of 30, divorced or separated, and employed at a blue-collar job.(60)

In general, the relative probabilities of causing or being involved in a crash increase dramatically as the driver's blood-alcohol concentration (BAC) increases. As Figure 5 illustrates, at a BAC of 0.05 percent the relative risk factor for crash involvement and causation is 1.5 times that at the 0.02 percent level. When BAC is 0.10 percent, the relative risk factor doubles for crash involvement and quadruples for causing a crash. With a BAC of 0.16 percent the likelihood of being involved in a crash is 4 times greater than at the 0.02 percent level and the likelihood of causing a crash is 8 times greater. Regardless of BAC levels, male drivers in the age groups of 18 to 24 years and 65 years and older are more likely to be involved in a crash than all other male drivers.(10)

A number of studies have shown that drivers who have been drinking heavily are much more likely to be involved in automobile accidents than are nondrinking drivers. The more serious the automobile accident, the more likely it is that alcohol is involved. There is evidence that driving fatalities are more closely associated with alcoholism and chronic alcohol abuse than they are with normal drinking. In fatal automobile accidents, a large proportion of the drivers had blood-alcohol levels high enough to suggest that they had chronic alcohol-related problems and were not just "social drinkers." Yet, the social drinker−driver is a major threat on the highway because: (1) they are so numerous, (2) they are not so easy to spot and defend oneself against; and (3) they often fail to recognize their limitations.

Individuals with chronic drinking problems are responsible for about two-thirds of the alcohol-related deaths on the highways. Young drivers and social drinkers with a high blood-alcohol level at the time of the accident cause the remaining one-third. In addition, many single-car driving fatalities are suspected to have been overt or unconsciously motivated acts of suicide. Excessive alcohol intake, generally of a chronic nature, is associated with one-third of all reported suicides. These figures say nothing of the people who are injured and possibly disabled. Disability injuries have been estimated to be 500,000 yearly. The costs of property damage, wage losses, medical expenses, and overhead insurance costs that result from these accidents must also be considered. Regardless of blood-alcohol concentration, accidents involving alcohol tend to be more severe in both property damage and personal injury than those unrelated to alcohol.

The problem of alcohol and driving is intensified by the fact that driving is becoming a more and more complex task. Contemporary driving is rarely "routine"; the complexity of the task is increased with higher density of traffic, accelerated speed, poor visibility or darkness, bad road conditions, faulty vehicles, and the unpredictable, dangerous actions of other drivers. Unfortunately, two

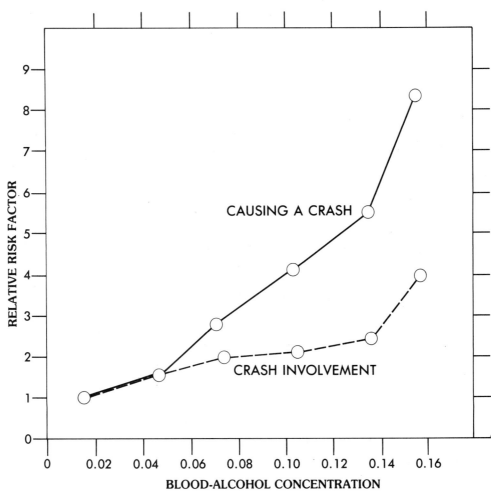

**FIGURE 5**
**Relative Probability That A Driver Causes and Is Inolved**
**In A Crash As A Function Of BAC Level**

SOURCE: Marc Aarens, Tracy Cameron, Judy Roizen, Ron Roizen, Robin Room, Dan Schneberk, and Deborah Wingard, *Alcohol Casualties and Crime,* special report prepared for National Institute on Alcohol Abuse and Alcoholism under Contract No. ADM 281-76-0027 (Berkeley, Cal.: Social Research Group, University of California, 1977).

NOTE: Relative to the probability that a driver with a BAC of less than 0.03% is in our causes a crash.

associated effects of alcohol on the drinking driver are to give him/her a heightened illusion of competence or increase his/her impulsiveness and recklessness while his/her abilities have been compromised. Intoxicated drivers, compared with sober ones, generally tend to use greater speed and less caution and to be more erratic.(143) Alcohol use is known to produce these common physiological and psychological manifestations that affect driving: impulsive responses and risk-taking; reduced sensory-motor coordination and reaction time; reduced tolerance to glare; underestimation of speed and distance; exaggeration of any emotional instability; reduced attentiveness, drowsiness. See Table 11 for the relationship between blood-alcohol concentration and driver behavior.

At present, there are national standards making mandatory legislation that defines the presumption impairment limit of blood-alcohol concentrations as not

### Table 11
#### Blood-alcohol concentration and driver impairment

| Blood-alcohol concentration | Common effects on driving ability | Approximate amount of liquor* |
|---|---|---|
| 0.02% | Mild changes occur. Many drivers may have slight change in feelings. Existing mood (anger, elation, etc.) may be heightened. Bad driving habits are slightly pronounced. | 1–2 oz. |
| 0.05 | Driver takes too long to decide what to do in an emergency. Inhibitions may be influenced. Shows a "so what" attitude, exaggerated behavior, and what appears to be loss of finger skills. In most states this blood-alcohol concentration may be considered with other competent evidence in determining whether the person is legally under the influence of alcohol. | 2–3 oz. |
| 0.10 | Driver exhibits exaggerated emotion and behavior—less concern, mental relaxation. Inhibitions, self-criticism, and judgment** are seriously affected. Shows impairment of skills of coordination. At this blood-alcohol level a driver is presumed "under the influence" in all states—and in many, 0.10% BAC is evidence of being "under the influence." | 5–6 oz. |
| 0.15 | Shows serious and noticeable impairment of physical and mental functions; clumsy, uncoordinated, the driver should wait 9–10 hours before driving. | 7–8 oz. |
| 0.40 | At this point most drivers have "passed out" (unconsciousness, clammy skin, dilated pupils). | Approximately 15–20 oz. |

*Beverages 90–100 proof.
**The effect of alcohol on judgment, inhibitions, and self-control, even in the lower blood-alcohol levels, is serious because (1) since self-criticism is affected early, the drinker often is unlikely to recognize any change in his behavior, and (2) he often feels more perceptive and skillful and, therefore, is likely to take more chances in passing, speeding, or negotiating curves (self-confidence increases as skill decreases—the worst possible combination).

greater than 0.10 percent. In order to prevent refusal to take a test on constitutional grounds of self-incrimination, an "implied consent" law must be passed. This is legislation based on a Supreme Court ruling that operation of a vehicle on a street or highway is a privilege, not a right, and that the granting of a driver's license can include the stipulation that the holder will take a chemical test if requested to do so by a law-enforcement officer. A driver who refuses a test may have his/her driver's license revoked for a designated period—usually six months to a year.[1]

Several ranges of blood-alcohol concentration are distinguished in American conceptions and laws. They differ, however, among jurisdictions. A concentration up to 0.05 percent (50 mg of alcohol per 100 ml of blood) is usually considered safe; the person is presumed to be unimpaired in his/her ability to drive. This level might be achieved by an average-sized man after two average drinks. Between 0.05 and 0.10 percent (50 to 100 mg of alcohol per 100 ml of blood) no presumption of impairment is made, but the blood-alcohol level may be presented in evidence in connection with other behavior of the driver to support a charge of being under the influence of alcohol. (In some European jurisdictions, especially in Scandinavian countries, a concentration of 0.05 percent is considered legal evidence of impairment.) In some American jurisdictions, a concentration of 0.08 percent is legally defined as evidence of impairment. In others, 0.10 percent is the legal standard for impaired driving or intoxication. In nearly all jurisdictions, 0.10 percent (100 mg of alcohol per 100 ml of blood) or higher is regarded as prima facie evidence of intoxication.(7)

Despite probable underreporting due to selective sampling and to legal and logistical problems, it seems safe to estimate that impaired drivers (0.10 percent or higher) are involved in 5 to 10 percent of the run-of-the-mill crashes and in 10 to 35 percent of the crashes involving serious injury. Injury to the driver is more likely after drinking, and both the probability and the severity of injury appear to increase as the amount of alcohol rises. The likelihood of being responsible for the crash is greater if the driver has been drinking. Higher blood-alcohol levels are associated with higher proportions of drivers responsible for the crashes.

Traffic safety is not the only problem associated with driving while impaired (DWI): there are financial risks as well. A DWI conviction can cause insurance difficulties for the driver: most insurance companies will not extend any type of driver's insurance without obtaining the driver's record, and most insurance companies in this country hesitate to insure drivers with alcohol-related traffic experiences (not only for DWI conviction.) A driver's insurance could be canceled as a result of a DWI conviction, and he/she may not be able to find a new company willing to insure him/her. Insurance premium rates go up for a driver convicted of DWI, because insurance coverage rates reflect the cost of medical care, repair bills, and court-awarded damages due to drunken driving. Alcohol-related experiences

[1]Robert Straus, ed., "Alcohol and Society," *Psychiatric Annals* 3, no. 10 (Oct. 1973): 88.

can change one's insurance status from "preferred" or "acceptable" risk to "questionable" or "unacceptable" risk.

Despite the dramatic evidence connecting drinking drivers and accidents, neither laws, punishment, nor appeals to intelligence, reason, and emotion have been effective deterrents to driving under the influence of alcohol. When legal charges are leveled against drinking or intoxicated drivers, it is difficult to get American judges and juries to return convictions. Sympathy and identification often seem to be more with the drunken driver than with his/her innocent victim. It is indeed a sad commentary that we allow the mass slaughter that occurs on the highways of America because of the drinking-driving problem. One solution that is being implemented in several foreign countries, notably Scandinavia and Great Britain, is the enactment and enforcement of very strong laws against drinking and driving. A driver with a blood-alcohol concentration of as little as 0.05 percent is legally under the influence of alcohol, and laws have made both loss of driving license and imprisonment mandatory for persons convicted of driving while intoxicated. (143)

Somehow, the attitude has developed in the United States that because it is a person's right to drink, it is a person's right to drive afterward. Whenever these "rights" are threatened, public sentiment in the United States seems generally resistant to efforts to protect the public's safety. As Dr. Robert Straus has indicated, "The rights to drive and to drink, at this point in time, appear to have a greater value in the hierarchy of American mores than the right of protection from the drinking driver."[2]

William N. Plymat, Sr., Executive Director of the American Council on Alcohol Problems, suggested a multifaceted prevention plan that involved lawmakers, police, court officials, alcohol advertisers, and the general public. Some of his suggestions have broad implications:[3]

*Advertisers and the media.* A new national ethic—one that frowns upon the use of *any* alcohol while driving—needs to be developed; the media can play a key role in the education and persuasion of the general public and the lawmakers. Instead of seeing glamorous ads implying the benefits and satisfaction of drinking, the general public would benefit from seeing ads that clearly point out the hazards of drinking and driving (by early 1982, such ads were beginning to make an appearance; one was even sponsored by House of Seagram). One bill before Congress in early 1982 would, if passed, discourage some of the pro-alcohol advertising by preventing companies from deducting the cost of such advertising at income tax time. The media can play still another important role in the prevention of drunk driving: it can give attention to new, stiffer penalties and can serve as a warning voice to those who are still considering drinking and driving.

---

[2]*Ibid.*
[3]William N. Plymat, Sr., "A Plan for Dealing with Drunk Drivers," *The Bottom Line* 5, no. 2 (Spring 1982): 7–14.

*Changing the laws.* By the beginning of 1982, ten states had passed "per se" laws—laws that made a specified blood-alcohol content an offense in itself. In these states there is no use arguing a drunk driving conviction: if the policeman finds that the driver's blood-alcohol content has reached the specified level, he/she simply informs the driver that *it is an offense.* The driver has no option but to plead guilty; there is no question as to guilt or innocence, no jury trial is needed, and no possibility exists of a driver's friend testifying and winning exoneration for the driver.

*Adhering to stiff penalties.* Many penalties can be levied for a conviction of drunk driving, even in states with "per se" laws. The driver's license may be revoked; chances are good that the driver will continue to drive without it. The driver may simply be arrested and a trial or sentencing date set; once the driver posts the required bail (as low as $300 in many states), he/she is free to leave the courthouse and drive again until sentenced. Even then, it is possible to persuade a judge to levy only a fine and to omit a jail sentence altogether.

According to Plymat, the best possible solution for deterrence is a mandatory jail sentence—clearly advertised and unwaveringly enforced. When a driver is arrested and found to have a specific blood-alcohol content, he/she is *automatically* jailed for a certain number of days, even for a first offense. In December 1980 the mandatory jail sentence was imposed in Cook County, Illinois, in an attempt to cut down on holiday traffic fatalities; heavy media coverage passed the word. The approach worked: fatalities during the two-week Christmas period dropped to 8 from 22 the year before; accidents involving personal injury dropped to 994 from 2,003 the year before.

While the penalty for first offenses will probably continue to be light (several days in jail), the penalty for repeated offenses, especially for drivers caught driving with a revoked license, could be much stiffer—an automatic jail term of 180 days *and* a fine of $500, for example. When such sentences become *automatic,* without appeal or chance of escape, we may begin seeing a drop in the incidence of drunk driving.

The national movement against drunk driving is gaining considerable momentum; one lobbying group, Mothers Against Drunk Driving (MADD), sponsors rallies and other educational efforts to sway public opinion against those who drive while intoxicated. During the Fourth of July weekend in 1982, for example, the group attempted to remind holiday travelers of the problems of drunk driving by strewing wrecked cars along major freeways in several states. Their efforts, and the efforts of groups like them, are contributing to the tide of public opinion against drunk driving that is beginning to surface.

## Home, Industrial, and Recreational Accidents

Alcohol also has been seriously implicated in death and injury resulting from home, industrial, and recreational accidents. A national survey found that 36 percent of regular drinkers and only 8 percent of nondrinkers reported two or more accidental injuries in the previous year. Heavier drinkers appear to have more accidents than other people, and alcoholics have a considerably higher rate of accidental death than the general population.

## Industrial Accidents

Occupational accidents affect a substantial portion of the population. Occupational accidents due to alcohol account for 18,000 deaths and 10 million injuries annually. Experimental evidence has shown that alcohol inhibits coordination and judgment, lengthens reaction time, and decreases motor performance and sensory skill in simulated industrial work. Studies show that problem drinkers are as much as three times more likely to be involved in industrial accidents than the general population.

## Aviation Accidents

A substantial percentage of general, noncommercial aviation crashes may be related to alcohol use at the time of the accident; data show that as many as 44 percent of the pilots who were involved in the accidents had been drinking.(10) Alcohol might contribute to aviation accidents and deaths by increasing the drinking pilot's tendency to take risks and inhibiting his/her psychomotor performance, which several investigators think occurs at BACs as low as 0.04. Unfortunately, corresponding studies are not currently available for commercial pilots.

## Drownings

Alcohol use is associated with up to 69 percent of drownings. Boating accidents could be caused by the poor judgment, faulty coordination, and lack of attention associated with alcohol use. Swimmers may take more risks, and the "pseudo-warmth" effect of alcohol may encourage people to stay in cold water too long. When drinking at home, a person might lose coordination, fall into a swimming pool or full bathtub, be knocked unconscious, and drown. Regardless of the specific situation, alcohol may depress the swallowing and breathing reflexes.

## Fire and Burns

Alcohol use and alcoholism have been implicated in the cause of fires and in the failure to detect or escape from them. Up to 83 percent of all fire fatalities and 62 percent of all burns involve alcohol use at the time of the accident; 53 percent of the fatalities and 23 percent of the burn victims were alcoholics. The number of young children and adults 65 years and older in fire deaths is disproportionately high, but it is among middle-aged fire victims that alcohol is often involved. One reason for these high figures is that alcohol lowers oxidation in the cells and increases a person's chance of succumbing to smoke inhalation and suffocation. Cigarette smoking is a major cause of fires, and in the general population a direct association exists between drinking and smoking. Alcohol is involved in nearly three times as many deaths from cigarette-caused fires as in deaths in fires resulting from other causes.

### Falls and Other Accidents

Balance and locomotor coordination are severely impaired in people who have consumed alcohol, thereby increasing the risk of falls. Alcohol has been found to be involved in up to 70 percent of all deaths and 63 percent of all injuries from falls. What little information exists suggests that alcohol is very common in many other types of accidents, including food asphyxiation deaths, hypothermia, frost injuries and deaths, snowmobile injuries, and tractor accident deaths.(10)

# Alcohol and Violence

Alcohol may be expected to release suppressed feelings of aggression and hostility. Recent studies do, indeed, show a correlation between alcohol intoxication and violent behavior. Half of all homicides and one-third of all suicides are alcohol related; they account for more than 14,000 deaths yearly. Some studies suggest alcohol is present in approximately 86 percent of homicide situations and others have found that 40 – 60 percent of the homicide victims had been drinking. Alcohol is also frequently involved in assaults and offenses against children. Estimates of alcohol involvement in reported assaults range up to 72 percent of offenders and 79 percent of victims. One study estimates alcohol involvement as high as 72 percent in robbery offenders.(10)

Statistical studies show that violence is often associated with immediate intake of rather large amounts of alcohol. Chronic heavy drinking is more likely to be associated with manifestations of self-destructive feelings such as depression, suicide, and immature and irresponsible behavior.

Here, as elsewhere, it is helpful to keep in mind the distinction between acute and chronic effects of alcohol. Expressions of aggression and hostility in response to alcohol are partly determined by psychosocial factors, such as the expectations of drinkers and others as to how alcohol will affect behavior.

Alcohol figures predominantly in less violent criminal behavior as well. For example, almost half of the 5.5 million arrests yearly in the United States are related to the misuse of alcohol. Drunkenness accounts for approximately 1.4 million arrests for disorderly conduct and vagrancy. This charge, used by some communities instead of a public drunkenness charge, accounts for an additional 665,000 arrests. Intoxicated drivers make up the 335,000 remaining arrests.

In addition, a recent U.S. study showed a dramatically high association between drinking and forcible rape. Results read at the 127th annual meeting of the American Psychiatric Association showed:

1. 50 percent of the rapists were drinking at the time of the rape and 43 percent were drinking heavily (ten or more beers or the equivalent).
2. 35 percent of the rapists were diagnosed, on stringent criteria, as alcoholics.
3. Alcoholic rapists as compared with nonalcoholic rapists were: (a) more likely to

be drinking at the time of rape; (b) more likely to have been using drugs in conjunction with alcohol at the time of rape; (c) more likely to have a history of prior use of drugs other than alcohol.

As Richard Rada points out, "It is, in fact, highly probable that in a high percentage of cases, control of the alcoholic sex offender's drinking behavior would in itself bring cessation of similar sex offenses."[4]

The cost to America's taxpayers for arrest, trial, and maintenance in jail of these drinkers has been estimated to be over $100 million a year.

It is important to understand that there is no direct casual connection between alcohol and violence. No alcoholic beverage presently known will, in and of itself, *cause* the taker to act violently. Alcohol can only modify bodily processes and behavioral capabilities that are already present. While alcohol may alter performance, it cannot be said to compel any particular act or form of social conduct, be it social charm or homicide. It is basically the personality of the user that determines the reaction. A substance is, in essence, only a catalyst. The alcohol is only one of the essential ingredients which determines its effects. Other important variables have been described as follows:

> The pharmacological action of alcohol is but one of the three factors that determine how a given person will react to that drug on a given occasion. The other factors are called "set" and "setting," and they are at least as important as the drug. Set is the psychologist's term for individuals' expectations of what a drug will do to him. It includes much of what we commonly call "personality." Setting is the total environment, physical and social, in which a drug is taken.[5]

It is quite possible for the combined effects of set and setting to overshadow completely the pharmacological action of a drug.

But while drugs only modify behavior and do not directly cause it, their involvement in acts of crime and violence cannot be overlooked. The relationship between crime, violence, and alcohol, be it causal or not, is frightening indeed.

As pointed out by the National Commission on the Causes and Prevention of Violence, it is clear that alcohol has identifiable effects on those who partake of it. These include, for some people, the removal or reduction of significant social inhibitions. Alcohol quickly enters the bloodstream and affects the central nervous system, removing some of the "controls" that generally operate on individuals. Functions such as judgment and complicated motor skills are affected first, followed later by more gross and semi-automatic motor skills, and finally by survival functions such as respiration. The "stimulation" generally associated with drinking should be properly understood as consequences of the *depressing* effect

[4]Richard T. Rada, "Alcoholism and Forcible Rape," paper read at the annual meeting of the American Psychiatric Association in Detroit, 1974.

[5]"The Role of Alcohol, Narcotics, Dangerous Drugs in Individual Violence," National Commission on the Causes and Prevention of Violence, *Crimes of Violence* 12 (Dec. 1969).

of alcohol on controlling and inhibiting brain mechanisms.(151)

Many "social drinkers" find themselves behaving "wildly" when they are drinking. This may lead to a very natural conclusion: Uncontrolled behavior of some criminals may be directly related to their drinking at the time they break the law. However, one can rarely say with certainty that a particular crime would not have occurred if the person had not been drinking. In other words, it is very difficult to say that violent behavior can ever be "caused" by a single factor. Highly complicated interactions of different factors, only one of which may be alcohol, generally are involved.

In summary, then, alcohol acts as a depressant, controlling and inhibiting brain mechanisms so that inhibitions are significantly reduced. In some individuals, the removal of certain inhibitions (e.g., fear of punishment or anxiety or guilt) may result in violent behavior. Nevertheless, these suggestive relationships cannot necessarily be construed as causal connections. Alcohol affects individuals differently; while for some individuals alcohol is a catalyst toward violence, for others it is not.

## Alcohol and Suicide

In 1981, 27,294 deaths in the United States were reported as suicides, making suicide a major cause of death in this country. It is estimated that as many as 10,000 of these deaths, or more than one-third, were related to alcohol.

Alcoholics (especially alcoholics who are drunk) are at especially high risk as possible suicides. The level of risk has been found to vary; one study reported it to be thirty times greater than the risk of suicide in the general population.(9)

Studies have shown that a significant number of alcoholics who committed suicide had experienced the loss of a close interpersonal relationship within six weeks or less of their death. In addition, the suicides studied tended to suffer from a long list of difficulties, ranging from health to legal to financial problems. The distribution of these events, as with the loss of a close interpersonal relationship, were skewed significantly toward the final weeks of the subject's life. It is suggested that interpersonal loss may be a predictor of suicide among alcoholics.

The mood-changing properties of alcohol have been seen as a possible link to suicidal actions. People who want to reduce depression often drink to do so, not realizing that large quantities of alcohol actually can increase both anxiety and depression. Other theorists suggest that alcohol could precipitate a suicidal act by depressing the critical life-evaluating functions of the ego, allowing unconscious self-destructive impulses to gain control.

Studies show that between 15 and 64 percent of those who attempt suicide and up to 80 percent of suicides had been drinking at the time of the event. For those with histories of problem drinking, these proportions are most variable, and range from 1 to 33 percent of suicide attempts and 2 to 48 percent of suicides. Many studies report that 20 percent or more of suicide victims (up to 25 percent of alcoholics) reported having attempted suicide before they either sought treatment or stopped drinking. Research also shows that alcoholics who committed suicide had a history of more suicide attempts than nonalcoholics, and alcoholics who attempt suicide more closely resemble actual suicides than do nonalcoholics who attempt suicide. These findings suggest that alcoholics who attempt suicide form a significant part of the population that eventually succeeds in committing suicide. It has been estimated that up to 9,000 alcoholics committed suicide in 1981. The use of alcohol in combination with other drugs is probably responsible for some proportion of accidental deaths as well as suicides.

Women have a higher rate of attempted suicide than men, while men have a higher rate of completed suicide than women.(9) Among alcoholic women the number of suicide attempts clearly exceeds that for the female population as a whole; recent data indicate that the rate of completed suicides among female alcoholics is twenty-three times the population rate. These findings suggest that the number of completed suicides among female alcoholics is significantly higher than for women in the general population.

Alcoholics are far more likely than nonalcoholics to attempt and commit suicide while drinking. The explanations for this phenomenon vary. Some theorists consider alcohol as an indication of a suicidal personality. Others feel that alcoholism itself, often may cause suicide. Most agree, however, that alcoholism often involves deterioration of important social relationships leading to social disintegration, loss of memory, and other precipitants of suicide.(10)

# Alcohol and Family Abuse

Child abuse, child neglect, child molesting, and marital violence are prevalent types of aggression in the family. Although empirical data on alcoholic involvement are quite limited, there are indications that intoxication is a precipating factor in many cases of child abuse. The largest American study on the subject reported that 38 percent of child-abusing parents had histories of drinking problems, and other studies have shown that up to 65 percent of child-abuse cases are alcohol related. Research also suggests that quarrels originating over one spouse's drinking eventually can result in physical aggression, although data are extremely limited. One study reported that 52 percent of violent husbands had histories of problem drinking or alcoholism.

Violence is not an isolated phenomenon that affects only one victim in a family. The "battering family" is frequently encountered by counselors, who report that a husband who beats his wife is often also a battering father, and he may well be the target of violence from his wife and even the children. Abused wives may also be child abusers. In one study conducted by Steward and de Blois, researchers questioned women whose sons were in treatment for child abuse at a psychiatric clinic; 65 percent of the mothers who had abused their sons had been abused by their husbands.(80) An Arkansas study by Spieker indicated that 31 percent of abusing husbands also abused the children.

A Minnesota study conducted by Carder included 100 abused wives who called a community agency hotline. It was found that 87 percent of the abusing men were alcohol users—35 percent daily drinkers and another 10 percent weekend drinkers. In addition, 71 percent of the women said they were also alcohol users, and most of the women reported frequent drinking.(80)

Most existing research seems to support the conclusion that alcohol abuse does not *cause* marital violence; the link is not one of cause and effect. Currently, the most widely accepted viewpoint is that alcohol abuse is a disavowal technique used by abusive husbands: in other words, some men may drink when they feel like beating their wives because they know that by being drunk, they will be released from responsibility both by their wives and by the rest of society.(71)

Recent research has suggested that child molesters may also often use drunkenness as an excuse for their offenses. This may be the result of alcohol's short-term effect of lessening awareness of the boundaries between acceptable and unacceptable behavior as well as the general social and physical deterioration associated with the continued abuse of alcohol.(9)

Another point is that alcohol acts to lessen inhibitions. Some alcoholics are particularly dangerous because rage is an important personality component, and the drinking is related to an attempt to "anesthetize"—to lessen the rage. But alcohol affects the higher centers of the brain and is actually a depressant of function. The result is that the rage increases—or at least the ability to contain it is lost—and assault becomes more likely.(71)

Three major points emerge from a review of the existing literature on alcoholism and domestic violence:

1. The repetitive cycle from generation to generation of both alcoholism and violence is present, possibly due to parental modeling. Behling's study indicated that 63 percent of abused children had at least one grandparent who was an alcoholic. In 41 percent of the cases where both child and spouse abuse occurred, one or both parents had been abused by an alcoholic or an alcohol-abusing parent. In 90 percent of the cases where a parent had been an abused child, alcohol was involved in that abuse.(46)
2. The spouse and child are equally likely to be victims of abuse.
3. There are similar personality characteristics of the attacker, the abuser, and children of alcoholics. Child abusers characteristically have a low tolerance for frustration, low self-esteem, problems with role reversals, difficulty experiencing pleasure, and lack of understanding of the needs and abilities of infants and children; they are also impulsive, dependent, immature, and depressive. Children of alcoholics are characterized by poor self-concept, are easily frustrated, often perform poorly in school, and are more likely to suffer from adjustment problems and problems of role reversal. Finally, alcoholics tend to be dependent, depressed, angry, impulsive, frightened, and immature, with poor self-concepts and self-images.

Studies have shown that there is a relationship between alcohol use and increased child abuse. Alcohol plays a part in one-third of all abuse cases. Although the child abuse may be physical, emotional, or sexual, many alcoholic parents realize that they have increased potential for these forms of abuse while intoxicated, and they therefore take more care not to engage in such forms of abuse. By far the most prevalent form of abuse among alcoholics is neglect of children—that is, erratic and inconsistent parenting. Many alcoholics have child-rearing problems, most of which fall within the category of inconsistent attention to children. This is not to imply that all alcoholics will, by virtue of their alcoholism, beat their spouses, nor that all alcoholics seriously abuse or neglect their children; we do know, however, that many alcoholics do have difficulties in child-rearing and in their marriages, leading to the potential for family violence.

The pattern continues from one generation to the next. Abused children often experience parental rejection, which may later lead to emotional and behavioral problems on the part of the child. These children who experience social and familial isolation and abuse early in life have a higher potential of becoming abusers and alcoholics themselves later in life.

Since the relationship between alcoholism and child abuse is somewhat elusive and sometimes overlooked during child therapy, special treatment approaches should be emphasized. First, children's services should be incorporated into alcohol therapy. Second, social agencies dealing with alcoholism should be educated to provide comprehensive treatment, to include child abuse. Third, those therapists who work with alcoholic parents should be educated to recognize the potential for child abuse among these parents. Fourth, there should be a continuation of research into prevention, intervention, and rehabilitation of alcoholic parents who are also child abusers.(80)

## Alcohol and Unborn Children

On June 1, 1977, the NIAAA released the following statement concerning the relationship between alcohol and birth defects:

Recent research reports indicate that heavy use of alcohol by women during pregnancy may result in a pattern of abnormalities in the offspring, termed the Fetal Alcohol Syndrome, which consists of specific congenital and behavioral abnormalities. Studies undertaken in animals corroborate the initial observations in humans and indicate as well an increased incidence of stillbirths, resorptions, and spontaneous abortions. Both the risk and the extent of abnormalities appear to be dose-related, increasing with higher alcohol intake during the pregnancy period. In human studies, alcohol is an unequivocal factor when the full pattern of the Fetal Alcohol Syndrome is present. In cases where all of the characteristics are not present, the correlation between alcohol and the adverse effects is complicated by such factors as nutrition, smoking, caffeine, and other drug consumption.[6]

Three University of Washington scientists studied a number of children born to alcoholic mothers; the children exhibited smallness for gestational age, retardation, failure to grow, smaller weight and head circumference, and distinct

[6]NIAAA, *Alcohol and Health,* Fourth Special Report to the U.S. Congres on Alcohol and Health from the Secretary of Health, Education, and Welfare, June 1978, p. 41.

patterns of abnormalities. The symptoms were classified as a specific syndrome known as *fetal alcohol syndrome* (FAS).

It has been found that alcohol ingested by the mother freely crosses the placental membrane and reaches the baby within one minute or less; in addition, alcohol also crosses the fetal blood-brain barrier. The fetus then retains the alcohol until the mother's alcohol concentration decreases, at which time fetal alcohol diffuses back across the placenta and returns to the mother's system. From there, the alcohol is oxidized and excreted from the mother's system. Blood recovered from several fetuses of mothers who had ingested alcohol showed that the fetuses had nearly the same blood-alcohol concentration as did the mothers, and it usually stays elevated nearly twice as long. (Different infants are affected differently, depending on the BAC of the mother and the infant's resistance to alcohol.)

Damage to the fetus from alcohol can occur before a woman even knows that she is pregnant. The first trimester of pregnancy is especially important in fetal development because vital organ systems are being formed; during this developmental time, the fetus is especially susceptible to the effects of any drug, including alcohol. Generally speaking, some of the critical times for organ development are as follows: 15−25 days into the pregnancy for the central nervous system, 24−30 days for the eyes, 24−36 days for the legs, and 20−40 days for the heart. Therefore, major structural damage could occur up to the eleventh week of gestation, a time during which a woman may not know or be entirely certain of her pregnancy. Thus, she may not alter her drinking patterns until after the fetus's organ formation is nearly complete. Alcohol continues to affect fetal development throughout the second and third trimester, too—so there is no safe time to drink during pregnancy.

FAS incidence is now placed at 1−2 cases/1,000 live births, with a possible partial expression of the syndrome in 3−5/1,000 live births. Evidence to date suggests that a woman who drinks 2 ounces of absolute alcohol per day has a 10 percent chance of having an FAS baby; women who drink more than 2 ounces have at least a 19 percent chance of having an FAS baby.

Conservative figures suggest an incidence of FAS of greater than 1 in 5,000 pregnancies—perhaps closer to 1 in 2,000, or two fully developed cases of FAS for every 100 women who drink more than 1 ounce of alcohol daily during early pregnancy. On this basis, FAS would be the third leading cause of birth defects with associated mental retardation, surpassed only by Down's syndrome (1 in 600) and spina bifida (1 in 1,000). Most important, of the three, only FAS is preventable.(10)

Parts of the syndrome may appear with these lesser amounts of alcohol consumption, weekend drinking, or heavy drinking during critical developmental periods of the pregnancy. As of yet, no absolutely safe level of alcohol consumption has been established. It must also be stated that women alcoholics have a 30−50 percent greater chance of having serious problems with the developing fetus than do nondrinking women.(77)

Furthermore, the mother may not be the only party implicated in the production and development of FAS in children. Fathers also have been found to play a definite role. A father who drinks heavily may also contribute to the syndrome because the alcohol he consumes may produce chromosomal alterations that affect his offspring.

Children with FAS generally exhibit alterations in development of bodily form and in growth that fall into eight categories:

*Prenatal growth deficiencies.* Even moderate drinkers (2 drinks per day) give birth to infants who average ½ pound less at birth than women who do not drink. Alcohol use by the mother during pregnancy contributes to an increased number of stillbirths, low birth weights, and prenatal mortality. Oddly enough, prepregnancy ingestion of high doses of alcohol can also lead to decreased birth weight of future children. The mother's use of alcohol seems to affect body length even more severely than weight, with length at birth being significantly shorter when alcohol is consumed during pregnancy.

*Postnatal growth deficiency.* Not only do FAS children show lesser body length and weight at birth than do normal children, they do not seem to catch up in the areas of weight gain, height, or head circumference even after birth. They exhibit many characteristics of the failure-to-thrive syndrome in that they have difficulty surviving and making neonatal adaptation.

*Delay of gross and fine motor control.* Typically, FAS children may manifest any of the following conditions in connection with this part of the syndrome: diminished muscle tone, jitteriness, poor sucking reflex, psychomotor disturbances, tremulousness, irritability, hyperactivity, poor grasp, poor eye-hand coordination, exaggerated reflexes, and increased muscle tension. Some of these symptoms—tremulousness, irritability, hyperactivity, exaggerated reflexes, and increased muscle tension—could very well be manifestations of an alcohol withdrawal syndrome in the infant.

*Varying degrees of mental retardation.* Retardation can range from borderline ranges of intelligence to severe retardation. Dr. Ann P. Streissguth of the University of Washington studied FAS children ranging in age from 10 months to 21 years. She found the average IQ to be 64, which falls within the mildly retarded category. However, she found that the overall IQ range was from 16 to 105.[7]

Mental retardation can be manifested later in life by a constellation of symptoms known as minimal brain dysfunction (MBD). MBD is one of the most pressing problems in contemporary medical practice because it affects an estimated 5 to 10 percent of the school-age population, or 5 to 7 million children in the United States. Furthermore, it is suspected that many MBD victims later

[7]Ann P. Streissguth, "Maternal Drinking and the Outcome of Pregnancy: Implications for Child Mental Health," *Grassroots,* Sept. 1978, Supplement, p. 30.

exhibit deviant, antisocial, and delinquent behavior.[8] MBD is characterized by the following symptoms, which appear several years after the FAS child is born: constant involuntary hyperactivity, short attention span, poor powers of concentration, impulsivity, inability to adjust to environmental changes, poor school performance (FAS children tend to score consistently lower in reading, writing, and spelling abilities), cognitive and perceptual problems, inability to follow through on tasks, and behavioral problems associated with school.[9]

*Facial abnormalities.* The face of an FAS child manifests distinctive characteristics, enabling physicians in many cases to identify an FAS child on the basis of facial features alone. Some of the most common abnormalities are microcephaly or abnormally small head (although hydrocephaly—abnormal fluid accumulation in the head—is an occasional variant), narrow eye slits, abnormally small eyes, epicanthic folds, strabismus and myopia, cataracts, retinal abnormalities, incomplete development of the upper jaw, diminished or missing philtrum, cleft lip and palate, short upturned nose, "fish mouth," sunken nasal bridge, and mild abnormalities of the external ear.

*Joint abnormalities.* The most common joint abnormalities in the FAS child are extra digits and abnormal palmar creases. There is also an increased frequency among FAS children of such positional limb deformities as congenital dislocation of the hip and club foot.

*Cardiac problems.* Ventricular septal defect is the most prevalent cardiac difficulty among FAS children, but some children also manifest an atrial septal defect.

*Minor genital abnormalities.* Table 12 provides a brief overview of the most common and consistent features of fetal alcohol syndrome.

# Prevention

The implications are clear: women of childbearing age must be alerted to the dangers of alcohol misuse. Such women must be educated about the dangers of alcohol use during pregnancy and during nursing, since alcohol readily enters breast milk, providing alcohol to the nursing infant.

Prevention of fetal alcohol syndrome has traditionally focused in three areas; of those, possibly the most effective is involvement and counseling by physicians and other health agencies. Since there is no level of alcohol use that is considered entirely safe during any period of pregnancy, counseling has emphasized abstinence from alcohol during pregnancy; in cases where the prospective mother insists on continuing to drink, health professionals urge keeping the amount of alcohol under two drinks a day and restricting all binge drinking. Women are told

---

[8]NIAAA, *Alcohol and Health,* p. 43.

[9]Bennett A. Shaywitz, "Fetal Alcohol Syndrome: An Ancient Problem Rediscovered," *Drug Therapy,* Jan. 1978, p. 107

---

*Table 12*
*Features of the fetal alcohol syndrome*

---

## Growth and Performance

- Prenatal onset growth deficiency, more pronounced in length than in weight
- Concomitant microcephaly (small head circumference) even when corrected for small body weight and length
- Postnatal growth deficiency in weight and length, usually below 3rd percentile
- Delay of intellectual development and/or mental deficiency (mean IQ from Seattle study = 64, range 16-92)
- Fine motor dysfunction (poor coordination)

## Head and Face

- Microcephaly
- Short palpebral fissures (narrow eye slits)
- Midfacial (maxillary) hypoplasia (underdevelopment of midfacial region)
- Flattened, elongated philtrum (middle of upper lip) associated with thin, narrow vermilion lip borders (highly specific to FAS)
- Minor ear anomalies including low set ears

## Limbs

Abnormal creases in the palm of the hand
- Minor joint anomalies
    —syndactyly (fingers or toes joined together)
    —clinodactyly (abnormal bending of fingers or toes)
    —camptodactylyl (one or more fingers constantly flexed at one or more phalangeal joints)

## Heart

- Ventricular and atrial septal defect (valve defects)

## Brain

- Absence of corpus callosum
- Hydrocephalus (excess fluid in cranium)
- Brain cell migratory abnormalities

## Other

- Minor genital anomalies
- Hemangiomas (benign tumors made up of blood vessels) in infancy

SOURCE: Data from Kenneth L. Jones and David W. Smith, "The Fetal Alcohol Syndrome," *Teratology* 12(1975):1-10.

---

that the chances of bearing a normal child increase proportionately as the amount of alcohol decreases.

Prevention efforts need to be increased, and they need to include efforts aimed at fathers as well.

# 4

Interaction of Alcohol
and Other Drugs

The wide spectrum of the effects of alcohol on the body and on behavior is well
documented; not as commonly recognized, but of critical concern, are the
problems that arise when alcohol is used in combination with other drugs.[1]
Particularly within the last three decades, there has been a considerable increase
in the use of pharmaceuticals, including self-prescribed, over-the-counter, and
illicit drugs, as well as those that are prescribed by a physician. Alcohol
consumption has increased during the same period; resulting in greatly expanded
opportunities for the problems associated with alcohol-drug combinations.

Of the 100 most-prescribed drugs, more than 50 percent contain at least one
ingredient known to react adversely with alcohol: many alcohol-drug combinations can result in severe health consequences, including death. Information from
the Drug Abuse Warning Network shows that more than 47,000 people who have
taken drugs and alcohol are treated in emergency rooms of hospitals each year.
And, more than 2,500 deaths yearly are attributed to the combination of alcohol
and various drugs.(105)

## Alcohol and Drugs in Medical Use

Adverse effects are not necessarily deliberate, although they may be in many
cases, when people attempt suicide or experiment with such combinations for

[1]This chapter is adapted from NIAAA, *Alcohol and Health,* Fourth Special Report to the
U.S. Congress on Alcohol and Health from the Secretary of Health, Education, and
Welfare, June 1978, pp. 47–51.

their mood-altering effects. In fact, most instances of adverse reactions are accidental. Although the effects of alcohol alone may be well known, that alcohol can interact detrimentally with other commonly used drugs is often overlooked. Even one or two drinks can have serious consequences for individuals taking various prescription drugs, or even aspirin. It is critical that patients who drink (even occasionally) inform their physicians of that fact, and that physicians in turn advise patients about situations in which alcohol should be avoided.

The issue of drug interactions with alcohol is important, too, in treating alcoholics and others who drink heavily. Heavy alcohol use results in a wide variety of physiologic and functional changes in the individual that may result in altered sensitivity to other drugs. For example, aspirin can produce massive gastric hemorrhage in the alcoholic, who typically has low prothrombin levels and alcoholic gastritis. Similar problems may be encountered when antidiabetic or anticoagulant agents are prescribed for alcoholics.

In addition, adverse consequences of alcohol-drug misuse are not strictly medical. Alcohol is perhaps best known as a central nervous system depressant, and as such, it impairs the performance of tasks requiring vigilance, speed of reaction, and coordination. When alcohol is combined with other sedatives or depressants—antihistamines, for example—this impairment can be exaggerated, and tasks such as driving vehicles or operating machinery can be especially dangerous.

## Alcohol and Drugs of Abuse

Combining alcohol with "drugs of abuse" is a special problem. These drugs are ingested specifically for their effects on the nervous system, and there is considerable potential for interaction with similar effects of alcohol. Reports collected from hospital emergency rooms and inpatient units, medical examiners, and crisis centers in 29 U.S. metropolitan areas show that alcohol use in combination with other drugs is a substantial problem. Of the approximately 200,000 drug crises reported annually in these areas, the second most frequent cause was alcohol in combination with other drugs of abuse. Medical examiners reported that 13 percent of all drug-related fatalities involved alcohol in combination with other drugs, again the second most frequent cause in the category.

Data from a recent nationwide survey indicate that drinkers are several times more likely than people who do not drink to use psychoactive substances nonmedically (Table 13). A sizeable proportion of persons using hallucinogens, cocaine, opiates, inhalants, and marijuana combine alcohol with these drugs. Among adults who ever have used marijuana, more than one-fourth report combining it with alcohol, as do roughly one-fifth of all cocaine users. The prevalence of combined use, however, is greater among regular or more frequent users of drugs or alcohol. One study of more than 10,000 persons arrested for drunken driving reported that a significant proportion of the drivers had been taking other drugs in addition to alcohol.

**Table 13**
**The use of other drugs among drinkers and nondrinkers of alcohol**

| Use of Other Drugs | Percentage of Youth: Ages 12 to 17 Years | | Percentage of Adults: Ages 18+ Years | |
|---|---|---|---|---|
| | Current Drinkers* | Not Current Drinkers | Current Drinkers* | Not Current Drinkers |
| Size of sample (unweighted base) | 302 | 684 | 1622 | 968 |
| Nonmedical psychotherapeutic pill user? | | | | |
| Yes | 18.8 | 6.5 | 18.9 | 9.4 |
| No | 81.2 | 93.5 | 81.1 | 90.6 |
| Ever used marijuana? | | | | |
| Yes | 44.3 | 11.8 | 31.4 | 6.9 |
| No | 55.7 | 88.2 | 68.6 | 93.1 |
| Ever used other illicit drugs? | | | | |
| Yes | 36.7 | 10.2 | 19.7 | 4.7 |
| No | 63.3 | 89.8 | 80.2 | 94.6 |

SOURCE: H. I. Abelson and P. M. Fishburne, *Nonmedical Use of Psychoactive Substances* (Princeton, NJ: Response Analysis Co., 1976)

*Those who report drinking alcoholic beverages within the past month.

# Drug Interaction

An *interaction* between alcohol and a drug is any alteration in the pharmacologic properties of either due to the presence of the other. Interactions may be (1) *antagonistic,* so that the effect of either or both agents is blocked or reduced; (2) *additive,* so that the net effect of the combination is the sum of the effects of the individual agents; (3) *supra-additive* (synergistic, or potentiating), so that the effect of the two agents in combination is greater than it would be if they were merely additive (probably the most important from a public health viewpoint, since the hazards of these combinations are greater than users expected); or (4) *independent,* so that drugs taken together act independently of each other although they are both present in the body at the same time. Present knowledge indicates that alcohol does not interfere with the actions of vitamins or oral contraceptives.

A fifth type of interaction can occur in alcoholics or heavy drinkers whose alcohol-related diseases (such as diabetes) may make them especially sensitive to other drugs. Furthermore, chronic alcohol use also can produce tolerance: that is, a fixed amount of alcohol has less of an effect than it would in the nonchronic user. In cross-tolerance, a fixed amount of another drug also has less of an effect in the alcohol user than in the nonuser.(10)

# Factors Determing Drug Response

The magnitude of the effect produced by a drug is a function of the quantity or dose of the drug present at its site of action at any given time. The more that is present, the greater the effect, up to the limit of the system to respond. Usually a drug does not reach its site of action instantaneously. Its accessibility is determined by the processes of absorption and distribution within the body. Nor does the presence of the drug at its site of action continue indefinitely. It is redistributed, metabolized, and/or excreted. At any given moment the response or magnitude of the drug effect is a function not only of dose but also of time, the time involved in getting the drug to and from its site of action. Dose and time are also important in interactions between two or more drugs. Each drug in the combination has its own dose time—response relationship. The interaction consequences can generally be predicted by considering the quantity of each drug one has taken and the time that has elapsed between taking the first and the second drug. Generally, the greatest interaction effect occurs when the two drugs are taken simultaneously, and it is generally true that the longer the interval between taking the drugs, the less likely that an interaction response will be observed.

A person's response to a drug or a combination of drugs is also affected by a number of other factors in addition to dose and time. Any of these factors can make an individual's response different from that of the "average" person or of the majority of the population. These include:

## Body Weight and Size

In general, smaller persons require smaller amounts of drugs than larger persons to produce effects of equal intensity. This is because larger persons have a larger volume or body mass in which the drug or drugs are distributed so that the effective drug concentration at the site or sites of action is less than that in a smaller person taking the same dose.

## Age

Individuals at the extremes of normal life, that is, infants and elderly persons, are often unusually sensitive to drugs. This apparent increase in drug sensitivity is associated with changes in rates of absorption, distribution, metabolism, or excretion. In general, the elderly tend to be particularly sensitive to narcotics, analgesics, and alcohol.

## Sex

Simply on the basis of weight, women may require smaller doses of drugs than men to obtain the same magnitude of response. However, with few exceptions, the response of men and women to the action of the drug or drugs is the same. At the same blood-alcohol concentration, the effects of alcohol are no different in women than in men.

### Nutritional State

Alcohol, unlike other drugs, can be used by the body as a source of energy. This supply of calories often suppresses the appetite and may lead to dietary deficiencies in heavy drinkers. A poor nutritional state, regardless of its cause, can produce altered drug sensitivities.

### General State of Health

Physiological variables such as changes in body temperature, water content, or pH of body fluids, may modify the effects of drugs in generally healthy individuals. Many chronic disease states such as high blood pressure and diabetes predispose individuals to adverse effects of drugs. In addition, these individuals are often taking specific drugs for control of the disease, symptom relief, or other therapeutic indications. Interactions of alcohol with these drugs and disease states are important but apply only to these patients.

### Psychological Factors

The mere act of taking a drug may produce effects of varying intensity that are unrelated to its pharmacologic action and cannot be attributed to its chemical properties. The best example is the often astonishing therapeutic effect of placebos—dummy or sugar pills—when a patient believes that they will bring relief. Drug effects, including those of drug combination, are also influenced by the mental set, response expected, and the setting or environment in which the drug is taken. Individual response to the general class of central nervous system depressants including alcohol, when taken for subjective purposes rather than for therapeutic purposes, is particularly prone to alteration by psychological factors.(150)

# Barbiturates

The well-known danger to human life from combined use of alcohol and barbiturates appears to result from a supra-additive interaction of the two. The combination of alcohol and barbiturates represents a greater hazard than the danger from either substance alone. In one study of human fatalities, the lethal dose of barbiturates was nearly 50 percent lower in the presence of alcohol than when used alone. Other studies confirm that the combined presence of alcohol and barbiturates, even in low doses, increases the potential for fatal, intentional, and accidental overdoses. Barbiturates and alcohol combined can cause significant respiratory suppression; coma and respiratory arrest occur at doses much lower than would usually be fatal. As a result, it is extremely difficult—even risky—to anesthetize alcoholics for surgery; doses normally needed for anesthesia may trigger respiratory arrest, coma, and death.

Alcohol and barbiturates also interact with regard to their behavioral effects. One study examined the interaction of alcohol and the long-acting phenobarbital; the complex reaction times were found to be increased sufficiently to be described as supra-additive. Alcohol also has been shown to affect people who had taken medium and short-acting barbiturates several hours before; they tended to fall asleep and to exhibit impaired motor performance. Simulated driving tests showed that combined alcohol and secobarbital resulted in considerably greater impairment of performance than either drug alone would have caused. The combination of alcohol and barbiturates can lead to so-called accidental suicide in which the confusion produced by ingestion of either drug can lead to an accidental overdose of the other drug.

Extensive animal studies support these findings. The combined effects on sleep, mortality rates, respiratory failure, and avoidance behavior were noted in many species, and the effects of the two drugs always were greater than those of either drug alone. A major source of this potentiation is the inhibition by alcohol of the enzymes that metabolize other drugs, so that the drugs are present in the bloodstream in higher than normal amounts. Synergism and tolerance may occur directly in brain tissue as well. These data indicate that barbiturates should not be used in the treatment of alcoholism.

# The Minor Tranquilizers

This class of psychotropic drugs is most likely to be combined with alcohol by the general population. People usually are unaware that tranquilizers are depressants of the central nervous system and that they can increase the detrimental effects of alcohol on performance, skills, and alertness.

## Meprobamate (Equanil, Miltown)

In combination with alcohol, meprobamate has been examined extensively for possible effects on skills related to driving. Decreased control of eye movement, body steadiness, and ability to perform on arithmetic and verbal mental tests, plus increased drowsiness and fatigue have been observed after combined alcohol-meprobamate use. The increased impairments occurred in time estimation, attention, reaction time, and alertness. Results of these studies on humans are corroborated by findings in animal research.

## Benzodiazepines

The most frequently used minor tranquilizers are the benzodiazepines, such as diazepam (Valium) and chlordiazepoxide (Librium). There is strong evidence that diazepam alone or in combination with alcohol is the cause of a great many driving accidents. Some studies have shown that the combination impairs reaction times and coordination ability more than when either drug is used separately. There is, however, little direct evidence of increased behavioral deterioration when alcohol and other benzodiazepines are combined. It seems that subjects are unaware of the increased impairment and incapable of judging it. Accordingly, those who use alcohol and diazepam should be informed of the possible debilitating effects resulting from combined use, particularly regarding the driving hazards.

Care should be taken when using or prescribing all drugs in this category, since there have been reports that some benzodiazepines, when combined with alcohol, have produced a severe hypotensive effect, leading to depressed cardiac functioning and respiratory arrest.

## The Major Tranquilizers

Typically, these potent tranquilizers are used for seriously emotionally disturbed patients. The most commonly used are the phenothiazines such as chlor-promazine (Thorazine) and thioridazine (Mellaril), and the alkaloids of rauwolfia, including reserpine (Serpasil). The major tranquilizers are central nervous system depressants and in combination with alcohol can produce severe, possibly fatal, depression of the respiratory center. Excessive drinking by a person who is also taking these drugs can lead to impaired hepatic functioning, which can result in toxic manifestations by a mechanism similar to that of barbiturates. Researchers caution against the use of the phenothiazines to control alcohol withdrawal since these drugs lower the seizure threshold and can induce hypotension, which can be exacerbated by alcohol.

When researchers examined the effect on motor skills of the interaction of alcohol with chlorpromazine, they learned that the combination lengthened reaction time. Animal studies indicate that chlorpromazine increased the effects of alcohol on respiration, motor activity, sleeping time, and the ability to perform avoidance and escape responses. There is also evidence that it may retard alcohol metabolism.

At least two studies have found that reserpine-alcohol combinations lengthen reaction time in humans. More substantial evidence from animal studies shows increased impairment with this combination.

## Antidepressant Drugs

Few studies have examined the combined effect of alcohol and antidepressant drugs. Monoamine oxidase inhibitors used as antidepressants, when combined with alcohol, can lead to a hypertensive crisis, with symptoms of nausea and severe headaches. Alcohol can also interact with these drugs in the brain, since both have major effects on brain neurotransmitters. Of the tricyclic antidepres-sants, those which are predominantly stimulants (for example, desipramine) have a tendency to slightly antagonize depressant effects of ethanol, while those which are predominantly depressants (amitriptyline, Elavil) can potentiate ethanol's depressant effects. Alcohol in combination with amitriptyline has been found to decrease motor coordination and reaction time. Tricyclic antidepressants also may lower the threshold for convulsions and should be administered cautiously during alcohol withdrawal.

## Stimulants

Although theoretically stimulants of the central nervous system such as caffeine and the amphetamines should antagonize the depressant effects of alcohol, this has been difficult to demonstrate in the laboratory. Stimulants may decrease the lethal effects of alcohol, but results of tests of a variety of behavioral, mental, and psychomotor tasks have been quite variable. In some cases combined use of alcohol with stimulants may produce hyperexcitability. It is particularly important to note that caffeine is at best only a weak antagonist of the depressant effects of alcohol; drinking coffee does not significantly improve driving performance in the intoxicated individual. Usually, when the effects of alcohol are reduced by stimulants, the reduction is small, is limited to only a few behaviors, or cannot be related to the drug.

Methylphenidate (Ritalin) is similar to the amphetamines in its interactions with alcohol. Pentylenetetrazol has been used to treat alcohol coma but has the dangerous effect of inducing convulsions.

Several other drugs, although not technically stimulants, have been suggested as possibly effective in reversing alcohol intoxication. These drugs, referred to as amethystics, include L-dopa, aminophylline, and propranolol, although more recent research indicates that propranolol's effects may be additive to those of alcohol.

## Anticonvulsants

Little work has been done on the interactions of alcohol with anticonvulsants such as diphenylhydantoin (Dilantin). Some evidence suggests that diphenylhydantoin may potentiate alcohol effects and is probably ineffective in controling convulsions associated with alcohol withdrawal. More importantly, chronic alcohol use may produce metabolic tolerance to anticonvulsants, and epileptics who are also heavy drinkers may not be receiving adequate dose levels of their anticonvulsant medication.

## Antihistamines

Antihistamines are used to control symptoms of allergy and motion sickness. Despite their sedative effect and their widespread over-the-counter sales, comparatively few studies have been made of the behavioral consequences of combining them with alcohol. However, the bulk of the existing evidence suggests at least an additive, and possibly a potentiating, interaction of the two. Clearly this combination should not be used when complex behavioral tasks, such as driving or operating machinery, are to be undertaken.

## Anesthetics

Studies indicate that care must be taken when using ether or chloroform to anesthetize alcoholics or other persons who have been ingesting alcohol. While greater amounts of these agents are necessary to induce adequate anesthesia in the presence of alcohol, a deeper narcosis is produced due to a supra-additive interaction. The result is increased sleep time and a greater possibility of death. In chronic alcoholics, a cross-tolerance to a wide variety of anesthetics has been observed.

## Ethanol Analogs

The ethanol analogs chloral hydrate and paraldehyde are sometimes used to treat alcoholics, the former as a hypnotic and the latter as a sedative in alcohol withdrawal. Both these drugs, however, have supra-additive effects when used with alcohol and can cause respiratory depression, cardiovascular changes, and death. The combination of chloral hydrate with alcohol has also been shown to impair performance on tests of psychomotor abilities.

## Morphine and Other Opiate Derivatives

Evidence suggests that most opiate derivatives, such as morphine and heroin, have a potentiating effect on the depressant effect of alcohol. Opiates have been reported to be involved frequently in deaths due to alcohol-drug combinations. In addition, chronic use of alcohol may sensitize the individual to the lethal effects of opiates, and vice versa. This is especially important, as a large proportion of heroin addicts and methadone maintenance patients are also heavy users of alcohol.

## Marijuana

Considerable evidence now indicates that the use of marijuana impairs human use of machines and driving, and that this impairment is greater when alcohol and marijuana are combined.

Researchers have found that both mental arithmetic scores and pursuit tracking ability were more impaired with alcohol and marijuana combined than with either drug alone. When a subject's attention was divided, the ability to monitor visual signals in central and peripheral vision was decreased. A marijuana-alcohol combination produced greater deficits of standing steadiness, manual dexterity, psychomotor skill, vigilance, information processing, and control of eye movement than did either drug alone. Those who use these drugs in combination should be alerted to this danger. Although there are no clinical reports of physiologic dangers associated with using marijuana and alcohol together, one study showed significant increases in both heart and pulse rates with combined use.

## Drugs Producing Alcohol Intolerance

Disulfiram (Antabuse) is the best known of the drugs that produce marked adverse and unpleasant reactions when combined with alcohol and that are used to promote abstinence in alcoholic patients. Calcium carbimide, sulfonylurea, and disulfiram apparently interfere with some aspect of the metabolism of alcohol, either the transformation of alcohol to acetaldehyde or its further subsequent metabolism. However useful in the treatment of alcoholism, this reaction can also be an unpleasant side effect of drugs used to treat other disorders.

## Other Interactions

Several classes of drugs, including various oral antidiabetic medications and antibiotics, may produce disulfiram-like reactions following alcohol ingestion.

Alcohol can also dangerously increase the anticoagulant properties of warfarin-type drugs, possibly by inhibiting enzymes that normally inactivate these drugs. It can produce an additive hypotension in individual's taking antihypertensive drugs (methyldopa, Aldomet), presumably because it produces renal and peripheral vasodilation. Patients being maintained on these types of medications should be advised to avoid using alcohol.

It has been suggested that alcohol dissolves the tars found in tobacco smoke, making them more available to body tissues, particularly in the head, neck, and esophagus. The resultant increase in risk for cancer is significant, since heavy drinking appears to be associated with heavy smoking. A similar mechanism may be responsible for the increased toxicity of other chemicals, such as metals and organic solvents (for example, carbon tetrachloride), with alcohol use.

Chronic alcoholics and heavy drinkers require special consideration when being treated for other disorders. The impaired liver function of these individuals may result in increased sensitivity and exaggerated responses to various drugs. For example, insulin and oral antidiabetic medications may produce extreme hypoglycemia in these patients. Anticoagulants can produce severe gastric hemorrhage in alcoholics. Conversely, cross-tolerance to other drugs, most notably other central nervous system depressants and anticonvulsants, may cause normally indicated doses of these medications to be ineffective.(9)

## How To Avoid Alcohol-Drug Interactions

Certain procedures can be followed to avoid alcohol-drug interactions, which are summarized in Table 14.

1. Patients should be honest with physicians about their drinking habits—present and past.
2. The patient should report changes in drinking habits to his/her physician. The balance between drug and alcohol use may be upset by changes in patterns, and the physician may have to make allowances.
3. Physicians should be asked about possible drug-alcohol interactions when they prescribe a new drug for a patient's use.
4. Patients should always check the containers on prescription drugs for warnings about the effects when the drug is combined with alcohol.
5. Patients should read all labels on over-the-counter drugs to see if there are possible drug-alcohol interactions.
6. A patient who is in doubt about taking over-the-counter or prescription drugs in combination with alcohol should ask the pharmacist when buying or refilling the drug.
7. Whenever the patient lacks specific information about alcohol interaction with a certain drug, he/she should be safe by not drinking.

**Table 14**
*Alcohol-drug interactions*

**NOTE TO THE READER:**

A legend appears to assist in reading this table. The underlined words are used to clarify the classifications of terms in this table.

**DRUG LEGEND**

| | **POSSIBLE EFFECTS OF COMBINING THIS DRUG WITH ALCOHOL** |
|---|---|
| **ANALGESICS**—Drug Classification | |
| Narcotics—Sub-Classification | |
| codeine (cough syrups w/codeine; (Trade Name) Novahistine-Expectorant; Phenaphen w/codeine) | Increased central nervous system (CNS) and respiratory depression |
| heroin—"junk"; "H"—(Slang Term) | Synergism of CNS depressant effect |
| meperidine (Demerol) | Respiratory arrest in large doses |
| methadone (Dolophine)—"Dollies" | Tolerance to depressant effects |
| **ANALGESICS** | |
| Narcotics | |
| codeine (cough syrups w/codeine; Novahistine-Expectorant; Phenaphen w/codeine) | Increased central nervous system (CNS) and respiratory depression |
| heroin—"junk"; "H" | Enhanced sedation |
| meperidine (Demerol) | Respiratory arrest in large doses |
| methadone (Dolophine)—"Dollies" | Tolerance to depressant effects* |
| morphine—"Dreamer"; "M" | |
| Non-narcotics | |
| Salicylates | |
| acetylsalicylic acid (aspirin; Excedrin) | Increased gastrointestinal (GI) blood loss and damage to stomach lining induced by aspirin |
| | Excessive alcohol intake and ingestion of aspirin may lead to severe GI bleeding |
| Other | |
| phenylbutazone (Butazolidin) | Enhanced deleterious effect on driving and psychomotor skills |
| d-propoxyphene (Darvon) | Increased CNS and respiratory depression |

*Effect is most likely to occur with chronic heavy consumption of alcohol.

## DRUG LEGEND

| | POSSIBLE EFFECTS OF COMBINING THIS DRUG WITH ALCOHOL |
|---|---|
| **ANTIANGINAL PREPARATIONS** | |
| Nitrates | Hypotension, resulting from enhanced dilation of blood vessels |
| nitroglycerin (Nitrong; Nitrostat) | Decreased blood pressure |
| pentaerythritol tetranitrate (Antora; Pentritol; Peritrate) | |
| Peripheral vasodilators | Possible disulfiram—like reaction |
| tolazoline (Priscoline) | |
| **ANTICOAGULANTS** | |
| bishydroxycoumarin (Dicumarol) | Unpredictable: occasional increased sensitivity to drug with acute intoxication |
| warfarin sodium (Coumadin; Panwarfin) | Decreased blood-clotting ability* |
| | Occasional moderate use of alcohol is unlikely to interfere with therapeutic effect in patients without liver disease |
| | Excessive alcohol use should be avoided |
| **ANTICONVULSANTS** | |
| clonazepam (Clonopin) | Enhanced CNS depression |
| diphenylhydantoin (Dilan; Dilantin) | Decreased drug effect* |
| | Possible seizures |
| **ANTIDEPRESSANTS** | |
| Tricyclic | Enhanced CNS depressant effects |
| amitriptyline (Elavil) | Impairment of motor skills related to driving or operating machinery following initiation of tricyclic therapy |
| desipramine (Norpramin; Pertofrane) | |
| doxepin (Sinequan) | |
| imipramine (Presamine; Tofranil) | |
| nortriptyline (Aventyl) | |
| protriptyline (Vivactil) | |
| Monoamine oxidase inhibitors | Mechanism unknown |
| isocarboxazid (Marplan) | Monoamine oxidase inhibits metabolism of tyramine in certain alcoholic beverages |
| pargyline (Eutonyl) | |
| tranylcypromine (Parnate) | |

## ANTIDIABETIC AGENTS

| Drug | Effect |
|---|---|
| Insulin (Iletin) | Increased sedative effects |
| | Nausea, vomiting, and headache |
| | Increased blood pressure |
| | Heart palpitations |
| | Hypertensive crisis (with certain drinks, e.g., Chianti wine and beer) |
| | Alcohol per se may cause hypoglycemia; in combination with insulin the effect may be augmented, resulting in increased drug effect |
| | Control of diabetes more difficult |
| | Possible severe hypoglycemia |
| chlorpropamide (Diabinese) | Possible disulfiram-like reaction |
| tolbutamide (Orinase) | Possible disulfiram-like reaction |
| | Increased hypoglycemic effect, particularly in fasting patients |
| | Decreased hypoglycemic effect with chronic alcohol use* |

## ANTIHISTAMINES

| Drug | Effect |
|---|---|
| Ethanolamines (prominent sedation) | CNS depression effects of drug synergized by alcohol |
| diphenhydramine (Benadryl) | Synergism of sedative effects (varies with class of antihistamine) |
| diphenylpyraline (Diafen; Hispril Spansule) | |
| Ethylenediamines (moderate sedation) | |
| methapyrilene (Histadyl; Nytol) | |
| tripelennamine (Pyribenzamine) | |
| Alkylamines (minimal sedation) | |
| brompheniramine maleate (Dimetane) | |
| chlorpheniramine maleate (Chlor-Trimeton; Coricidin) | |
| Phenothiazines (moderate sedation) | |
| promethazine (Phenergan; Synaglos) | |

*Effect is most likely to occur with chronic heavy consumption of alcohol.

| DRUG LEGEND | POSSIBLE EFFECTS OF COMBINING THIS DRUG WITH ALCOHOL |
|---|---|
| **ANTIHYPERTENSIVE AGENTS** | |
| Alpha-methyldopa (Aldomet) | May increase sedation with initial treatment |
| Guanethidine (Esimil; Ismelin) | Enhanced postural hypotensive effect may produce dizziness or fainting spells |
| Rauwolfia alkaloids deserpidine (Enduronyl; Harmonyl) reserpine (Butiserpazide; Hydromox; Serpasil) | May increase sedation with initial treatment |
| Paragyline (see ANTIDEPRESSANTS, Monoamine oxidase inhibitors) | |
| **ANTI-INFECTIVE AGENTS** (including those commonly called antibiotics) | |
| Chloramphenicol (Chlormycetin) | Possible disulfiram-like reaction |
| Griseofulvin (Fulvacin U/F) | Possible disulfiram-like reaction |
| Isoniazid (Nydrazid) | Decreased effect with chronic alcohol use |
| Metronidazole (Flagyl) | |
| Furazolidone (Furoxone) | Possible disulfiram-like reaction |
| Penicillin | No reported drug interaction |
| **CENTRAL NERVOUS SYSTEM STIMULANTS** | |
| Cocaine—"Coke" | No interactions have been reported |
| Amphetamines (Benzedrine)—"Bennies" (Biphetamines)—"Black Beauties"; "Speed" | Antagonizes CNS depression |
| Dextroamphetamines (Dexedrine)—"Dexies"; (Eskatrol) | No motor coordination improvement—as with alcohol alone |
| Methylphenidate (Ritalin) | |
| Caffeine (contained in certain pain killers (Aspirin Phenacetin Caffeine capsules; Empirin; No-Doz) (soft drinks; coffee) | |
| Nicotine (cigarettes) | Clinically important drug interaction not established |
| **HALLUCINOGENS** | |
| Cannabis (marijuana)—"Pot;" THC; "Hash" | Additive effect |

Lysergic acid diethylamide—"LSD"; "Acid"

Mental and motor impairment

Reported but questionable precipitation of LSD flashbacks

Mescaline—"Mesc"
Psilocybin—"Mushrooms"

No reported drug interaction

**ORAL CONTRACEPTIVES** (Noromyl; Ortho-Novum; Ovral)—"The Pill"

No reported drug interaction

**SEDATIVE-HYPNOTICS**

Barbiturates—"Downers"
  amobarbital (Amytal)
  butabarbital (Butisol)
  pentobarbital (Nembutal)
  phenobarbital (Luminal and various others)
  secobarbital (Seconal)—"Reds"

Enhanced CNS and respiratory depression

Cross-tolerance to sedative effect among sedative-hypnotics and with alcohol*

Potentially lethal combination in large doses

Nonbarbiturates
  chloral hydrate (Felsules; Noctec)—"Mickey Finn"
  Chloralbetaine (Beta-Chlor)
  ethochlorvynol (Placidyl)
  glutethimide (Doriden)
  methaqualone (Quaalude; Sopor)—"Rorer"
  carbromal (Carbrital)
  flurazepam (Dalmane—see TRANQUILIZERS, minor)

Nausea

Vomiting

**TRANQUILIZERS** (also used as muscle relaxants)

Minor
  chlordiazepoxide (Librium; Libritabs)
  clorazepate (Trankene)
  diazepam (Valium)
  flurazepam (Dalmane)
  lorazepam (Ativan)
  oxazepam (Serax)
  prazepam (Verstran)

Caution should be used when driving or operating machinery

At social drinking levels, there is usually minimal synergism of CNS depression

At more than social-drinking levels, increased sedation and CNS depressant effects

Cross-tolerance to sedative effect*

*Effect is most likely to occur with chronic heavy consumption of alcohol.

| DRUG LEGEND | POSSIBLE EFFECTS OF COMBINING THIS DRUG WITH ALCOHOL |
| --- | --- |
| hydroxyzine (Atarax; Vistaril)<br>meprobamate (Equanil; Miltown)<br>tybamate (Solacen; Tybatran) | Additive or synergistic increase of CNS depressant effect |
| Major<br>chlorpromazine (Thorazine)<br>prochlorperazine (Compazine)<br>trifluoperazine (Stelazine)<br>thioridazine (Mellaril)<br>perphenazine (Trilafon)<br>haloperidol (Haldol) | Additive CNS depression (sedation prominent)<br>Impairment of muscle coordination and judgment; caution should be used when driving or operating machinery |
| VITAMINS | No reported drug interaction; in alcoholism, however, malnutrition is often noted |
| MISCELLANEOUS<br>Antimalarials<br>quinacrine (Atabrine, Mepacrine)<br>Disulfiram (Antabuse) | Blocks alcohol metabolism<br>Disulfiram-like reaction<br>Disulfiram plus alcohol, even small amounts, produces flushing, throbbing in head and neck, nausea, vomiting, breathing difficulties, sweating, and other problems.<br>In severe reactions there may be serious cardiovascular and respiratory problems convulsions, and death.<br>Disulfiram should NEVER be administered until the patient has abstained from alcohol for at least 12 hours. |

Muscle relaxants (see TRANQUILIZERS, minor)

SOURCE: NIAAA, *The Community Health Nurse and Alcohol Related Problems*, U.S. Department of Health, Education, and Welfare, 1980, pp. 153-60.

---

*Effect is most likely to occur with chronic heavy consumption of alcohol.

# 5

# Problem Drinking and Alcoholism

According to a major study of American drinking practices, more than two-thirds of the adult population, or about 98 million people, drink alcoholic beverages at least occasionally. The overwhelming majority of those who drink do so responsibly, but there are some whose drinking gets out of hand, endangering themselves and those around them. The NIAAA has indicated that about one in ten of the 98 million Americans who drink is now either a full-fledged alcoholic or at least a problem drinker. Thousands of the problem drinkers are under 21. Among those with drinking problems are men and women, young and old, from all socioeconomic backgrounds, religions, races, and occupations. What distinguishes these individuals from the rest of the drinking population is a matter of some disagreement and considerable research.

To those who believe in abstinence, the drinking of any alcoholic beverage in any amount is excessive drinking. To the majority, however, problem drinking occurs when anyone drinks to such an excess that his/her ability to control his/her actions and to maintain a socially acceptable life adjustment is impaired.

The extent of this kind of drinking has been expressed in terms of the number of people involved, the number of traffic accidents, the rates of manpower losses, juvenile delinquency, and deaths, and the size of the financial burdens on the community. While such figures have been widely accepted as scientific fact, most of these measurements are only rough estimates. For example, alcoholism has been frequently cited as the fourth ranking public health problem in America, surpassed only by cancer, heart disease, and mental illness. But there is no accepted ranking of diseases as "public health problems." If such a listing could be prepared, it is not known exactly whether alcohol would properly be ranked fourth, second, tenth, or third. Whatever its rank, alcoholism is one of our major public health problems; it is responsible for thousands of deaths annually and shortens the average alcoholic's life by ten to twelve years. It has been suggested that only about 10 percent of all alcoholics live to be 70 years of age, and about 50 percent die before the age of 51.

## Defining Alcoholism and Problem Drinking

Alcoholism is a complex problem, and this in itself creates considerable difficulty for those who would deal with it.

It is a problem for the alcoholic. It is a problem for the family and closer friends. It is a problem for the community and the neighborhood. It is a problem for the state and for the nation that must pay the human costs—the costs of personal and community disruption and the costs of planning for prevention and control measures. It is a problem for the professionals and those allied to them, who must provide treatment services for the victims of acoholism.(31)

Realistically, then, the problem drinkers are those who cause significant damage to themselves, their families, or their communities because of drinking. Some are clearly addictive drinkers or alcoholics.

It is estimated that there are 9.3 to 10 million problem drinkers, including alcoholics in the adult population—or 7 percent of the nation's 145 million adults 18 years and older. (About 75 percent of the population over age 17 uses alcohol occasionally—i.e., socially or sacramentally—or abusively.) This estimate includes both those who are alcoholics and those who are otherwise disabled as a result of alcohol. In addition to the nation's alcoholics, an estimated 14 percent of the adult male population and 3 percent of the adult female population are problem drinkers.

There are also an estimated 3.3 million problem drinkers among youth in the 14–17 age range—19 percent of the 17 million of this age group. Youth are not generally included in the 10 million adult estimate because their alcohol problems are apparently different from those of adults. Alcohol problems among youth tend to be acute rather than chronic. For example, they usually involve drinking-driving episodes and belligerence rather than alcohol-related medical illnesses and addiction per se. However, all teenagers, regardless of their drinking patterns, obviously represent the population of future adult problem drinkers; they therefore represent an important target for effective alcohol-abuse prevention programs.(9)

Chronic problem drinking is thought to encompass such features as frequent intoxication and binge drinking, symptomatic drinking (including signs attributed to physical dependence and loss of control), psychological dependence, disruption of normal social behavior patterns, problems with spouse, relatives, friends, neighbors, employers, or the police.(8)

Problem drinkers are those who are not only psychologically dependent, but also physically dependent and have developed some degree of tolerance. *Physical dependence* manifests itself as the drinker continues to ingest quantities of alcohol and repeatedly exposes nearly every tissue of his/her body to blood-alcohol mixture. Soon the cellular structures in the brain and elsewhere in the body begin to adapt to the presence of alcohol, and increasing amounts of alcohol become necessary to produce physical and behavioral effects. This adaptive phenomenon of tolerance to alcohol is much like the adaptation of insects to insecticide.

Paradoxically, in the later steps of alcohol addiction there frequently is a reversal of tolerance. The addict needs less alcohol than he/she once did to get the same effects. The cause of this phenomenon is not known, although some investigators spectulate that the prime reasons for loss of tolerance are the progressive brain damage and the destruction of liver cells with their ability to detoxify alcohol. Completely terminating the intake of alcohol and observing the alcoholic's reaction in the form of a withdrawal syndrome dramatically demonstrates physical dependence.(50)

Dunn and Hedberg describe *behavioral dependence,* also called emotional or psychic dependence, in the following way:

> This type of dependency is a learned preference for alcohol. As other addictive drugs, alcohol causes several immediate effects experienced by some drinkers as pleasant and positive—physical calm, ease, relaxation, or euphoria. Furthermore, alcohol usually facilitates social assertiveness or approach behaviors and alters many unpleasant moods or states of being such as anxiety, depression, boredom or irritability. Also, alcohol consumption commonly reduces physical pain—real or imagined—that may be toally unrelated to drug usage, such as that resulting from back injury. These effects can be considered positive or pleasant by the drinker and serve as a basis for a positive conditioned response.[1]

Apparently, these associations are stored in the neural memory system, and as the individual continues to use alcohol to gain positive effects, a habit gradually develops. Thus, the drinker learns to depend on alcohol for its effects.

In addition, the list of problem drinkers must include those who are apparently not addicted to alcohol—who show no symptoms of dependency—but whose drinking has nonetheless created serious personal or family problems.

Within our society at large, problem drinking is usually recognized as such whenever anyone drinks so much that his/her ability to control his/her actions and maintain a socially acceptable life adjustment is impaired. Several authorities in the alcohol field have suggested some behavioral criteria that characterize the person who drinks to much:

1. Anyone who must drink in order to function or to cope with life has a drinking problem.

---

[1]Robert B. Dunn, and Allan G. Hedberg, "Treating the Two Faces of Alcoholism," *Modern Medicine,* 10 June 1974, pp. 35–36.

2. Anyone who, by his/her own personal definition or that of family and friends, frequently drinks to a state of intoxication (four times a year) has a drinking problem.
3. Anyone who goes to work intoxicated has a drinking problem.
4. Anyone who is intoxicated and drives a car has a drinking problem.
5. Anyone who sustains bodily injury requiring medical attention as a consequence of an intoxicated state has a drinking problem.
6. Anyone who, while under the influence of alcohol, does something he/she contends he/she would never do without alcohol has a drinking problem.
7. Anyone who must drink in order to get to and perform his/her work has a drinking problem.
8. Anyone who comes in conflict with the law as a consequence of an intoxicated state has a drinking problem.(5,8)

# Describing Problem Drinkers[2]

Many Americans drink alcohol as they live life—rapidly and under tense circumstances. At those two indigenous American institutions—the cocktail party and the commuter bar—drinking is usually done standing, the alcoholic beverage is gulped rapidly with the barest minimum of food, and the general aim is to reach the desired end point of "being high." Even more significant is the fact that this pattern is condoned; in the United States it is frequently all right to drink just for the purpose of getting drunk.

In this age of psychiatric sophistication, Americans conveniently forget that a state of drunkenness is a state of illness. Paradoxically, a dose of alcohol can be used as a form of self-medication.

From time to time, for example, we are called to perform an activity we wish to but cannot. Our conscious desire to perform is overwhelmed and incapacitated by unwelcome inhibitions. Alcohol is an easy releaser; the hounding inhibitions melt quickly before its chemical presence. The actor may bring himself to the otherwise terrifying center stage; the lecturer can speak; the author can write; and the sexually frigid can respond. This group of alcohol drinkers is growing because it seems that the demands of increasingly complex situations require alcohol to ease the way. Unfortunately, alcohol is a fickle ally, and increased amounts may lead to states of intoxication and responses not appropriate for the circumstances. In an increasingly complex society, the danger that alcohol will be called upon to fulfill a tranquilizing role must be guarded against.

Another common experience is to find people who use alcohol to lift depression, to dull the inner pain, and dispel the sense of ugliness within them. Some find that liquor provides what they seek and become fearful of giving up the bottle for fear that the pain will return. On the other hand, some patients find that

[2]Adapted from an article by Morris E. Chafetz, *Preventive Medicine* 3 (1974): 5–10, and presented in the Second Special Report to the U.S. Congress on Alcohol and Health.

alcohol actually deepens their depression. They respond to the deepened depression by imbibing more and more of the liquor, hoping to achieve the relief they seek.

Another kind of alcohol user is the person who employs alcohol to blur his/her perceptions. When such an individual becomes aware that some socially forbidden impulses are coming too close to the surface, he/she may use alcohol heavily. In this circumstance, the alcohol may obliterate the discomforting feelings, or it may dissolve inhibitions to the point where a person permits himself/herself to act on instincts.

One common type of alcohol drinker is the individual who uses alcohol to sustain a psychological system of defenses. Here, the "blackout" phenomenon is usual. In other words, repressed unconscious desires become a reality during intoxication, but the drinker has no recollection when sober of what has transpired. People with a sober characterological attitude of complete kindness, nonexistent hostility, and abject passivity will, with liquor, become brutal, hostile, and aggressive. Once the effects of the liquor are gone, however, they undergo what appears to be a form of selective amnesia, as they express incredulousness at descriptions of their behavior while intoxicated.

Alcohol for a certain segment of the population has one goal worth drinking for: oblivion. The inhabitants of this unhappy drinking state down their drinks in a state of bliss. To them, reality is terror, and a dream state of narcosis is the only way to continue.

Another alcohol drinker is the individual who is more tolerable to his/her social unit when intoxicated than when sober. This syndrome is seen most often in configurations where nonalcoholic, extremely dominating mates or parents exist. On the one hand, the nonalcoholic mates or parents appear to suffer greatly as a consequence of the alcoholic state of the other. If treatment or extraneous events result in sobriety, however, the healthy members become proportionately more disturbed as the alcoholic member becomes less dependent on alcohol. What becomes clear is that the pathological drinking behavior of the alcoholic person was a cover-up for the disturbances in another.

Less obvious is that subgroup of individuals who, although heavily under the influence of alcohol, do not seem so to the casual observer. This type of individual can carry on highly complicated business and social activities and seems to be none for worse for drinking. Only when a fall in blood alcohol level occurs does the person suddenly return to the original state of awareness. This person, upon regaining the nondrinking self, has no inkling of people, places, or events that have transpired for hours, days, or weeks. Then, not only is he/she stunned by sudden situations, but innocent sharers or that "other" personality are confronted with a new individual in an old body.

If we are to make any headway in reducing these unhealthy ways in which alcohol is used psychologically and socially, we must come up with bold ideas that face the problem directly.

We know that the influences that can mediate the imbibing of a definite amount of alcohol are innumerable. The psychological, physical, and social factors that determine our response to a given quantity of alcohol are not consistent from individual to individual, nor within the same person at separate times. Since responses to alcohol are unpredictable, it is easy to see why drinkers who use alcohol to achieve a delicate balance between feeling good and feeling sick often cross the border and suffer complications, and why the hairline or end-point difference between responsible drinking and unhealthy drinking is a tough target to hit.

## Definition of Alcoholism

Alcoholism has been called a disease. In the broadest sense of the word, it *is* a disease—a disabling condition, progressive in nature and manifested as a syndrome with interrelated biological, emotional, social, spiritual, and behavioral aspects. On this point most experts agree. However, there is no formal definition of alcoholism or of an alcoholic person which is universally or even generally accepted. Perhaps the definition most widely considered as authoritative is that of Mark Keller of the Center of Alcohol Studies at Rutgers University:[3] "Alcoholism is a chronic disease or disorder of behavior characterized by the repeated drinking of alcoholic beverages to an extent that exceeds customary dietary use, or ordinary compliance with the social drinking customs of the community and which interferes with the drinker's health, interpersonal relations, or economic functioning.

The World Health Organization defines alcoholism as an addiction to alcohol. Alcoholism is characterized by a compulsion to take alcohol on a continuous or periodic basis to experience its psychological and physical effects and sometimes to avoid the discomfort of its absence. Tolerance may or may not be present. The fact that a person is addicted to alcohol implies a probable impaired behavioral responsiveness to social control.

Another important concept described by Dr. Ebbe Curtis Hoff of the Medical College of Virginia is based on three facets:

1. There is loss of control of alcohol intake. The victim finds himself/herself drinking when he/she intends not to drink or drinking more than planned.
2. There is functional or structural damage, physiological, psychological, domestic, economic, or social.
3. Alcohol is used as a kind of universal therapy, as a psychopharmacological substance through which the problem drinker attempts to keep life from disintegrating.(6)

One more psychiatrically oriented definition which combines descriptive

---

[3]NIAAA, *Alcohol and Alcoholism: Problems, Programs and Progress,* National Institute of Mental Health, PHS Publication No. (HSM) 72-9127 (1972), p. 9.

criteria with a suggestion concerning the origins of alcoholism as a chronic behavioral disorder is that of Chafetz and Demone:[4]

> We define alcoholism as a chronic behavioral disorder which is manifested by undue preoccupation with alcohol to the detriment of physical and mental health by a loss of control when drinking has begun (although it may not be carried to the point of intoxication) and by a self-destructive attitude in dealing with personal relationships and life situations. Alcoholism, we believe, is the result of disturbance and deprivation in early infantile experience and the related alterations in basic physio-chemical responsiveness. The identification by the alcoholic with significant figures who deal with life problems through the excessive use of alcohol, and a social, cutural milieu which causes ambivalence, conflict, and guilt in the use of alcohol.

The National Council on Alcoholism suggests that alcoholism fits the definition of disease given in *Dorland's Illustrated Medical Dictionary,* 24th edition: "A definite morbid process having a characteristic train of symptoms; it may affect the whole body or any of its parts, and its etiology, pathology, and prognosis may be known or unknown."

One way of defining an *alcoholic* is by using the three criteria set up by the NIAAA:[5]

1. Alcohol consumption—generally, an alcoholic consumes more than 120 drinks per month; more than 10 million people in the United States are classified as alcoholics based on the criteria of consumption.
2. Adverse effects—generally, an alcoholic suffers adverse effects (such as social impairment, psychological problems, physical disease, days missed from work, and other negative consequences) as a result of drinking; almost 8 million Americans are classified as alcoholic based on the "negative consequences" criterion.
3. Alcohol dependence—some people lose control, becoming physically dependent on the alcohol; 4-6 million Americans are classified as alcoholics based on this criterion.

Obviously, the criteria represent three different approaches to defining alcoholism; while all three are present in some cases, a person may be classified as alcoholic based on only one (such as consumption, without dependence or adverse effects).

Dr. Marvin Block, an authority on alcoholism, suggests that one of the most interesting ways of classifying alcoholics was developed and delineated by E. M. Jellinek, perhaps the greatest authority on alcoholism who ever lived. He named the types with the letters of the Greek alphabet. They fall into five main categories:

---

[4]*Ibid.*

[5]"How Many Alcoholics?" *The Bottom Line on Alcohol and Society,* Vol. 5, No. 1 (Winter 1982), p. 7.

*Alpha type.* The alpha alcoholic is psychologically dependent. He/she uses alcohol to gain courage, to remove self-consciousness, and to deal with inhibitions. This type of alcoholic is using alcohol to make life more bearable. It is purely a psychological reliance, for the purpose of relieving psychic pain.

*Beta type.* The beta alcoholic is not psychologically dependent. As this individual drinks alcohol, it produces an adverse affect on the lining of the stomach causing gastritis, or it may cause a swelling of the nerve sheaths which brings about neuritis (or, when it affects more than one nerve, polyneuritis.) These conditions are painful, and the alcohol is responsible for the pain. Thus, the beta alcoholic is in pain caused by the alcohol and, in turn, he/she continues to drink to relieve the pain. If the individual drinks enough, alcohol acts as an anesthetic and affects the brain much as ether, chloroform, or other anesthetic drugs would, but much more slowly.

*Gamma type.* This is the most common type of alcoholic in the United States. A gamma drinker has all the characteristic marks of alcoholism: psychological dependence, physiological dependence, and the development of tissue tolerance. When tissue tolerance develops, it takes more and more alcohol to produce the effect he/she desires. There are no accurate figures available, but it is estimated that 90 percent of the alcoholics in the United States fall into this classification.

*Delta type.* Even though this type of individual drinks alcohol over long periods of time and in excessive amounts, there is no psychological dependence. But because of the chronic, heavy use of alcohol, the tissues become dependent on alcohol. The drinker becomes physiologically dependent. He/she suffers withdrawal if alcohol is taken away, is just as alcoholic and as physiologically involved as the gamma type. This type of alcoholic is found particularly in countries such as Chile and France where it is common to drink wine instead of water. Such a person may drink wine all of his/her life and never be withdrawn from it. Sometimes this type is unaware of being alcoholic until he/she is removed from alcohol by chance and suffers delirium tremens.

*Epsilon type.* This type of alcoholism is most predominantly found in the Scandinavian countries. This drinker is often referred to as the "spree," "binge," or "fiesta" drinker. He/she may drink nothing between sprees and then go on binges of drinking, lasting anywhere from three days to weeks or longer. This type of drinker is just as alcoholic as those in other classifications, even though he/she does not drink between sprees. When this person does drink, he/she loses control, and keeps on drinking until it gets out of hand or until unconsciousness is reached.(25)

Whatever the definition used, the population of alcoholic and problem drinkers is sufficiently large to warrant attention as a major public health problem in the United States. Although criteria and estimates vary considerably, it is generally thought that about 9 to 10 million people in the U.S. are alcoholics or problem drinkers. Of those, depending upon the definition used, the number of actual alcoholic individuals has been estimated to be somewhere between 6 and 10 million.

# Attitudes About Alcoholism[6]

Through the years a variety of attitudes and definitions concerning the problem of alcoholism have been expressed. The following models as presented by Siegler, Osmond, and Newell are an expression of some of the most common attitudes. These models are simple method of classifying the attitudes and related theories. They are not theories themselves. However, the number and variety of the models suggests that the problem of alcoholism has not been solved to everyone's satisfaction.

## The Impaired Model

*Definition.* An alcoholic is a drunk, souse, topper, tippler, soak, lush. When he/she gets drunk, he/she is plastered, bombed, stoned, tight, oiled.

*Etiology.* Some people are just that way for unknown reasons.

*Behavior.* Drunks are repulsive and dirty; nice people do not like to get close to them. Sometimes they are comical. They fall down, talk to lamp posts, try their door key in the wrong house, get their words mixed up, and so forth. But it is wrong to laugh at them and make fun of them because they cannot help it.

*Prognosis.* There will be no change.

## The "Dry" Moral Model

*Definition.* Alcoholism is a moral failing, not an illness. It is the natural penalty for drinking.

*Etiology.* Alcoholism occurs because drinking occurs. Some strong-willed people can apparently drink without becoming alcoholics. But the social risk in drinking is too great to allow any acceptance.

*Behavior.* The alcoholic behaves immorally because he/she drinks.

*Treatment.* There are many ways to try to get an alcoholic to stop drinking, including forcing church attendance, firing him/her from the job, pouring whiskey down the sink, marrying him/her off to someone strong enough to control him/her, divorce, shunning him/her, ridiculing him/her, giving him/her aversion treatments, and so forth. In short, behavior therapy. Fines and jail sentences may help.

*Prognosis.* The prognosis is poor unless a way is found to threaten alcoholics or punish them so that they stop drinking. The only hope is to make

---

[6] This section is adopted from Miriam Siegler, Humphrey Osmond, and Stephens Newell, "Models of Alcoholism," *Quarterly Journal of Alcohol Studies,* 29 (1968): 573–581.

alcohol unavailable. Young drinkers should have the example of the alcoholic before them.

## The "Wet" Moral Model

*Definition.* Alcoholics are drinkers who do not obey the rules of the drinking society. They behave badly when drunk, and they cannot hold their liquor. Alcoholism is an unacceptable form of drinking behavior.

*Etiology.* It is a mystery why some people who drink become alcoholics.

*Behavior.* The behavior of alcoholics is antisocial. They spoil the happy, congenial occasions that social drinking can provide.

*Treatment.* Everybody in the drinking society including the alcoholic knows how to treat alcoholics: by juggling around rewards and punishments. A spouse may refuse sex, refuse to speak, withhold the family money, reduce housekeeping standards. His/her doctor may give him/her hell, tell the alcoholic to grow up and not be a crybaby, and so on.

*Prognosis.* If only the right formula of rewards and punishments could be found, everything would be all right. Otherwise, prognosis is gloomy.

## The Alcoholics Anonymous Model

*Definition.* Alcoholism is an incurable, progressive, and often fatal disease. Alcoholism is also a spiritual problem for alcoholics. Alcohol is a poison to an alcoholic though not to others. An alcoholic is a person whose life has become intolerable through the use of alcohol. AA is a close community of those afflicted with this disease.

*Etiology.* Alcoholics are emotionally impaired people who drink to compensate for their inadequacies and then, because of their body chemistry, become addicted to alcohol, creating a circular process of further inadequacy and further drinking.

*Behavior.* At the height of his/her drinking career, the behavior of the alcoholic derives largely from the need to get enough to drink to control withdrawal symptoms. Earlier variety of behavior is due to complex physical, mental, spiritual problems of an enduring nature.

*Treatment.* The best treatment for an alcoholic is permanent, continuous involvement in AA.

*Prognosis.* With the help of AA, alcoholism can be arrested although never cured. Without AA, the prognosis is usually hopeless.

## The Psychoanalytic Model

*Definition.* Alcoholism is a symptom of a deep, underlying neurosis. Alcoholics are addictive personalities.

*Etiology.* Since the alcoholic is an infantile person, the key to understanding his/her inability to achieve maturity lies in early emotional experiences.

*Behavior.* The behavior of the alcoholic is to be interpreted as a symbolic means of expressing unconscious conflict.

*Treatment.* For alcoholism, as for all neurosis, psychotherapy is required.

*Prognosis.* The prognosis for alcoholics is not encouraging.

### The Family Interaction Model

*Definition.* Alcoholism, like drug addiction and schizophrenia, is best seen as a form of family interaction in which one person is assigned the role of the alcoholic while others play the complementary roles, such as the martyred wife, the neglected children, the disgraced parents, and so forth. As this deadly game is played by mutural consent, any attempt to remove the key factor, the alcoholic, is bound to create difficulties for the other family members, who will attempt to restore their former game.

*Etiology.* As these family games are circular and self-reinforcing, it is useless to inquire how it began. In general, the basic personality inadequacies are transferred from generation to generation. The behavior of the alcoholic and other family members is a series of moves in a continuous and long, drawn-out family game.

*Treatment.* Family therapy is the only treatment.

*Prognosis.* Prognosis depends on the availability of family therapy. With it the prognosis is good; without it, poor.

### The "Old" Medical Model

*Definition.* Alcoholism is a serious, progressive, and eventually fatal disease which is incurred by the immoral behavior of excessive drinking.

*Etiology.* The etiology of alcoholism is the excessive drinking of alcohol. The reason for the immoderate drinking is unknown. Alcoholics seem to be unable to control themselves.

*Behavior.* Alcoholics are destroying their lives and ruining their bodies by drinking so much, and this is immoral.

*Treatment.* The doctor's problem in the treatment of acute states of illness in alcoholism is the management of the patient in a toxic state. Attention must be given to systemic dehydration, cirrhosis of the liver, nutritional deficiencies, and so on.

*Prognosis.* The prognosis is poor because the patient will not care for himself/herself.

### The "New" Medical Model

*Definition.* Alcoholism is a progressive, often fatal disease, possibly hereditary. Alcoholics are ill people whose body chemistry is such that they can become addicted to alcohol. In emergency treatment, alcoholism must be distinguished from schizophrenia depressions, head injuries, and so forth.

*Etiology.* It appears that alcoholics may have a defect in metabolism, possibly involving one of the major amino acids. There are probably also psychological and sociocultural contributing factors.

*Behavior.* Much of the alcoholic's behavior stems from the alcoholic's need to control withdrawal symptoms.

*Treatment.* Any treatment which helps the alcoholic abstain from drinking is valuable, provided that it does not impair his/her health.

*Prognosis.* Prognosis at the present time is not good. However, there is hope that medical science will provide new information, new treatments, and preventive measures.

## Causes of Alcoholism

The term *alcoholism* is intended to encompass the range of social and health problems which occur when the use of alcohol contributes to their development. The use of alcoholic beverages becomes alcoholism when it is combined with (or aggravates) behavior injurious to the individual's role in and responsibility to his/her and work and his/her role as a member of society.

It may be self-defeating to begin to discuss a disorder of this sort by stating that there is a lack of agreement among the experts as to its precise nature. Alcoholism has been variously described as an allergy, a physical disease, an addiction, and a mental illness. It is uncertain whether the disorder is an entity in itself or a symptom. Its causes have been attributed to a predisposition, because of inherited nervous disability; to the presence or absence of some chemical in the body; to individual reaction; to environmental stress. There are proponents of all of these explanations, singly or in combination, and it is encouraging to know that research is in progress along many lines.

Meanwhile, it is important to know that the experts do agree on one major point: Alcoholism is *not* related to willful misconduct. Those who have learned most about the subject through study, observation, and experience have discarded the long-standing relegation of problem drinking to the category of bad behavior. They agree that it is a disorder or an illness made up of a complex of physical, social, behavioral, spiritual, and psychiatric aspects.

It is also generally recognized that the following characteristic actions of alcohol increases its addictive potential: [7]

1. Acts primarily on the brain.
2. Produces adverse symptoms on awareness and psychological or psycho-

[7] G. G. Nahas, "A Pharmacological Classification of Drugs of Mouse," *Bulletin on Narcotics*, Vol. XXXIII, No. 2, 1981, p.p. 5-6

motor performances.

3. Produces a pleasurable reward by relaxing inhibitions, altering sensory perception and relieving unpleasant feelings.

4. Acts as a "powerful reinforcer" inducing a craving and compulsive alcohol oriented behavior.

5. Frequent, daily use is associated with tolerance.

6. Abrupt interruption of chronic long-term use is often associated with an abstinence syndrome (delirium tremens), which may be mild or severe.

7. Frequent, daily use over a long period of time is associated with an increased incidence of physical and/or mental illness.

Even though there is a lack of agreement among the experts as to its precise nature, there are a number of theories which have been advanced in an attempt to identify the etiology (cause) of alcoholism. The following is a brief overview of the most common theories as presented in the First Special Report to the United States Congress on Alcohol and Health.(1)

## Physiological Theories

Some researchers explain chronic heavy alcohol intake in terms of physiological or biological mechanisms. They try to come to grips with such phenomena as addiction, habituation, tolerance, physical dependence, loss of control and craving, and "appetite" for alcohol by examining physiological functions and processes, either by experimental studies or by observation of naturally occurring cases. Even though research to date has not located any chemical, physiological, or genetic factor as a cause of alcoholism, the possibility that a physical factor exists cannot be ruled out, and further investigations are essential.

The three main physiological theories are as follows:

*Genetic theory.* It has been hypothesized that alcoholism may be inherited. This idea is popular among some because alcoholism appears to run in some families. It is suggested, therefore, that an alcohol-prone individual may have inherited the susceptibility to being influenced adversely by ingested alcohol. This theory would suggest a liability stemming from biochemical predisposition.

Two different forms of inherited alcohol problems that have distinct genetic and environmental causes have been identified in recent research.[8]

One type of alcohol problem is called male-limited because it tends to be passed only from fathers to sons. It is highly hereditary regardless of environment and limited to men whose natural fathers have records of extensive treatment for combined alcohol abuse and criminal behavior.

[8] Cloninger, Robert C., "Researchers Investigating Inherited Alcohol Problems," NIAAA Information and Feature Service, National Clearinghouse for Alcohol Information of The National Institute on Alcohol Abuse & Alcoholism, August 30, 1982.

The other is referred to as milieu-limited because of the role environment plays in the frequency and severity of its development. It affects both men and women and is usually associated with mild alcohol abuse and minimal criminal behavior on the part of the natural parents.

Both hereditary and environmental factors seem to play a role in the development of alcoholism. Researchers found that, if the natural parents of adopted children were alcoholic, the children ran a greater risk of becoming alcoholic despite being raised by nonalcoholic adoptive parents. However, if the natural parents were not alcoholic and the adoptive parents were, the risk was not increased.

The male-limited form of alcohol abuse accounted for only about 24 percent of the adopted men with alcohol problems in the study. Passed from father to son, this type of alcohol abuse was highly hereditary despite adoptive environment. Drinking problems of the fathers of this group began early in life—usually in adolescence—and recurrent abuse often interfered with work and marriage and led to crimes of violence such as assault and wife beating. Sons of this type of alcoholic faced a ninefold increase in risk. About 18 percent of the sons of men with this type of alcoholism developed alcohol problems, compared with about 2 percent of the general population.

Although environmental factors seemed to have little effect on the risk of developing this type of alcohol problem, they may have influenced the severity of the problem. The natural fathers of these adoptees had a record of extensive treatment for alcohol problems while the sons had a record of recurrent problems but not treatment, indicating, possibly, a milder form of illness, the researchers said.

The risk among the male adoptees of developing this type of alcohol problem varied from 13 to 26 percent, depending upon environment. Although "alcohol abuse is mild in most cases and usually does not require treatment . . . more severe disability requiring hospital care may occur in susceptible sons who are exposed to particular postnatal environments, especially sons from the sociocultural background associated with low occupational status."

The biological fathers of these men had a history of heavy drinking that began in their 20s or 30s and gradually progressed to a state of physical dependence in middle age. The fathers may have had medical problems associated with their drinking, but were usually able to maintain jobs and families. Problems were mild, criminal behavior was minimal, and often there was no history of treatment. The natural mothers of adoptees with this type of problem, in contrast with the mothers of those with the male-limited form, sometimes also had a history of mild alcohol problems and convictions for minor crimes.

This milder milieu-limited type of alcohol problem also appeared to be inherited by women, most often from their mothers. Among adopted daughters whose natural parents had alcohol problems, 6.7 to 7.7 percent (depending on environment) developed alcohol problems compared with 2.3 percent in the general populations.

Although both fathers and mothers with mild forms of problems had daughters who became alcoholic, daughters whose mothers had problems stood out as much more susceptible.

Additional supporting research is needed.

*Genetotropic theory.* The genetotropic theory of alcoholism combines the concept of a predisposing genetic trait and a nutritional deficiency. It is postulated that because of an inherited defect in metabolism, some people require unusual amounts of some of the essential vitamins, and because they do not get these large amounts of vitamins needed in their diet, they have a genetically caused nutritional deficiency. The theory is that those who have these unmet nutritional needs develop an abnormal craving for alcohol. In this case the need is met by alcohol, and the consequence is alcoholism. According to this theory, then, alcoholics are those with a genetically caused nutritional deficiency.

*Endocrine theory.* The endocrine theory of alcoholism suggests a dysfunction of the endocrine system. Similar symptoms found in alcoholics and patients with endocrine disorders suggest that some failure of the endocrines might be causally related to the onset of alcoholism. If alcohol ingestion places stress on the body, chronic heavy drinking could cause hyperactivity of the pituitary gland, eventual exhaustion of the adrenal cortex, and, consequently, a breakdown in the functions regulated by the adrenal hormones. Again, the experimental and clinical research does not provide adequate support for this theory in a cause-and-effect relationship.

*Abnormal metabolites in the brain theory.* A new theory on the causation of alcoholism has recently come to light, it hypothesizes that some individuals have an abnormal metabolite in the brain, which may cause the production of an addictive state by alcoholic beverages. In studies done with rats, the laboratory animals were injected with a brain amine known as THP (tetrahydropapveroline). Once injected, the rats drank alcoholic solutions in increasing amounts that finally reached the excessive stage. Interestingly enough, the animals had previously rejected the alcohol before administration of THP.(58)

## Psychological Theories

Theories in this area assume that alcoholism is a symptom of an underlying personality or emotional disorder. The one specific personality disorder frequently seen in alcoholics is being antisocial. However, the general consensus is that no one personality type is a prerequisite for becoming an alcoholic.

The three main psychological approaches are as follows:

*Psychoanalytic theory.* The basis for the psychoanalytic theory rests on three major theoretical positions: (1) the view that alcoholism results from one or more of three unconscious tendencies: self-destruction, oral fixation, and latent homosexuality; (2) the view that alcoholism represents a struggle for power; and

(3) the idea that alcoholism develops as a response to inner conflict between dependency drives and aggressive impulses.

*Learning theory.* The learning theory has its foundation in the idea that learning by reinforcement explains alcoholism. This theory considers alcohol ingestion a reflex response to some stimulus, a way to reduce an inner drive such as fear or anxiety.

*Personality trait theory.* Psychological research has also attempted to define the causes of alcoholism in terms of an "alcoholic personality." It is postulated that in the prealcoholic state, a personality pattern or constellation of characteristics would be discernible and should correlate with a predisposition toward alcoholism.

It is believed by some people, then, that alcoholics are psychologically "different," that they possess a number of traits which, combined, make up the "alcoholic personality." There is, however, no agreement on the identity of these traits, or certain knowledge that they are the causes or results of excessive drinking.

It has been suggested by Fox that alcohol is an alcoholic's means of adjusting to what seems to him/her to be an intolerable combination of personal dynamics and interpersonal relationships. Regardless of the markedly diverse underlying psychopathology or environmental circumstances, alcoholics have many difficulties in common. Some of the more obvious of these are:

1. Lack of any real identity except as an alcoholic.
2. Relatively low ego strength.
3. A tremendous ability to remain unaware of their own feelings.
4. Marked feelings of insecurity and isolation with subsequent needs to control.
5. Inability to anticipate delayed gratification, and the learned pattern of relief of discomfort by alcohol.

Hoff suggests the following concerning mental changes in alcoholism:[9]

Although the psychopathology in alcoholism varies with the individual, the chronic alcoholic does tend to develop along a particular "character matrix." Certain pre-existing mental traits, present before the alcoholic actually takes to drinking, frequently become increasingly pronounced as excessive amounts of alcohol are taken. For some reason, the alcoholic cannot and does not use the neurotic traits of the relatively well-adjusted or the overt symptoms of the psychoneurotic to deal with his anxiety in times of stress. Rather, he find his solution in alcohol.

Table 15 exhibits some of the mental and personality changes frequently encountered in the alcoholic patient. Yet, if there is a prealcoholic personality, its

---

[9] Ebbe Curtis Hoff, *Aspects of Alcoholism* (Philadelphia: J. B. Lippincott Co., 1963), p. 63.

## Table 15
### Common mental and personality traits in the alcoholic

| Traits | Their expression |
|---|---|
| Low Frustration Tolerance | For people who do not tolerate frustration well, for whatever reasons, the urge to escape that frustration can be compelling—and alcohol usage may provide the escape hatch. |
| Inferiority feelings | Chronic, continual feelings of inferiority usually develop due to early childhood experiences, such as being over protected, spoiled or neglected by parents. The rush of confidence following an alcohol-induced high, seems like wonderful magic to the person who has serious feelings of inferiority. |
| Fearfulness | Fear of being embarrassed, of conflict with other people, of being alone—may be very painful and very hard to shake. For the person who believes alcohol may relieve daily fear, the power of expectation seems to make that wish come true. |
| Unrelieved boredom | This wish to escape boredom probably accounts for as much alcohol abuse among young people as any kind of emotional pressure. |
| Feelings of powerlessness | The image of power, and success projects a distorted idea of what people should demand of themselves. Alcohol seems to bring on feelings of strength or assertiveness. |
| Emotional Dependency | Dependency in this sense means a tendency to look for help which comes from outside oneself—rather than from one's own strength and intelligence. People who depend most heavily on the strength and knowledge of other people are also those most likely to depend heavily on alcohol. |
| Egocentricity | Self-centered view of problems—extreme narcissism, primary concern with self and need to drink; in later stages, promises or does anything to maintain the supply of alcohol. |
| Paranoid ideas | Accusations of marital infidelity by alcoholic mate, offers of help and expressions of concern misinterpreted as "picking on" him/her. |
| Ambivalence | Expressions of love as well as of annoyance and hostility toward mate, family members, and friends; alternating attitudes whereby he/she seeks, and then rejects, treatment and/or help. |
| Inconsistency | Excessive deviations in behavior, often impulsive in nature; undependable at home, at work, and in other situations, all because of drinking which must be done; extraordinary fears. |
| Lack of insight | Rationalizations and tendency to blame others and the environment for the compulsive need to drink; creation of myth that he/she can control drinking; attitude of indifference to cover up feelings of shame and degradation. |
| Arrogance and defiance | Grandiosity of thought and of discourse, masking feelings of in- |

PROBLEM DRINKING AND ALCOHOLISM

| Traits | Their expression |
|---|---|
| | feriority and inadequacy; aggressive acting out of resentments and hostility agains family, friends; and others, often leading to fights; sadistic traits. |
| Moods of depression | Deep feelings of guilt, remorses, and self-accusation after a bout; general avoidance of discussion or admission of drinking; occasional outbursts of self-disgust and desire to stop; masochistic inclinations. |

SOURCE: The Addictive Personality, Human Relations media (New York) 1979, p. 24 and Ebbe Curtis Hoff, *Aspects of Alcoholism* (Philadelphia: J. B. Lippincott Co., 1963), p. 63.

specifications are poorly defined, often contradictory, and seem to apply broadly to all mental illness. Knowledge of the role played by psychological factors in alcoholism also awaits further research.

## Sociological Theories

Cultural and national groups have different rates of alcoholism. Some of the groups with apparently high rates of alcoholism are the Americans, the northern French, Poles, northern Russians, Swedes, and Swiss. Groups with an apparently low incidence include the Chinese, southern French, Greeks, Italians, Jews, Portuguese, and Spaniards. Sociologists and therapists have sought to explain these differences by examining the attitudes and values of the different populations.

Two sociological theories have been proposed to explain these differences in relation to alcoholism:

*Cultural theory.* Bales proposed three ways in which cultural and social organizations can influence the rates of alcoholism: (1) the degree to which the culture operates to bring about inner tensions or acute needs for adjustment in its members; (2) the sort of attitudes toward drinking the culture produces in its members; and (3) the degree to which the culture provides suitable substitute means of satisfaction.(19)

*Deviant behavior theory.* The concept of alcohol abuse as deviant behavior seems to be receiving more attention. It has been suggested that there are three main reasons for social concern about alcohol: (1) the intrinsic properties of alcohol as a drug over which one may lose control; (2) the symbolic or cultural traditions attached to drinking which permit relaxation of social and personal controls; and (3) the widely held view that alcohol use is associated with socially undesirable behavior.

Thus, viewing alcoholism as deviant behavior would mean viewing the alcoholic person as someone who, through a set of circumstances, becomes publicly labeled a deviant and is forced by society's reactions into playing a deviant role.

Dr. Albert Ulmann has suggested that the rate of alcoholism is low in groups in which the drinking customs, values, and sanctions are well established, known to, and agreed upon by all. By contrast, groups with marked ambivalence toward alcohol and no agreed-upon ground rules tend to have a high alcoholism rate. When such conflicts exist with their pressures, guilt feelings, and uncertainties, the alcoholism rate may be very high. As pointed out in a report by the National Institute of Mental Health, research has shown that in groups that use alcohol to a significant degree, the lowest incidence of alcoholism is associated with the following habits and attitudes:[10]

1. The children are exposed to alcohol early in life within a strong family, religious group, or other support group. Whatever the beverage, it is served in very diluted form and in small quantities, resulting in low blood-alcohol levels among the drinkers.
2. The beverages commonly, although not invariably, used are those containing relatively large amounts of nonalcoholic components, which also keeps blood-alcohol levels low.
3. The beverage is considered mainly as a food and usually consumed with meals, again resulting in low blood-alcohol levels.
4. Parents present a constant example of moderate drinking.
5. No moral importance is attached to drinking. It is considered neither a virtue nor a sin.
6. Drinking is not viewed as a proof of adulthood or virility.
7. Abstinence is socially acceptable. It is no more rude or ungracious to decline a drink than to decline a piece of bread.
8. Excessive drinking or intoxication is not socially acceptable. It is not considered stylish, comical, or tolerable.
9. Perhaps most importantly, there is wide and usually complete agreement among members of the group on what might be called the ground rules for drinking.

There is probably no single cause of alcoholism. As many theorists suggest, an approach to the problem should incorporate ideas from two or more hypotheses. Generally, such an approach selects from each of the broad areas of physiology, psychology, and sociology. A tentative model may be developed as suggested by Plaut:[11]

A problem drinker is an individual who:
1. Responds to beverage alcohol in a certain way, perhaps physiologically determined, by experiencing intense relief and relaxation.
2. Has certain personality characteristics such as difficulty in dealing with and

---

[10] Correctional Association of New York and International Association of Chiefs of Police, *Alcohol and Alcoholism: A Handbook.* (New York: The Christopherson Smothers Foundation Inc., 1966), p. 8
[11] Thomas Plaut, "Alcohol Problems," A Report to the Nation by the Cooperative Commission on the Study of Alcoholism (New York: Oxford Press, 1967).

overcoming depression, frustration, anxiety.

3. A member of culture that induces guilt and confusion regarding what kinds of drinking behavior are appropriate is more likely to develop trouble than will most other persons.

Even though we do not know the underlying causes of alcoholism, there is enough known at present about the treatment and rehabilitation of alcoholic people to make a difference in their lives and that of their families.

# The Warning Signs of Alcoholism

Individual variation makes it impossible to present a complete list of signs and symptoms uniformly characterizing the early stages of problem drinking. However, Dr. Seldon Bacon, an authority on alcoholism, regards the following as the common, almost universal indications of the development of alcoholism in the American drinker:[12]

1. The individual begins to drink more than the other members of his group.
2. The individual begins to drink more frequently than others.
3. With increasing frequency, the individual goes beyond the allowed license for drinking behavior.
4. He begins to experience "blackouts" or temporary amnesia during and following drinking episodes.
5. He drinks more rapidly than others. He gulps his drinks.
6. He drinks surreptitiously and sneaks drinks.
7. He begins to lose control as to time, place, and amount of his drinking. He drinks—and often gets drunk—at inappropriate times and places when he did not intend to.
8. He hides and protects his liquor supply so he will never be caught short.
9. He drinks to overcome the hangover effects of his prior drinking.
10. He tries new patterns of drinking as to time, place, amounts, and what he drinks.
11. He attempts "geographical" cures by moving to new locations, or "traveling" cures by seeking out different drinking groups—usually of a lower social status.
12. He becomes a "loner" in his drinking. Ingestion of alcohol becomes the sole purpose of drinking.
13. He develops an elaborate system of lies, alibis, excuses, and rationalizations to cover up or to explain his drinking.
14. He has personality and behavioral changes—even when not drinking—which adversely affect his family situation, his friendship groups, or on-the-job relationships. Accidents, job losses, family quarrels, broken friendships, and trouble with the law may take place, not just when he is under the influence of alcohol, but even when he is not.
15. Characteristics of the final phases are obvious and tragic: extended binges, physical tremors, hallucinations and deliria, complete rejection of social reality, malnutrition with accompanying illnesses and diseases—and an early death.

---

[12] Kenneth A. Rouse, "Detour in Alcoholism Ahead," Kemper Insurance Company booklet (Long Grove, Ill., 1972), p. 4.

It must be understood that alcoholism may be present without blackouts or any of the other popularly accepted symptoms of addictive drinking. In general, an individual may be considered an alcoholic if he/she continues to drink even though drinking consistently causes physical illness, headache, gastric distress, or hangover, or consistently causes trouble with spouse, employer, or the police.

# The Alcoholism Label

A general description of the variables involved in labeling a person as an alcoholic individual is given in a report prepared for the Cooperative Commission on the Study of Alcoholism: [13]

1. The quantity of alcohol consumed. It is obvious that there can be no alcoholism without alcohol. But quantity alone is an insufficient dimension for attaching the alcoholism label. There have been numerous attempts to define alcoholism only in terms of quantity of consumption. The standards are as numerous as the number of quantifiers.

2. The rate of consumption. One pint of hard liquor consumed during a ten-hour period causes a qualitatively different behavioral pattern than the same amount consumed during a one-hour period. Therefore, drunkenness is a function of the rate of consumption as well as absolute quantity.

3. Frequency of drinking episodes. A person who gets drunk three or four times a year is less likely to be labeled an alcoholic than someone who gets drunk every week. Frequency of drunkenness is one factor determining the extent to which alcohol-induced dysfunction can occur.

4. The effect of drunkenness upon self and others. A man who commits deviant sex acts or beats his wife while drunk is more likely to be labeled an alcoholic than a man who quietly gets drunk and leaves others alone. That is, the effect of the drunkenness on others, the reaction of others to the drunkeness, is a determinant of how and if the individual is labeled an alcoholic.

5. Visibility to society's significant labeling agents. The police, the judiciary, school personnel, welfare personnel, employers, and, in some situations, social peers and helping agents, such as psychiatrists, physicians, lawyers, and others are the key instruments of alcoholic labeling.

6. The total social matrix of the person. There are different norms for different classes and status groups in the social system. Social contacts are a key determinant of whether a person will be labeled an alcoholic and, therefore, be reacted to as an alcoholic. For each individual case, however, a proper diagnosis of alcoholism requires the services of an expert.

More recently, the National Council on Alcoholism has taken a step toward settling the legal and medical question of whether alcoholism is a disease and identifying the variables necessary in labeling a person an alcoholic. By establishing a set of criteria for the diagnosis of alcoholism, a 14-member Committee of the National Council on Alcoholism (chaired by Dr. Samuel C. Kaim, Staff Director of the Veterans Administration's section on alcoholism and

---

[13] NIAAA, *Alcohol and Alcoholism,* p. 18.

related disorders) compiled a definition. The guidelines are designed not only to put the diagnosis of alcoholism on a standardized basis, but to avoid overdiagnosis—to guard an individual from the presumption of alcoholism unless clear-cut, reproducible data are available to confirm it.(43)

The guidelines are presented in two tracks: Track 1, the physiological and clinical; and Track 2, the psychological and attitudinal manifestations. These two tracks are listed separately and criteria for both classifications fall into "major" and "minor" categories. *Major criteria* are symptoms that represent conclusive evidence of physiological or psychological dependence while *minor criteria* are symptoms usually associated with, but not necessarily indicative, of, alcoholism. The committee indicated that there is no rigid uniformity in the progress of alcoholism, but that early diagnosis is helpful in treatment and recovery; therefore, their criteria are separated into "early," "middle," and "late." Besides identifying early and late symptoms, the committee graded each item according to its degree of implication in the presence of alcoholism, as follows:

*Diagnostic Level I.* Classical, definite, obligatory; a person who fits this criteria must be diagnosed as being alcoholic.

*Diagnostic Level II.* Probable, frequent, indicative; a person who satisfies this criteria is under strong suspicion of alcoholism. Other evidence should be obtained.

*Diagnostic Level III.* Potential, possible, incidental; these manifestations are common in people with alcoholism but do not by themselves give a strong indication of its existence. They may arouse suspicion but significant other evidence is needed before the diagnosis is made.

See Tables 16 and 17 for the criteria as presented by the National Council on Alcoholism.(43)

---

### Table 16
### *Major criteria for the diagnosis of alcoholism*

| Criterion | Diagnostic level |
|---|---|
| TRACK I. PHYSIOLOGICAL AND CLINICAL | |
| A. Physiological dependency | |
| 1. Physiological dependence as manifested by evidence of a withdrawal syndrome when the intake of alcohol is interrupted or decreased without substitution of other sedation. It must be remembered that overuse of other sedative drugs can produce a similar withdrawal state, which should be differentiated from withdrawal from alcohol. | |
| a) Gross tremor (differentiated from other causes of tremor) | 1 |
| b) Hallucinosis (differentiated from schizophrenic hallucinations or other psychoses) | 1 |

| Criterion | Diagnostic level |
|---|---|
| c) Withdrawal seizures (differentiated from epilepsy and other seizure disorders) | 1 |
| d) Delirium tremens. Usually starts between the first and third day after withdrawal and minimally includes tremors, disorientation, and hallucinations. | 1 |
| 2. Evidence of tolerance to the effects of alcohol. (There may be a decrease in previously high levels of tolerance late in the course.) Although the degree of tolerance to alcohol in no way matches the degree of tolerance to other drugs, the behavioral effects of a given amount of alcohol vary greatly between alcoholic and nonalcoholic subjects. | |
| a) A blood-alcohol level of more than 150 mg [per 100 ml] without gross evidence of intoxication. | 1 |
| b) The consumption of one-fifth of a gallon of whiskey or an equivalent amount of wine or beer daily, for more than one day, by a 180-lb. individual. | 1 |
| 3. Alcoholic "blackout" periods. (Differential diagnosis from purely psychological fugue states and psychomotor seizures.) | 2 |
| B. Clinical: major alcohol-associated illnesses. Alcoholism can be assumed to exist if major alcohol-associated illnesses develop in a person who drinks regularly. In such individuals, evidence of physiological and psychological dependence should be searched for. | |
| Fatty degeneration of liver in absence of other known cause | 2 |
| Alcoholic hepatitis | 1 |
| Laennec's cirrhosis | 2 |
| Pancreatitis in the absence of cholelithiasis | 2 |
| Chronic gastritis | 3 |
| Hematological disorders: | |
| Anemia: hypochromic, normocytic, macrocytic. Hemolytic with stomatocytos's low folic acid | 3 |
| Clotting disorders: prothrombin elevation, thrombocytopenia | 3 |
| Alcoholic cerebellar degeneration | 1 |
| Wernicke-Korsakoff syndrome | 2 |
| Cerebral degeneration in absence of Alzheimer's disease or arteriosclerosis | 2 |
| Central pontine myelinolysis Diagnosis only possible postmortem | 2 |
| Marchiafava-Bignami's disease | 2 |
| Peripheral neuropathy (see also beriberi) | 2 |
| Toxic amblyopia | 3 |
| Alcohol myopathy | 2 |
| Alcoholic carimyopathy | 2 |
| Beriberi | 3 |
| Pellagra | 3 |

TRACK II. BEHAVIORAL, PSYCHOLOGICAL, AND ATTITUDINAL

All chronic conditions of psychological dependence occur in dynamic equilibrium with intraspsychic and interpersonal consequences. In alcoholism, similarly, there

| Criterion | Diagnostic level |
|---|---|

are varied effects on character and family. Like other chronic relapsing diseases, alcoholism produces vocational, social, and physical impairments. Therefore, the implications of these disruptions must be evaluated and related to the individual and his pattern of alcoholism. The following behavior patterns show psychological dependence on alcohol in alcoholism:

| Criterion | Diagnostic level |
|---|---|
| 1. Drinking despite strong medical contraindication known to patient | 1 |
| 2. Drinking despite strong, identified, social contraindication (job loss for intoxication, marriage disruption because of drinking, arrest for intoxication, driving while intoxicated) | 1 |
| 3. Patient's subjective complaint of loss of control of alcohol consumption | 2 |

SOURCE: Reprinted with the permission of: (a) The National Council on Alcoholism; (b) *The American Journal of Psychiatry* (Vol. 129, pps. 137-146, 1972), the American Psychiatric Association and the American College of Physicians; (c) *The Annals of Internal Medicine*, Vol. 77, pps. 249-258, 1972. Copyright 1972.

### Table 17
### Minor criteria for the diagnosis of alcoholism

| Criterion | Diagnostic level |
|---|---|
| TRACK I. PHYSIOLOGICAL AND CLINICAL | |
| A. Direct effects (ascertained by examination) | |
| 1. Early: | |
| Odor of alcohol on breath at time of medical appointment | 2 |
| 2. Middle: | |
| Alcoholic facies | 2 |
| Vascular engorgement of face | 2 |
| Toxic amblyopia | 3 |
| Incidence of infections | 3 |
| Cardiac arrhythmias | 3 |
| Peripheral neuropathy (see also Major criteria, Track I, B) | 2 |
| 3. Late (see Major criteria, Track I, B) | |
| B. Indirect effects | |
| 1. Early: | |
| Tachycardia | 3 |
| Flushed face | 3 |
| Nocturnal disphoresis | 3 |
| 2. Middle: | |
| Ecchymoses on lower extremities, arms, or chest | 3 |
| Cigarette or other burns on hands or chest | 3 |
| Hyperreflexia, or if drinking heavily, hyporeflexia (permanent hyporeflexia may be a residuum of alcoholic polyneuritis) | 3 |
| 3. Late: | |
| Decreased tolerance | 3 |

| Criterion | Diagnostic level |
|---|---|
| C. Laboratory tests | |
|    1. Major—Direct: | |
|      Blood-alcohol level at any time of more than 300 mg/100 ml | 1 |
|      Level of more than 100 mg/100 ml in routine examination | 1 |
|    2. Major—Indirect: | |
|      Serum osmolality (reflects blood alcohol levels): every 22.4 increase over 200 mOsm/liter reflects 50 mg/100 ml alcohol | 2 |
|    3. Minor—Indirect: | |
|      Results of alcohol ingestion: | |
|        Hypoglycemia | 3 |
|        Hypochloremic alkalosis | 3 |
|        Low magnesium level | 2 |
|        Lactic acid elevation | 3 |
|        Transient uric acid elevation | 3 |
|        Potassium depletion | 3 |
|      Indications of liver abnormality: | |
|        SGPT elevation | 2 |
|        SGOT elevation | 3 |
|        BSP elevation | 2 |
|        Bilirubin elevation | 2 |
|        Urinary urobilinogen elevation | 2 |
|        Serum A/G ration reversal | 2 |
|      Blood and blood clotting: | |
|        Anemia: hypochromic, normocytic, macrocytic, hemolytic with stomatocytosis, low folic acid | 3 |
|        Clotting disorders: prothrombin elevation, thrombocytopenia | 3 |
|      ECG abnormalities: | |
|        Cardiac arrhythmias: tachycardia: T-waves dimpled, cloven, or spinous: atrial fibrillation: ventricular premature contractions: abnormal P waves | 2 |
|      EEG abnormalities: | |
|        Decreased or increased REM sleep, depending on phase | 3 |
|        Loss of delta sleep | 3 |
|        Other reported findings | 3 |
|        Decreased immune response | 3 |
|        Decreased response to Synacthen test | 3 |
|        Chromosomal damage from alcoholism | 3 |
| TRACK II. BEHAVIORAL, PSYCHOLOGICAL, AND ATTITUDINAL | |
| A. Behavioral | |
|    1. Direct effects | |
|      Early: | |
|        Gulping drinks | 3 |
|        Surreptitious drinking | 2 |
|        Morning drinking (assess nature of peer group behavior) | 2 |
|      Middle: | |
|        Repeated conscious attempts at abstinence | 2 |

| Criterion | Diagnostic level |
|---|---|
| Late: | |
| Blatant indiscriminate use of alcohol | 1 |
| Skid Row or equivalent social level | 2 |
| 2. Indirect effects | |
| Early: | |
| Medical excuses from work for variety of reasons | 2 |
| Shifting from one alcoholic beverage to another | 2 |
| Preference for drinking companions, bars and taverns | 2 |
| Loss of interest in activities not directly associated with drinking | 2 |
| Late: | |
| Chooses employment that facilitates drinking | 3 |
| Frequent automobile accidents | 3 |
| History of family members undergoing psychiatric treatment; school and behavioral problems in children | 3 |
| Frequent change of residence for poorly defined reasons | 3 |
| Outbursts of rage and suicidal gestures while drinking | 2 |
| Anxiety-relieving mechanisms, such as telephone calls inappropriate in time, distance, person, or motive (telephonitis) | 2 |
| B. Psychological and attitudinal | |
| 1. Direct effects | |
| Early: | |
| When talking freely, makes frequent reference to drinking alcohol, people being "bombed," "stoned," etc., or admits drinking more than peer group | |
| Middle: | |
| Drinking to relieve anger, insomnia, fatigue, depression, social discomfort | 2 |
| Late: | |
| Psychological symptoms consistent with permanent organic brain syndrome (see also Major Criteria, Track I, B) | 2 |
| 2. Indirect effects | |
| Early: | |
| Unexplained changes in family, social, and business relationships: complaints about wife, job, and friends | 3 |
| Spouse makes complaints about drinking, reported by patient or spouse | 2 |
| Major family disruptions: separation, divorce, threats of divorce | 3 |
| Late: | |
| Overt expression of more regressive defense mechanisms: denial, projection, etc. | 3 |
| Resentment, jelousy, paranoid attitudes | 3 |
| Symptoms of depression, isolation, crying, suicidal preoccupation | 3 |
| Feelings that he/she is "losing his/her mind" | 2 |

## Alcoholism Risk

The Criteria Committee on the National Council on Alcoholism also pointed out that epidemiological and sociological studies show that the following factors indicate high risk (there is not complete agreement on its extent) for the development of alcoholism: (43)

1. A history of alcoholism in the family, including parents, siblings, grandparents, uncles, and aunts.
2. A history of teetotalism in the family, particularly where strong moral overtones are present and where the social environment of the patient has changed to associations in which drinking is encouraged or required.
3. A history of alcoholism or teetotalism in the spouse or the family of the spouse.
4. Coming from a broken home or a home with much parental discord, particularly where the father was absent or rejecting but not punitive.
5. Being the last child of a large family or in the last half of the sibship in a large family.
6. Being a member of a group (for example, the Irish and Scandinavians) recorded as having a higher incidence of alcoholism than others (such as Jews, Chinese, and Italians). (It is necessary to remember that alcoholism can occur in people of any cultural derivation.)
7. Having female relatives or more than one generation who have had a high incidence of recurrent depression.
8. Heavy smoking; heavy drinking is often associated with heavy smoking (the reverse is not necessarily true).
9. Having a higher incidence of disruptive experiences—death in the family or separation or divorce of the parents—during childhood.

## The Common Symptoms of Alcoholism

Individual patterns of alcohol abuse may vary considerably, making diagnostic procedures may be complex; nevertheless, it may be helpful to present the common symptoms of alcoholism in three traditional stages. These stages usually take the form of a downward progression, sometimes referred to as the steps of alcoholism.

*Early or prodromal stage.* Heavy drinking, "blackouts," loss of control, attempts at abstinence, furtive drinking, preoccupation with drinking, drinking in gulps, evasiveness about drinking.

*Middle or crucial stage.* Excuses for drinking, lone drinking, antisocial behavior, acute hangovers, morning drinking, poor health, job loss, loss of control of drinking, extravagant or grandiose behavior, aggressive behavior, persistent remorse, periodic total abstinence, attempted changes in pattern of drinking, increasing preoccupation with alcohol, loss of outside interests, self-pity, contemplation of or attempt at geographic escape, unreasonable resentments, protection of alcohol supply (in other words, hides bottles), neglects proper nutrition, hospitalization, decrease of sexual drive, alcoholic jealousy.(10)

*Late or chronic stage.* "Benders," deficiency diseases, delirium tremens, loss of tolerance, ethical deterioration, impairment of thinking, drinking with social inferiors, vague indefinable fears, inability to perform simple muscular tasks without alcohol, obsessive drinking, uses of alibis and rationalizations that fail, admission of defeat.(10)

Figure 6 provides an overview of the typical stages in the development of alcoholism as well as steps often involved in the rehabilitation process.

## Early or Prodromal Stage

Many alcoholics begin as social drinkers, gradually increasing their intake; others appear to be "alcoholic" almost from the first drink. ("It seemed to mean more to me than it did to my friends.") The beginner alcoholic tends to take up with a crowd that likes to drink heavily and with some regularity. He/she will get "high," especially on weekends; sipping changes to gulping; and sneaking a couple of extra drinks just to make sure he/she will have enough becomes routine.

*"Blackouts."* This is a clear symptom of the early stages of alcoholism. A blackout is an interval of temporary memory loss during which a person remains conscious and active and may even appear sober, but later has no recollection of where he/she was or what he/she may have done or said.

*Loss of control.* The drinker is unable to control his/her drinking. He/she gets drunk in the "wrong" places and at the "wrong" times. He/she can still stop himself/herself from drinking for days, weeks, or even months, but once he/she starts he/she has no control over how much he/she will drink or how long the drinking episode will continue. Up to this point, it is still possible for some potential alcoholics to pull back from the brink of alcohol addiction. Beyond this point, they are dependent and recovery will be difficut.

*Attempts at abstinence.* The early symptoms of alcoholism may last an average of ten years or less before giving way to middle-stage symptoms. Toward the end of this period the family usually begins to realize something is wrong. Family tensions develop and the alcoholic, particularly in the early alcoholic, blames his/her problems on everything except alcohol. Sometimes, after a loss of control of drinking, he/she recognizes with the help of others that drinking is an important part of his/her problems. He/she decides to stop drinking and succeeds for a time. Family tensions ease, and fear lessens until "next time."

A physician may find certain physical symptoms that may not be immediately recognized as alcoholism but that can, at any rate, indicate that alcoholism may be present. These symptoms are heartburn; morning cough with intense paroxysms; tachycardia (excessively rapid heartbeat) with or without high blood pressure; tremor in middle age; purpura or ecchymoses (subcutaneous hemorrhage, bruising); anxiety, tension, and stress; insomnia; and hyperglycemia.

## Middle or Crucial Stage

*Excuses for drinking.* After a successful spell of abstinence, the alcoholic recovers self-confidence to some degree. He/she decides he/she has licked the problem ("just one won't hurt") and one drink leads to another and finally to a binge. The alcoholic becomes uneasy about this and seeks to excuse his/her behavior with elaborate explanations of why on this or that occasion he/she simply had to drink.

*Lone drinking and antisocial behavior.* Feeling guilty about drinking, the alcoholic now starts to avoid people whom he/she feels are critical of him/her. It is now much more comfortable to drink alone or in secret, hiding drinks if necessary. Family rows occur. The alcoholic blames the family for his/her drinking, and drinks more because of the way he/she claims they treat him. Resentment of real or imagined attitudes on the part of others may express itself in hostility and destructive actions.

*Acute hangovers and morning drinking.* Hangovers by this time are no joking matter. They involve acute suffering, including piercing headaches, feelings of guilt, and morning-after jitters. As a result, the alcoholic starts drinking in the morning. This helps the hangover victim feel better, but the additional alcohol only adds to the fundamental problem. In time, morning drinking becomes a regular habit, hangover or not.

*Poor health and job loss.* Drinking becomes the alcoholic's main obsession. Proper eating is neglected.

As previously mentioned, alcoholic beverages contain little food value beyond their calorie content. And, for a variety of reasons, nearly all alcoholics diminish their regular food intake while drinking. Alcohol suppresses appetitite, usually irritates the gastric mucosa, and promotes euphoria; none of these is conducive to good nutrition.

One study showed that an alcoholic reduces total calorie intake by about one-third. Other nutrients were reduced in about the same proportion. And, as indicated by Dr. Frank Iber of Tufts University School of Medicine:[14]

> Essentially all alcoholics, or others using alcohol as a substantial portion of their daily calorie intake, are apt to become malnourished because alcohol calories replace other more valuable food forms such as protein, water-soluble vitamins, and minerals.

> To compound the problem, alcoholics have a diminished ability to make glucose from fat or protein as normal persons do. This reason alone explains why fasting for even as brief a time as eight hours may produce hypoglycemia sufficient to produce a coma in the alcoholic.

> The drinking alcoholic ingests and utilizes too little protein, B vitamins, and minerals. But this is not all: When his condition has persisted for many months, his

[14] Frank Iber, "In Alcoholism, the Liver Sets the Pace," *Nutrition Today,* Jan./Feb. 1971, p. 7.

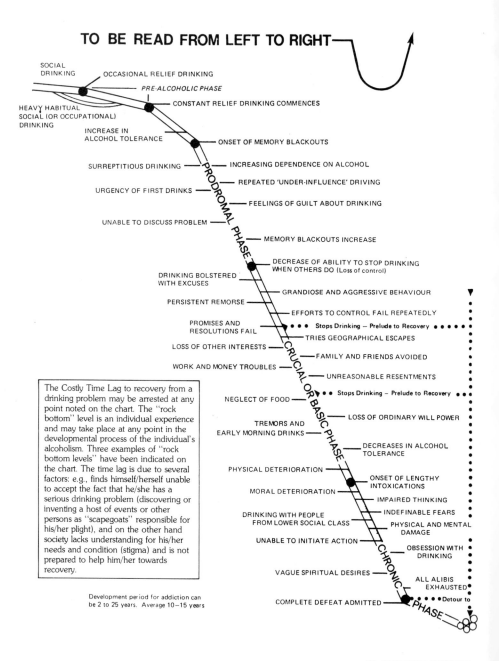

## TO BE READ FROM LEFT TO RIGHT

SOCIAL DRINKING

OCCASIONAL RELIEF DRINKING

*PRE-ALCOHOLIC PHASE*

HEAVY HABITUAL SOCIAL (OR OCCUPATIONAL) DRINKING

CONSTANT RELIEF DRINKING COMMENCES

INCREASE IN ALCOHOL TOLERANCE

ONSET OF MEMORY BLACKOUTS

SURREPTITIOUS DRINKING

INCREASING DEPENDENCE ON ALCOHOL

URGENCY OF FIRST DRINKS

REPEATED 'UNDER-INFLUENCE' DRIVING

FEELINGS OF GUILT ABOUT DRINKING

UNABLE TO DISCUSS PROBLEM

MEMORY BLACKOUTS INCREASE

PRODROMAL PHASE

DECREASE OF ABILITY TO STOP DRINKING WHEN OTHERS DO (Loss of control)

DRINKING BOLSTERED WITH EXCUSES

GRANDIOSE AND AGGRESSIVE BEHAVIOUR

PERSISTENT REMORSE

EFFORTS TO CONTROL FAIL REPEATEDLY

PROMISES AND RESOLUTIONS FAIL

• • • Stops Drinking – Prelude to Recovery • • • •

TRIES GEOGRAPHICAL ESCAPES

LOSS OF OTHER INTERESTS

FAMILY AND FRIENDS AVOIDED

WORK AND MONEY TROUBLES

UNREASONABLE RESENTMENTS

CRUCIAL OR BASIC PHASE

• • Stops Drinking – Prelude to Recovery • • •

NEGLECT OF FOOD

LOSS OF ORDINARY WILL POWER

TREMORS AND EARLY MORNING DRINKS

DECREASES IN ALCOHOL TOLERANCE

PHYSICAL DETERIORATION

ONSET OF LENGTHY INTOXICATIONS

MORAL DETERIORATION

IMPAIRED THINKING

INDEFINABLE FEARS

DRINKING WITH PEOPLE FROM LOWER SOCIAL CLASS

PHYSICAL AND MENTAL DAMAGE

UNABLE TO INITIATE ACTION

OBSESSION WITH DRINKING

CHRONIC

VAGUE SPIRITUAL DESIRES

ALL ALIBIS EXHAUSTED

• • • Detour to

COMPLETE DEFEAT ADMITTED

PHASE

The Costly Time Lag to recovery from a drinking problem may be arrested at any point noted on the chart. The "rock bottom" level is an individual experience and may take place at any point in the developmental process of the individual's alcoholism. Three examples of "rock bottom levels" have been indicated on the chart. The time lag is due to several factors: e.g., finds himself/herself unable to accept the fact that he/she has a serious drinking problem (discovering or inventing a host of events or other persons as "scapegoats" responsible for his/her plight), and on the other hand society lacks understanding for his/her needs and condition (stigma) and is not prepared to help him/her towards recovery.

Development period for addiction can be 2 to 25 years. Average 10–15 years

**OR OBSESSIVE DRINKING**
(possibly to point of no recovery—

## FIGURE 6
### A Chart of Alcohol Addiction and Recovery*

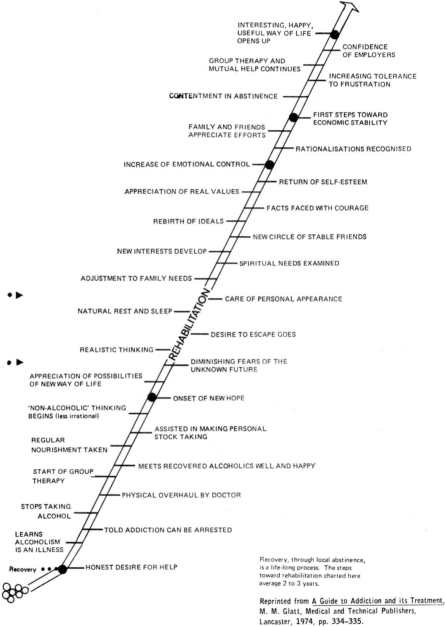

INTERESTING, HAPPY, USEFUL WAY OF LIFE OPENS UP

CONFIDENCE OF EMPLOYERS

GROUP THERAPY AND MUTUAL HELP CONTINUES

INCREASING TOLERANCE TO FRUSTRATION

CONTENTMENT IN ABSTINENCE

FIRST STEPS TOWARD ECONOMIC STABILITY

FAMILY AND FRIENDS APPRECIATE EFFORTS

RATIONALISATIONS RECOGNISED

INCREASE OF EMOTIONAL CONTROL

RETURN OF SELF-ESTEEM

APPRECIATION OF REAL VALUES

FACTS FACED WITH COURAGE

REBIRTH OF IDEALS

NEW CIRCLE OF STABLE FRIENDS

NEW INTERESTS DEVELOP

SPIRITUAL NEEDS EXAMINED

ADJUSTMENT TO FAMILY NEEDS

CARE OF PERSONAL APPEARANCE

NATURAL REST AND SLEEP

REHABILITATION

DESIRE TO ESCAPE GOES

REALISTIC THINKING

DIMINISHING FEARS OF THE UNKNOWN FUTURE

APPRECIATION OF POSSIBILITIES OF NEW WAY OF LIFE

ONSET OF NEW HOPE

'NON-ALCOHOLIC' THINKING BEGINS (less irrational)

ASSISTED IN MAKING PERSONAL STOCK TAKING

REGULAR NOURISHMENT TAKEN

START OF GROUP THERAPY

MEETS RECOVERED ALCOHOLICS WELL AND HAPPY

PHYSICAL OVERHAUL BY DOCTOR

STOPS TAKING ALCOHOL

LEARNS ALCOHOLISM IS AN ILLNESS

TOLD ADDICTION CAN BE ARRESTED

Recovery

HONEST DESIRE FOR HELP

Recovery, through local abstinence, is a life-long process. The steps toward rehabilitation charted here average 2 to 3 years.

Reprinted from A Guide to Addiction and its Treatment, M. M. Glatt, Medical and Technical Publishers, Lancaster, 1974, pp. 334–335. Courtesy of E. & S. Livingstone Limited.

CONTINUES IN VICIOUS CIRCLES
irreversible mental or physical deterioration)

small intestine's absorptive capacity for fats, fat-soluble vitamins, folic acid, thiamine, and proteins is seriously impaired.

In one respect, alcohol in the body acts as a carbohydrate and increases the body's requirements for the B vitamins. Alcohol also increases the urinary losses of amino acids, magnesium potassium, and zinc.

The middle-stage alcoholic's health may be undermined and he/she may need some hospital treatment. He/she has constant trouble in work, social, and family life. Finally he/she loses or leaves his/her job. If nothing intervenes to stop the process of alcoholism, he/she enters the late stage of the disease.

## Late or Chronic Stage

*"Benders."* Prolonged bouts of drinking mark the fully developed alcoholic. These are periods of hopeless, helpless, blindly compulsive drinking and drunkenness which may last for several days. Nothing appears to matter except continuing the oblivion as long as possible. Everything is sacrificed: family, money, friends, health. The alcoholic may even resort to stealing to get alcohol. By now the signs are obvious, his/her behavior clearly indicating he/she is a sick person who needs understanding and help. By now the alcoholic is in such a state that instead he/she makes enemies, evokes distrust and even hate. After a bender, the alcoholic may sober up and remain sober for a period of days, weeks, and even months, but unless he/she gets adequate help and understanding in overcoming the inner drive to drink, his/her benders will probably continue and become progressively worse. Without treatment the alcoholic is faced with a bleak, drunken future which may be relieved only by early death or mental instability. Nevertheless, the deterioration can be arrested along the way at any point where the alcoholic can be persuaded to recognize that he/she can no longer live without alcohol and to accept help.

*Deficiency diseases.* During this stage it is not uncommon to see problems of malnutrition, fatty liver, cirrhosis of the liver, alcoholic hepatitis, brain damage, and other alcohol-related health problems.

*Decrease in tolerance.* It appears that a combination of prolonged drinking and malnutrition may cause damage to the tissue of the liver—the organ that detoxifies or metabolizes alcohol—and if sufficient liver damage occurs, the efficiency of the liver is considerably reduced and the person develops a reverse tolerance. The alcoholic becomes drunk on less alcohol than was previously needed because of the inability of the liver to metabolize the alcohol as efficiently as before.

*Delirium tremens or "DTs".* This is the withdrawal illness or abstinence syndrome that occurs in the minority of alcoholics (5-8 percent) who are actually physically dependent upon the drug, having used it daily for weeks or months in large and increasing doses so that their body cells adapt to it. When the alcohol is no longer available or the amount is sharply reduced, DTs occur. The symptoms include visual hallucinations, auditory hallucinations (see Figure 7), disorienta-

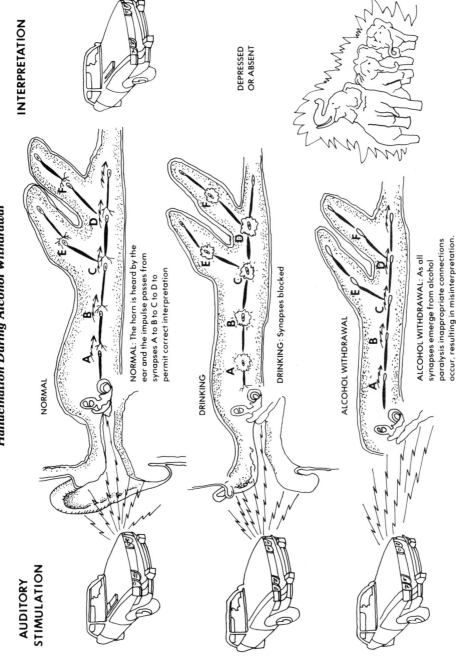

**FIGURE 7**
*Explanations of Auditory Hallucination During Alcohol Withdrawal*

AUDITORY STIMULATION

INTERPRETATION

NORMAL

NORMAL: The horn is heard by the ear and the impulse passes from synapses A to B to C to D to permit correct interpretation

DRINKING

DRINKING: Synapses blocked

DEPRESSED OR ABSENT

ALCOHOL WITHDRAWAL

ALCOHOL WITHDRAWAL: As all synapses emerge from alcohol paralysis inappropriate connections occur, resulting in misinterpretation.

SOURCE: Adapted from Frank Iber, "In Alcoholism, The Liver Sets the Pace," *Nutrition Today* (January/February 1971): 6.

tion, confusion, delusions, tremors, restlessness, and other symptoms lasting several days.

Dr. Victor notes that the initial signs of withdrawal usually begin as early as 7 to 8 hours after the person's last drink; they peak within 24 hours and begin to subside in 48 hours. This phase of withdrawal is basically benign and is usually managed symptomatically. But in a small proportion of cases, after about 48 to 72 hours without alcohol, the person may become profoundly confused; he/she has vivid hallucinations, psychomotor and autonomic system overactvity in the form of tachycardia, sweating, fever—in other words, delirium tremens. During this later phase, between 5 and 15 percent of the alcoholics will die. See Figure 8 for explanation of withdrawal phases.

**FIGURE 8**
*Two Phases of Withdrawal and Their Symptoms*

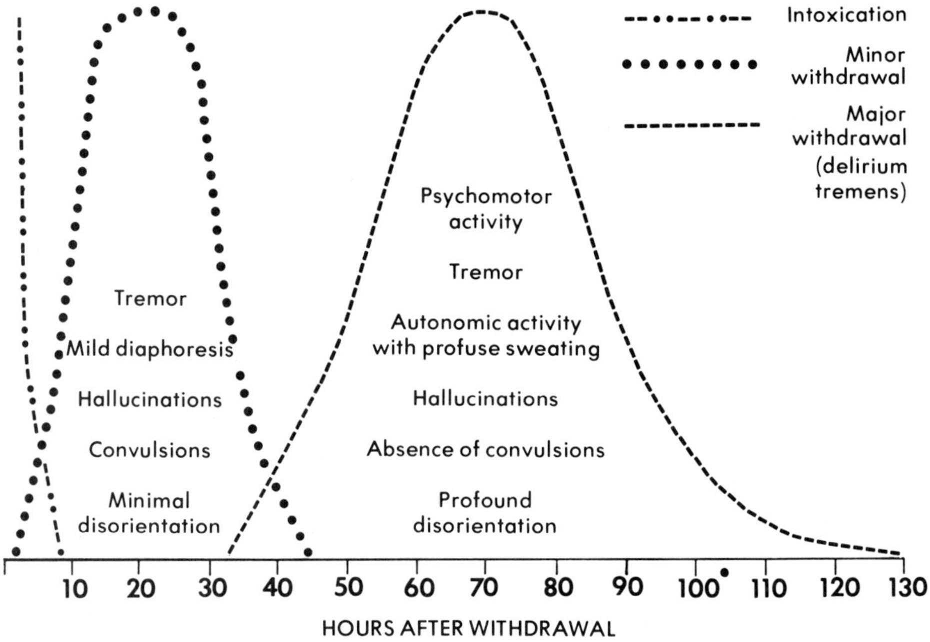

SOURCE: Maurice Victor, "Managing Alcoholism," *Drug Therapy* (July 1973): 60.

The withdrawal syndrome has four common characteristics:

1. The severity of the syndrome is dependent upon the length and the extent of the drinking problem.
2. Reduction in alcohol consumption could cause withdrawal symptoms to appear.

3. Any alcoholic beverage can cause the syndrome.
4. The syndrome may be caused by an event beyond the patient's control (i.e., the patient could be in an accident and as a result of hospitalization be unable to continue his drinking patterns).

Table 18 summarizes many of the ideas previously presented in this chapter.

# Common Myths About Alcoholism (45)

*Nothing can be done unless the alcoholic "wants to stop drinking."* This emphasis upon a sudden and absolute break from alcohol as a prerequisite for treatment suggests that the very goal which may be beyond the current capability of the alcoholic must already have been achieved. In other words, he/she must be halfway well before he/she can be helped to go the rest of the way. This requirement does not apply in other categories of acute or chronic illness when treatment intervention is essential. Treatment attempting to discover the relationship of the drinking problem his/her real needs and directed toward an understanding of what he/she would strive for if not handicapped by the problem is, in fact, based on building his/her capacity for control. This is possible in periods of sobriety.

*The alcoholic must hit "rock bottom" (i.e., lost job, home, family, health) before he/she will want to get well.* Total destruction of every positive aspect of his/her life is a poor base for a program of treatment or rehabilitation. As in all disorders, early intervention can be rewarding. The symptoms or signs are recognizable; the informed employer, union counselor, spouse, or board official may require that the alcoholic accept treatment as a condition of continuing his/her job, family relationships, or probation. The emphasis is thus placed upon acceptance of treatment, on rewards or satisfaction rather than penalties.

*It is hopeless to treat alcoholism in any case. A patient may reform for a while but always slips back.* This attitude is born of the stigma of alcoholism and fostered by unrealistic, unscientific expectations in a chronic condition. We do not consider treatment of tuberculosis or heart disease hopeless because the patient has reoccurrences. Many alcoholics do, in fact, succeed in living their lives without a reoccurrence of any personal, social, or economic disaster due to drinking. Emphasis on "reform" rather than on treatment of a disorder is another reflection of the prevalent attitude of the alcoholic as an "offender." An individual with any chronic disease, including alcoholism, needs treatment.

*Alcohol itself is the only cause of alcoholism. If it were removed, there would be no alcoholism.* The first part of this statement is a myth in itself; the great majority of people who use alcohol do not become alcoholics. The second part of the statement is related to a wish for a simple answer, an easy way out, a means of escaping the need to confront and explore a very complex and difficult area of human life. These myths are related, to some degree, to the problem of

## Table 18
### Indications of alcohol-related problems

| FAMILY | SOCIAL | PHYSICAL | OCCUPATIONAL | DRINKING BEHAVIOR | LEGAL |
|---|---|---|---|---|---|
| Quarrels over drinking | Loss of interest in activities not directly associated with drinking | Hangover (malaise, red eyes, hand tremor) | Work pace more spasmodic | Gulping drinks | Driving while under the influence of alcohol |
| Physical abuse | | Alcohol or mouth wash on breath | Avoiding boss associates | Shifting from one alcoholic beverage to another | Frequent auto accidents |
| Decreased socialization with friends | Not seeing customary friends | "Accident prone"— fractures, cuts, burns, etc. | Neglecting details formerly attended to | Admits drinking more than peer group | Other offenses— assault, disorderly conduct, property crimes, public drunkenness, reckless driving |
| History of divorce | Seeking out new "friends" with similar drinking preferences | Vague, minor complaints, especially in women | Job changes (frequently) | Drinks to relieve anger, depression, etc. | |
| Withdrawal of children | | | | | |
| Reluctance of children to bring friends home | Marked behavioral change after drinking | Blackouts (no memory of events though not passing out) | Frequent absences from work | Repeated conscious efforts at abstinence | Referral to alcohol safety action program |
| School or other behavioral problems in children; super straight | Irritability | | Disappears in afternoon | Blatant, indiscriminate use of alcohol | Under-age purchasing of alcoholic beverages |
| Family history of alcoholism, abstinence, broken home | Sensitive to comments from others about drinking | *Injuries, especially when treatment is delayed 24 hours | Neglected household tasks | Drinking alone | |
| | | Hospitalization for: peptic ulcer, gastritis, pancreatitis | Falling grades | Hiding bottles | |
| Woman recently separated, divorced, children leaving home | Inappropriate telephone calls | | Frequent absence from school | Not measuring drinks | |
| | Personality change, poor judgment, inability to concentrate, memory impairment | Laboratory findings (early) BSP retention 10-15% serum enzymes uric acid 10-15% | | Drinking before going to a social function | |
| Signs of fetal alcohol syndrome in newborns and young children | | | | Not know how many drinks one has had | |
| Financial worries | | | | Intoxication | |

SOURCE: NAIAAA. *The Community Health Nurse and Alcohol Related Problems,* U.S. Department of Health, Education, and Welfare, 1980, p. 58.

*You can assume that a person has alcohol-related problems if the continually has injuries and then doesn't bother to seek medical treatment for the injuries. This lack of seeking treatment obviously points to the fact that the person was in an intoxicated condition when he/she was injured and was either not concerned with the injury or was unable to seek help immediately. A person who does not seek medical attention for an injury for more than 24 hours may have waited to regain sobriety before seeking treatment.

motivating the alcoholic. They serve as an excuse for not dealing with the problem at all.

*Most alcoholics are found on skid row.* A firmly entrenched belief in some quarters is that most, if not all, alcoholics are on skid row, the most dilapidated section of almost every large community, and that most, if not all, skid row inhabitants are alcoholics. Consequently, it has been thought that eradicating skid row would eradicate alcoholism, and the end of alcoholism would mean the end of skid rows. From research, it is obvious that most excessive drinkers are not skid row derelicts. More than 70 percent of them reside in respectable neighborhoods with their husbands or wives, try to send their children to college, and attempt to perform effectively at their jobs and in their families. It has been estimated that less than 5 percent of the alcoholics in the United States would be found on these so-called skid rows. Some studies suggest that it is even less than 3 percent.

*Only the "psychological cripples" will become problem drinkers and develop into alcoholics.* This is a myth believed by many and taught by some professionals. It is one that must be dispelled if our preventive education efforts are to succeed. Dr. L. Harold Caviness, founder of the mental health unit at the Battle Creek Sanitarium, says[15] "We are asked to believe, Don't worry, normal, well-adjusted people don't become alcoholic, only pre-addictive personalities." However, you will find the list growing quite long: oral-dependent persons, psychopaths, compulsive personalities, very tense and sensitive people, maladjusted and psychotic, latent psychotics, people with a low frustration tolerance or serious defects in self-esteem, insecure men with unbearable doubts about their inadequacy in manliness, anxious persons "needing" to pretend bravery, shy people "needing" instant sociability and extroversion. Let me point out that many of these people will not recognize themselves as marked for alcoholism until they are already addicted and then they have a "need" to deny it."

*Young people cannot be alcoholics.* More than one-half million alcoholics are teenage or younger. One branch of AA tells of a 12-year-old boy who recently celebrated one year of sobriety. It is not one's age nor how long one has been drinking that determines whether or not an individual is an alcoholic.

*An individual cannot be an alcoholic if he never drinks until after five in the afternoon.* Granted, many alcoholics and problem drinkers feel the need of a drink in the morning. And some individuals who persist in taking three-martini lunches may be on shaky ground. But just because one does not choose to drink until after five o'clock gives no assurance that one may not be an alcoholic. Alcoholism has little to do with the time of day one consumes alcohol.

---

[15] Harold Caveness, "The Effects of Alcoholism on the Central Nervous System and Personality," *Report on Alcohol* (Winter 1972).

*Alcoholism is strictly a male disease.* Twenty years ago, alcoholism was six times more prevalent among men, but now the ratio is nearly even. More women than ever use alcohol today. Statistics also show that many women who were secret alcoholics are now coming "out of the closet" to seek treatment and help.

*An individual cannot be an alcoholic if he/she has never been in trouble with the law because of drinking.* Not everyone who drinks excessively gets in trouble with the law. Besides, an arrest for public intoxication or drunken driving may not indicate the first time a person has been drunk and caught by law enforcement officials. Getting arrested for an alcohol-related offense may be a blessing in disguise because it may cause an alcoholic or a problem drinker to realize that his/her drinking patterns are out of control and therefore motivate him/her to seek help.

*Alcoholics drink only distilled spirits.* Beer does have a lower alcohol content than either wine or distilled spirits, but it is proportionately as intoxicating or addicting as wine or spirits. Those alcoholics who are beer drinkers drink large quantities of beer. Wine, on the other hand, generally has at least twice the alcohol content of beer per ounce. What is the type of alcohol most often consumed in the country of the world having the highest alcoholism rate? Wine. It is the alcohol that imposes the risk of alcoholism—not the type of beverage.

*The person who drinks only on weekends cannot be an alcoholic.* Many alcoholics do consume alcohol daily, but others confine their drinking strictly to weekends. In the final analysis, alcoholism is not determined entirely by when or how often a person drinks, but rather what happens when he/she drinks (for example, losing control when drinking).

*An individual cannot be an alcoholic if he/she claims, "I can take or leave alcohol. I can quit anytime."* Those who make such statements usually realize that they have some sort of drinking problem. Those who are not alcoholic have no need to go on the wagon. Problem drinkers make such statements because they wish to prove that they are in control of their drinking habits. Usually, such statements indicate short-term sobriety only.

*An individual cannot be an alcoholic if he/she is in good health.* Many who drink excessively for years do not show overt signs of health damage, but in the long-term scheme, damage will show up. In addition to suffering such health problems as cirrhosis, central nervous system changes, and cardiovascular damage, most alcoholics die eight to ten years before their time.(13)

## Recovery from Alcoholism is Possible

Although much remains to be learned about the cause, scope, treatment, and prevention of alcoholism, it has been shown that recovery from this devastating illness is definitely possible. Hundreds of thousands have recovered and are leading happy, successful, productive lives without alcohol. It is no longer regarded, as it once was, an incurable, hopeless condition beyond human reach.

Today, for the alcoholic and those affected by his/her illness, the all-important single fact to know about alcoholism—and upon which to act—is this: alcoholism is a treatable disease. The alcoholic is a sick person and can be helped to a successful recovery.(130)

## Sources of Help—for the Alcoholic and for Those Concerned With His/Her Recovery

Local and county hospitals.

The local alcoholism information center, or council on alcoholism; or the National Council on Alcoholism, Inc., 2 Park Avenue South, New York, N.Y. 10016.

The local central office of Alcoholics Anonymous, or Alcoholics Anonymous, Box 459, Grand Central Station, New York, N.Y. 10017.

The Al-Anon Family Groups Council, 115 East 23rd Street, New York, N.Y. 10010.

The family service agency in your community.

The state agency (in 50 states) concerned with alcoholism. It may be an independent commission, or a division within the state department of public health or department of mental health.

The local AFL-CIO Community Service Committee, or AFL-CIO Community Service Activities, 211 East 43rd Street, New York 17, N.Y. 10017.

A bishop, pastor, priest, or spiritual advisor. (In many instances, physicians and clergymen have had special professional training and experience in the treatment of alcoholism.)

Local community mental health center.

A doctor or psychiatrist.

The local Office of Rehabilitation Services.

The county Mental Health Association, or National Association for Mental Health, 10 Columbus Circle, New York, N.Y. 10019.

The National Clearinghouse for Alcohol Information, Box 2345, Rockville, MD. 20852.

Veterans Administration, Alcohol and Drug Dependent Service, 810 Vermont Avenue, N.W., Washington, D.C. 20420.

For additional information about the kinds of services offered by some of these and other organizations and agencies, see Table 19.

***Table 19***
***Services for the alcoholic and his/her family***

| Name, address | Services |
|---|---|
| Alcoholics Anonymous<br>PO Box 459, Grand Central Station<br>New York, N.Y. 10017<br>(Local groups throughout the United States)<br><br>Information on AA for physicians:<br>Dr. Lewis K. Reed, Secretary<br>International Doctors in<br>Alcoholics Anonymous (IDAA)<br>1905 Volney Rd.<br>Youngstown, Ohio 44511 | Offers help by bringing alcoholics in touch with former alcoholics. A new member is introduced to an AA meeting by an experienced member. Anonymity is ensured. Many AA groups are limited to a single profession or interest groups. For information, write to the address at the left or call the AA in your local telephone directory. |
| Alcohol and Drug Problems<br>Association of North America<br>1130 17th St NW<br>Washington, D.C. 20036 | Provides information and publications on alcoholism and alcoholic treatment centers |
| Al-Anon Family Groups<br>Headquarters, PO Box 182<br>Madison Square Garden, New York, N.Y. 10010<br>(Chapters in most major cities) | Offers help to the families of alcoholics. Anonymity is ensured. |
| The National Council on Alcoholism<br>733 Third Ave<br>New York, N.Y. 10017<br>(Chapters in most major cities) | Provides information on member groups and other agencies, including a catalog of publications on alcoholism. Publishes the *Labor-Management Alcoholism Journal* (bimonthly) |
| The National Institute on Alcohol Abuse<br>and Alcoholism, National Clearing House<br>for Alcohol Information<br>PO Box 2345, Rockville, Md. 20852 | Provides listings of private and public treatment facilities in each state |
| Christopher D. Smithers Foundation<br>41 E 57th St<br>New York, N.Y. 10022 | Provides numerous pamphlets, especially on the topic of alcoholism programs in companies and industry |
| Association of Labor-Management<br>Administrators and Consultants on<br>Alcoholism, Inc (ALMACA)<br>11800 Sunrise Valley Drive, Suite 410<br>Reston, Va. 22091 | Helps set up and administer alcoholism programs in corporations, labor unions, or government agencies; also provides consulting services |

# 6

# Social Problems and Excessive Drinking

The men and women with drinking problems constitute a small portion of the American population, but the misery that they cause themselves and others is enormous. If one considers only the personal costs of drinking, the price is exorbitant.

Dangerous drinking patterns are not the only ones that can lead to drinking problems, nor will everyone who drinks and endangers self and others necessarily become a problem drinker. What is certain is that a person with these dangerous drinking practices runs a much higher risk of running into problems.

Although there is little consensus on how to define and measure drinking-related problems, one useful way to describe the problem is in terms of the consequences to self or others. A drinking-related problem is one that is occasioned by the use of alcoholic beverages and results in harm to oneself or others. Under this definition, any problem closely associated with drinking can be considered a drinking problem. Some 10 million adults are classified as problem drinkers, but many other drinkers also experience some kind of problem connected with their drinking.

Drinking problems can be more or less serious depending on the severity and/or frequency of the adverse consequences associated with drinking. Drinking repeatedly in ways that cause harm to self or others is obviously a matter of more concern than doing so once or twice in a lifetime. Most lists of drinking-related problems include categories that are familiar to all of us:

*Interpersonal problems*—with spouse and family, with relatives, with friends

143

and neighbors; *social problems*—with fellow employees and employer, with creditors, with police; *personal problems*—with one's ability to function properly, with one's ability to stop drinking once he or she has started, with one's ability to forego drinking, with one's health.

This list brings us around full circle. Drinking to make up for damaged ego and human needs can make it even more difficult ever to fulfill these needs. Drinking heavily and constantly because of hate for the job can make a person incapable of performing on a more desirable job. Drinking because of marital problems makes the problems worse. Drinking because a person considers himself/herself a failure makes it less likely that he/she will ever be a success. In a phrase, drinking to substitute for frustrated human needs makes it harder to achieve the real thing. Figure 9 is an adaptation of Abraham Maslow's hierarchy of needs, and it shows the problems that can be compounded by drinking.

# Health and Mortality of Alcoholics

The words *alcohol* and *mortality* are likely to conjure up some vivid images—the squeal of brakes and sickening crash on the "drunk driving" TV messages, the derelict dying in a flop house in a bout of delirium tremens, or perhaps a teenager dropping dead after gulping down a quart of whiskey on a bet. All of these are dramatic ways of "dying of drink," and there are many others—but most people who die "before their time" from drinking too much do not die in such dramatic ways.

Causes of death are often indeterminate or multiple. Similarly, types and gradations of drinking behaviors are varied and numerous, so it is reasonable to expect different patterns of drinking behavior to be associated with different patterns of mortality.

The relationship between alcohol and death can be direct, as in the case of an overdose, or indirect, as in accidents where the physical or mental state produced by the alcohol puts the drinker at higher risk. The relationship can be long-term, as in the physiological deterioration of the liver, or short-term, as in homicide or suicide performed under the influence of alcohol. In practice, different kinds of relations between alcohol and death will often be superimposed. It should be noted that even when an association is found between a particular pattern of drinking and mortality, it does not necessarily follow that the drinking caused the death.(8)

The life expectancy of alcoholics is estimated to be shorter by 10-12 years than that of the general public. Studies indicate that the mortality rate of alcoholics is at least two-and-one-half times greater, and they suffer from a disproportionate number of violent deaths. According to the latest national figures, alcoholism, with alcoholic cirrhosis and alcoholic psychosis, has accounted for about 0.7 percent of all deaths. Alcoholism appears as the cause of death on more than 13,000 death certificates yearly, not to mention the 350,000-500,000 deaths in which alcoholism is indicated as a complicating factor—when in reality it is often the underlying cause. The National Council on Alcoholism states that the effects of

**FIGURE 9**
*Maslow's Hierarchy of Needs and*
*Alcohol-Related Problems*

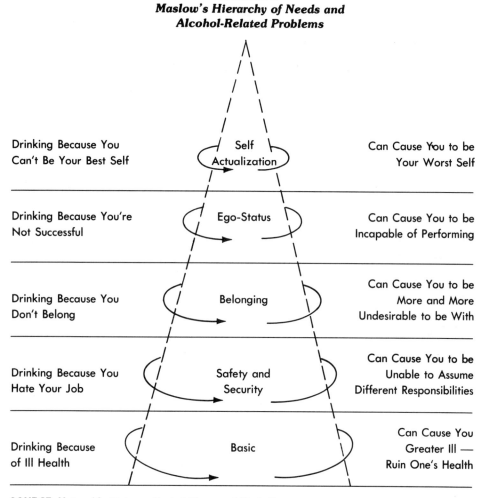

| Drinking Because You Can't Be Your Best Self | Self Actualization | Can Cause You to be Your Worst Self |
| Drinking Because You're Not Successful | Ego-Status | Can Cause You to be Incapable of Performing |
| Drinking Because You Don't Belong | Belonging | Can Cause You to be More and More Undesirable to be With |
| Drinking Because You Hate Your Job | Safety and Security | Can Cause You to be Unable to Assume Different Responsibilities |
| Drinking Because of Ill Health | Basic | Can Cause You Greater Ill — Ruin One's Health |

SOURCE: National Institute on Alcohol Abuse and Alcoholism.

alcohol are responsible for 30,000 deaths per year in the United States—more than any other problem except heart disease and cancer.(69) Individuals with drinking problems are known to have many chronic and even fatal diseases which are related to drinking.

Sidney Pell, Ph.D., and C. A. D'Alonzo, M.D., of DuPont's medical staff reported to the convention of the American Medical Association on a study of 992 DuPont employees with known or suspected drinking problems. These employees were matched by age, sex, job, and geographic location with 992 others who were either social drinkers or abstainers. Table 20 shows the number suffering from various chronic diseases.

**Table 20**
*Dupont study of chronic diseases: Heavy drinkers vs.*
*social and nondrinkers*

| Disease | Heavy drinkers | Social and nondrinkers | Percentage increase |
|---|---|---|---|
| Hypertension | 333 | 148 | 125% |
| Cirrhosis | 29 | 1 | 2,800 |
| Stomach ulcer | 74 | 39 | 90 |
| Duodenal ulcer | 106 | 78 | 36 |
| Nephritis | 53 | 35 | 50 |
| Asthma | 38 | 23 | 65 |
| Bronchitis | 34 | 26 | 30 |
| Diabetes | 35 | 22 | 59 |
| Gout | 30 | 18 | 39 |
| Neuritis | 98 | 63 | 57 |
| Coronary disease | 75 | 59 | 27 |
| Other heart disease | 123 | 104 | 18 |
| Cerebrovascular | 16 | 8 | 100 |

SOURCE: Walter Krusich, "Alcohol and Health: A Casual or Causal Relationship," *Report: A Quarterly Bulletin Concerned with the Effects of Alcohol Consumption,* American Businessmen's Research Foundation 27, no. 1 (Spring 1969): 6.

## Problem Drinking and the Family

The attempts to rehabilitate problem drinkers have often focused upon the alcoholic as an individual, separate from his/her family. But for every alcoholic there are usually five or six other people related by family or business who are also affected by—and are often precipitating factors in—the alcoholic's problem. Alcohol is a family illness that should be treated in a family setting. It is not merely a question of the physical and mental state of the problem drinker himself. At least 36 million people share alcohol problems secondhand. *A recent Gallup Poll shows that 33 percent of the U.S. families surveyed reported "drinking troubles."* For a detailed description of the effects on the family, See Figure 10.

Those who work with alcoholic people recognize the familiar terms for the psychological and behavioral aspects of alcoholism—denial, confusion, shame, guilt, anxiety, obsession, self-pity, depression, remorse, low self-esteem, blame, social isolation, anger, loss of control, violence, inconsistency, progression, attempts to manipulate, attempts to control the drinking. A fact less easily recognized is that these words also describe the parallel behavior of the alcoholic person's family members—spouse, parents, and children as well as others whose interactions with the alcoholic person constitute a close relationship. Most alcoholic people live and interact with their families, and the impact of their illness on the family structure is devastating.(150)

Sharon Wegscheider has designed the scheme in Table 21 to show the parallel nature of the alcohol dependent's true feelings and the family members' feelings as reactions to the dependent's behavior.

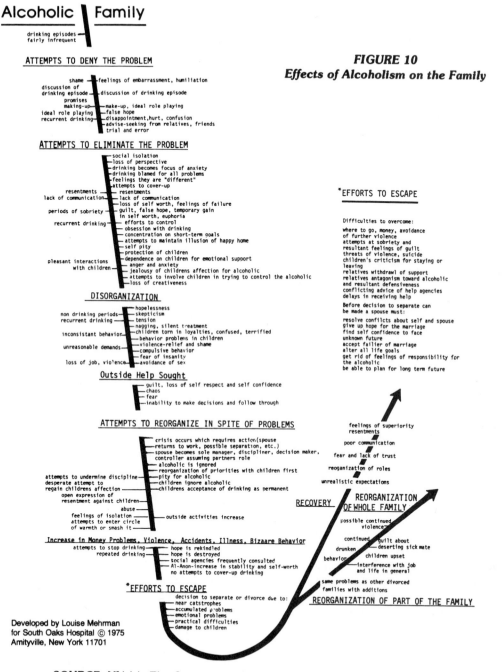

**FIGURE 10**
*Effects of Alcoholism on the Family*

SOURCE: NIAAA, *The Community Health Nurse and Alcohol Related Problems*, U.S. Department of Health, Education, and Welfare, 1980, p. 89.

**Table 21**
**Parallels between the alcoholic's feelings and behavior**
**and family member's feelings**

| Dependent's true feeling | Dependent's behavior | Family members' feelings |
|---|---|---|
| Guilt, self-hatred | Self-righteousness, blaming | Guilt, self-hatred |
| Fear | Aggressiveness, anger | Fear |
| Helplessness | Controlling (of others) | Helplessness |
| Hurt | Abusiveness | Hurt |
| Loneliness, rejection | Rejecting | Loneliness, rejection |
| Low self-worth | Grandiosity, criticalness | Low self-worth |

SOURCE: Sharon Wegscheider, *Another Chance: Hope & Health for the Alcoholic Family,* Science & Behavior Books Inc., Palo Alto, CA, 1981 p. 83.

Healthy family structure depends upon the mature relationship of responsible parents. In this atmosphere, the children, who will identify and copy parental behavior, learn basic communication skills enabling them to function responsibly within the family and society. In alcoholic families, there is frequently a decline in efforts to communicate constructive feelings. Rather, most efforts to communicate center on negative attempts to control behavior. In the home of an alcoholic person, communication is frequently in half-truths and white lies because the nonalcoholic parent needs to protect the children from the truth about the drinking parent. Children soon begin to perceive that parents do not always mean what they say and do not always say what they mean. They are victimized by the desire to believe in their parents, particularly the one who is alcoholic. And with the continued broken promises, they begin to lose faith in verbal communication and depend instead upon actions. These children learn to act out their impulses, following the model of the alcoholic parent. They learn to rely on themselves and may not develop trust in others.(52)

Children of alcoholics have a high frequency of alcohol misuse, antisocial behavior, neurotic systems, and psychosomatic complaints. A variety of complex factors may interact to produce disturbances in these problems, including the personality characteristics of both the alcoholic and nonalcoholic parents, family disorganization, the sociocultural position of the family, and possibly a genetic predisposition to alcoholism. In one study, it was found that children of alcoholic fathers were more likely to be admitted to inpatient and outpatient medical facilities for illnesses with no apparent organic cause. It appears, too, that parental alcoholism may be related to delinquency and hyperactivity in children. Most studies assessing psychological functioning of a sample of alcoholics have shown a high incidence of emotional disturbance.

Studies show that children are most susceptible to the effects of parental drinking at the age of 6 or 7, in early adolescence, and again in later adolescence. And children of alcoholic parents have specific attitudes regarding alcoholism in the family. Generally, they find an alcoholic mother more detrimental than an alcoholic father. Children tend to display more behavioral and emotional problems when the mother is an alcoholic also.(2)

When marital problems, financial stress, or unfulfilled needs push a parent into the vicious circle of alcoholism, the delicate family structure is damaged and all family members suffer the consequences. For example, if the alcoholic spouse is the father, his oldest son may identify his father as an irresponsible figure. Mother cleans up after him when he is sick from drinking. She bails him out of jail and somehow pays the bills and buys the food when he is unemployed. If the wife is the alcoholic spouse, the oldest daughter is often expected to assume the traditional duties of cleaning house, taking care of the younger children, and "mothering" her own mother. Thus, children of problem drinkers are forced to assume roles they are not ready to fill. When the daughter marries early to escape her overwhelming responsibilities and finds she has not learned to cope with marital problems, she may turn to drinking as a buffer just as her mother did. The son may turn to drinking or other delinquent behavior to get attention that his inebriate father is unable to provide.

It is interesting to note that, just like the mother described above, the spouse of the alcoholic can become what is termed an *enabler*. He or she tries to help the alcoholic by wanting to care for him/her, by wanting to help someone with a problem, and by generally taking over some of the dependent person's role or task so that the dependent person does not have to face any consequences of his/her sometimes irresponsible behavior. This may go so far that the enabler gives up his/her own needs and concerns to care for the dependent person. Such behaviors on the part of the enabler do not help the alcoholic but instead keep the alcoholic going.

If the alcoholic is to be treated successfully, the enabler must also be treated. If the enabler is treated and ceases to function, the responsibility falls back on the alcoholic, who then must decide whether or not to get well. He/she then becomes the leader in a sense while the family members and enabler relinquish their role as leaders and become followers.(159)

This child-parent identification pattern may explain why alcoholism tends to "run in the family." Most researchers feel that it is a learned coping behavior rather than a genetically inherited phenomenon.

Because alcoholics are moody people, they present models of tremendous inconsistency for children. Depending on the alcoholic's immediate need, he/she can be either quite strict or very open and liberal, quite accepting of particular behavior or very rejecting. As a result, a child is never sure what reaction his/her behavior will evoke. The child is bound to push limits because he/she does not know where the limits really lie. Because of the alcoholic's inconsistency and, therefore, the family's inconsistency, there are no clear-cut rules and regulations in the homes of many alcoholics.

In an alcoholic's family, the sober partner can cause as much injury to the children as the problem drinker can. The spouse of an alcoholic often directs anger, shame, and verbal abuse at the problem drinker and the children rather than concentrating on rescuing self and family from the situation. The alcoholic reacts to this with more drinking, and attempts to hurt those closest to him/her, feeling successful when the partner reacts with anger, tension, and feelings of inadequacy. The children are caught in the middle, waiting for at least one parent to provide some emotional security. They need the love and approval of both parents but are torn inside by their loathing of the inconsistent behavior.

Repeated studies have shown that children of alcoholics are more prone than other children to delinquency, anxiety neurosis, depression, hostility, and sexual confusion. Children who do not follow these paths and seem to have made a better adjustment also may have difficulties. These children often develop rigid, moralistic codes of behavior. They are often driving, energetic, and demanding, experiencing difficulty in accepting limitations and failures. They need to dominate in order to defend themselves against internal signs of weakness or passivity.(82)

The family situation is vital in the rehabilitation of the alcoholic. As long as the drinker has emotional control over his/her spouse and is protected from taking responsibility for his/her problem, there is little hope that he/she will improve.

As previously indicated, there are approximately 36 million people who share alcohol problems secondhand. But we should look at it another way: There are 36 million potential helpers who have a personal stake in helping a relative or friend find a way to healthy living.(140)

The person who sets out to help a troubled drinker, be it a friend or relative, may at first feel quite alone and possibly embarrassed, not knowing where to turn for help. We have preserved many wrong ideas and attitudes about problem drinking and alcoholism. Many people still label both as moral weaknesses to be hidden and endured in silence. Fortunately, the moral stigma has now begun to fade as more people learn that alcoholism is an illness that can be treated, with good odds for recovery. Half to three-quarters of those who seek treatment recover or show marked improvement. Alcoholism is becoming recognized as the most untreated treatable illness in America.

Help is now available in most communities for the troubled drinker who goes or is guided to treatment. With know-how, compassion, patience, the person with "someone close" can play a key role in his or her turn-about treatment and recovery.

Help and support can be given in three stages: (1) learn about the illness and sources of treatment; (2) guide the "someone close" to treatment; and (3) support the person during treatment and after.(140) Doing this demands effort, patience, and, most important, genuine personal concern.

## Learning About Problem Drinking

Many people who live with them every day do not know and understand the signs of problem drinking and of the illness of alcoholism. They are honestly baffled by the problem drinker's behavior. Why does the person act this way? What are the differences between a social drinker and one who is dependent on alcohol? When is the "someone close" in danger? And of critical importance, what are the early signs of drinking trouble, which, if heeded in time, could avert alcoholism and related major life problems?[1]

Anyone who is wondering if there is a drinking problem within his/her family should ask himself/herself the following questions. If one is convinced there is a drinking problem, answering the questions is a must.

1. Do you lose sleep because of someone's drinking?
2. Do many of your thoughts revolve around the drinking situations and problems resulting because of that person's drinking?
3. Do you try to control the drinking by asking for promises to stop drinking?
4. Do you make threats?
5. Do you have increasingly negative attitudes toward the person?
6. Do you mark, hide, or empty bottles of liquor or medication?
7. Do you think that everything would be o.k. if the drinking situation changed?
8. Do you feel alone, rejected, fearful, angry, guilty, exhausted?
9. Are you feeling an increasing dislike of yourself?
10. Do you find your moods fluctuating as a direct result of the drinking?
11. Do you try to deny or conceal the drinking situation?
12. Do you cover and protect for the person?
13. Do you feel responsible and guilty for the drinking behavior?
14. Are you beginning to or have you withdrawn from friends and outside activities?
15. Have you taken over responsibilities that used to be handled by the other person?
16. Are financial problems increasing because of the drinking?
17. Do you find yourself trying to justify your feelings and behavior in reaction to the drinking behavior?
18. Do you have any new physical symptoms like headaches, indigestion, nausea, shakiness?
19. Do you feel defeated and quite hopeless?
20. Is your sexual relationship negatively affected by the drinking situation?
21. If there are children in the home, are they showing any stress and behavior changes that could be related to the drinking situation?

Three or more "yes" answers mean there is a drinking problem. Professional or expert help is needed.

With fewer than three "yes" answers it would still be good to see someone. When concern develops about another family member's drinking, it is good to talk

---

[1]The next three sections are adapted from reprinted from Alcohol, Drug Abuse and Mental Health Administration, *Someone Close Drinks Too Much,* DHEW Publication No. (ADM) 74-23, pp. 5-7.

with a person who is able to determine whether there is a problem with drinking.(193)

Reading some of the factual booklets about drinking, alcohol misuse, and alcoholism that are now available can give many of the answers.

Looking for answers in the home community, however, has three added benefits. First, the information is immediately available and may be made to fit the particular situation by face-to-face discussion with the information giver. Second, it identifies and should open the doors of community sources of help and counseling treatment and rehabilitation. Third, taking some action to help a relative or friend may ease the frustration of just standing by.

The home search may take some doing because alcoholism treatment services have not yet been started in every community. In most, however, information and help can be obtained from one or more of the groups identified and listed at the end of the preceding chapter.

Sometimes the quickest grasp on the local situation may be gained by joining a group such as Al-Anon. These family members and friends of problem drinkers usually know where help is available. They also share practical suggestions on day-to-day living with one who has a drinking problem. Al-Ateen groups offer similar help to younger members of families with alcohol troubles. If help cannot be found near home, information about the nearest sources may be obtained from the county public health office, county medical society, and designated state agency for alcoholism, or by writing to the National Clearing House for Alcohol Information, Washington, D.C.

Help with alcoholism problems has come to many communities because residents needed it, could not find it, and finally demanded it.

## Adjustment and the Family of an Alcoholic

There are seven stages of adjustment that the average family of an alcoholic goes through:

*The family tries to deny the existence of the problem.* The nonalcoholic parent often covers up the alcohol-related behavior of the alcoholic parent; during this stage, periods of sobriety occur. Eventually, it becomes evident to the nondrinking partner that the alcoholic has a drinking problem.

*The family members who are not alcoholic begin to approach the alcoholic verbally and behaviorally.* They try reasoning, pleading, threatening, promising, demanding, and lecturing. The family avoids embarrassing situations by removing themselves from social situations. The partner who is not alcoholic frequently stops buying liquor, tries to hide it, or locks it up. Unfortunately, home remedies executed by the family rarely work.

*The family becomes disorganized.* The attitude of family members increasingly is "What's the use?" The non-drinking partner begins to feel unloved and ineffective as a marriage partner, and the children feel rejected.

*The family attempts to reorganize, despite the obvious problems.* The spouse who does not drink (or who is not alcoholic) starts assuming the duties once filled by the alcoholic. The alcoholic eventually and gradually becomes excluded from family activities.

*The family members physically separate themselves from the alcoholic in a desperate attempt at solving the problem.* Many of the attempted separations do not last: the spouse and children return because of the problems of relocation. (The problem is especially severe when the mother tries to leave, since she may not be able economically to support herself and the children.)

*If the separation becomes permanent, the family reorganizes:* roles and responsibilities of each member are reviewed and reassigned.

*If the parent decides to stop drinking, acceptance and reorganization must ensue.* Family members often adopt a "wait and see" attitude, watching to see if the alcoholic's period of sobriety will last.

# Guiding the Problem Drinker to Treatment

Even after a helper seeks service on behalf of an alcoholic, the alcoholic may not cooperate at once by going for treatment. If there is one thing true of problem drinkers, it is that, as with all people, each one is different—different in human needs and responses, as well as in their reasons for drinking, their reactions to alcohol, and their readiness for treatment. A person who knows a good deal about the alcoholic's unique qualities and way of life and who has made the effort to gain some understanding of the signs and effects of problem drinking, should be in a better position to consider a strategy for helping the alcoholic.

The helper should be active and get involved, talking about the drinking problem honestly and openly. It is easy to be too polite or to duck the issue by saying, " After all, it's their private affair," but it is not polite or considerate to let someone destroy his/her family and life. Most people with drinking problems really want to talk it out.

It is important to reject certain myths that in the past have done great harm to alcoholic people and hampered those who would help them. These untruths come from ingrained public attitudes that see alcoholism as personal misconduct, moral weakness, or even sin. They are expressed in such declarations as, "Nothing can be done unless the alcoholic person wants to stop drinking," or, "The alcoholic person must hit rock bottom,"—that is, lose health, job, home, and family "before he/she will want to get well again." These stubborn myths are not true and have been destructive. One may as well say, "You can't treat cancer or tuberculosis until the gross signs of disease are visible to all."

The truth is that with alcoholism, as with other kinds of acute and chronic illness, early recognition and treatment intervention are essential and rewarding.

The family members must be compassionate and patient, but must be willing to act. Experience shows that preaching does not work. A nudge or a push at the right time can help, but also shows that the helper cares. Push may even come to shove when the troubled drinker must choose between losing family or job or going to treatment. (All persons should be given the right to stay sick before they are given the right to be well.) Thousands of alcoholic persons have been helped when a spouse, employer, or court official made treatment a condition of continuing family relationships, job, or probation. A helper cannot cure the illness, but when the crucial moment comes, the helper can guide the person to competent help. When attempting to guide or while waiting for the "right time" to approach the problem of alcoholism with a friend or relative, family members should consider the following do's and don'ts.

## Do's and Don'ts for the Family [2]

Alcoholism is frequently referred to as a "family illness," because within the confines of the family, alcoholism commonly causes major difficulties and emotional harm. In the treatment of the problem drinker, family attitudes present obstacles which must be removed before recovery can begin.

Both the family and the alcoholic should be helped to face the reality of their situations, and they should decide which familial interactions are constructive and which are destructive. Poor family attitudes often intensify the alcoholic's need to escape into drink and to strengthen his/her distorted view of himself and others.

By the time the problem drinker is seen by a professional, the family has often done more harm than good with "home treatment" methods of lecturing, weeping, pleading, and various other emotional appeals. As a result, the professional will often decide to include the wife (or husband), as well as other family members, within the scope of the therapeutic efforts in an attempt to restore their psychological balance and to help them develop a realistic insight into the existing problem as an illness.

Family members should follow these valuable rules when dealing with their alcoholic:

### Do's

1. Learn the facts about alcoholism—a variety of authoritative booklets for the laymen are available through the AMA, Chicago; the National Council on Alcoholism, New York; and other organizations. Attend meetings of AA and Al-Anon Family Groups with an open mind to learn and benefit from the experiences of others.
2. Develop an attitude, reflecting insight, to match the facts that you have learned about alcoholism and the alcoholic.
3. Test your attitude by taking honest personal inventory of yourself: Are you convinced that alcoholism really is a disease? Is your approach to the alcoholic one of love, indifference or rejection?

[2]Adapted from Ebbe Curtis Hoff, *Aspects of Alcoholism* (Philadelphia: J. B. Lippincott Co., 1963), pp. 61–63.

4. Discuss the situation with a trusted layman—a clergyman or social worker—or a person who has experienced some phase of alcoholism, either as an alcoholic or as a family member.
5. Take it as a matter of course when your alcoholic stops drinking, either as a result of self-help or of formal treatment; observe complete alcohol abstinence yourself, because drinking on the part of the nonalcoholic mate is unconsciously resented by the alcoholic and may make him/her resume drinking.
6. Establish and maintain a healthy atmosphere in the home, with a sympathetic place in the family circle for the alcoholic member.
7. Encourage new interests and participate whenever possible in recreational or occupational activities enjoyed by your alcoholic; encourage him/her to see old friends.
8. Be patient and live one day at a time: alcoholism takes a long time to develop; recovery does not happen overnight. Accept setbacks and relapses with equanimity. Keep on trying.
9. Approach the alcoholic about his/her drinking problem only when he/she is sober—for example, shortly after a bout, when hangover, depression and remorse are present.
10. Discretely place injurious objects out of sight and attempt to withhold car keys when your alcoholic becomes intoxicated.
11. Explain the nature of alcoholism as an illness to children in the family; try to spare their seeing the alcoholic parent in an extremely intoxicated state.
12. Advise local bartenders and police, whenever possible, about your alcoholic's condition to help prevent community incidents and embarrassments.
13. Try to remain calm, unemotional, and factually honest in speaking with the problem drinker about his/her behavior and its day-to-day consequences.
14. Refuse to ride with the alcoholic person if he/she insists on drinking and driving.
15. Encourage treatment but allow the alcoholic to make his/her own choice.
16. Go to the treatment group with the alcoholic person.

## Don'ts

1. Don't preach, nag, lecture, and assume a "holier-than-thou" attitude; with the alcoholic's characteristic low tolerance of frustration, such will probably cause him/her to escape more and more into alcoholism.
2. Never use emotional appeals such as "If you love me"; they only tend to increase feelings of guilt and the compulsive need to drink.
3. Be sure not to make threats you do not intend to carry out or will not be able to follow through.
4. Do not look upon your alcoholic as a moral weakling or completely take over his/her responsibilities, leaving him/her with no sense of importance or value.

5.  Do not shelter your alcoholic from situations where alcohol is present: do not hide bottles or pour liquor down the sink. Such acts only impel him/her to establish a secret supply hidden from you and certainly do not aid him/her in successfully facing the everyday temptation of drinking in our society.
6.  Never extract promises or place your alcoholic in a position where he/she must be deceitful. Pledges, readily given and broken, intensify the alcoholic's guilt feelings and loss of self-respect.
7.  Be sure not to argue or put the pressure on the alcoholic when he/she is drinking or intoxicated—the response is usually one of negativism and even violence. Never resort to physical violence or punishment.
8.  Never be overconfident or expect a recovery that is either immediate or complete.
9.  Do not cover up or make excuses for the alcoholic person or shield him/her from the realistic consequences of his/her behavior.
10. Try not to be a martyr, or feel ashamed or at fault. These attitudes will only serve to destroy objectivity and usually are sensed by the already remorseful, suspicious alcoholic.
11. Avoid making an issue over, or standing in judgment of, the method of recovery selected by your alcoholic.
12. Never use the children as tools or turn them against the alcoholic in an attempt to cope with your problems.
13. Never drink along with the problem drinker.
14. Above all, do not accept guilt for another's behavior.

## Supporting the Problem Drinker [3]

Treatment attempts to discover the relationship of the person's drinking problem to his/her real needs: an understanding of what he/she would really strive for if he/she were not handicapped by his/her problem. One goal is building up his/her capacity for control which becomes possible in periods of sobriety.

Persons with drinking problems have the same needs as all other people, food, clothing, shelter, health care, job, social contact and acceptance, and particularly the need for self-confidence and feelings of self-worth and dignity. This is where "support" comes in. What seems to be needed most is a warm, human concern. The kinds of support given depend, of course, on finding out from the alcoholic person himself/herself what is needed. Strained family and friend relationships, money troubles, worry about job or business, sometimes matters that may seem trivial, all confuse his/her life situation and may contribute to the drinking problem. Moral support in starting and staying with treatment, reassurances from employer or business associates, willing participation by spouse or children in group therapy sessions are examples of realistic support. The long-range goal is healthy living for the alcoholic person and his/her family.

---

[3]The next two sections are adapted from *Someone Close Drinks Too Much,* pp. 12-13.

Physical health, social health, emotional health, and spiritual health are objectives we all share. This happy ending is not necessarily reached with the achievement of sobriety. Many recovered persons will succeed in living a good life without a recurrence of any personal, social, or economic disaster due to drinking. Others may have setbacks and will continue to need compassionate support and help.

# The Family and Chances of Recovery

Three out of four alcoholic men and women are still married, living at home, holding on to a job, business or profession, and are reasonably well-accepted members of their communities. For those in this group who seek treatment, the outlook is good. Regardless of life situation, the earlier treatment starts after drinking troubles are recognized, the better the odds for success. Many therapists now use rehabilitation as a measurement of outcome. Success is considered achieved when the patient maintains or re-establishes a good family life and work record and a responsible position in the community. Relapses may occur but do not mean that the problem drinker or the treatment effort has failed. A successful outcome on this basis can be expected for 60 to 80 percent, depending upon the personal characteristics of the patient, early treatment intervention, competence of the therapist, availability of hospital and outpatient facilities, and the strong support of *family, friends, employer, and community.* "It is doubtful that any specific percentage figure has much meaning by itself," says one authority. "What does have a great deal of meaning is the fact that tens of thousands of such cases have shown striking improvement over many years."

# Drinking Behavior in the Family

We should remember that problem drinkers come from families that often show these beliefs and attitudes: (1) ground rules for drinking are vague and inconsistent; (2) one set of rules holds for men, another for women; (3) one parent favors drinking, the other opposes it; and (4) if children have been using pep pills, marijuana, and similar drugs, parents seem relieved when these children turn instead to alcohol abuse.(3) The results of such practices and attitudes are often the following:

1. Children experiment with alcohol in their middle or late teens, usually away from home.
2. Young people become accustomed to drinking on irregular occasions (such as the weekend "beer bust") and to drinking large amounts on an empty stomach. They rarely drink mainly with meals.
3. Children see both adults and young people drink to escape from emotional and uncomfortable situations, and they adopt these practices for themselves.
4. Children see pressure placed on others to drink. To them, not to drink is scorned as a sign of cowardice or unfriendliness.
5. Young people boast of their drinking prowess.
6. Young people drink to win acceptance from their peers or to prove

something—their manliness, glamour, sex equality, or independence from their parents.
7. Intoxication is viewed as comical or socially acceptable.
8. Tragically, the message that children get from their parents is, "Drink as I say, but do not as I do."(3)

It is vitally important that each family discuss and then decide on a set of ground rules that each member can follow comfortably. Families must agree on how all members—parents and children alike—will or will not drink, why they will use alcoholic beverages, and how they will react to those who abstain, those who drink moderately, and those who overindulge. It is imperative to keep family communication lines open.

Parents and teachers cannot sit back and delegate the entire responsibility to the government, the medical profession, churches, and schools, although each of these may influence decision-making.

Answers to the following questions may also affect decision-making and personal choices:

1. Do our present alcohol laws and community standards actually prevent drinking problems, or do they make excessive drinking appear glamorous?
2. When an entertainer jokes about his own heavy drinking, does this make overindulgence seem socially acceptable?
3. How can young people be helped to evaluate and analyze alcohol advertising for truths and half-truths? What's the hidden message of advertisements that extol one brand as "a man's drink," or that use such phrases as "for a romantic evening?"
4. Do our schools give alcohol education based mainly on scare statements (warnings that scarcely impress young people who see their parents drink moderately at home) or do they provide the facts on drinking as unemotionally as they would offer a basic science course? Do they help young people in their own decision-making?(3)

To help prevent irresponsible drinking, children must develop healthy attitudes starting in early childhood. These attitudes can be developed most effectively within families, if parents are prepared to react honestly and openly, and through well-planned alcohol education programs in schools. Each should support the other.(3)

Remember, however, that what parents do is far more important than what they say.

## Family Intervention Technique in the Treatment of Alcoholism

Bernie Boswell and Sandy Wright have recently developed a unique approach to the problem of alcoholism as it relates to the family. Their program, "The Cottage," which was originally developed in Salt Lake City, Utah, continues to be one of the more innovative and exciting programs in preventive and treatment efforts. A description and philosophy of the program is presented here as written by the founders and directors, Boswell and Wright: [4]

It has become increasingly apparent that a large part of the problem of alcohol abuse is the behavior of certain key persons living close to the one with the drinking problem. This is especially true in family situations. Family members often are harmfully "supportive" to the alcoholic, ameliorating his crisis, covering for him, rescuing him, and generally perpetuating the very behavior which they claim is so troublesome to them. It is also clear that in most cases they are unaware that they are doing this. Their attempts to help the alcoholic are sincere, but misled. It can be extremely frustrating to work with the problem drinker alone, even when he *does* originate treatment, which is rare. A change is desperately needed in the family context, the natural environment.

Through this relatively innovative new program, it has been learned that the traditional treatment approach in alcoholism, the medical model of removing the problem drinker from his home or natural environment, giving him treatment in a recovery center, hospital or outpatient clinic, and then returning him to his environment, is indeed inadequate. Even in cases of medical emergency for withdrawal from alcohol, some very encouraging approaches to home detoxification under medical supervision are showing unusual success.

Additionally, there is the very real confusion of "who has the problem?" By far, the vast majority of calls for help come from family members, relatives, and friends. When asked if the problem-drinker will come in for treatment, the reply is "Oh no! He doesn't think he has a problem." One then has to ask himself, who *does* have the problem?

In cases like these, a group meeting with the significant others is, at least, one possible opportunity of affording help to a family. Those living with an alcoholic must learn to focus *away* from his drinking, and onto being responsible for themselves, so that they are not looking to the behavior of another person as a solution to their own problem. Many times those living with the alcoholic have a more serious problem than the alcoholic. He has become the family scapegoat. In the majority of cases, family members need to learn to *stop trying to change the alcoholic* or get him sober. This means they must learn *not* to feel responsible for his behavior, and this isn't an easy task.

We feel that the entire family or context around the person with the drinking problem, can profit from education and treatment. It simply does not make sense to treat the symptoms evidenced by any given individual, and then return him to an untreated environment which initially fostered the condition.

*Treating the whole family.* The need to treat the entire family, or system,

[4]This section is reprinted from Bernie Boswell and Sandy Wright, "A Family Intervention Technique in the Treatment of Alcoholism," published under the aspices of the Environmental Education and Treatment Association, Inc. (1973), pp. 1-8.

when one individual is having symptoms, is essential. Many workers in family therapy have found it difficult to treat the symptoms of any given individual outside of an environment which expects and reinforces the symptoms. Family therapists, more recently, have discouraged hospitalization of the identified patient, noting that it can increase his sense of dependence and inadequacy, and can have definitely prolonging effects on his dysfunction. Jay Haley, who has done pioneering work with schizophrenic families, has stated:

> An essential part of the medical model was the idea that a person could be changed if he were plucked out of his social situation and treated individually in a private office or inside a hospital. Once changed, he would return to his social milieu transformed because he had been "cleared" of the intrapsychic problems causing his difficulties . . . the focus of family treatment is no longer on changing an individual's perception, his effect, or his behavior, but on changing the structure of a family and the sequences of behavior among a group of intimates . . . The problem is to change the living situation of a person, not to pluck him out of that situation and try to change *him*.

Treating, modifying and altering the environment of the "sick" member must direct itself impartially to all members of that context, with the spotlight being shared equally by all. In work which Virginia Satir did with a delinquent family member, she observed:

> Other family members interfered with, tried to become part of, or sabotaged the individual treatment of the "sick" member, as though the family had a stake in his sickness. The hospitalized or incarcerated patient often got worse or regressed after a visit from family members, as though family interaction had a direct bearing on his symptoms. Other family members got worse as the patient got better, as though sickness in one of the family members were essential to the family's way of operating.

Experience has shown in working with alcoholism families, that a similar process goes on. It has been repeatedly observed that if the alcoholic stops drinking, this does not bring about the solution which everyone had anticipated. In fact, conditions may get worse. Often when an alcoholic stops drinking, the nonalcoholic spouse will become depressed, so that we see something of a "seesaw" phenomenon. The dysfunction in the family can actually be augmented when there isn't a drinking problem to focus to. It becomes obvious that in families with an alcohol problem or similar behavioral disorder, the *strong family member needs to soften*. And unfortunately, society usually supports and reinforces the "strong" one.

After working with schizophrenic families for some length of time, Satir observed:

> The symptom of any family member at a given time is seen as a comment on a dysfunctional family system. The wearer of the symptom, the identified patient, is seen as signaling distortion, denial, and/or frustration of growth.[5]

---

[5]Jay Haley, *Changing Families: A Family Therapy Reader* (New York & London: Grune & Stratton, 1971), p. 127.

*The Cottage Meeting*—what is it? The Cottage Meeting is a small, informal gathering of concerned individuals held in the home of the person seeking help for an alcoholic, or for himself in relation to an alcoholic. It is a technique for family intervention in the condition of alcoholism in which many individuals are playing roles in the dysfunction. The host invites the group members, and is asked to include as many of the involved family members, relatives, friends and significant others as he can assemble. An effort is made to assemble the key figures in the total context in which the alcoholic is situated, especially those individuals who might be playing the roles described by Joseph Kellerman and Eric Berne (following). The goal is to educate and treat the *whole situation, background, or environment* relevant to the person with the drinking problem.

A Cottage Meeting is usually initiated when a family member calls into an alcoholism information center for help. Since the person with the drinking problem is often still denying that he has a problem, the meeting usually is held without the problem drinker in attendance. He may later desire treatment, and can then be included with his family as well as be given individual help.

Family members are urged to view the alcoholism as an illness, and they are given information about community services where they can turn for help. When Cottage Meetings are utilized specifically as a family intervention procedure, those present are encouraged to explore the roles they might be playing in the total problem, and are then helped to modify their behavior toward the alcoholic, both their actions and reactions, as well as their attitudes and verbal communications. Concepts from transactional analysis are especially helpful, at this point, and the group is educated to the game of "alcoholic." Sometimes there are deep feelings toward the alcoholic, perhaps anger and rage, and it can be helpful to family members to get these feelings out.

Each situation is unique, and must be explored in a unique way. The theme running throughout subsequent meetings is: "the only way you can change the behavior of another individual, is to change your own behavior."

*Concepts from transactional analysis.* The following concepts in alcoholism have been so helpful in working with family members, that they will be included here. These concepts are borrowed from Joseph L. Kellerman and are supplemented, where appropriate, by those of Eric Berne and Claude Steiner. The following statements are fundamental to family intervention in the treatment of alcoholism:

1. Alcoholism is a social dysfunction, always involving two or more persons.
2. The primary aspect of the condition of alcoholism is denial.
3. Denial is present in all persons surrounding the drinking member.
4. Recovery from alcoholism may be best initiated by someone other than the alcoholic.

See chart entitled "Environmental Alcoholism—The Illness of Denial." (Table 22)

The clinical picture of a family with alcoholism is that one person drinks too much and gets drunk. Significant others react to his drinking and its

---

### Table 22
### *Environmental alcoholism—the illness of denial*

---

1. Alcoholism—a social illness, usually involving two or more persons.
2. The primary aspect of alcoholism is denial.
3. Denial is present in all people surrounding the drinking person.
4. Recovery from alcoholism may best be initiated by someone other than the one who is drinking.

The four stages in the family with alcohlism:

1. **Denial** — Everyone denies that there is an alcoholism problem. Family members try to hide the alcoholism both from each other and from those outside the family.
2. **Home** treatment — Everyone tries to get the alcoholic to stop drinking. Hiding bottles, nagging, threatening, persuasion and sympathy are tried. Home treatment always fails because of the efforts made are toward changing the behavior of someone else.
3. **Chaos** — The problem becomes so critical that it can no longer be denied and hidden. Neighbors and friends become aware of the alcoholism. Role reversal takes place within the family.
4. **Control** — The spouse or family member takes complete control of and complete responsibility for the alcoholic. If still living within the family, the drinking member becomes an emotional invalid.

Some characteristics of alcoholism—the illness

1. Marked personality change when drinking.
2. Loss of control of drinking—of amount, time and place.
3. Unhealthy dependencies.
4. Low tolerance for tension.
5. Deep underlying sense of inadequacy.

---

consequences. The drinker responds to this reaction and drinks again. There is constant verbal contradiction of what is actually going on. The alcoholic denies his drinking problem and the spouse continues to make verbal threats which are not carried out. This sets up a merry-go-round of blame and denial, a downward spiral which characterizes alcoholism. To understand alcoholism, we must look not at the alcoholic alone, but view the entire condition, with its supporting cast of players. See chart entitled "ALCOHOL . . . 'IC' or 'ISM'?" (Figure 12) for depictions of the following characters.

*1. Enabler* (rescuer) The one who sets up the rescue operations. He saves the alcoholic from the crisis. He cannot bear to allow the alcoholic to suffer the consequences of his own behavior. This denies the alcoholic the process of learning by correcting his own mistakes, and conditions him to believe there will always be a protector who will come to his resuce.

*2. Provoker* (persecutor) Usually a member of the opposite sex. Can be the spouse, and is sometimes the mother. The persecutor is hurt and upset by the drinking episodes, but in spite of everything, holds the family together. She sacrifices, adjusts, never gives up, never gives out, never gives in, but never forgets. Sometimes called the "adjuster."

*3. Victim* (patsy) The one who is used. The Victim suffers the consequences of the alcoholic's irresponsible actions. This can be the boss, employer or business

**FIGURE 11**
*Alcohol . . . "ic" or "ism"?*

## ...IC

**DENIAL**
**DEPENDENCY**
**SELF-CONDEMNATION**
**SHAME**

## ...ISM

**COUNTER-DENIAL**
**COUNTER-DEPENDENCY**
**SELF-RIGHTEOUSNESS**
**BLAME**

**ENABLER
(RESCUER)** The one who sets up the rescue operations to save the alcoholic from any crisis. This denies the alcoholic the process of learning from his own mistakes.

**PROVOKER
(PERSECUTOR)** The one who is hurt and upset by the drinking episodes, but, in spite of everything, holds the family together. The provoker sacrifices, adjusts, never gives up, never gives out, never gives in, but never forgets.

**VICTIM
(PATSY)** The one who 'used'. The Victim suffers the consequences of the alcoholic's irresponsible actions. He can be an employer, business partner, or family member. The Victim gets the work done when the alcoholic is absent.

**REMOVE COUNTER-DENIAL**
**REMOVE COUNTER-DEPENDENCY**

**REMOVE SELF-RIGHTEOUSNESS**
**REMOVE BLAME**

partner. The Victim is the person who is responsible for getting the work done, if the alcoholic is absent.

Kellerman has identified four stages which a family will generally progress through, before outside intervention is sought. A description of these stages is also given to the family seeking help. See chart entitled "Effective Living Skills." (Figure 12)

*1. Denial.* Everyone denies that there is an alcoholism problem. Attempts are made, by family members, to hide the alcoholism both from each other and from the outside world. Denial can last up to seven years after the problem is critical.

*2. Home treatment.* All efforts possible are made to get the alcoholic to stop drinking. Bottles are hidden, threats are made, nagging, coercion, and sympathy are tried. Home treatment lasts about two years before outside help is sought.

*3. Chaos.* The problem erupts outside of the family. Neighbors and friends become aware. Perhaps the police are called to the home. The condition can no longer be hidden or denied. *Role reversal* takes place. The problem drinker may completely abdicate his position in the family. The wife may become the bread winner and begin to make the major decisions.

*4. Control.* The nonalcoholic spouse, or family member, takes complete control of the family, and takes responsibility for the alcoholic. The alcoholic ceases to function as a family member and, if still living with his family, will do so as an emotional invalid, removed from any real communication with the family.

The roles in the game of "alcoholic" and the stages in the family breakdown are explained at length to members of the family and the context. Mainly the process of dealing with the nonalcoholics in the condition of alcoholism is one of education and re-learning. If the individual wearing the symptom, the drinking member, is present, the procedure is just the same. He also is allowed to view the condition objectively, which, by itself, reduces his guilt and has therapeutic value. Some of the focus and blame is automatically taken off him as the attention is drawn to the total family system.

*Self-responsibility of family members.* Emphasis in Cottage Meetings with the family is to get the individuals present to stop focusing on the alcoholic's drinking behavior and to begin focusing on themselves as a solution to their own problem. They need to learn to accept alcoholism as a condition which they didn't cause, and they can't cure. They must surrender the feeling of personal responsibility for the drinking member and begin to allow him to suffer the consequences of his drinking. If their perception can be altered to see that a "hands-off" policy really expresses care and concern and not rejection, this new perception alone can actually help the alcoholic out of his dilemma of dependency.

We do not emphasize alcoholism as an illness, but rather as a learned behavior. The prognosis is more optimistic and in keeping with a "health" model. This allows the significant others to look at their own attitudes, reactions to and

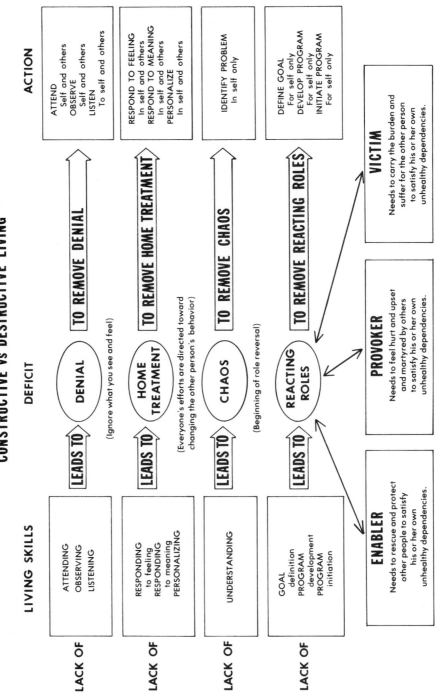

**FIGURE 12**
*Effective Living Skills*

CONSTRUCTIVE vs DESTRUCTIVE LIVING

interactions with the alcoholic, as possible reinforcers of the condition and to begin to alter them.

Efforts are made at once to reduce the anxiety and guilt about alcoholism which is prevalent in the family. It may take an enormous amount of courage for a husband, or wife, to cease acting as a support to the drinking person, to see that this is not love but is actually perpetuating the condition. At this point, family members need to explore and endeavor to break their own dependencies, and to see themselves as self-reliant enough to survive the loss of those dependencies.

A great deal of work is needed with the family in exploring and strengthening their own individual self-awareness, self-reliance, and self-responsibility. In a sense, they have been just as dependent on the problem drinker and his symptoms as he has been on their support. Alcoholism is a condition of mutual dependencies. It is always a problem of more than one person. Members who appear strong may very much have needed the one with the symptoms to bolster them.

The Cottage Meeting, as a family intervention technique, is one way of bringing individuals seeking help for another, to focus on their problems (not those of another person, or an absent person), and to gain the strength and freedom to seek solutions to that problem which will be most beneficial to themselves. As an individual focuses less on another person, and more upon his own feelings, the environment is automatically modified to some extent and changes can be expected in the behavior of others in the family system. In this way, the treatment of the total condition is underway.

*Social network intervention and alcoholism.* Some of the more recent therapeutic techniques in the field of family therapy are moving beyond not only the identified patient, but beyond the traditional family unit in their approach to family crisis. Ross Speck and Carolyn Attneave have begun intervening into the entire social network when one family is troubled. They call it "a way of healing through retribalization."

In social network intervention, everyone in the kinship system or tribe is assembled: all friends, neighbors, extended family members, relatives, and anyone who is of significance to the family or individual who offers the presenting problem. Up to 50 people might be gathered together at one time and in one place. A team of network intervenors (3 or 4) then goes to work to bring the network together. This might take several intense sessions of discussion, interaction and psychodynamic exploration. In these sessions, the difficulties experienced by the family in crisis are talked about and explored within the larger network. The larger group begins to see itself as a functioning organic unit, with a sense of connectedness between individuals. This is called the "retribalization" process. The results of social network intervention can range anywhere from dramatic psychological breakthroughs to practical solutions for the family in crisis.

Speck and Attneave believe that the problem of any one individual can be traced back to dysfunction in the entire social network. They state:

Traditionally, the individual has been regarded as the "sick" one; more recently, the family has been identified as a "sick" unit. Our experience is that in some instances the entire social network causes and perpetuates pathology, scapegoating the individual and/or family.

One of the most interesting and relevant features of social network intervention is a phenomenon called the network effect. The network effect follows retribalization. The entire group seems to revive or create a *healthy* social matrix which can then deal with the problems and crises of its members in a positive and helpful manner. This often leads to practical solutions. The renewed network, itself, takes the responsibility for solving the problem of its troubled family or troubled family member. Treating the entire social network is one of the goals of intervention. Speck and Attneave state further:

> The social network is a relatively invisible, but at the same time a very real, structure in which an individual, nuclear family, or group is embedded. There are malfunctioning social networks as well as malfunctioning families and individuals. The retribalization goal of social network intervention attempts to deal with the entire structure by rendering the network visible and viable, and by attempting to restore its function. Thus, the social network becomes the unit of treatment or intervention—it becomes the "patient"—and the success or failure of the therapy will require new modes of evaluation.

In Cottage Meetings, achievement in this same intervention of a malfunctioning unit is being demonstrated. The context and environment of the drinking family member is the target of treatment. The success of the intervention can hardly be evaluated solely in terms of whether or not an alcoholic modifies his drinking behavior. Something larger goes on—families will pull together into a new and functioning solidarity, and can together, with mutual supportiveness, seek solutions to their own crises, or those of individuals in their context. There is no question that the same phenomenon that Speck and Attneave call retribalization occurs in ongoing Cottage Meetings—even with the primary client still absent. The network effect often surfaces after that family has stopped focusing to the alcoholic, and has become more able to accept the drinking behavior, rather than trying to modify it.

In keeping with the health model and health emphasis, labeling is avoided whenever possible, especially the label, "alcoholic." This minimizes scapegoating, and maximizes focusing to the entire context or system. Social network intervention, used in alcoholism, is not so much a matter of getting the network together around an alcoholic family, as getting the network together around a "person with a problem, and the problem happens to be alcohol." De-emphasizing alcoholism as a special condition in its own right, and treating it simply as another of the "isms" which are symptomatic of dysfunctioning families and dysfunctioning networks, is a more positive and realistic approach with a more optimistic prognosis.

If, as Speck and Attneave suggest, the entire social network causes and perpetuates pathology, and further scapegoats the individual and the family, then the entire social network needs to be treated or it will continue to spawn "sick" families and "sick" people.

The Cottage Meeting approach is another entrance into the social network system, where labels can be forgotten in a real effort to hear each other, to communicate in a real way, and to find health-giving and responsible relationships with others.

# Alcohol Use and Abuse Among Women

Conservative estimates of the number of adult women with alcohol-related problems range from 1.5 million to 2.25 million, while it is conjectured that as many as 900,000 are alcoholics. That estimate is probably low, though, because many researchers believe that nine out of ten female alcoholics go undetected today.

Why?

There are a number of reasons. Treatment programs are clearly male-oriented. Even though the number of male and female social drinkers are about even, an attitude that "nice girls don't drink" still prevails in many circles. Many female alcoholics are housewives who can easily hide their problems. Of those who do seek help, many (as high as 85 percent) complain to their physicians about the physical and emotional symptoms of alcoholism in hopes that the physician will make a correct diagnosis.

Finally, society is much more protective of women than men—and there is a distinct double standard as far as drinking is concerned. Men are allowed to drink openly to relieve stress, boredom, and loneliness; women are not. The sight of an intoxicated man is common and accepted; people are disgusted and outraged at an intoxicated woman.

The facts remain: women *do* suffer drinking problems, and an increasing number of women *are* alcoholics. As women's status and roles evolve to meet new social conditions, there is renewed concern about alcoholism. The fact that nearly all young women drink stands in stark contrast to the dominance of abstention among older women, and it is undoubtedly a twentieth-century phenomenon. The higher rate of drinking, of course, increases the potential for a greater number of alcoholics.

Given these concerns, there is considerable interest in the social factors that contribute to alcoholism among women, and in whether these social factors are related to broader changes occurring in women's roles. In particular, a central question is whether the extension of women's roles to include traditional male roles will increase or reduce alcohol-related problems among women.

Although many social factors determine a woman's lifestyle, among the most important are age, marital, employment, and socioeconomic status. Some of these factors may also influence drinking behavior.

One recent study has shown that the proportion of women who drink drops considerably with increasing age, regardless of other social factors. However, there is a higher incidence of heavier and problem drinking in the 35–64 age group than either the younger or older age groups. The sole exception to this pattern occurs for divorced and separated women in the under-35 age group.

The effect of marital status varies with the age group. Among women under 35, there is little difference between single and married women, but divorced and separated women have the highest incidence of heavier and problem drinking of any group. However, where comparisons are possible, the older women who are divorced, separated, and widowed show lower problem rates than those who are married. Since the divorced status is likely to be more recent for the younger woman than for the older one, the study suggests that the crisis of divorce or separation rather than the status of being divorced is responsible for elevated rates of heavier and problem drinking for younger women. Among married women under 65, those who are working have higher rates of heavier and problem drinking than those who are not employed outside the home, regardless of socioeconomic status. This finding may stem from peer pressures in the working situation to drink more frequently accompanied by few inner constraints not to do so. An alternative explanation associates elevated rates with conflicts stemming from the dual demands of the roles of wife and employee.

The same study has also suggested that lifestyles can be categorized into how much or how little they exemplify traditional ideas of women's roles. Traditional American role expectations for a woman have included being a wife and mother and, if she works, a secretary, nurse, or a teacher. Nontraditional roles include being single, childless, or having a career such as business executive or lawyer. A woman who breaks with tradition is generally exposed to societal pressures to conform, and some drinking patterns may emerge as a reaction to this role conflict.

A sex-role index was devised to classify women 30 to 64 years of age into in-role and out-of-role groups. To be out of role, a woman had to be nontraditional on at least three of the five criteria. The results comparing the two groups indicated that in-role women are more often drinkers but out-of-role women are more often heavier and problem drinkers regardless of socioeconomic status. Another study showed that for women in traditional female occupations, personal sex-role characteristics were the most significant predictors of higher levels of drinking. For women in traditionally male occupations, the level in the organization and salary were the sole predictors of higher drinking levels.

Women are subject to stresses in life that are different from those of men. Not only are their roles different, but so are related factors such as behavior, goals, self-images, and life experiences. Some specific stresses women face that have been related to alcohol abuse are as follows:

*Home stresses.* Many women give up a career and career goals to be at home with a family. Home crises such as family health problems and too many children cause this woman to be dissatisfied with her choice of remaining at home. This situation can be a precursor to problem drinking.

*Work stresses.* The work world has a definite male orientation and as such imposes excessive pressure and loneliness upon career women. Such factors can cause increased drinking among women.

*The overburdened woman.* Many women maintain two roles—maintaining a home and holding a full-time job. The double role can cause undue stress, which may cause a woman to seek relief in alcohol.

Women are also subject to other stresses and personal crises that may precede the onset of excessive drinking:

*The empty nest stage of life.* The period when all the children have left the home is stressful for many women. Many mothers feel that they are left behind and devoid of any reason for being. Drinking makes this empty life seem more bearable.

*The loneliness of the single life.* Even though many single women find life extremely fulfilling, there are still lonely times during holidays, weekends, and after work. Single women may ask themselves, "If I choose to work rather than marry, what can I do about those lonely times that will inveitably come? Will my life be complete if I don't bear children? Will I be fullfilled without the company of a husband?" Going to singles bars and drinking alone tend to alleviate some of these thoughts and some of the loneliness.

*Menopausal crises and postpartum depression.* These are two problems that may present a woman with unusual stress. Drinking may help to relieve the feelings of stress, depression, and the emotions that accompany these episodes.

Attempts to define a typical female alcoholic personality have been disappointing. The only traits identified so far are poor self-concept and low self-esteem; while women alcoholics are in many ways a heterogeneous group, many had at least one alcoholic parent.

Physiological factors may also influence the incidence of alcoholism among women. Men require nearly twice as much alcohol to get intoxicated as women, but women seem to absorb alcohol more quickly than men, and so they become intoxicated more rapidly. Many women attain their peak blood-alcohol concentration and become more obviously intoxicated during the middle of the menstrual cycle, when hormone levels are highest. Also, because of hormonal and other physiological factors, women tend to be more susceptible to some of the damaging effects of alcohol, such as liver disease.

It is not surprising that until recently, alcoholic treatment programs were ill equipped to deal with women alcoholics. Historically, women have received low-priority attention in nontraditional areas, thereby establishing a cultural protective device for women who are problem drinkers. Families and medical professionals frequently have tended to disguise female alcoholism under less embarrassing diagnoses, effectively eliminating treatment. Another barrier to treatment is the well-documented fact that women who spend more time at home than men do tend to drink at home alone, therefore less visibly.

Encouraging signs for women's treatment do exist. More women are entering treatment and initial studies of posttreatment behaviorial changes indicate positive prognoses in many cases.(10)

# Alcohol Use and Abuse Among the Elderly

Abstinence is more common among older people. Some of them are lifelong abstainers. Others have given up drinking for reasons of health or because they live in environments where alcoholic beverages are not available.

Some of the healthier and more active elderly are likely to be drinkers. Experiments in providing alcoholic beverages in a social setting to older persons (non-problem drinkers) living in nursing homes and residences for the aged yielded some beneficial effects and caused no apparent harm. However, those in a controlled environment such as a nursing home do not represent the typical elderly population.

Alcoholism is less frequent among the elderly than among the young, in part because many problem drinkers do not survive to old age. But some people become problem drinkers only when they grow old and for reasons, directly connected with aging. As the proportion of older people is growing, alcoholism among the aged may become an increasingly important problem. In fact, alcoholism is one of the two biggest health problems among the elderly.

A significant number of people 60 years old and older have problems with alcohol. Up to 10 percent of the general elderly male population are problem drinkers, and approximately 10 percent of alcoholics in treatment are age 60 or older. In contrast, only 2 percent of the elderly female population are heavy or problem drinkers. As many as 1.6 million Americans over 65 may be alcoholics.

What is known about older problem drinkers indicates that their alcohol abuse differs in character from abuse by younger persons. Elderly alcoholics can be distinguished as belonging to one of two groups: those who began drinking at an early age and those who began drinking later in life. The "early-onset" alcoholics have more in common with the younger alcoholics as regards reasons for drinking and patterns and amount of consumption; "late-onset" alcoholics usually drink in response to the stresses of aging. Older alcoholics in general drink more in response to external rather than personality factors.

Elderly alcoholics generally consume less alcohol than younger ones, although they are more likely to drink daily. They have also been somewhat contradictorily characterized as tending to drink alone, at home, and to go on binges. Most elderly alcoholics seldom engage in more than mildly severe drinking, characterized by intoxication no more than once a month and only minimal related functional problems.

There are many reasons for the decrease in the consumption with increasing age. The capacity to consume alcohol declines with age, probably due to failing metabolism. The aged are often isolated, so there are fewer social occasions at which alcohol consumption is encouraged or sanctioned. Economic factors may play a part in limiting consumption as well. There also seems to be some correlation between age at onset of excessive alcohol use and later abstinence. Those who had developed drinking problems before age 40 tended to stop drinking by the time they reached their 70s; those who developed problems later did not stop.

Alcoholism in the elderly, at least "late-onset" alcoholism, can be regarded as symptomatic of a society that de-emphasizes a legitimate, comfortable, useful role for the aged. Researchers agree that the most common reasons for alcohol abuse by this age group include depression, loneliness, feelings of uselessness, bereavement, and loss of self-esteem. Retirement from a full, lifelong career can leave the older person feeling cast aside, obsolete, and old overnight. The desire for escape is, as in younger alcohol abusers, the primary reason for alcohol abuse by senior citizens.

Heavy drinking by the aged is particularly dangerous for several reasons. Most obvious is that the body systems of the aged are in a general state of decline. Those who have engaged in heavy drinking for many years may continue habits cultivated when their physiologic processes were more efficient, not realizing their decreasing capacity. This can put further strain on the liver and kidneys and exacerbate problems in almost all body systems: heart disease, for example, is definitely aggravated by alcohol.

Another deadly complication of alcohol use by the elderly is the very real possibility of drug interaction. The elderly consume a disproportionate amount of prescription and over-the-counter drugs, often self-administering excessive quantities. Alcohol-drug interaction is a serious potential problem: many drugs lose their therapeutic value when combined with alcohol; some combinations can cause death.

Alcohol use by elderly persons with medical problems can be harmful in another way. The somewhat anesthetic effect of alcohol can serve to mask pain that would otherwise be an indicator of an acute condition, such as the warning angina provides of heart attack.

A variety of complications that range in seriousness from minor to severe are the side effects of alcohol abuse in the elderly. Alcoholics may suffer from self-neglect, falls, confusion, and behavior that precipitates family quarrels.

There are numerous problems encountered in attempting to treat the elderly alcoholic, some of which are quite basic. There is widespread disagreement regarding how alcoholism itself should be defined, and, as we have already established, the elderly alcoholic does not necessarily manifest the classic symptoms of the disease. The most common definition—psychological or physical addiction—is difficult to employ: psychological addiction is hard to quantify, while the physical addiction theory normally defines addiction in terms of severe withdrawal symptoms, overlooking lesser withdrawal symptoms of varying intensity.

Diagnosis of alcoholism based on the quantity consumed and the frequency of consumption is no more reliable. Due to cultural differences in acceptable levels of drinking, it is difficult thus to identify or define deviant behavior.

A third definition of alcoholism involves the presence of certain social problems related to alcohol consumption. Unfortunately, most of these problems are not applicable to the elderly or stem from factors relating to aging itself rather than to alcohol abuse.

Diagnosis of alcoholism in the elderly is further complicated by the fact that persons displaying it are apt to hide themselves. Some feel that they have a limited time left to them and that they should be allowed to "enjoy" it as they wish. Worse, many are hidden by their families.

Once the elderly alcoholic is identified, there is some confusion as to where he/she should be treated—at an alcoholism treatment center or a facility for the elderly. Aside from reluctance on the part of the alcoholic and his/her family, there are other reasons why the alcoholism treatment center is not the best place for this particular client.

As was discussed previously, the older alcoholic's problem differs from that of younger problem drinkers. He/she views alcoholism differently. His/her reasons for drinking and his/her pattern of drinking are different. Being in treatment with a group much younger than himself/herself may intensify feelings of being old and out of place.

A recent study examined needs among the elderly for mental health and alcoholism treatment centers, and the advantages of extending Medicare coverage for treatment at these facilities. The results indicated that Medicare provider status for treatment centers would provide less expensive, more easily accessible mental health care to the elderly. Such a provision would, however, require an increased number of professionals with special training, orientation, and sensitivity to meet the particular problems faced by the elderly.

Alcoholism treatment centers are often reluctant to treat the elderly patient. Agencies often devote more attention to those clients who are able to demonstrate successful recovery in terms of restoration to gainful employment.

It has been determined that the most efficacious way of treating the elderly alcoholic is at centers for the elderly and through treatment at home. Although medical treatment for alcohol and age-related problems is of great importance, social therapy (since it treats the problems that generally cause older persons to drink) seems to be the most beneficial for the client. This involves the use of antidepressive medication for the clinically depressed, group socialization, and home visiting. Antabuse therapy is usually not needed for this group.

Concern for alcoholism in the elderly is growing and study of the problem is being given increasing attention, providing perhaps the best hope for ameliorating the situation.

Because of the special problems confronting the older drinker, information, resources, and expertise among agencies, and individuals need to be well coordinated and relevant to the issues involved. Policy-makers, legislators, program planners, and administrators can play a major role in developing a projected course of action.

# Incidence and Severity of the Native American Alcohol Problem

It is estimated that over one-half of the Native American population are consistent and excessive alcohol users. Thus, alcohol is considered the most serious health, social, and economic problem among Native Americans today.(60) The alcoholism death rate for the Native American and the Alaskan native during the past few years has ranged from 4.3 to 5.5 times the U.S. rate for all races.[6]

Roughly two-thirds of the alcoholism deaths among the Native American population are the result of cirrhosis of the liver with associated alcoholism. Another 30 percent result from alcoholism, and the remainder are due to alcoholic psychoses.

Historically it is generally agreed that Native Americans north of Mexico were unaware of distilled alcoholic spirits before the arrival of the Europeans in the 16th and 17th centuries, although some evidence exists that fermented beers and wines were used in some religious rites. Since Native Americans had little or no contact with alcohol in beverages, they did not develop cultural means for dealing with its problems; thus their lack of ways to control drinking made them easy victims of alcohol. For thousands of years western cultures have used alcohol for social and religious purposes and have established ways of regulating behavior more fully than has the Native American population. The lack of cultural norms has resulted in dangerous patterns of drinking among Native American groups. First, the use of alcohol as a focus for group activity has developed. A great deal of sharing of alcohol exists within Native American groups, with heavy pressure to give and accept freely from others. Many fear that if they fail to comply, they will incur social disapproval and rejection. Second, aggressive behavior often develops under the influence of alcohol. The same behavior would evoke rejection, disapproval, and punishment if the individual were not intoxicated. Large amounts of alcohol appear to produce feelings of despondency, self-hatred, fear, and violence. This may be one reason why half the people of all races who commit suicide and a third of those who lose their lives in murders have had significant amounts of alcohol in their bloodstreams at autopsy.

Unfortunately, the Native American male, like those in many other minority groups, usually works in menial, low-status jobs if he can find employment at all. He has virtually no chance to become self-assertive and experience feelings of personal worth. Moreover, conditions and attitudes prevail that make it easy for him to feel that a low level of performance is expected and that he is presumed to be irresponsible and unreliable. As a result, there are few avenues open for feeling self-worth other than gaining acceptance through fellowship in a drinking group. Available jobs are fewer once an individual becomes an alcoholic and gets to be known as such, and his income is lower if he does find work. Job security is extremely uncertain and frequently work is only temporary. In many instances there appears to be little advantage in working as opposed to obtaining welfare assistance; in point of fact, the receipt of welfare money can be an even more reliable source of income than working. When new industries are established on

[6]Adapted from National Institute of Mental Health, Division of Special Mental Health Programs, *Suicide, Homicide, and Alcoholism Among American Indians: Guidelines for Help,* DHEW Publication No (HSM) 73-9124, pp. 4-9.

reservations, they often employ only women; the men are thus left at home, which adds to feelings of emasculation and lack of responsibility as a family leader. Even when men are employed, they may be required to work at the same jobs as women, which contributes to lack of self-esteem, annoyance, animosity, disgust, and self-hatred. Women too are subjected to many stressful situations, including being the recipients of abuse from alcoholic husbands. By and large, women are less likely to develop alcoholism than men in most Native American communities for the reasons outlined above. Suicidal attempts are frequent among Native American women, however. When they move to cities, Native Americans feel detached from the security of their own surroundings and removed from their relatives and friends, and they frequently do not adapt well to urban living as it is now constituted for them. Many will return home discouraged, while others may drift from one slum to another in a large city. The result is an increase in the likelihood of drinking (and more recently drug abuse), with suicide and homicide as potential outcomes.

In one Native American community in the Northwest, records were kept during one year showing accidents related to drinking. Eighty percent of the auto accidents, 31 percent of accidental injuries, 94 percent of the fights involving injury, and all 35 suicide attempts were shown to be related to drinking. The Indian Health Service staff believes these figures to be conservative. A study in a southwestern Native American tribe showed that 47 percent of suicides involved intoxication at the time of or just before the act occurred. It has been shown that 43 percent of all arrests in the United States were related to drinking but the comparable figure for Native Americans was 76 percent. Drunkenness alone accounted for 71 percent of total Native American arrests. Nonalcoholic arrests were only slightly above the U.S. average. In a state penitentiary Native Americans comprised 34 percent of the inmate population, although in the total state census they comprised only 5 percent of the population. The majority of crimes were committed while under the influence of alcohol. The problem has existed for a number of years, as is shown by the fact that as far back as 1959, all 36 Native American prisoners in one federal prison had been convicted of murder or manslaughter while intoxicated.

Native American suicide rates appear to be twice the national average. Estimates place these alcohol-related suicides among Native Americans at 75-80 percent.(60) Social factors contributing to suicide and alcoholism consist of cultural identity conflicts, loss of tradition and heritage, prejudice and discrimination, movement away from spiritual interests, and peer-group pressures among adolescents.

Political factors include government paternalism and suppression by a dominant society. Such factors inhibit Native American self-expression, decision-making, and control of individual destiny.

Situational factors are contained for the most part in other aspects of the suicide profile. Time spent in boarding schools and the frequency of disrupted family units are particularly relevant.

In relation to education, 10 percent of all Native Americans over the age of 14 have not attended formal schools in white areas; nearly 60 percent have less than an eighth-grade education. It is difficult for Native Americans to attend schools because of racism on the part of white teachers, a white cultural bias as to what is important to learn and know (such as being on time), a language barrier, a lack of academic tradition (Native Americans had no formal schools for thousands of years), and the problem of isolation in remote areas. Forty-two percent of Native American children drop out before completing high school—a rate that is almost twice the national average.

In schools, Native Americans are subjected to a curriculum based on white educational materials. They find it difficult to identify with Anglo middleclass values. Their textbooks project cultural stigmas, as in stories of the cavalry and the Native Americans. There are few books written by Native Americans for Native American children.

The educational environment plays a major role in suicide among young Native Americans. Blocked educational opportunities; lack of exposure to extracurricular activities such as sports and interest groups; lack of interest and disinclination to try anything innovative among older white teachers; little change in curriculum over time; the separation from friends and relatives of students coming from far distances, and restriction of freedom—all contribute to the suicide and alcoholism problem among young Native Americans at boarding schools.

We must view the suicides and the alcoholism problem of the Native American as symptoms of a severe and often fatal disturbance. In attempting to provide solutions we must become cognizant of the clues that are frequently present, for they are more than merely clues—*they are cries for help.* We must alert ourselves to the causes and contributing factors such as unemployment, inadequate housing, an oppressive educational system, cultural conflicts, and loss of identity. These are the roots of the frustration that manifests itself in drinking and self-destruction.

Where can the answers be found? The answers lie within the Native American people themselves. Native Americans want to realize their *personal potential* by controlling their own future, making their own decisions, and involving Indian people in the implementation of these decisions. Every minority group destined to progress must reach this state of responsibility to renew and maintain cultural pride in its heritage, as well as promote individual self-esteem and motivation to succeed. Only by working together to develop themselvs and their enivornment can the Native Americans hope to solve these devastating social problems and restore a new dignity to their people, for they, like all human beings, must have *something to live for.*

## Alcohol Use and Abuse Among Black Americans

Black Americans constitute the largest ethnic minority group in the United States. Although Black Americans have been represented in national surveys of drinking practices and problems, they seldom have been the focus of research designed to analyze alcohol use and abuse in terms of their cultural norms, values, and beliefs, nor have the cultural variables that distinguish Black subgroups from one another been differentiated.

Alcohol appears to play a role in influencing crime in urban and rural Black communities. Blacks are more likely than whites to be victims of alcohol-related homicide. Some researchers attribute the apparently disproportionate devastation caused by alcoholism in the Black community to the widespread "ghettoization" and victimization of Blacks in the United States. The situation is seen as a separation and alienation of many Blacks from the common goals, purposes, and rewards of the larger society.

A major barrier to treatment of alcoholism among Blacks has been the lack of development of culture-specific treatment programs for Black alcoholics. Further research could center on specific areas of investigation, including patterns of alcohol use, social context of that use, definitions of alcohol abuse, and help-seeking patterns among Blacks. There is also a need for data concerning middle—and upper-class Blacks.(9)

## Alcohol Use and Abuse Among Hispanics

Across-the-board findings relating to Hispanics is difficult: the Hispanic population of the United States comprises a number of subgroups that differ widely in national origin and culture, and most research efforts tend to concentrate on only a small number of the individuals involved. Nevertheless, studies indicate that the extent of problem drinking among the Spanish-speaking population tends to be greater than among the general population, a finding supported by high alcohol-associated arrest and mortality data.[7] Problem drinking may be caused in part by the stress of acculturation—difficulty in learning English, lack of success in finding employment and housing, and prejudice and discrimination. Poverty rates are high among Hispanic Americans, and alcohol-related problems seem to run proportionately high. Alcohol use and abuse may also be related to minority-group status and its attendant discrimination and prejudice.

## Alcohol Use in the Gay Community [8]

While precise estimates of the number of gay alcoholics and alcohol abusers are not yet available, clinical and community observations suggest that these numbers may be substantial. The social structure of the gay community encourages drinking; the gay bar is the community center, and studies have shown that the largest portion of social time is spent in bars or at parties where alcohol is available. Other factors center on the stigma associated with both alcoholism and homosexuality. Further research is needed to bring about increased understanding and appropriate, sensitive intervention.

[7]NIAAA, *Alcohol and Health,* Second Special Report to the U.S. Congress from the Secretary of Health, Education, and Welfare, June 1974, p. 86.
[8]*Ibid.,* p. 88

## The Cost of Alcoholism to Industry

In recent years, industrial leaders had calculated industry's loss through alcoholism at $8 billion. New reports say the cost is near $16-20 billion, and that 6 percent of the average company's work force may be problem drinkers. In some industries, the percentage may even be higher. State and local government agencies lost another $6-8 billion because of drunken employees. According to some estimates, more than half the nation's alcoholics are employed. Yet, unless they can overcome their illness, most cannot function to their fullest ability and may eventually become unemployable.

An article in *Addictions* states the extent of the alcohol problems on industry: "An individual can be an employer whether he has 10 or 1,000 employees. But if he has 10, and one of them is incapacitated on the job that makes up 10% of his total work force. If that same worker is disruptive, he affects the morale, and possibly the earnings, of 100% of the work force."[9] Each such employee costs the company conservatively about 25 percent of his/her salary in absenteeism, tardiness, spoiled materials, and reduced effectiveness.(35) In addition, the industrial alcoholic is responsible for about 10 percent of deaths and injuries on the job—in fact, there are two to five times the occurrence of on-the-job accidents among alcoholics.(116)

Other industrial problems, impossible to show numerically, include friction with co-workers, lowered morale, bad executive decisions, and deteriorated public and customer relations. Excessive drinking unquestionably results in the loss of trained and experienced employees. This can be especially damaging to companies, since alcoholic employees are usually middle-aged, with many years of service behind them. Such experienced workers are among the most valuable assets of any firm. Because of this, many companies have found it cheaper to try to cure an alcoholic worker than to fire him/her. The NIAAA is helping industrial firms, as well as state and local governments, to develop alcoholism treatment and rehabilitation programs.

It is obvious that it is costly for a company to tolerate alcoholism. A list of direct and indirect loss areas would include the following:[10]

1. Absenteeism
2. Accidents
3. Bad decisions
4. Clowning, horseplay, fighting
5. Discharges
6. Dissention in work groups
7. Early retirements

[9]Milan Korcok, "Alcohol on the Job—What's Being Done," *Addictions* 22 (Winter 1975):5.

[10]*Company Controls of Drinking Problems: Studies in Personnel Policy,* Research Report No. 218 from the National Industrial Conference Board, Inc. (New York, 1970), p. 8.

8. Garnishments
9. Increased benefit costs
10. Lost sales
11. Lowered work efficiency and morale
12. Overtime payments necessitated by absent workers
13. Safety hazards
14. Supervisory time lost with alcoholic workers
15. Unfavorable public relations in the community

Companies have demonstrated that these losses and problems can be reduced by alcohol control programs, and that the costs of operating these programs are well below the benefits attained. The chart entitled "How It Works" [Figure 13] shows how a corporate alcoholism program that aims for early detection operates. The supervisor has a key role in setting the program in motion by discussing a change in work performance with employees. If a health-behavioral problem such as alcoholism is suspected, the employee is referred to the medical department of the company or to his/her family doctor. Often the supervisor briefs the medical department on signs observed suggesting that something is wrong, although the supervisor may not have discussed drinking with the employee.

According to Dr. Milton A. Maxwell, who has made intensive studies of the early identification of problems in industry, there are as many as 44 on-the-job signs which may appear in the problem drinker in industry. These are often characteristic of early- or middle-stage alcoholism. Fifteen of the most common on-the-job drinking signs are:[11]

1. Hangovers on the job
2. Morning drinking before going to work
3. Absenteeism, half-day or day
4. Increased nervousness, jitteriness
5. Drinking at lunchtime
6. Hand tremors
7. Drinking during working hours
8. Late to work
9. More unusual excuses for absences
10. Leaving work early
11. Leaving post temporarily
12. Avoiding boss or associates
13. More edgy and irritable
14. Using "breath purifiers"
15. Longer lunch periods

The employed problem drinker exhibits a combination of unsatisfactory performance and almost certain progressive deterioration if the condition goes unchecked. Conscientious management should neither tolerate nor ignore

[11]Kenneth A. Rouse, "Detour—Alcoholism Ahead," Kemper Insurance Company booklet, 1964, p. 2.

**FIGURE 13**
*How A Corporate Alcoholism Program Works*

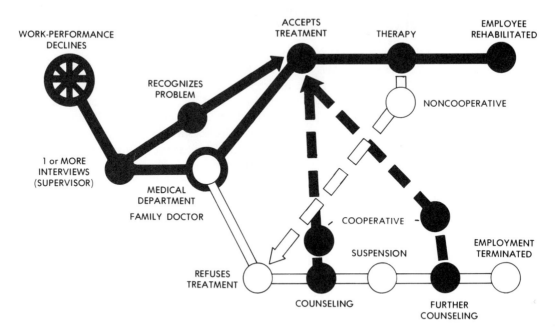

SOURCE: Adapted from *Company Controls for Drinking Problems: Studies in Personnel Policy,* Research Report No. 218 from the National Industrial Conference Board, Inc. (New York, 1970), p. 8.

him/her. Positive action by the employer, which is treatment-oriented, results in the retention of valued employees and eliminates excessive costs created by them.

Experience has shown that successful early identification programs for employed problem drinkers are based on five essentials:(7)

*A written policy* which specifies the procedures for identifying and confronting employees who may have drinking problems. This should include recognition by the organization that alcoholism (more usefully called "problem drinking") in the employment setting is a health problem, and that employees with that problem will not be penalized for seeking help.

*Specific channels* within the work organization, including designation of a program coordinator, whereby identified problem drinkers are counseled and, if necessary, referred to appropriate resources in the community for help in dealing with their problem.

*Training of managers and supervisors* regarding their responsibilities in implementing the program.

*Education of the entire work force* concerning policy, procedures, and the provision of help—without penalty—for problem drinking.

*Cooperation between management and labor unions* and other employee organizations in providing support for the program, its implementation, and its continuity.(19)

The early corporate programs, although few, have afforded an opportunity to develop strategies in the occupational area based on experience. The strategy recommended to organizations seeking clues for successful operation of an occupational program is based on the following four elements.[12]

*Recognition.* In most instances, problem drinking by an employee will show up in impaired job performance and absenteeism before the appearance of the severe classical symptoms of alcohol dependence. When supervision is competent, these early but repeated signs—poor work, patterned or suspicious absenteeism, or both—are easily recognized in spite of efforts by the employee to conceal them.

*Documentation.* Impaired performance sets the stage for intervention. Unlike most other social relationships, the link between the employer and employee is contractual. Repeated instances of inadequate job performance constitute a breach of this contract.

*Confrontation.* Problem drinking, accompanied by impaired performance, often occurs in employees who, having worked for years in one organization, have intense psychological and economic investment in their jobs. Confrontation of such an employee is a momentous event when fortified by documented inadequacy of job performance and the clear possibility that disciplinary action will be taken if he/she does not take steps to bring his/her performance back to an acceptable level documented jointly by labor and management. This confrontation usually precipitates a crisis which can motivate the employee to do something about the problem. Often he/she responds by accepting help offered by the organization, rather than face possible adverse action that may shatter his/her central life role. In many instances the confrontation undermines the basic rationalization which enabled the employee to avoid recognizing his/her problem—the notion that drinking did not affect his/her work ("If I am doing my job, I can't be one of those . . .").

*Offer of assistance.* The amount and kind of assistance offered depends on the capability and circumstances of the employer. Implementing a program to identify and help the problem drinker recover his/her health may require an investment in new personnel and procedures, additional supervisory training, and employee education. If the program is correctly viewed as a means of regaining the productivity of skilled employees—in whom the organization already has considerable investment—it is an asset to typical company goals. In many cases, the program can be located in existing personnel or medical departments.

---

[12]NIAAA, *Alcohol and Health,* p. 170.

Even on a short-term basis, industry's helping alcoholics can pay handsome dividends. Table 23 shows the employee benefits one company experienced by providing an alcoholic treatment program for 101 employees with drinking problems.

### Table 23
### Benefits of an alcoholism program for industry

|  | Before Treatment | After Treatment | Percentage Change |
|---|---|---|---|
| Lost Work Hours | 47,182 | 24,185 | −49% |
| Sickness and accident benefits | $33,339 | $23,861 | −29% |
| Leaves of absence | 112 | 49 | −56% |
| Grievances | 26 | 6 | −78% |
| Discipline | 102 | 38 | −63% |
| Accidents | 51 | 9 | −82% |

SOURCE: William S. Dunkin, "From the Boiler to the Boardroom—Getting Booze Off the Company's Back," *Listen,* pp. 7-8.

## Cost to the Nation*

The President wants a balanced federal budget, in spite of declining tax revenues. As a result, Congress has been forced to cut back in public services, with alcohol programs being one of the target areas for spending reductions.

As a result of the economic downturn of the past two years, state budgets for alcohol programs are also facing cutbacks or, at best, continuation programs, most of which are barely making a dent in combatting alcohol problems.

When alcohol program personnel plead for the money they need for prevention and treatment programs, they are often told . . . "We can't spend the money we do not have."

That answer may or may not seem logical, depending on your point of view. One viewpoint is that we have no choice about paying the cost of the alcohol problems. In one way or another, society *will* pay the costs.

The choice we face, according to this point of view, is *how* we will meet the cost of alcohol problems in society.

Of course it is more humane to prevent alcohol problems, and to get alcoholics into treatment so that they can return to society as productive, tax-paying citizens.

It is not only more humane, in this viewpoint, it is also more cost-effective to invest money in prevention and treatment programs.

Whether you agree with this logic or not, it is important to consider the cost of alcohol problems to society. Of course there are no precise methods to do this, but

*This Section is adapted from: *The Bottom Line,* American Businessmen's Research Foundation, Vol. 4, August 1980, pp. 10-16.

in the information which follows, we have attempted to revise and update the best data which is available today on the cost of alcohol problems to society.

And, we have suggested what seems to us to be a logical approach for generating more revenue to invest in alcohol programs.

The first reliable national cost figures for alcohol problems were reported in the Department of Health, Education and Welfare's Second Special Report to the U.S. Congress on *Alcohol and Health,* which was released in June, 1974. Based on figures supplied through a study financed by the NIAAA, the cost of alcohol problems in the U.S. for 1971 were pegged at $25.37 billion (Table A).

### Table A
### 1971 Alcohol-Related Expenses

| | |
|---|---|
| Lost Production | $9,350,000,000 |
| Health and Medical | 8,290,000,000 |
| Motor Vehicle Accidents | 6,440,000,000 |
| Alcohol Programs, Research | 640,000,000 |
| Criminal Justice System | 510,000,000 |
| Social Welfare System | 140,000,000 |
| Total | 25,370,000,000 |

## Second Study

In the Department of Health, Education and Welfare's Third Special Report to the U.S. Congress on *Alcohol and Health,* (June, 1978), the economic cost of alcohol problems to society was pegged at $42.75 billion. The period studied was 1975, which, when compared to the previous period studied (1971), showed an increase of 68.5 percent. (Table B)

### Table B
### 1975 Alcohol-Related Expenses

| | |
|---|---|
| Lost Production | $19,640,000,000 |
| Health and Medical | 12,740,000,000 |
| Motor Vehicle Accidents | 5,140,000,000 |
| Violent Crime | 2,860,000,000 |
| Social Responses | 1,940,000,000 |
| Fire Losses | 430,000,000 |
| Total | $42,750,000,000 |

All categories reflected higher costs in the 1975 study, except the figure for motor vehicle accidents.

This decreased, as a result of a more conservative approach in the methodology and, to some degree, a changed pattern of social behavior on the highways. Even though the cost figure for alcohol-related accidents decreased in the 1975 study, the amount was still significant.

## Lost Production

The largest economic cost, amounting to some $19.64 billion, was in the area of lost production of goods and services. This figure was derived from three separate factors:

1) Lost market production amounting to $15.46 billion.
2) Lost military production amounting to $411 million.
3) Lost future production from excess mortality in 1975 amounting to $3.77 billion.

The lost market production figure was computed by estimating the difference in average household income between those households which have a male alcohol abuser and those who do not. The NIAAA study offers a breakdown of these loss differences for various age levels from 21-59. (Table C)

### Table C
### Estimated Lower Earnings in 1975 of Households Having an Alcohol-Abusing Male Parent, According to Age

| Age Group | Total Households Including a Male | % Households With Male Alcohol Abuser | Households With Male Alcohol-Abuser Parent (est.) | Differences in Average Household Income (est.) | 1975 Lower Earnings Due to Alcohol Abuse (est.) |
|---|---|---|---|---|---|
| 21-29 | 7,941,000 | 27.6% | 2,191,700 | $2,122 | $ 4,650,000,000 |
| 30-39 | 11,502,000 | 16.7% | 1,920,800 | 2,275 | 4,370,000,000 |
| 40-49 | 12,290,000 | 15.1% | 1,855,800 | 2,494 | 4,630,000,000 |
| 50-59 | 10,821,000 | 13.6% | 1,471,700 | 1,278 | 1,810,000,000 |
| Adjusted 1975 Total (estimated) | | | | | $15,460,000,000 |

SOURCE: NIAAA

## Conservative Figures

The cost estimate figures for lost production were conservative for several reasons. First, they took into account only males between the ages of 21 and 59. Workers under 21 and over 60 were not included in the NIAAA cost study, and both of these omitted age segments do experience a significant number of alcohol problems.

In general, lost production was considered in terms of the goods and services that usually flow through the traditional market system. When alcohol abuse lowers a worker's productivity, the goods and services not produced as a consequence do not appear in the marketplace.

However, individuals also produce goods and services in nonmarket areas such as within the household, and society also suffers considerable economic loss of these goods and services, too. The NIAAA study made no attempt, though, to estimate the alcohol-related losses resulting from nonsalaried problem drinkers such as housewives.

With the growing number of working women at all age levels, and with recognition of problems of alcohol abuse among women, the production loss figure stated by the NIAAA is indeed conservative. In reality, it should probably have been from 25 percent to 30 percent higher, if women and those under 21 and over 60 were included.

## Health and Medical

The second largest cost of alcohol problems was for health and medical care. Excess mortality is particularly high for alcoholism and cirrhosis of the liver, the disease usually associated with alcohol abuse. But significant alcohol related mortality rates also result from several other causes including heart disease, cancer, pneumonia and stomach and duodenal ulcers. Given the pattern of excess mortality, the researchers indicated that one would logically expect considerable excess morbidity as well. These illness costs were computed by type of expenditure in Table D.

### Table D
### Estimated National Health Expenditures as a Result of Alcohol Abuse in 1975, According to Type of Expenditure

| Type of Expenditure | Total Adult Population Expenditures | Expenditures Resulting From Alcohol Abuse | Expenditures Resulting From Alcohol Abuse As A Percentage Of Total Expenditures |
|---|---|---|---|
| Health Service and Supplies: | | | |
| Hospital Care | $ 42,300,000,000 | $ 8,400,000,000 | 19.9% |
| Physicians' Services | 17,900,000,000 | 1,300,000,000 | 7.3% |
| Dentists' Services | 6,200,000,000 | | |
| Other Professional Services | 1,700,000,000 | 120,000,000 | 7.3% |
| Drugs and Drug Sundries | 8,900,000,000 | 280,000,000 | 3.2% |
| Eyeglasses and Appliances | 2,000,000,000 | | |
| Nursing Home Care | 8,800,000,000 | 190,000,000 | 2.2% |
| Expenses for Prepayment and Administration | 3,900,000,000 | 780,000,000 | 19.9% |
| Government Public Health Services | 2,500,000,000 | 390,000,000 | 13.1% |
| Other Health Services | 3,000,000,000 | 330,000,000 | 13.1% |
| Research and Medical Facilities Construction | 6,100,000,000 | 780,000,000 | 13.1% |
| Training and Education | 2,300,000,000 | 170,000,000 | 7.3% |
| | $105,600,000,000 | $12,740,000,000 | 12.1% |

Of the $12.74 billion spent for alcohol-related health services, the largest share, or $8.4 billion, went for hospital care. This meant that approximately $1 in every $5 spent in the U.S. for hospital care in 1975 went for alcohol-related problems.

Expenditures for dentists' services and eyeglasses and appliances were omitted from the NIAAA study, due to the difficulty of getting accurate cost data. As a result, health care costs in the NIAAA study would also be on the conservative side, because the researchers indicated that the available literature revealed little about proportionate costs attributed to alcohol abuse. The total costs of health care due to alcohol abuse and alcoholism in the health care field, therefore, are understated by this amount.

## Motor Vehicle Accidents

The third largest economic cost assessment was the $5.14 billion which resulted from alcohol-related minor vehicle accidents. Alcohol affects drivers by impairing their vision, coordination and judgment, and tends to increase the risk of motor vehicle accidents in proportion to the blood alcohol concentration of the driver.

The presence of alcohol is also associated with more severe crashes, tending to intensify the consequences when accidents do happen.

The NIAAA cost figure for motor vehicle accidents was based on a National Highway Safety Administration (NHSA) study of motor vehicle crashes in 1975 which showed a cost to society of $37 billion. Excluding less tangible items, this figure was reduced to $29 billion. Defining alcohol abuse in terms of blood alcohol concentration above 0.05%, this resulted in a cost figure of $6 billion.

From that $6 billion figure the researchers subtracted the cost of lost production, hospital care and premature death which was computed elsewhere, with $5.14 billion remaining as a conservative estimate of the direct costs of alcohol-related motor vehicle crashes in 1975.

## Violent Crime

Various studies indicate a relationship between alcohol use and crime. In the case of homicide, a blood alcohol level above 0.10% has been found in 67% of the offenders. In cases of forcible rape, 24% of the offenders were determined to be drinking at the time of the crime. For aggravated assault, it was estimated that alcohol was present in 30% of the offenders, representing the midpoint of the range of estimates derived from several research studies.

The NIAAA researchers estimated that the economic cost of violent crime in the U.S. during 1975 was approximately $3.3 billion. This figure was derived from a modification of the cost of crime reported by the President's Commission on Law Enforcement and Administration of Justice. Costs associated with alcohol in crimes of homicide, forcible rape and aggravated assault amounted to $2.1 billion.

Costs of the response of the cimrinal justice system were estimated at $760 million. This resulted in a total estimated cost for violent crime of $2.86 billion.

Consistent with their practice of erring on the conservative side, the NIAAA research team included no cost figures for unreported crime which might be associated with alcohol, nor did they estimate a cost figure for the considerable property damage done by vandals under the influence of alcohol.

## Social Response Costs

The estimated cost of social response systems to alcohol problems was computed by the NIAAA researchers at $2.7 billion, from which the costs of criminal justice system responses to violent crime were deducted, leaving a net cost of $1.94 billion.

Social responses to alcohol problems can be divided into two general kinds of government programs—direct and indirect. Direct programs are those specifically established to combat alcoholism through case-finding, prevention, treatment, rehabilitation, research and education. Indirect programs include expenditures directed at alleviating various social problems, such as social welfare programs which are called for because of alcohol problems.

In the other cost estimates, the concern was with the cost of the problem itself, but under this category, the concern was with the cost of society's responses to a particular problem.

The five areas of social response which were convered by the NIAAA study are shown in Table E.

### Table E
### Estimated Costs of Social Responses to
### Alcohol Problems

| | |
|---|---|
| Social Welfare System | $1,273,800,000 |
| Alcohol Programs | 74,700,000 |
| Highway Safety Programs | 29,200,000 |
| Fire Protection | 392,000,000 |
| Criminal Justice (Nonviolent Crime) | 170,100,000 |
| Total | $1,939,800,000 |

## Social Welfare Costs

Estimates for the alcohol abuse costs of the social welfare system were based on those parts most likely to include a significant response specifically to alcohol abuse. They included 5 areas.

1) Unemployment Compensation Programs
2) Public Assistance Programs Providing Income Maintenance
3) Special Income Maintenance Programs, such as Emergency Relief
4) Workmen's Compensation Programs
5) Other Special Welfare and Social Service Programs

Excluding transfer payments that constitute nearly 90% of the expenditures, the total real costs of these components of the social welfare system were estimated to be $5.3 billion. A significant proportion, amounting to $1.3 billion, was estimated to be associated with alcohol abuse.

## Highway Safety Program Costs

Alcohol abuse increases the risk and intensifies the consequences of motor vehicle accidents and fires. Economic costs are manifested in the loss of life, personal injuries, and property damage.

Society responds to these real costs by expending considerable sums on highway safety and fire protection programs. In a study by Berry and others, it was estimated that 18.5% of the cost of automobile accidents and 11.2% of the cost of fires in 1975 were attributable to alcohol abuse.

## Nonviolent Crime Costs

Because alcohol abuse is associated with crime, particularly violent crime, the social system includes a criminal justice component to cope with this antisocial behavior.

In 1975, some $17.2 billion was spent within the criminal justice system. It was estimated that nearly $1 billion was attributable to problems of alcohol abuse. The major proportion of this cost was computed under the cost of violent crimes, and the remainder, for nonviolent crimes, was shown by the NIAAA research team under this section of their report.

## Fire Losses

The economic cost of alcohol-related fires in 1975 was estimated to be about $604.4 million, or approximately 11% of the estimated total economic costs of fires.

Approximately $107.3 million reflects double counting that has already been estimated under lost production and health care costs and therefore was deducted from the total costs in this section, resulting in a net cost of alcohol-related fires in 1975 of $434.1 million.

Despite the limitations of research in this area, this estimate approximates the cost of fires that can reasonably be attributed to alcohol abuse. Alcohol abuse may contribute to the cause of fire in the first place, and it may serve to intensify the consequences.

There is evidence that alcohol abuse contributes to the number of fire fatalities and burn injuries.

Included in the $604.4 million estimate are approximately $206 million as a result of lost production from premature death, $119.7 million in medical costs, $15.1 million in lost production from personal injury, and $209.6 million from property damage.

The estimate of the cost of fire fatalities may have been too conservative, because it was based on the lowest proportion of fatalities in which alcohol served to impede escape.

## Updating Alcohol Problem Costs

The total estimated cost of alcohol problems to society in 1975 of $42.75 billion was based on six areas in which reasonable estimates could be developed.

These estimates by the NIAAA researchers tended to understate the true economic impact, as has been noted in several areas of the investigation.

The NIAAA policy was that it would be better to be on the conservative side than to open themselves to accusations of exaggeration.

Although there are no more recent studies to give a current figure on economic costs of alcohol problems, it would seem reasonable to apply the change in the Consumer Price Index (CPI) to the 1975 figures to bring them up to date.

In our judgment, this would represent a conservative approach, since the 1975 figures were 68.5 percent higher than the 1971 figures in the two NIAAA studies.

At the same time, the CPI rose by only 32.9 percent in this four-year period.

## Estimating 1981 Costs of Alcohol Problems

Based on the 1967 index (1967=100), the Consumer Price Index rose from 161.2 in 1975 to 281.1 for 1981, for an increase of 74.3 percent.

By applying this 42.7 percent increase to the NIAAA's 1975 cost figures, we have what is shown in TABLE F.

### Table F
### 1981 Alcohol-Related Expenses

| | |
|---|---|
| Lost Production | $34,232,520,000 |
| Health and Medical | 22,205,820,000 |
| Motor Vehicle Accidents | 8,959,020,000 |
| Violent Crime | 4,984,980,000 |
| Social Responses | 3,381,420,000 |
| Fire Losses | 749,490,000 |
| TOTAL | $68,513,250,000 |

1981 expenses estimated by Hafen

## "Study" Questions Validity of NIAAA Data

A 165-page "study" has been submitted to the Department of Treasury and to the Department of Health and Human Services of the federal government questioning the validity of NIAAA data not only concerning the cost of alcohol problems, but other NIAAA estimates which give some indication of the seriousness of alcohol problems in our present society.

The "study" was conducted by the Columbia University School of Public Health and concluded:

". . . there is little sound basis for such claims as there being upwards of 10 million problem drinkers, including alcoholics, in the adult population and that their number is increasing; that there are 1.5 to 2.25 million problem drinkers among women, that there are over 3 million problem drinkers among youth; and that heavy consumption of alcohol by pregnant women leads consistently to a cluster of birth defects — the so-called Fetal Alcohol Syndrome (FAS); that half of all motor vehicle accident fatalities are alcohol-related; and that the cost of alcohol abuse in 1975 was $43 billion."

It ought to be obvious that no one has a head count on the number of problem drinkers and alcoholics in the U.S. (or anywhere else) and that it is virtually impossible to come up with irrefutable data in all the various areas of alcohol-related problems.

However, the NIAAA research does present what we feel is a sound and reasonable estimate for such things as the costs of alcohol-related problems to society.

All the researchers are not in agreement, but the NIAAA data errs on the conservative side, without exception. If anything, the NIAAA figures understate the dimensions and costs of alcohol problems.

And, whereas the Columbia University School of Public Health is indeed a prestigious institution, we would still question the conclusions of this study, as well as others which are funded by the liquor industry.

One reason why we question the conclusions of such studies is that DISCUS has an unblemished record of never having one of their research projects come up with conclusions which are contrary to the liquor industry philosophy. . .

1) That alcohol problems are overstated. They are not really as bad as the government (or anyone else) would have you believe, and

2) That it isn't the alcohol that causes the problems. It's people, the environment or something else.

## Where do you get the Money for Alcohol Programs?

In an effort to balance the federal budget and perhaps even offer some form of a tax cut, both the President and Congress are indeed faced with a dilemma . . . Should they cut government-financed services, or is there a way to provide adequate funding for needed services such as alcohol programs while sticking with a balanced budget?

Our suggestion is to provide funding for alcohol programs through an increase in taxes on beer, wine and distilled spirits at the federal level.

There is nothing new about this idea . . . it has come up with a fair degree of consistency over the past decade, but each time it has been defeated by Washington's powerful liquor lobby.

Douglas Metz, Executive Vice President of the Wine and Spirits Wholesalers of America recently commented on the liquor lobby's victory in the current session of Congress by stating. . .

"Attempts to include an increase in the federal tax on alcoholic beverages as a part of a $4.2 billion package of tax increases to balance the fiscal year 1981 budget have failed.

Strong grassroots (liquor) industry opposition, including objections from wholesalers in states having Senators and Congressmen on the two Congressional tax writing committees, have helped forestall consideration of a 20 to 50 percent increase in taxes on beverage alcohol."

There are four persuasive reasons why alcohol taxes should be increased at the federal level in order to provide alcohol program funding.

1) Federal taxes on beer, wine and distilled spirits have remained unchanged for nearly 30 years. The last tax boost for alcoholic beverages came in 1951.

2) The prices for alcoholic beverages have remained relatively stable in our inflationary economy, largely because brewers, vintners and distillers have had no increase in their tax rates.

For example, the Consumer Price Index overall rose by 74.3 percent from 1975 to 1981.

At the same time, prices for alcoholic beverages rose only 25.8 percent. Since beer, wine and liquor are luxuries, not necessities, in the consumer budget, it would not be out of line to boost alcohol taxes, at least to keep liquor prices in line with the rest of the CPI.

3) Alcohol revenues have not kept pace with the increasing cost of alcohol problems. Our conservative estimate of the cost of alcohol problems to society, based on the NIAAA research data and the CPI indicates an increase in the cost of alcohol problems in the U.S. of $25.7 billion from 1975-1981. At the same time, estimated alcohol revenues have gone up only $7.2 billion, from $9.7 to $16.9 during the same five-year period. Alcohol revenues (national, state and local) have gone up only 43.1 percent in the past five years, while the CPI has increased 74.3 percent.

4) Taxes paid on alcoholic beverages are "voluntary taxes," and most of these taxes are paid by the persons who need help from alcohol programs. It is generally accepted that a small number of drinkers consume a large percentage of beer, wine and spirits in the U.S. An ABMRF analysis of NIAAA data on drinking practices concluded that 10 percent of the drinking age population consumes 73 percent of the beer, wine and liquor in the U.S. Within this 10 percent of the drinking age population are the problem drinkers and alcoholics, a large share of the target population for alcohol programs. Any increase in taxes would be borne disproportionately by this group of drinkers who would, in effect, be prepaying for services and programs they need in advance, through the taxes on their drinks.

## Stumbling Blocks to Acceptance

One of the chief stumbling blocks to any tax increase on alcoholic beverages is the liquor industry itself. Their objections are based on two factors. . .

1) Any increase in taxes raises prices, and may cut down on sales. (Although this argument may seem contradictory to another philosophy of the liquor industry which is that prices, as well as liquor control laws, age laws, etc. really have no impact on how much people drink.)

2) Specific objection will come to any liquor tax increase which might either be earmarked for alcohol programs or which might be mentioned by lawmakers as an "offset" for an alcohol program expenditure. The liquor industry objects to the association between alcoholic beverage taxes and alcohol programs because of the implication that it might be *alcohol* that causes the problems of alcoholism, drunk driving, etc. (Acceptance of that could lead to further controls on the products they manufacture and market.)

The second major stumbling block to increased alcohol taxes as the basis for more adequate alcohol program funding comes from what we would term the "Prohibition Hangover."

This phenomenon of the "Prohibition Hangover" has several aspects, but as it relates to alcohol taxes and alcohol programs, it causes people, particularly in the alcohol programs field, to resist the tie-in, on the basis that such a move signals a "return to Prohibition."

Alcohol program personnel who hold to this philosophy feel that any connection between the product (beer, wine, spirits) and the problem (alcoholism, drunk driving, etc.) is a "simplistic" approach, one which returns us to the Probhition Era, when society equated the product with the problem.

## We Will Pay, One Way or Another

Our objection to cutting back on funding for alcohol programs is based on the philosophy that society will pay, one way or another, for alcohol problems. The $68 billion figure which we arrived at by applying the CPI to the NIAAA's 1975 data, we feel, is a modest estimate of what these problems are costing our society today.

Much better that we mount programs of prevention and treatment to deal with these problems, so that there would be a reasonable chance of preventing some from suffering, and returning others from their life of suffering to become useful, productive citizens.

And what better way to pay for such programs than to let those who voluntarily *choose* to drink pay for these programs. There is evidence that increased prices would cut down some on alcohol consumption, but then that in itself might serve as a means of preventing alcohol problems.

# 7

# Treatment
# of Alcoholism

A report from the National Institute on Alcohol Abuse and Alcoholism indicated that alcoholism is the country's most untreated treatable disease; as many as two-thirds of its victims can recover. (6) And these statistics could be higher if more people were guided to and received the appropriate treatment.

Yet there persists in our society a number of myths and misunderstandings that make it difficult for alcoholics to seek and obtain the help they need. We still think of alcoholism as a weakness rather than an illness, an attitude which encourages problem drinkers and their families to hide their "sins" instead of facing the problems and seeking treatment. And many people—laymen and medical personnel alike—still consider alcoholism untreatable, and the person with alcohol problems intractable and unwilling to be helped. None of these assumptions are true. Alcoholics Anonymous (AA) took the lead in shifting away from the "misconduct" concept of the disorder and toward a treatment approach. They saw that something far more complicated than bad behavior was involved in alcoholism, and that the traditional "treatment" of punishing the offender neither helped him nor deterred others. An important part of their approach was the identification of alcoholism as an illness.

## Complexity of Treatment

The causes of alcoholism are so many and appear in such differing constellations from person to person that one cannot consider treating alcoholism as if it were a single illness with an identifiable and specific etiology, a known course, and a

195

proven response to a particular chemical agent or medical treatment. Alcoholism is the result of complex and interacting factors. About the only characteristic shared by most of the alcoholic population is a pattern of repeated alcohol abuse that acts as a form of self-treatment for the sufferer.[1]

The kinds of people afflicted with alcoholism are probably as varied as humanity itself, and a variety of treatment techniques have been developed. Yet other, new forms of treatment are being developed. Although each technique has its partisans, the critical research has not been done to demonstrate convincingly which approach works best with which specific person.

There is some general misunderstanding about the pain experienced by the alcoholic person. Sometimes we forget this, however, and view the alcoholic person only as a fun-loving, irresponsible, and childish person who is given over to the immediate gratification of every impulse. As a matter of fact, such a being exists within every one of us. Yet on reaching maturity we have to deny this part of ourselves. Thus when it looks as though the alcoholic person is not playing the game of adulthood fairly, we get angry with him/her and attempt to teach him/her a lesson or to give him/her the "good-old-kick-in-the-pants" treatment. Sometimes this creates an ambivalence in those who treat the alcoholic patient—an ambivalence based on an overt and conscious wish to help the alcoholic patient, and a covert and unconscious wish to punish him/her. These conflicting feelings may distort a treatment program.

## Pain of Alcoholism

The pain the alcoholic person feels is the pain of self-loathing and humiliation . . . from loss of the respect of his family and friends . . . from growing isolation and loneliness . . . from the awareness that he is throwing away much of his unique and creative self and gradually destroying his body and soul. He doesn't usually mean to get drunk, really drunk—he just wants to take the value from alcohol. Getting drunk, really drunk as only an alcoholic person becomes, is a nightmare of lost memories, retching, vertigo, the shakes, and a profound melancholy of regret. Sometimes it becomes a living nightmare of terrifying visions, screaming accusatory voices, and convulsions.

Who would seek such experiences knowingly? From the intrapsychic viewpoint, heavy drinking is a form of adaptation or adaptive repair that has gotten out of control. Maladaptive symptoms are developed and maintained tenaciously because they are useful. For example, a phobia is developed as a way to hide a serious neurotic fear behind some irrational fear, such as fear of heights or of closed spaces or of water. The irrationally feared thing is then avoided so that awareness of the underlying neurotic fear can be avoided. In addition, once stuck

---

[1]The first three sections are adapted from NIAAA, *Alcohol and Health,* First Special Report to the U.S. Congress on Alcohol and Health from the Secretary of Health, Education, and Welfare, DHEW Publications No. (HSM) 72-9099, p. 71.

with such a problem-solving technique, the unhealthy coping mechanism can be used for secondary advantages such as avoiding responsibilities.

## Value of Alcoholism

Alcohol has many such advantages. Indeed, it is the ubiquitous and quick problem-solving potential of this substance which is our major problem. In small doses for social drinkers, it gives a pleasantly softening and mood-elevating effect that facilitates social interaction. A slight "buzz" is experienced as pleasurable. For the alcoholic person, however, a "big bust" has become a necessity for survival. It may provide euphoria to relieve apathy and sadness, a reduction of apprehension when more and more of life seems too stressful, or oblivion to blot out loneliness and disappointment. For some, it may provide a deliciously prolonged state of self-pity and destruction with which to punish someone.

More attention needs to be directed to the "value" of alcohol in helping the alcoholic individual cope—albeit in a sick way—with some of his most deeply hurting problems. Therein lies the dilemma: The devastating effects of alcoholism are so obvious that we are bewildered by patients' apparently evading or frustrating the best treatment efforts. But when heavy drinking is seen as an adaptive phenomenon, we are not so perplexed that people can actually treat themselves this way. This view opens up therapeutic opportunities. But it also brings a humble sense of respect for the symptom—alcoholism—and the knowledge that the solution will not be smiple or easy. A few lectures on the evil effects of alcohol will not suffice, nor will increasing life's pain by punishment. Having accepted the reality of alcoholism as a chronic and often recurring sickness, one becomes more tolerant of relapses—the so-called "slips"—by the patient and, at the same time, more optimistic about the long-range benefits of treatment.

## Treatment and Motivation of the Alcoholic[2]

Several studies have shown that both professionals and laymen view the alcoholic as a person who "chooses" to drink and therefore entraps him/herself in alcoholism. Since the alcoholic person begot his/her alcoholism, the argument goes, it remains his/her responsibility and choice to lift himself/herself out of it by his/her own bootstraps; accordingly, nothing can be done by way of therapeutic intervention for him/her until he/she undertakes his/her own rehabilitation.

It is paradoxical yet understandable that the alcoholic person is thought to act with intent and choice when, in fact, the essential characteristic of his/her illness is that he/she is disabled from directing his/her actions, especially where alcohol is concerned. But the layman and professional alike see him/her as suffering from a

[2]This and the next section are adapted from NIAAA, *Alcohol and Health,* Second Special Report to the U.S. Congress from the Secretary of Health, Education, and Welfare, June 1974, p. 145.

self-"chosen" condition, and this gives rise to the impression that an alcoholic person who does not deliberately "choose" treatment will not profit from it.

It is notable that successful alcoholism programs are those that have an aggressive outreach. Alcoholic persons do respond to treatment alternatives when they are offered. It has been demonstrated that the failure of treatment often does not lie in the patient's poor motivation but rather in failure to provide treatment alternatives and to maintain close contact with him/her.

# Trends in Treatment of Alcoholism

Significant progress toward improving the care provided for alcoholic people may be made, not only by developing new and better treatments, but also by bettering the systems under which care is delivered.

Treatment and rehabilitation should seek to disrupt the alcoholic's pattern of alcohol abuse, reestablish stability in life, help him/her recognize and accept his/her problem, establish new behavior patterns, and build continuing support for his/her new life. In other words, therapy should prepare the alcoholic to live comfortably as a nondrinker and develop effective living skills.

"Tremendous efforts have been made to help sufferers realize that it is possible to live without the drug (alcohol) to which they have become addicted and that comparative comfort is attainable without pursuing a drug effect that, at best, is transitory and, all too often can lead to a broken life."[3]

Treatments of alcoholism have tended to be based on one of two common policies. Some treatment centers, like some private practitioners, specialize in some single modality: disulfiram (Antabuse), or conditioned reflex, or behavior modification, or group therapy, or psychodrama, or individual counseling, or diet control, or any other of the dozens of possible techniques. The patient has to fit the treatment. If he/she does, he/she is helped. But if it was not suitable for him/her, the effort has mostly gone to waste. Other treatment centers have the opposite sort of policy. Their patients are exposed to a variety of methods of a salad-like mixture: group therapy, religious counseling, psychodrama, individual counseling, conjoint-spouse sessions, relaxation lessons, didactic lectures, disulfiram—and, often AA meetings. The idea is that "something" may work. Quite often, something does. This is sometimes evidenced by the fact that the patient continues to attend AA meetings after he is discharged.

The problem with both of these policies is the waste of human resources and the lack of economy. The single-specialty method wastes staff as well as patient resources in treating individuals not suited to the particular method. The multiple-method center wastes its resources in applying several unnecessary treatment modalities to each of its patients.

Recent national surveys have indicated that indeed a community alcoholism

---

[3]Marvin A. Block, "Don't Place Alcohol on a Pedestal," *Journal of the American Medical Association,* May 10, 1976, p. 2103.

rehabilitation program needs to have a variety of methods and resources available. But to be effective does not require exposing every patient to all the possible treatments. Instead, adopting a social-systems approach, a community-oriented program should take into account the differences among the patients, as well as the interactions of the several components in the society, and systematically seek to fit the appropriate treatment to each individual.

This idea was expressed thirty years ago. Its implementation on a broad scale, however, has become possible only recently with the movement toward community-oriented programs. Under such programs it is possible to match certain types of patients to the most suitable types of helping facilities or agencies or programs or methods of treatment. Undoubtedly treatment programs could maximize their effectiveness by clearly identifying the type of alcoholic population they propose to serve, the goals most feasible for that population, and what methods can be expected most nearly to achieve those goals. Undoubtedly, success rates could be maximized if the expectations of a group of patients are sensibly matched to the helping resource. And, in this context, it would become possible to carry out tightly designed evaluations that would clearly measure the effectiveness of each program.

## General Systems Theory[4]

A general systems theory approach can help to clarify the complexities of alcoholism. In the field of human actions, the general systems theory holds that behavior is composed of several layers of action and reaction, with each layer related to other layers that are more or less complex—or above or below it—in a systems hierarchy. Thus we cannot treat disordered behavior by assigning ultimate cause to one system, and then treating that system. Rather, multiple interacting systems must be taken into account.

Unfortunately, the systems approach precludes any easy answer. But the process of searching for answers is the "childhood" of any science and may be the forerunner of successful solutions.

The systems to be reviewed for therapeutic opportunities in the field of alcoholism are:

Biological
    Biochemical-celluar
    Organ-body
Intrapsychic
Interpersonal
Social
    Small group
    Large Group
Societal

[4]Adapted from NIAAA, *Alcohol and Health,* First Special Report, p. 72.

## Biological: Biochemical-cellular

The ill effects of alcohol on the body rather than the basic phenomenon of alcoholism itself have been of greatest interest to medical investigators and physicians, possibly because they feel more at home in this field. Some physicians confuse the treatment of alcohol intoxication with the treatment of alcoholism; nonmedical people are as much in error by thinking that the treatment of intoxication is not important in the treatment of alcoholism itself. Nevertheless detoxification, which is actually only the treatment of acute medical symptoms, is a vital first step in helping alcoholic individuals.

Much is known today about the metabolism of alcohol and its pharmacological, metabolic, physiological, and biochemical effects on the human body. Improved detoxification processes have reduced the mortality and morbidity rate of severe intoxication and postintoxication states. The usual procedure is to use anticonvulsant drugs and sedative compounds to prevent seizures and delirium tremens during the period when alcohol-withdrawal symptoms are manifest. High-potency vitamins and general supportive care are also standard components of treatment at this stage.

Patients must be examined carefully to detect possible head injuries, tuberculosis, the development of pneumonia or other infection, or metabolic or electrolyte disorders. Sound sleep is sought with compounds that increase dream sleep, since a deficit in dream sleep during and immediately following intoxication may be a factor in acute agitation, hallucinosis, or delirium tremens.

For many years, a medical axiom held that alcoholic patients are dehydrated. The patients were therefore treated with large amounts of intravenous fluids. Recent research has demonstrated that a rising blood-alcohol concentration does indeed lead to dehydration. But if there is no diarrhea, vomiting, or unusual degree of perspiration, a drop or flattening curve of blood alcohol actually leads to overhydration. Thus, fluids are now given orally in many small drinks according to the patient's need to shake his/her thirst.

Ending the after-pains of intoxication more quickly has long been a goal of everyone who ever got drunk. Many home remedies exist; none are effective. Administration of fructose sometimes speeds the metabolism of alcohol. But the central nervous system disorders and metabolic symptoms of acute postintoxication states may require a week or more—long after the alcohol has disappeared from the body—for complete physiological recovery.

Hospitals that accept alcoholic patients for detoxification are reducing both illness and death following acute alcoholic episodes. Despite positions taken by the American Medical Association and the American Hospital Association, however, some hospitals and physicians still avoid the responsibitility for detoxification, and health insurance is often inadequate to cover its costs.

## Biological: Organ-body

Long, excessive use of alcohol has deleterious effects on the various organ systems such as the heart, pancreas, liver, peripheral nerves, brain, and body cells in general. Alcoholic hepatitis is now thought to be the precursor of cirrhosis. Acute heart failure in alcoholism has a very poor prognosis if the individual continues to drink.

The general social and physical deterioration of the alcoholic person finally results in the "skid row" bum caricature. Only a small minority of alcoholic individuals ever reach this level. Because of their utter helplessness and visibility, however, large amounts of money have been spent in their incarceration and arrest, while little treatment effort has been expended in their service. While the future of these forlorn people is not bright, their further deterioration might be halted by setting up long-term facilities that offer roofs and food and people who care, as well as relief from loneliness, to these unfortunate individuals without homes.

For the great majority of alcoholic persons whose fate is by no means sealed, prompt and continued medical supervision is essential. Cessation of drinking and nutritional rehabilitation are the first order of treatment. Those who have suffered injuries to the central nervous system may need organ retraining to help compensate for irreversible damage. Failure to provide adequate medical care may result in premature death in many individuals, possibly by an average of ten to twelve years.

## Intrapsychic

Many professionals treating persons with alcoholism base their techniques on the assumption that the disorder is a result of emotional or unconsciously motivated factors. This assumption is controversial. Since intrapsychic factors are studied by inference and other indirect means, hard confirming information on the validity of this theory is difficult to collect. The view that alcoholism is an intrapsychic disorder is involved in the same debates as those surrounding the typology of emotional and mental disorders, and is subject to the same degree of criticism by many persons who object to seeing it thus classified.

At this time, well thought-out and conclusive studies on the effects of various psychological treatment techniques are lacking, equivocal, or contradictory. The poor design of followup studies is discouraging, making it difficult to practice effective matching of patients and techniques.

Putting aside parochial arguments among psychotherapeutic schools, however, most therapists agree that a vital part of any treatment program is the opportunity offered the alcoholic person to develop trust in someone. The alcoholic individual generally appears to be lonely and guilt-ridden. Beneath a facade of conviviality, he yearns for a trusting and nonjudgmental helping person upon whom to become dependent. This dependency is often accompanied by such distrust from earlier disappointments in life that the alcoholic person must challenge any new-found helper to see if this caregiver will be found wanting—like all others who came before.

Individual therapy is the preferred mode of therapy for some people. But the course of individual treatment is often rocky and fraught with peril to the therapeutic alliance. For example, the alcoholic patient's repeated testing of the relationship is often so intense and continuous, it may result in fulfillment of the patient's fear and in reinforcing his/her view that no one can be trusted, no one can help. Another way of explaining this interaction is gleaned from the transactional analysis viewpoint that sees the alcoholic person engaged in a game or series of manipulations to accomplish his/her goal of making human contact. For the alcoholic patient to recover, the therapist must be a better game-player and be able to block destructive moves.

Psychotherapists do not agree whether total abstinence is an absolutely necessary goal and the only measure of success in the treatment of alcoholism. The abstinent alcoholic patient may present so many other disabilities that just giving up drinking may be an inadequate criterion for recovery. Abstinence has long been deemed the first essential step in psychological rehabilitation, but opinions keep appearing to suggest that some alcoholic persons can become normal drinkers while, at the same time, increasing their psychological and interpersonal health in other areas. This viewpoint disturbs many therapists, who fear that each alcoholic patient will see himself/herself as the exception who can become a controlled drinker. Figure 14 gives a schematic representation of this dilemma.

Who is qualified to treat the alcoholic patient? Some feel that an alcoholic person who has recovered from the illness is best qualified since he/she has a deep, personal understanding of the problem. Members of many professional disciplines disagree with this viewpoint. They agree that the recovered alcoholic person may have an initial advantage in establishing rapport, but fear that the depth of his/her understanding will be limited by the blind spots and prejudices of his/her own battle with the disorder.

This controversy is less partisan today than formerly. In our guild partisanship, we must not lose sight of one fact: In the foreseeable future, sufficient numbers of trained professionals will not be available to care for the nation's mental health needs, including the control of alcoholism. We must train sufficient paraprofessional personnel to augment the professional work force. Recognition of the value of volunteer and indigenous groups is growing; no better example exists than AA. Fortunately, the therapeutic disciplines and AA have met, heard, and learned from each other.

Most therapists agree that recovered alcoholic persons can be of great value as counselors, but that professional guidance is essential. The risk of having alcoholic individuals (or, for that matter, any person suffering an intrapsychic illness) treated by inadequately trained personnel is that the latter may, often unconsciously, develop strong feelings that can be destructive to the patient. The inclination of the alcoholic patient to continuously challenge his/her therapeutic helper, plus his/her tendency to relapse, can be a severe test for anyone. These acts on the part of the patient may provoke destructive hostility, or defensive permissiveness to cover the hostility, on the part of counselors improperly prepared to recognize and handle these feelings. And permissiveness can be just

**FIGURE 14**
*The Dilemma in Treating Alcoholism*

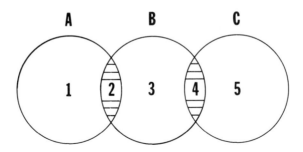

Circle A represents patients who have stopped drinking.
Circle B represents patients who have shown improvement in some
  facets of their lives.
Circle C represents patients who continue drinking.

---

The overlap of these groups produces five subgroups:

Area 1 represents the patients who have stopped drinking but show no other
form of improvement.

Area 2 represents the patients who have stopped drinking and show other
forms of improvement.

Area 3 represents the improved patients whose improvement is not demonstrably related to changes in their drinking practices.

Area 4 represents the patients who show other forms of improvement
although they are still drinking.

Area 5 represents the patients who continue drinking and show no improvement at all.

SOURCE: Reprinted from NIAAA, *Alcohol and Health,* First Special Report to the U.S. Congress on Alcohol and Health from the Secretary of Health, Education and Welfare, DHEW Publication No. (HSM) 72-9099, p. 74.

as destructive as hostility since it does not permit the therapist to set realistic and firm limits on the patient.

Group therapy has a wide acceptance in alcoholism treatment programs. This type of treatment is attractive for today's developing community alcoholism programs because it is usually less expensive than individual therapy. But group therapy should be attractive not because it costs less but because it can prove effective in treating alcoholism. It cuts across three systems—intrapsychic, interpersonal, and the social small group—permitting the alcoholic patient to see himself/herself more honestly, to view his/her relationship to other important figures more clearly, and to feel he/she is an integral part of a social system.

This type of therapy ranges from groups with intensive psychoanalytic orientation, where unconscious motivations (even utilizing dream analyses of both patients and therapists) are probed, to community groups where problems of group living are paramount and the group itself has the function of effecting significant changes in the lifestyles of its members.

A form of group therapy now increasingly used with alcoholic patients is one involving a confrontation process. At some level of understanding, the alcoholic person himself/herself is quite aware that he/she is destroying his/her life's potential. Alcohol, however, has become such a vital self-treatment he/she dares not admit the harm inflicted on himself/herself by use of alcohol. The alcoholic tries to kid others so they will reflect back to his/her own hope that drinking is not really such a serious problem. This denial of his/her drinking problem is so obvious it may simply look like a lie to an observer.

The inability to face up to the reality, however, is largely an unconscious mechanism and needs to be attacked as the first order of therapeutic business. An individual psychotherapist may find all attempts to break through the patient's defenses deflected by the desperate alcoholic patient who reasons, "After all, what does he/she really know about it?" In the group setting, however, similarly afflicted people confront each other with the fact that each one is, indeed, in the same boat. How obvious the rationalizations of someone else seem! Confrontation with these transparencies by one's own peers seems less threatening and is easier to accept, especially when a patient can move back and forth between being the confronter and the confronted. The presence of the professional therapist prevents the session from deteriorating into scapegoating or ganging up on a patient who is not yet ready to "take on" the full implications of this type of therapy.

Sometimes role-playing or psychodrama facilitates group therapy. Let's just pretend, the therapist suggests, you are the rebellious son, the cast-out daughter, the long-suffering wife, the overprotective mother, the indifferent father. Roles are interchanged skillfully. This is make-believe and patients can "ham it up," playing the roles as they appear in their imaginations. They are assuming the parts of other people, and thus they do not bear the threat of self-revelation. But how real and revealing the stage action is to both the group-audience and the players! Poignant and change-effecting therapeutic sessions often involve a sudden coalescence of love and support by the group, sometimes following a tearful breakthrough of long-hidden emotions revealed by an actor.

Varieties of sensitivity training and marathon techniques have also emerged in recent years to be incorporated in some therapy groups. These techniques increase the feeling, tone, and intimacy of groups of alcoholic patients. These modifications seem to fit in with theoretical assumptions about the group therapy process. The only reservations in applying these methods more often are adequate screening of patients who can benefit from these group therapy methods and the need for trained group leaders.

Sensitivity groups have the general purpose of exploring the here and now of how the members feel about each other. The members gain a learning experience by seeing how each comes across to others. This encourages the patients to drop their individual facades and to become more honest in their interpersonal relations, first within and then outside of the group.

As its title implies, the marathon group meets over a prolonged period, lasting perhaps forty hours. A patient may be able to keep his/her mask intact over a short interval, but this becomes increasingly difficult to maintain as time lengthens. Pretenses tend to break down and real feelings come out.

Learning theory has been brought into the field of alcoholism treatment with the hypothesis that alcoholism is maintained because it is learned and reinforced as a behavior that engenders important rewards. In trying to account for the persistence of alcohol dependence or addictive drinking, it is always tempting to extrapolate from common experience of alcohol-induced euphoria and to imagine that for the alcoholic person the immediate pleasure of drinking negates the prospect of its many aversive social and health consequences. The profound depression, dysphoria, and anxiety observed in the alcohol-dependent person during the course of chronic heavy alcohol ingestion challenges this type of simplistic explanation. Instead, some learning theorists hold that acceptance by the alcohol-dependent person of the consequences of his/her gross use of alcohol suggests that the pain he/she is seeking to assuage is extreme, and that it is this assuagement which constitutes the "immediate reward," thus overriding the foreseeable but delayed punitive consequences.

Treatment based on learning theory involves the use of positive or negative reinforcement techniques, or both kinds, as the behavioral therapist tries to help the patient alter alcoholic behavior by retraining his/her form of learning response. Aversive therapy is a form of negative reinforcement; it consists of giving the patient a painful experience and associating it with the use of alcohol. If successful, any consideration of drinking thereafter reflexively evokes a mental association with the painful or aversive stimulus, and the idea of drinking is rejected.

Three examples of this type of therapy are:

1. Nausea-inducing drugs in which an emetic agent is administered shortly before the patient sips his favorite alcoholic beverage, which results in prolonged vomiting (with an average duration of 45 minutes). The sequence is repeated two to three times per treatment session, with treatment sessions being scheduled every day for three or four days. One-year abstinence rates are reported at 60% with this treatment method.
2. Electric shock, with an objective of eliminating or drastically reducing alcohol consumption by pairing alcohol repeatedly with painful electrical impulses. Effects of this type of therapy tend to be short-lived and modest.
3. Unpleasant images in which the patient imagines aversive consequences while he imagines drinking. He also imagines successfully overcoming the urge to drink. Practice sessions twenty times a day are required of the patients. The usefulness of this type of treatment is uncertain.(60)

As is true of other aversive techniques, the enduring effectiveness of these negative reinforcement methods is unsure unless they are backed up with other forms of help. They are not popular with some professionals for fear they might be unknowingly used to vent unconscious hostile feelings toward alcoholic patients.

Typically, the patient who uses aversive therapy is one who has a high level of education, who comes from a high socioeconomic status, who has an intact marriage, who is successful in keeping conflict out of his life, and who thinks of alcoholism as a medical disease.(16)

Alcoholic behavior can be triggered by certain cues which are difficult to resist. In a type of therapy known as the cue-exposure techinque, the alcoholic is exposed to his "cues" in a clinical setting and then is helped to resist succumbing to the drinking urge by the therapist. The hypothesis is that by using this technique, the professional can extinguish craving and help the alcoholic or problem drinker resist excessive drinking. Such a technique would be especially effective for alcoholics who have been on an abstinence regime, as the great majority of these individuals will take a drink of alcohol within two years of detoxification.(50)

Modes of positive reinforcement based on learning theory, which would make not drinking a more rewarding experience than drinking, could be expected to prove more effective in altering behavior. Specific techniques in applying this aim have only begun to be developed experimentally by behavior therapists, although in essence this aim underlies most psychotherapeutic programs as they try to develop increased self-esteem, group approval, and renewal of human contacts.

Work therapy has been successful for some alcoholics in that it provides some of the same satisfactions as alcohol. Primarily, work therapy relieves tension, depression, and loneliness. In addition, it provides other positive benefits such as consuming the alcoholic's attention, absorbing his/her interest, allowing for self-expression and emotional release, centering his/her imaginations on something creative, and producing end results the person can be proud of.

Conflicts that arise between behavioral therapists and other psychological schools are not over the question whether reward reinforces while punishment deters behavior. That is self-evident. The issue concerns what really constitutes reward and punishment. The psychoanalytic theorist would hold that for the obsessively guilty, pain and punishment could be rewarding while success could be painful.

Much accommodation is being made today between learning and other motivational theories. The difference, as well as the growing accommodation between the schools of thought, may be illustrated by the following models. In an attempt to bring about certain responses, the behavioral therapist manipulates the stimuli to be fed into the "black box" (the brain with all its complexities and unknowns) and the responses that are emitted; the black box itself does not interest him/her. On the other hand, the concerns of the psychoanalytically oriented therapist and his/her patient are with the black box itself and with the conflicts and motivations contained in it. This therapist avoids applying stimuli and does not try to establish desirable responses; his/her quest is for insight, which he/she believes will allow the needed behavioral changes.

Other techniques that have been tried in the treatment of alcoholism include the use of hypnosis and LSD. Hypnosis can be used to explore feelings and memories that are not readily available to conscious experience but play an important role in precipitating drinking episodes. Posthypnotic suggestions can be given that make abstinence seem pleasurable and drinking painful. This use of hypnosis is an extension of the important impact a therapist can have upon his/her patient through suggestion and exhortation.

LSD has been utilized to evoke dramatically the patient's awareness of buried emotions and his/her human qualities. While some controversy remains, LSD treatment does not appear to offer significant help to alcoholic patients, and surveys of hospital-based programs show that LSD, hypnosis, and aversive therapies are not widely used.

Psychoactive drugs have made a major impact on the treatment of important psychiatric disorders since the early 1950s. These drugs, along with changes in community attitudes about mental illness, have been significantly responsible for the steady decline in numbers of hospitalized psychiatric patients. Most impressive has been the impact of the phenothiazines, a group of major tranquilizers, on schizophrenia and, more recently, lithium salts in the treatment and prevention of manic-depressive psychosis. Less certain is the relative balance of good and harm from the use of the minor tranquilizers in softening the blows of everyday life that are experienced in an exaggerated way by neurotic patients.

Thus, enthusiasm over the antidepressant or mood-elevating drugs has diminished. Much uncertainty exists about the use of chemical compounds to modify the anxiety and depression that reflect the intrapsychic stress experienced by alcoholic persons. The use of sedative and tranquilizing compounds may be essential in treating alcohol-withdrawal syndromes and to prevent delirium tremens; their long-term use, however, is fraught with a risk of addiction in the very individuals who are already prone to an addictive response. Therefore, most experienced physicians use such drugs judiciously, usually reserving them for crisis situations. Which drugs are best is controversial, and the placebo effects of drugs are sufficiently high to make it difficult to demonstrate a superiority for any one drug that can be repeated by many investigators and clinicians.

Since 1948, one drug—disulfiram (Antabuse)—has had a major impact on the treatment of alcoholism. It remains a favorite of many physicians because it often relieves the compulsiveness and obsessiveness of well-motivated patients so other forms of therapy can be used. Others seem reluctant to use it. Disulfiram is, in itself, a relatively inert compound. But it has the effect of interfering with the metabolism of alcohol after its first conversion to acetaldehyde in the liver, by blocking the further breakdown of the acetaldehyde. This results in an increased amount of acetaldehyde in the blood. Since acetaldehyde is very toxic, severe and even dangerous symptoms develop if alcohol is consumed when disulfiram is present in the body.

Symptoms begin appearing with 5−15 minutes after alcohol ingestion. The patient feels a warmth in the face; the skin turns red from the upper chest up; a pulsating headache often appears and neck constriction is felt. Nausea and copious vomiting generally occur within 30−60 minutes; sweating occurs when nausea appears, the person becomes pale, his/her blood pressure drops, and he/she experiences difficulty in breathing. There may be complaints of chest pain, dizziness, blurred vision, weakness, marked uneasiness, confusion, and syncope (fainting, loss of consciousness). Symptoms generally last from one-half hour to several hours and are usually followed by a deep sleep.(99)

Symptoms of disulfiram therapy differ in intensity and duration depending upon the individual taking the therapy, the dosage and duration of the disulfiram ingested, and the amount of alcohol taken into the body. Because of these signs and symptoms that accompany Antabuse therapy, alcoholics undergoing this type of treatment carry a card like that in Figure 15. Disulfiram is slowly removed from the body, and a patient who has taken this medication must wait several days after discontinuing it before he/she can drink safely.

There may be side effects with disulfiram therapy. Mild side effects include fatigue, dizziness, skin problems, headache, impotence, gastrointestinal disturbances, and a peculiar odor and taste. More serious side effects are psychiatric disorders such as organic brain syndrome and psychosis. If the disulfiram dosage is decreased, the prevalence of side effects will be reduced.

Disulfiram therapy is not recommended for everyone. Those with cirrhosis, nephritis, epilepsy, goiter, pregnancy, other drug addiction, diabetes mellitus, asthma, and blood diseases should be cautious or advised not to take disulfiram.

Physicians who prescribe this drug might demonstrate the danger of drinking to the patient by having him/her undergo a mild disulfiram-alcohol reaction under carefully controlled conditions, but usually a careful explanation is adequate.

The drug itself is not a sufficient therapeutic program. Combined with other psychological rehabilitative techniques, disulfiram can be a most useful tool, but it is not a panacea. In the motivated alcoholic patient, it can "buy time" when he/she has an impulse to drink. During that interval he/she has time to reconsider his/her best long-range interests.

Disulfiram is not a drug to be used without careful concern for the medical state of the patient. While it causes relatively few serious side effects in itself, a person in a weakened state might have an attack of acetaldehyde poisoning if he/she drank an alcoholic beverage while taking disulfiram. This could be dangerous for a person suffering from such conditions as arteriosclerotic heart disease, cirrhosis, severe kidney disease, diabetes mellitus, or any serious debilitating medical disorder. Careful medical examination and psychological considerations should precede the prescription of this compound.

The question of hospitalization for the alcoholic patient is usually generally agreed on when he/she is acutely intoxicated, or suffering from serious medical complications that would require hospital care even if he/she did not abuse alcohol or suffer from alcoholism. The reluctance of many general hospitals and

**FIGURE 15**
*Wallet card distributed by Ayerst Laboratories to be*
*carried by persons taking antabuse.*

I am on ANTABUSE® (disulfiram) therapy. If I am disoriented, too ill to give a history, or unconscious, I may be having a serious ANTABUSE (disulfiram)-alcohol reaction. Do not administer alcohol, paraldehyde, or any mixture with an alcohol content.

FOR INFORMATION ON TREATMENT OF A REACTION, ▶
PLEASE SEE REVERSE SIDE

---

My name is _____

Address _____

City and State _____ Tel. _____

**PLEASE TRY TO CONTACT**

Doctor _____

Address _____

City and State _____ Tel. _____

Suggested emergency measures to help counteract an ANTABUSE (disulfiram)-alcohol reaction should include the usual supportive measures to restore blood pressure and to treat shock. Inhalation of oxygen intravenous antihistamine or intravenous ephearine sulfate.

**AYERST LABORATORIES**                    Please see other side ▶
                                           Printed in U.S.A.      7902

physicians to accept this responsibility discriminates, in effect, against the indigent patient. The private patient, who usually has a family doctor, can gain admission to a hospital—though his/her diagnosis may be masked by vague phrases such as gastrointestinal disorder or fever of undetermined origin. A psychiatric hospital may admit him/her as having an acute depressive reaction.

Sometimes, the indigent patient may be cared for in a detoxification center operated by city authorities, such as in St. Louis or Washington, D.C. A local city or county hospital may also have a detoxification center. Too often, however, the unofficial detoxification center is the city jail, where medical care for the person in an acute alcoholic episode is likely to be a matter of chance.

Whether or not detoxification is needed, hospitalization for rehabilitative and psychological care is not always available in state mental hospitals and private psychiatric hospitals. Most specialists agree that hospitalization is indicated if the patient needs detoxification, is suicidal, homicidal, or unable to terminate a drinking bout unless removed from the source of alcohol by temporary confinement. Not all professionals agree, however, that hospitalizing the alcoholic person for other reasons is indicated; they fear a regressive sheltering or institutionalizing effect of the hospital which may run counter to the need to learn to live in the normal community. Uncertainty also exists as to whether the alcoholic patient should be housed with other psychiatric patients or placed in a special hospital or special unit.

Hospitalization does have the major advantage of getting hold of the alcoholic person long enough to begin instituting various therapeutic techniques that can then be continued after discharge. For example, interpersonal and social small-group system intervention such as family therapy and AA can be started during this time, and a foundation laid for necessary aftercare.

## Interpersonal

This system falls between the intrapsychic and the social small-group systems, blending imperceptibly into each. Interpersonal therapy focuses on marital and family disorders and how they relate to the alcoholic person's marital partner or family member. It consists of give-and-take with important people in the patient's life today, rather than in the past, although those early love and hate experiences show up as a shadow over what the patient is doing now.

In caricature, for example, the wife of the alcoholic man is portrayed as a long-suffering, work-worn, red-eyed, self-sacrificing woman forever bewildered by her once-generous husband's alcoholic debauchery and irresponsibility. Scratching the surface a bit in interpersonal therapy, however, may reveal a rather steely woman, contemptuous of her husband and secretly pleased with her dominant role in the family. Surprisingly, this may not be her first marriage to an alcoholic man.

Further investigation might reveal some dynamics of her past relationships—the intrapsychic system. These would suggest she was acting out old shadows of disappointment in her father's failure to be strong and reliable. She neurotically recreates this scene in her present life by choosing alcoholic mates. If her unconscious choice of a mate does not quite meet the picture of her father—for example, if the spouse turned out to be insufficiently weak—she would subtly undercut and push her husband along the desired path to irresponsibility.

These dynamics can be mirrored when the nonalcoholic partner is the husband. Superior and indifferent treatment of a wife can leave a woman with a growing loneliness and rage, finally culminating in her hidden alcoholism—that is, not hidden from her husband, but ignored by him and hidden by both of them from the world. How mismatched this intact and successful man seems to be with his now slovenly and brain-damaged wife. He must keep her from public view.

Yet, after loud proclamations that this drinking will no longer be tolerated, a nonalcoholic spouse may even be detected sympathetically slipping gin into the hospital for the alcoholic partner now under care for alcoholism. Or, take the example of the physician's wife struggling to avoid her destructive drinking which has become a public humiliation to her husband. Her husband asks her to buy champagne for their wedding anniversary because he forgot her problem after only a month of abstinence on her part!

In this marital situation, one prediction holds: The nonalcoholic spouse will unconsciously resist attempts of the alcoholic partner to recover. Subtle, or even not to subtle, means may be employed to undercut progress. If, despite these pressures, the alcoholic partner manages to recover, the effects may be devastating for the mental health of the spouse.

Attractive as these theoretical assumptions may be, life—fortunately—is not that simple. Many wives and husbands of recovered alcoholic persons are delighted by the change; marriages are preserved, and great efforts are expended to encourage prolonged recovery. In other words, the variables are too many to allow accurate prediction.

A broader view holds that the nonalcoholic partner, even with many unresolved needs, is faced with an immediate reality: A chronically inebriated husband or wife. Assuming that the causes lie more with the inebriate individual, to what advantage can this situation be used unconsciously by the nonalcoholic spouse? Faced with a painful reality, this spouse may seek some secondary gain to make up somewhat for the losses. Maybe, when intoxicated, the alcoholic spouse is more, or less sexually directed . . . more, or less, generous . . . more, or less, communicative . . . or more, or less, intimate. Or, the wife may be faced with a great disappointment in her husband: She can no longer depend on him for support. She is forced to assume a greater and greater share of his responsibilities until finally, she is both mother and father in the house—a position she may find herself unconsciously enjoying.

Meanwhile, the alcoholic spouse may painfully be beginning to move toward recovery. The long-term results might be very much to the advantage of the spouse. For the short run, however, she may not be so willing to relinquish the secondary gains. Her husband demands to take back his man-of-the-house responsibilities. But can she be sure? Will this be just another brief attempt on his part, to be followed by another, even more painful disappointment? She hesitates, holds on to the reins, and gives only half-hearted support to his efforts. He wants back now; she is not sure. He feels rebuffed and hurt and may go back to drinking. This sequence may be repeated several times.

Because so many variables are involved in the differing constellations of marriages, the tendency is growing to treat the couple rather than just the alcoholic partner. An immediate resistance that has to be resolved is the belief of the nondrinking spouse that he or she is not really in need of help but is coming just to help the other. A first attack on this resistance is to point out that it is the marriage which is the patient; the alcoholism of one partner is merely the symptom of a sick marriage. Before long, the complementary pathology of the nonalcoholic spouse is usually in full bloom, ready for therapeutic attention.

This approach may be widened to include other or all members of the immediate family. What role do children play in perpetuating a parental drinking pattern? A disdainful "Is Dad drunk again?" could be a startling confrontation leading toward greater motivation to become well. Unfortunately, the question is more likely to be received with shame and resentment, both good reasons "to really tie one on!" The son's loss of self-respect as he sees his identification model crumbling may require painstaking rebuilding, which may be facilitated if he can participate with his father in the therapeutic reconstruction of the self-esteem of the entire family.

Sometimes the significant other, possibly the addictor, needs to be identified and, if possible, brought into the picture. This could be Mom, Dad, or the mistress who finds her lover more responsive when he is drunk. These significant others are more difficult to bring into a therapeutic situation than a spouse. If the addictor cannot be involved and persists in his or her role, the alcoholic patient may have to be helped to make a clean break for self-survival.

Offshoot organizations of AA have been effective in this area of involving family members and helping them. Al-Anon, an organization for spouses of alcoholic patients, is available whether or not the alcoholic partner is in AA or part of some other rehabilitation procedure. The great value derived from such an organization is to learn that one is not alone in this predicament and to take advantage of other spouses' trial-and-error attempts at better adjustment. It is hoped that greater understanding by the spouse may lead to ways to help the alcoholic partner toward treatment. Al-Ateen is a parallel organization for the teenage children of an alcoholic parent; Al-Atots is for still younger children.

## Social: Small Group

Not only do all of us have intrapsychic and intimate interpersonal experiences, but we also live in small social groups such as friends, acquaintances, clubs, neighbors, and interest groups that extend outside our families. Such contacts play a major role in maintaining identification roles and self-esteem, and in offering opportunities for controlled and healthy releases of impulses. Unfortunately, the slow progression to alcoholism usually results in a loss of such contacts. Friends cease to be; old drinking buddies cannot and do not wish to keep pace; neighbors are disdainful. The alcoholic person, already struggling with a waning sense of personal worth, progressively becomes alienated and lonely. He/she may project responsibility upon others for his/her social rejection. Within himself/herself, however, is only too aware of where the responsibility lies, thus confirming the worst of his/her already low self-appraisal.

*Alcoholics Anonymous (AA).*[5] The prime example today of treatment provided within small group settings that take these factors into account is AA, the

---

[5]Adapted from NIAAA, *Alcohol and Health,* Second Special Report, p. 153.

major influence for the past 30-odd years in gaining acceptance of the disease concept of alcoholism. The aim of AA members is to help each other maintain their sobriety and to share their recovery experience freely with anyone who may have an alcohol-related problem. The AA program basically consists of "Twelve Suggested Steps" designed for personal recovery from alcoholism. Several hundred thousand alcoholic people have achieved sobriety in this way, but members recognize that their program is not always effective with all alcoholic individuals, and that some persons may require professional counseling or treatment.

AA is concerned solely with the personal recovery and continued sobriety of individuals who turn to this fellowship for help. The organization itself engages in no research, no medical or psychiatric treatment, nor endorsement of any causes, although members often participate in such activities as individuals. Organization-ally, AA's policy is one of "cooperation but non-affiliation" with other organizations concerned with the problems of alcoholism. AA is self-supporting through its own groups and members; contributions from all outside sources are declined. Members preserve personal anonymity in the newspapers, films, broadcasts, and other public information media.

To some, AA has at times appeared defensive about the roles of professional groups in the field of alcoholism. These fears have largely disappeared as AA members and the professions have come to know one another better. Mutual appreciation, cooperation, and understanding have emerged as a result of better communication between AA and other groups in the field of alcoholism.

AA keeps no membership records and provides no hard statistics. Thus, it is sometimes difficult to verify or explain its success in scientific terms. Nevertheless, it is easy to see why AA should and does work so often. The fellowship seems ideally suited for the guilt-ridden and lonely person lying beneath the facade of good nature assumed by many alcoholic individuals before coming into AA. This is not surprising, as AA was developed by people who had experienced similar feelings.

Founded in 1935 by two hopeless alcoholic persons—a stockbroker and a surgeon—AA has proved that hundreds of thousands of people can and do recover from alcoholism, and go on to become productive citizens. While AA has no formal religious dogma, most AA members rely on a spiritual approach—a Higher Power greater than themselves. For some, this reliance may well be the most important factor in their recovery. The "Big Book" of AA is well worth reading. Many alcoholic persons, however, are not able to take the first step of AA: "We admitted we were powerless over alcohol—that our lives had become unmanageable." They need other forms of therapy before they can be motivated to accept the AA program.

The person who does stay with the program also relies on the help of other alcoholic individuals as he/she sets out on a course of making amends for previous wrongs. He/she turns to helping others (Twelfth Stepping) not only for the sake of others (the professional viewpoint), but for his/her own continued personal sobriety. All of this activity occurs in a fellowship with others like himself/herself who are in the process of recovering; in this fellowship he/she is unconditionally accepted as a peer.

AA has been described as a loosely knit, voluntary fellowship of alcoholics gathered together for the sole purpose of helping themselves and each other to get sober and stay sober. It has also been pictured as serving its members first as a way back to life and then as a design for living. Widely publicized since the early 1940s, it has more than 7,000 local chapters, with one in almost every sizable town.

AA, historically, has probably been the most effective modality in helping alcoholic people achieve sobriety and it remains outstandingly influential. Many methods are known to help alcoholic patients to stop the destructive drinking. A great many therapists regard AA as the most useful adjunct to any treatment, especially in helping to maintain the gains of the beginning of treatment. The importance of treating the entire family has been recognized in the formation of Al-Anon, Al-Ateen, and Al-Atots as adjuncts to AA for adult relatives, teenage sons and daughters, and younger children of alcoholic persons. An interesting recent development in several cities has been the establishment of clubs where alcoholics and their spouses can go for social events as well as modified group therapy. It is possible that this represents the trend noted elsewhere for couples and families to receive help together rather than separately, and the recognition that the issue in families is not how a ''healthy'' spouse deals with a ''sick'' partner, but how they cope together with a mutual interactional problem in which alcohol plays an important role. These subsidiary groups do not teach nonalcoholic relatives how to manipulate the alcoholic family member. Instead, they concentrate on helping the relatives appreciate and deal with their own feelings toward alcoholism and the alcoholic person. As a byproduct of this experience, nonalcoholic family members assist in recovery rather than aggravate the illness.

Important to the AA approach is an admission by the alcoholic of his/her lack of power over alcohol. He/she must have hit what is termed ''rock bottom,'' finding himself in a desperate and totally intolerable situation. For some this realization may come when they have lost everything and everybody. For others, it may occur when they are first arrested by the police or warned by their employer. At this point, this individual must decide to turn over his/her life and will to a power greater than his/her own. Much of the program has a spiritual but nonsectarian basis.

The average AA group member is male, between the ages of 31 and 50, and is in a sales or managerial position professionally. He initially came to AA because of another AA member and attends an AA meeting three or more times a week.

During the early years of AA, some members rigidly insisted that ''only an alcoholic can understand an alcoholic,'' and there was minimal cooperation between AA workers on the one hand and physicians, clergymen, and social workers on the other. With the accumulation of more experience and knowledge, however, most AA members no longer hold these concepts, and cooperation with therapists in the professions has been increasing.

The AA program is based on the famous Twelve Steps:
We:
1. Admitted we were powerless over alcohol—that our lives had become unmanageable.
2. Came to believe that a Power greater than ourselves could restore us to sanity.
3. Made a decision to turn our will and our lives over to the care of God as we understood Him.
4. Made a searching and fearless moral inventory of ourselves.
5. Admitted to God, to ourselves, and to another human being, the exact nature of our wrongs.
6. Were entirely ready to have God remove all these defects of character.
7. Humbly asked Him to remove our shortcomings.
8. Made a list of all persons we had harmed and became willing to make amends to them all.
9. Made direct amends to such people wherever possible, except when to do so would injure them or others.
10. Continued to take a personal inventory and when we were wrong promptly admitted it.
11. Sought through power of prayer and meditation to improve our conscious contact with God as we understood Him, praying only for knowledge of His will for us and the power to carry that out.
12. Having had a spiritual experience as a result of these steps, tried to carry this message to alcoholics and to practice these principles in all our affairs.

*Halfway houses.* Another form of small group therapy for alcoholic persons is represented by the halfway house, which has been developed to fill the serious gap that has arisen between hospital and outpatient services. The middle-class patient, for example, usually returns to or continues with his/her family. Many alcoholic persons, however, have lost old attachments. After detoxification and with good motivation toward rehabilitation, they unhappily run into the demoralizing situation where no one wants them and they have no place to go.

Other patient characteristics are that the individual generally has a partial high school education, engages in labor or technical jobs, shows a great degree of marital disintegration, is unable to cope with conflict and stress, and is a "low-bottom" alcoholic (though not a skid-row alcoholic).(116)

Originally instituted for various types of emotional disorders, the halfway house has probably performed its greatest service for the alcoholic patient. Generally, this patient can look back to a better experience of integration than, for example, the person with a long history of schizophrenia, and has greater potential to return to at least his/her former level of functioning. The alcoholic individual on the road to recovery may remain in a halfway house from several weeks to several months. Here he/she has an opportunity to continue confrontation group therapy, obtain proper nutrition, and take a breathing spell while he/she job-hunts or undertakes a vocational rehabilitation program. At the halfway house he/she has a built-in group of acquaintances and is encouraged to extend his/her social circle. Very often, the halfway house has a strong AA or spiritual orientation that provides him/her with vital support. Perhaps one of the greatest values of a halfway house is that it offers a "dry island" to which the recovered alcoholic person may retreat. Here, in association with others to whom he/she relates, he/she temporarily insulates himself/herself from community, family stresses, and drinking stimuli during his/her hours away from work.

An example of a halfway house would be the Compass Club. The Compass Club list of rules may be a pattern for other halfway houses:

1. One drink and you're out.
2. Eat morning and evening meals in the club.
3. Observe the 11 P.M. curfew nightly.
4. After the 72-hour restriction is up, go out and find work.
5. Pay $3 a day rent, $21 a week.
6. Go to all mandatory meetings and group discussions.
7. Talk to counselors about drinking problems.
8. Attend outside AA meetings.
9. Perform cleanup and maintenance details as assigned.
10. Be cooperative.(99)

Halfway houses may be part of a public network of rehabilitation services, or operated by nonprofit voluntary groups. Unfortunately, halfway houses are in short supply. This is especially true for women, for society often forgets that women also have alcohol-related problems.

A day hospital falls between a halfway house and a hospital. The halfway house is for the person with no place to go, but who does not need a hospital. The day hospital is for the person who does have a place to go, is not quite ready to go there yet, but does not need full-time care.

In the day hospital, the alcoholic patient continues with group therapy, engages in resocialization, participates in vocational rehabilitation programs, and gradually increases his/her community contacts. He/she returns home nights and weekends, gradually decreasing the proportion of time spent in the day hospital.

The night hospital or weekend hospital is a reverse variation on this theme. Perhaps the individual can return to a job which presents few stresses for him/her, yet needs time before he/she can return to where his/her real stresses lie—in marriage and family.

A major roadblock to greater use of halfway houses and day or other partial hospitalization techniques is the failure of health insurance to realize that these approaches are less expensive alternatives to full-time hospital care. It is hoped that this penny-wise, pound-foolish attitude will be changed.

*Activity groups.* The goal of treatment in activity groups is to improve self-concept by increasing physical health through such activities as fishing, organized sports, dancing, arts and crafts, hiking, bowling, and bridge playing. People are brought together and practice positive social interaction. The activities also function as nonthreatening outlets for hostility and aggression.(99)

## Social: Large Group.

The estimated 10 million people in our midst with alcohol-related problems undoubtedly have a major impact on such large social groups as industry, the military, and our driving, flying, and boating populations. This is especially relevant when we consider the lack of realism in such traditionally held viewpoints as, "Alcoholics are bums so they don't hold down jobs in our business or factory"; or, "Alcoholics are too poor to own automobiles, and those who do are too foxy to drive after drinking."[6]

The fact that less than 5 percent of people with alcohol-related problems are on skid row makes it obvious that most alcoholic individuals are in the work force. And most of them, like most of us, do own automobiles and do drive.

Within the work world, rehabilitation programs have several essential elements: (1) casefinding; (2) confrontation; (3) motivation; and (4) followup. A relatively easy person to identify is the individual whose job performance shows increasing impairment due to a behavioral problem which expresses itself through such symptoms as recurrent absenteeism, vague physical complaints, poor on-the-job interpersonal relationships, and decreasing efficiency. The issue is not so much the education of supervisors in early casefinding (they have a pretty good idea of who is in trouble), as it is in their companies' establishing policies and procedures that allow them to take corrective action. It should be noted that the criterion for company action is the employee's job performance and not his/her use of alcohol. Similarly, the only criterion of successful response is improved job performance.

When impaired job performance indicates alcohol abuse or alcoholism may be involved, a company with an alcoholism program refers the individual to medical or personnel counseling services. These services may be an integral part of the company, or they may be community-based services that are used by the company under contract or other agreements. The assistance offered to the employee in this instance should not differ from that offered in cases of job impairment due to other disease-related conditions.

As in many other health and welfare plans, labor and management agreement is essential to the development of industrial alcoholism programs. There are several accepted procedures for implementing such programs. In general, an employee is offered and urged to accept a designated health service for diagnosis of a condition that may possibly be affecting his/her work. Such a health service identifies the nature of the problem and recommends an appropriate treatment course. In the case of alcoholism, this recommendation may be referral to a specified alcoholism clinic, a psychiatrist, AA, or other appropriate caregiver. During this confrontation, the employee is given a clear choice of either improving his/her job performance or facing administrative disciplinary procedures. The offer to assist him/her is expressed firmly, but it must be accepted voluntarily. If treatment is accepted, the worker must show a reasonable effort to pursue treatment, and his/her work performance must also

[6]Adapted from NIAAA, *Alcohol and Health,* First Special Report, p. 80.

show improvement. If his/her performance continues impaired and he/she manifests little concern in obtaining treatment, the normal administrative procedures based on deteriorating work performance take their course. If sincere treatment effort fails to improve his/her work, then the issue of disability retirement may have to be resolved. In cases where performance improves although no treatment is undertaken, no company action is warranted beyond monitoring the level of work to ensure that the problem does not repeat itself.

Early identification of the alcoholic employee is essential. A program at one company has already resulted in a 63 percent reduction in absenteeism; at another company substantial rehabilitation has been achieved in 65 percent of the workers diagnosed as needing treatment for alcoholism. In both companies, early identification was stressed.

The cost of industry alcoholism programs is negligible compared with the cost of no program. The alcoholic worker, for example, is likely to be an older and more experienced employee. Studies in one large company showed that two-thirds of employees identified as alcoholic persons had from 5 to 15 years of service. In another company, such employees average 22 years of service. Losing such workers is expensive; so is the cost of continued job impairment. But since these employees have much to lose in terms of seniority, the leverage for constructive on-the-job intervention is great.

When it comes to coping with alcohol-related traffic accidents, one form of positive intervention being tried out in many communities is therapy offered as an alternative to punishment, to the person arrested for driving when intoxicated. A full range of community services is being utilized, just as for the worker who is offered treatment instead of immediate job dismissal. Considering all the previously mentioned complexities of therapy, one standard and rigidly applied program is not likely to be successful. The U.S. Department of Transportation is now funding pilot projects to discover what orientation might be effective. Traditional techniques of jail, fine, and license revocation have not been successful. Neither have the well-intentioned but naive attempts to alter this situation by a few lectures on the evils of "Demon Rum." Though they may act as if they didn't know the facts, the bulk of the "students" are all too knowledgeable about the effects of alcohol, but they are caught up in an addictive illness.

## Societal

Ours is a society ambivalent about its drinking habits. Nearly one-third of our adult population does not drink at all, but most people drink at least occasionally. Of the population that drinks, an uncertain proportion wonders whether drinking may be morally evil. For many, even social drinking requires a defiant pull away from old family attitudes of abstinence. On the other hand, we have groups for which controlled drinking is the norm, but some may be undergoing changes from traditional customs toward uncontrolled drinking.

An overall coordinating agency for services is needed in most communities. Otherwise, gaps in service will exist through which many alcoholic persons will fall, or costly duplications will occur. This coordination can be accomplished under the umbrella of a public health department, a comprehensive health or mental health organization, or some similar group. An important part of the coordinating body is a high visible community education and referral service, similar to those affiliated with the National Council on Alcoholism. This referral service is a place to which to turn for help in finding the right spot to enter the treatment network. It can be used both for self-referrals and to assist clergymen, physicians, courts, teachers, social agencies, and other health professionals coming in contact with people who have drinking problems or are addicted to alcohol.

An essential first level of treatment is detoxification for the acutely intoxicated person. Some communities might prefer a detoxification center, perhaps operated by a public health department, from which a patient can be referred to rehabilitative resources. Others might prefer to develop detoxification treatment at each community general hospital. A hospital will be necessary for those who are a risk to themselves or others, or for those who must be hospitalized so they can obtain a handle on the beginning of long-range rehabilitation. A network consisting of general hospital psychiatric units, private freestanding psychiatric hospitals, and publicly supported mental health units—whatever is locally appropriate—must be developed. Detoxification is merely emergency treatment, representing the first step toward recovery for the acutely intoxicated person. Unfortunately, the only medical service offered by many communities to alcohol abusers and alcoholic persons is a detoxification service, and even when continuing services are provided, facilities are so inadequate that they discourage people from seeking, accepting, or continuing treatment.

AA should be encouraged to participate in the system at an early point and then be reintroduced along the way for those who need special help before they can accept the AA fellowship. AA groups can be established at detoxification units, general and psychiatric hospitals, and clinics. As soon as possible, the patient should be out of a hospital; indeed, the majority will not need a hospital at all. For those still requiring much support, or without personal attachments, halfway houses and a partial hospitalization program should be developed.

Outpatient care may run the gamut from AA, to special alcoholism clinics, to general psychiatric clinics, to private practitioners with special interest and skills in treating alcoholic persons. Therapy must be directed at both intrapsychic and interpersonal problems, sometimes with involvement of spouses and other family members.

Community consultation is essential for a well-functioning program. Professionals should be available to offer help at major casefinding points: the municipal court, the city jail, welfare departments, hospital emergency rooms, and social agencies. Consultation for education programs should be available to schools, clergymen, service clubs, and interested social groups.

Despite the best efforts of this community network, some alcoholic persons will be in an irreversible state. For these people, social centers and sheltered living will have to be provided.

Many communities will find it necessary to bring in special organizations that work best with certain minority or ethnic groups. Indigenous workers should be trained and available as therapeutic intervenors at each step in the network of services.

In general, alcoholics and alcohol abusers who need adequate medical coverage and health and social resources do not have the same services available—either from the private or public sectors of the nation—as persons with other illnesses. This has been due, in part, to this historic reluctance to commit incentive, personnel, or funds to this area of need. It is also due to the lack of clear-cut diagnostic procedures which can be used to determine the existence of the illness, alcoholism. Surprisingly, an inventory of resources will show that many of the needed treatment facilities actually exist in most communities. What is lacking is organization, coordination, cooperation and, most important, a dedication to see the alcoholic individual as a person worthy of care. Given some outside grant funding, the cost of supplying the missing links may be within grasp. Operational costs for the community will not be heightened; in fact, they will prove much less expensive than failure to operate such a system. Private health insurance carriers, through state regulatory bodies, should be forced to remove clauses in their policies that discriminate against alcoholism. The cost of providing care for the medically indigent patient will be minimal compared with ultimate public costs of neglecting him/her.

No one knows what proportion of alcoholic patients can be helped by a system providing such continuity of care. As with many medical and social disorders, alcoholism tends to be a chronic ailment with a myriad of causative factors. Control is the practical goal. Recovery may be temporary, but is vital to survival while it lasts, and temporary improvement allows optimism that control can be gained. To date, at any given time, a cross-section of alcoholic patients shows one-third much improved (not only in alcohol-related behavior, but in general living comfort), one-third experiencing some lesser benefit, and one-third unchanged. A slice across the sample at another time will show considerable shifting back and forth among these sectors. With such a success rate at present, we can expect our efforts to be correspondingly rewarded as we muster knowledge and resources in the future.

# Chances of Recovery [7]

In evaluating the future outlook of alcoholics, many therapists divide patients into three broad groups.

*The psychotic alcoholics.* These are patients, usually in state mental

[7]Adapted from Public Health Service, National Clearinghouse for Mental Health Information, *Alcohol and Alcoholism,* U.S. Department of Health Education, and Welfare, PHS Publication No. 1640, pp. 37–38.

hospitals, with a severe chronic psychosis. They may account for 5 to 10 percent of all alcoholics.

*The skid row alcoholics.* These are the improverished "homeless men" who usually no longer have—or never did have—family ties, jobs, or an accepted place in the community. They may account for 3 to 8 percent.

*The "average" alcoholics.* These are men and women who are usually still married and living with their families, still holding a job—often an important one—and still are accepted and reasonably respected members of their community. They account for more than 70 percent of the alcoholics.

From the scanty information available, it would appear that the prognosis for chronic psychotic and skid row alcoholics is poor, and that less than 10 to 12 percent can obtain substantial aid from ordinary therapy. For the average alcoholic, the outlook is far more optimistic. Here, three different yardsticks of control have been utilized.

*Complete cure.* By strict definition, this would mean that the alcoholic would become able to drink normally or socially, using alcohol moderately and under complete control. Most specialists hold that no alcoholic can ever learn to drink moderately and regard statements to the contrary as unwise or dangerous. However, other specialists hold that the potential for returning to normal or controlled drinking is higher for the alcoholic whose drinking is somewhat controlled than for the totally uncontrolled alcoholic.

*Permanent abstinence.* For most therapists, the goal of treatment is complete abstinence from alcohol, in any form and under any condition, for the rest of the patient's life. According to available information, only a small percentage—perhaps less than 20 percent of all treated patients—have been able to maintain absolute abstinence for more than three to five years. In certain highly selective industrial and business groups, the rate of abstinence may be as high as 50 percent.

*Rehabilitation.* Recently, some leading therapists have been using a different basis of measurement in which success is considered achieved when the patient maintains or re-establishes a good family life, a good work record, and a respectable position in the community, and is able to control his/her drinking *most of the time.*

Depending on the motivation and intelligence of the patient and his/her determination to get well; the competence of the therapist; the availability of whatever hospital or clinic facilities; tranquilizers and other drugs which may be needed; and the strong support of family, employer, and community—a successful outcome can be expected in many cases.

"It is doubtful that any specific percentage figure has much meaning in itself," says Dr. Seldon D. Bacon, director of the Center of Alcohol Studies at Rutgers. "What has a great deal of meaning is the fact that tens of thousands of such cases have shown striking improvement over many years."

There is no evidence that any particular type of therapist—physician, clergyman, AA worker, psychologist, or social worker—will achieve better results than another. The chances for a successful outcome apparently depend more on the motivation of the patient and the competence of the therapist than on the type of psychotherapy employed. The earlier that treatment is begun, the better are the prospects for success, although some patients have been treated successfully after many years of excessive drinking.

# Delivery and Evaluation of Treatment Services[8]

Continuing care may be provided in various settings at different times or a combination of arrangements may be needed by a particular person. At present there are available six major treatment stances that broadly cover the myriad of various techniques.

*Acute detoxification*—treatment of the acute intoxication and withdrawal syndromes needed by almost all patients.

*Chronic detoxification*—needed (usually in a controlled environment) by all patients suffering from intermediate or chronic brain syndromes.

*Environmental manipulation*—for those individuals who exist in a very high-risk drinking culture or those locked into a very destructive interpersonal situation.

*Supportive therapy*—should be built into all aspects of treatment but may be the only appropriate modality at certain points of recovery for certain patients.

*"Internal change" therapy*—A broad concept that covers the wide range of treatment techniques employed by those trained in psychiatry and the behavioral sciences. These are considered more glamorous techniques by most young therapists but are not appropriate in the early phases, if at all, for a substantial number of persons with alcoholism. If these techniques are the exclusive treatment modality of a program, it will be capable of delivering services to a narrow segment of the patient population.

*Treatment of the counter alcoholic*—this may be spouse, parent, offspring, landlady, homosexual partner, etc. It is the person or persons with whom the patient has mutual dependency and whose dynamics need the alcoholic's drinking almost as much as the alcoholic does.

The key to successful treatment lies in appropriately timing the right combination of these modalities to meet the individual's needs at any given phase of his recovery process. A major shortcoming of delivery systems, to date, is that they usually utilize only one or two of these treatment stances. If the remainder are

---

[8]Adapted from Vernelle Faux, "Recommednations for Detoxification Services," *Proceedings: On Alcoholism Emergency Care Services,* National Institute on Alcohol Abuse and Alcoholism.

available in the community, they are not visibly connected or interrelated for the patient. Sometimes the patient may sense the competitive either-or attitudes of his/her would-be helpers and many sense that they are considered failures or not motivated if they do not respond to a particular modality at a particular time. The setting or settings within which these treatment stances can be provided are variable and should be flexibly used to meet the individual's needs. They include such things as:

1. Hospital-based inpatient and outpatient services.
2. Rehabilitation centers providing 24-hour care, with the day and night hospital components.
3. Halfway house living arrangments and programs.
4. Specialty outpatient clinics.
5. Multipurpose outpatient clinics with definable services for alcoholics.

Regardless of setting, the program must have certain essential characteristics including:

1. Available medical attention.
2. Reasonable accessibility to patients—for example, public transportation and adequate parking.
3. Peer group identity—that is, they should be earmarked and accepted as alcoholism services by staff and patients and not be competed for by other patient populations.
4. "On demand" concern—if at all possible they should operate seven days a week, spread across day-evening hours, and provide walk-in attention. The patient under stress, struggling to keep from returning to alcohol for relief, should be able to go to his treatment resource at any time and find help. It is not realistic to expect many patient to be able to maintain themselves with only a weekly appointment program. During stress they may need to be able to be there all day every day. At other times, two group sessions a week may be sufficient.
5. Assistance with various aspects of his/her total problem—staff should have expertise in a wide range of areas such as physical, emotional, situational, work, family, legal, and other problems. The program should be structured in a way that makes these services easily available as parts of a whole, and not isolated or competitive components in the patient's eyes.

See Figure 16 for an overview of community services for alcoholism.

Regardless of the type of treatment used, several ideas should be stressed with the therapist involved:

1. Do not give up if the treatment used does not work the first time.

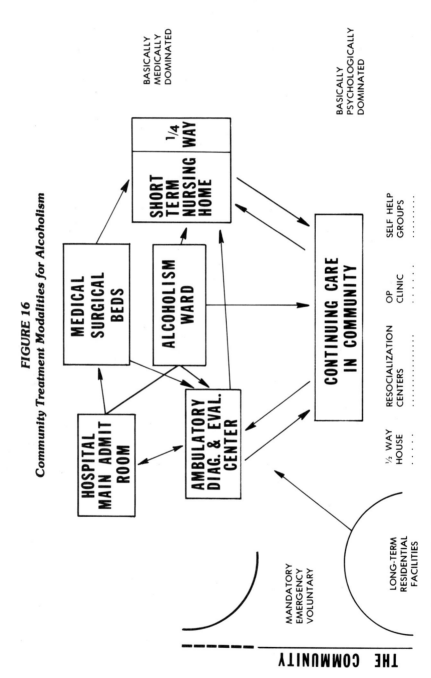

*FIGURE 16*
*Community Treatment Modalities for Alcoholism*

SOURCE: Reprinted from Vernelle Faux, "Recommendations for Detoxification Services," *Proceedings: On Alcoholism Emergency Care Services,* National Institute on Alcohol Abuse and Alcoholism.

2. Do not preach or moralize to the alcoholic.
3. Do not use anger or silence with the patient.
4. Stress the positive aspects of therapy.
5. Confront the alcoholic about his problem and offer suggestions for solving the problem without causing the patient a loss of dignity.
6. Do not underestimate alcoholism as a disease.
7. Do not delay in helping an alcoholic get into appropriate therapy.
8. Warn the alcoholic about foodstuffs and medications that contain alcohol.
9. Respect the alcoholic's appraisal of the situation.
10. Warn the patient about the taking of other drugs during therapy.(21)

# Treatment Outcome[9]

Evaluation is being increasingly recognized as critical for the continued expansion and improvement of treatment programs. Individuals and organizations with life-and-death power over such programs are requiring quantitative evidence of effective impact on clients as well as efficient and economical management. In general, the treatment of alcoholism is often looked on with skepticism and pessimism.

Conventional wisdom has held that there was no very effective therapy for alcoholism and that differences among treatment methods were inconsequential. This attitude is undoubtedly due to the low rate of success reported in evaluations of various treatments. Most of these studies, however, have had serious methodological flaws which distort the record of actual effectiveness of treatment in alcoholism.

The first major flaw is failure to discriminate between the rehabilitation potential of different alcoholic populations. For example, it is estimated that among alcoholic inhabitants of skid row a total rehabilitation rate of only 5 to 10 percent may be expected, but in business and industry, problem drinkers have a high total rehabilitation potential, as high as 80 or 90 percent. Another facet of this flaw is cost-effectiveness. Very intensive therapeutic programs for excessive drinkers with low recovery potential will not show much success, but more modest programs for high-potential patients will usually have considerable cost-effectiveness.

A second flaw arises from the limited perspective of treatment personnel evaluating their results solely on the basis of their own one-time experience with a patient. It is natural for a therapist or clinic, when a patient drops out before having shown definite signs of recovery, to write him/her off as a therapeutic failure. This assumes that the patient was not benefited at all. But as one commentator has noted, this assumption may be erroneous, for "most therapists' successes are built on the preceding therapists' failures. So your failure can be the next therapist's success; which means, you haven't accomplished nothing." In other words,

[9]Adapted from NIAAA, *Alcohol and Health,* Second Special Report, pp. 154-155.

evaluation based on what happened between time one of any treatment undertaking and any particular subsequent time X does not necessarily reveal the total effect of the therapeutic effort. The payoff may be in having laid a necessary foundation for the success that will—again erroneously—be attributed exclusively to the next therapeutic effort. This error is partly responsible for the discouragement that some therapeutic personnel feel about the "low rate" of success with alcoholic patients.

A third flaw involves the target of treatment. Since excessive drinking is what appears to bring the alcoholic patient to treatment, rehabilitation programs have often focused solely on the drinking. This approach ignores other serious problems in the patient's life that may be influencing his/her drinking behavior and which, unless they are dealt with, may make recovery from the alcoholism impossible.

A fourth flaw concerns the criterion of success. Success can be measured effectively only in the light of specified goals. In turn, the definition of treatment goals is intimately related to the therapeutic needs of specific alcoholic populations and to the available methods of treatment. The differential definition of treatment goals in alcoholism, however, has only recently come under consideration.

## Recommendations for Detoxification Proceedings[10]

Initially, the alcoholic visits the physician weekly for 15 to 20 minutes, when the medical symptoms such as nervousness, insomnia, appetite, weight, and sense of well-being are explored. Some supportive psychological counseling is done and warnings with regard to the physical damage of acoholism are given. Ongoing treatment by a tranquilizer such as chlordiazapoxide or diazapam occurs and continues for a period of at least several weeks to a few months. This type of regimen is often fairly effective.(99)

The ideal continuing care program would be in easy commuting distance from the patient's home, work, and family; open and available to him/her at least 12, if not 24, hours a day, 7 days a week; and staffed by an interdisciplinary team who view him/her as their mutual or shared responsibility for as many months, or years, as he/she needs their services.

Some of the obvious measures of effectiveness of detoxification programs are:

1. The ease with which patients with all kinds of manifestations of alcohol abuse can get into the program. This includes ambulatory and voluntary, or coerced and intoxicated patients, as well as those on a stretcher who may not even know where they are being taken.
2. A low incidence of severe medical complications such as seizures, aspiration protracted DTs, acute cardiac arrest, etc. If a real cross-section of the patient

---

[10]Adapted from Vernelle Faux, "Recommendations for Detoxification Services."

population is being served, these complications will occur. If the detoxification service—both directly provided and appropriately backed up by a range of medical-surgical services—is medically effective, the incidence and the severity of these problems will be lessened.

3.  The proportion of patients who leave the detoxification asepct of care without having adequately begun the continuing care phase reflects the effectiveness of the psychosocial component of a detoxification program. The medical intake phase of a comprehensive program cannot be evaluated by such things as percentage or number of readmissions, patients still sober at the end of a given period of time, etc.

Results of the above three criteria will vary widely with the characteristics of the patient population being served. More often than not, they cannot be compared with other similar programs for this reason. The most reliable yardstick is a comparison of the results in these three areas from time to time, within the same program, using built-in devices to determine if and when the patient population of the program actually changes rather than staff views of the patients changes.

An indirect but important measure of a program's effectiveness is the stability of staff accompanied by change and diversification of program. Programs with high staff turnover never get past the formative stages and expend most of their energies on themselves, not on their patients. Programs that become stereotyped and grind out the same services, year in and year out, communicate their boredom and sense of futility to their patients. In either case, the number of "cases" may continue to pile up, but the amount of effective services delivered continues to decline. Above all else, in developing services for alcoholics now or in the foreseeable future, we should keep clearly in mind that we do not have answers to many questions regarding the disease and its treatment, much less its prevention. Each program should build in an ongoing evaluation designed for growth rather than reporting, as well as the kind of support and flexibility that encourages teaching, experimentation, change, and research, both within the facility and out in the community.

# 8

# Preventing Alcohol Problems and Alcoholism

Preventing alcohol problems and alcoholism in our country is a major public health goal, but its realization rests ultimately in the private decisions and behavior of every citizen. Our nation has tried legal prohibition of alcohol and rejected it. Some states are still experimenting with controlled sales of alcoholic beverages, and minors are still denied the legal right to drink. Until recently, the weight of objective evidence suggested that such legal controls have had little effect on use and abuse of alcohol.(6) However, the findings of a recent study completed in Michigan showed that the lower age of majority (18 years) did serve to increase alcohol consumption among Michigan's newest adults, the 18-21-year-olds. The study indicated that after the legal drinking age was lowered, the average 18-20-year-old was consuming an extra six-pack of beer per weekend and an extra bottle of liquor per month.(111) Other research reports by the Alcohol Safety Action Program in Washtenaw County, Michigan, support the comments of Dr. Wolfgang Schmidt, Associate Research Director of the Addiction Research Foundation of Ontario: "Since imposition of the new drinking age laws, significantly more young drivers are being involved in accidents and are being killed, and the carnage can be directly related to their drinking—not to increased police sensitivity, or across the board increases in motor vehicle accidents.[1]" As a

[1]*Report on Alcohol,* American Businessmens' Research Foundation 32, no. 4 (Winter 1974): 31.

result, like Michigan, there is a move in many states to raise the drinking age back to 21.

Moral exhortations and scare tactics have for the most part met with failure. People continue to drink, and a small but significant percentage drink to excess. Yet, there is some evidence that accumulation of facts, with effective education of the public, can and does make a difference. For example, doctors, who have more access to knowledge of the effects of smoking, have significantly reduced their cigarette use.(6)

# Definition for Prevention Programs

Prevention programs should begin by defining the alcohol-related problems they seek to prevent. In today's society, the programs do not include prohibition as a goal; instead, they seek to minimize alcohol-related problems and to reduce the negative consequences of drinking. They recognize that most alcohol-related problems fall within five general areas: (1) chronic illness or disability resulting from prolonged, excessive drinking; (2) acute health problems related to a specific drinking bout; (3) injuries, death, and property loss caused by accidents and crimes related to drinking; (4) failure of the chronic, excessive drinker to fulfill his/her role in the family or on the job; and (5) mental problems such as depression and anxiety related to drinking.

Once the mass of alcohol problems is broken down into distinct alcohol-related behaviors requiring modification, the approach to preventing those problems must be determined. According to public health principles, problems are seen as stemming from an interaction of three factors—the host, the agent, and the environment. Intervention at any or all of these points is appropriate for prevention of a problem. The public health model for dealing with alcohol problems is as follows: *host*—the individual and his/her knowledge about alcohol, the attitudes that influence drinking patterns in the drinking behavior itself; *agent*—alcohol, its content, distribution, and availability; *environment*—the setting or context in which drinking occurs in the community and mores that influence the drinker. Although strategies focusing on any of the three factors may overlap or complement work directed at the others, the public health model provides a useful framework for understanding and organizing prevention programs.(9)

Table 24 uses the public health model to suggest specific prevention techniques directed at the host, agent, and environment.

# Self and Prevention of Alcoholism

A great deal has been said about how outside forces influence thinking and sometimes create difficulties—especially in the area of problem drinking. But each person has *some* control over the kind of person he/she becomes and whether or not drinking patterns become dangerous and gain control.

Abraham Maslow's studies of self-actualizing personalities might be a good

### Table 24
### Targets for prevention activities directed to host, agent and environment

| Host | Agent |
|---|---|
| Teach problems of alcohol in the schools | Examine whether legislation concerning where, when, and how alcohol may be sold and consumed can be changed to reduce alcohol abuse |
| Develop interactive skills (values clarification, decision making. etc.) | Manipulate control policies to decrease or stabilize per capita consumption by restricting availability through a variety of strategies such as |
| Provide alternatives to increase individual self-confidence and inner resources (i.e. hobbies sports) | • a strict pricing policy<br>• limiting on-premises drinking<br>• lowering alcohol content of beverages |
| Educate adults to be responsible hosts/hostesses | • limiting numbers of retail and wholesale outlets<br>• enacting and enforcing strict zoning regulations |
| Identify youths having drinking patterns inconsistent with peers for the purpose of early intervention. | Encourage cooperation between alcoholism personnel and alcohol beverage control boards |
| Provide information about sources of help for teenagers suffering personal or family drinking problems | Assess the influence of advertising and counter advertising on drinking behavior |

#### Environment

Arrange settings where alcohol is consumed to minimize abuse (lighting, seating arrangement, music, food)

Change cultural meaning of drinking to encourage drinking in conjunction with other activities, discourage it as focus of activity

Encourage responsible role-modeling by parents who drink

Develop sanctions against drunken behavior

Improve economic, cultural, and other qualities of life in the community

Encourage educational system to be more responsive to students' personal needs

Decrease consequences of abuse (e.g. provide rides home for intoxicated individuals)

Educate retailers of alcoholic beverages about their legal and ethical responsibilities

SOURCE: NIAAA, *Guide to Alcohol Programs for Youth,* U.S. Department of Health and Human Services (1981).

starting place for prevention of drinking problems. The following summary might point out how well you match up with Maslow's ideal and might help identify some areas you'd like to work on.

Self-actualized people:

1. are realistic. They do not enjoy constant pipedreams. They recognize their circumstances but do not allow their lives to be dictated by circumstances. They work for their goals.
2. take things in stride. They are down to earth. They accept themselves, others, and the world for what they are. They are aware of what is right, what is wrong, and what is possible.

3. are spontaneous. They are not always uptight. They are themselves. They allow others to be themselves.
4. are not on an ego trip. They do not begin every sentence with "I." They are problem-centered, not self-centered.
5. do not get swallowed by life. They respect their own need for privacy and detachment. They know their own personal limitations. They pace themselves. They do not burn themselves out before their time.
6. are "awe-ful." They appreciate people and events in a fresh way. As beholders, they have a lot of beauty in their eyes.
7. can run deep. They do not focus constantly on the superficial. They can see below the surface of things.
8. identify with mankind. They are not religiously, ethnically, racially, or any-other-kind-of-ly parochial.
9. have a few profound relationships. They are known and loved deeply by a few special people.
10. are democratic. They elicit respect and take into account the feelings, desires, and aspirations of others, even when they do not have to.
11. do not confuse means and ends. They would never say and really mean: "I would do anything in the world to . . ." They do not have their price.
12. laugh at life situations, not people. Their sense of humor is not hostile. It is philosophical.
13. are open to the new. They are creative and like to see creative things and be around creative people. They are not easily threatened.
14. do not follow the Joneses. They do not conform. They have their own standards and stick by them.
15. rise above problems. They are not submissive. They are not satisfied simply to cope with problems; they work to remove them.

## Alcohol Education and the Family

The most influential teachers of responsible or irresponsible drinking are parents. Children tend to follow the drinking customs of their families and cultures. Many children see drinking occurring harmlessly in their homes as a part of adult behavior. In some families, even young children are allowed to drink with their families on special festive occasions. Children from such backgrounds are unlikely to accept a hard-line campaign against all alcohol as a "poison"—or the notion that drinking is immoral—and they are likely to become drinkers themselves. Fortunately, such individuals generally do not have problems as adults in controlling their drinking behavior—even though they may drink considerably. On the other hand, children from families in which there is ambivalence toward alcohol—either because parents differ in their attitudes, or because theory and practice disagree—run a greater risk of developing drinking problems as adults. A recent study by Dr. Forest S. Tennant, involving five thousand young adults, suggests that those who drink alcohol at home before the age of 15 are likely to have a problem with alcohol later on.(127)

Since the family is the ideal setting in which to instruct and influence children as to their future drinking patterns, parents might consider some of the following ideas that may make alcohol education within the family more effective:

1. Parents should examine with utmost honesty their own attitudes toward drinking.
2. Parents should learn the truth about alcohol from authoritative sources such as books, pamphlets, and professionals, and should encourage their children to do so.
3. Parents should set a good example for their children in conversation and behavior: never push drinks on people who do not want them; drink moderately; and serve nonalcoholic drinks during social gatherings at home.
4. Parents should discuss the subject of alcohol fully and frankly with their children. Avoiding the subject, even though parents are abstainers themselves, is shirking an important duty. Children must be given the facts, be allowed to make their own decisions, and be allowed to draw their own conclusions.
5. Parents should acquire factual knowledge about alcohol, its use, and its non-use.
6. Parents should work toward responsible positions and attitudes of their own regarding alcohol.
7. Parents should be consistent in what they say and in what they do regarding alcohol.
8. Parents should help children view alcohol objectively, as a substance that can be used either without harm or destructively.
9. Parents should teach children some fundamental causes of problem drinking.
10. Parents should promote respect for other persons who practice responsibility toward alcohol in a different way, whether through use or non-use.(17)

Lynn Lott, founder and director of Petaluma's Family Education Center, would add the following suggestions that may minimize the danger of alcohol and other drug abuse among children. These suggestions are based on the fact that alcohol and drug abuse more likely stem from a family setting in which there is a lack of parental concern, there is parental permissiveness or domination, there is a lack of ability to cope with stress, and there is a feeling of alienation. The use of Lott's guidelines make for a family in which children are more contributing and participating members of the family structure.

1. The family foundation should be built on feelings of trust and friendship among family members. Discussions that are calm and take place in a friendly atmosphere are much more effective than nagging and yelling.
2. An effort should be made to set aside specific times for parents and children to participate together in family activities. Sports activities, vacations, picnics,

and other outings are perfect for family interaction.

3. Family councils are good sources of sharing for family members. Such meetings should be encouragement for each family member to share feelings and ideas.

4. Parents should capitalize on children's strengths. When children perform tasks in an especially efficient manner, they should be complimented. Children should, as much as possible, work on tasks with which they have some expertise and interest.

5. Children should be encouraged to develop decision-making skills by being allowed to make decisions in appropriate situations. Even young children can participate in this process by deciding, for example, whether they would rather wear a green shirt or a blue shirt. Older children, naturally, will have more weighty decisions in which to participate.

6. Parents should become informed, learning as much as possible about alcohol use and abuse and about the dangers of abuse among children and teenagers.

7. Parents should refrain from using words that are absolutes—like *always* and *never*. More appropriate words imply that there might be a gray area rather than just black or white—like *might* or *could*.

8. Parents should be honest at all times with their children, especially concerning alcohol use and abuse. Parents should express their feelings about potential alcohol use and the effects of alcohol.

9. With the help of the children, parents should set limits and rules for alcohol. There should always be consequences for not following the rules, and parents should be prepared to follow through in helping to enforce the consequences of broken rules and limits.

10. Children are different, and therefore may decide to live differently from a parent's style of life. Parents should accept this and not condemn children. A parent must still love the child, even if the parent does not like the way the child acts.(168)

## Peer Approaches to Prevention: [2]

Strong peer interaction and influence is a normal, necessary, and healthy part of adolescent development. This natural tendency to rely on peers provides an opportunity to channel that very force toward healthy behavior and the promotion of the survival, maintenance, and growth of the individual. Peer groups have outstanding potential as an effective method for preventing problem behavior because they can readily be tailored to deal with so many of the factors

[2]Adapted from Alcohol, Drug, and Mental Health Administration, *Adolescent Peer Pressure—Theory, Correlates, and Implications for Drug-Abuse Prevention,* DHHS Publication.

related to stress reduction, building coping skills, and modifying situational constraints outlined previously. For example, the following types of peer programs can help to address many different factors associated with alcohol/drug and adolescent problem behaviors.

1. Positive peer influence programs can help to channel peer pressure in positive directions; they can also help to develop and enhance self-esteem and problem-solving and decision-making skills.
2. Peer teaching programs address the need not just for useful information and skills among teenagers, particularly in relation to academic success in school, they also provide participating young people with meaningful roles and real-world responsibilities at a time when they are increasingly isolated from such roles and responsibilities in the prolonged adolescence of the peer culture.
3. Peer counseling/facilitating/helping programs assist young people in solving problems and coping with some of the challenges with which they are inevitably confronted in modern society; family problems and problems with friends and school are commonly dealt with in these kinds of programs.
4. Peer participation programs can function as a link between the world of peers and the world of adults by providing peers with real-world tasks and responsibilities and adult guidance in accomplishing them.

In short, peer programs can address all the major variables—stress, skill deficiency, and situational constraints—that have been identified as being closely related to problem behavior. The growing popularity of peer-group strategies in schools and youth-service programs across the country attests to the effectiveness of these approaches, and research evidence has also begun to support such approaches.

By providing as many opportunities as possible for healthy development and by minimizing risks, we can reduce young people's vulnerability to alcohol and other problem behavior. Since anything that severely obstructs the survival, maintenance, or growth of an individual may lead to negative outcomes, an effective approach to the prevention of problem behavior calls for many kinds of simultaneous efforts. Prevention should work to minimize avoidable stress, abuse, and loss in the lives of young people. It should provide a wide range of constructive coping skills—skills that can promote healthy social and emotional development and thus help in the management of unavoidable stresses. Further, prevention should reduce the impact of situational factors that encourage drug and alcohol abuse.

Peer group approaches show great promise in accomplishing many of these ends. Peer programs can help young people to become more competent, to make meaningful contributions to their peer groups and their communities, and, most important, to gain experience in functioning as effective and concerned human beings.

## Those Who Assist Youth[3]

To help young people come to grips with the meaning of alcohol in their lives, adults need to establish an open, sharing, trusting atmosphere. Teenagers need to deal with their feelings and values since this subjective dimension—not facts—determines how and why people use and abuse alcohol.

Achieving a warm, accepting relationship with teenagers can be as natural to youth workers as breathing, but a few suggestions may still be welcome. Alcohol project directors speak with striking similarity about the personal qualities important in adult workers. These key factors include:

*Honesty and openness.* The adult who works with adolescents must be prepared to give them honest feedback about their behavior and to provide a model of self-awareness. When the adult leader is pleased or disappointed, he/she should tell the young people. An adolescent's trust is based on confidence that the adult means what he/she says and says what he/she means. Without honesty there is no trust, and without trust there is no cooperation. It also helps teenagers to get to know the adult leader on a personal level. Teens love to hear short personal anecdotes.

*Respect and ability to listen.* When teens talk—listen! The adult leader should make eye contact, smile, avoid sarcasm or sarcastic tone of voice, face the speakers squarely, make sure each member of the group is heard, and insist that teenagers also respect each other's feelings and ideas. Adults need to deal with the fact that they may respect some teenagers easily while finding it hard to respect others. An important part of this respect is really believing in the teenagers' capabilities—in their ability to make their own responsible choices and to carry out their own ideas and plans.

*A sense of humor.* Teens respond to a light touch; humor also makes life easier for the sponsor. Although alcohol is a serious issue, a project can still be fun rather than dull or grim. Jokes, cartoons, refreshments, recreation breaks, personal anecdotes, a funny prop—all can contribute to a positive, productive atmosphere. Teenagers also enjoy taking photos or videotape films of themselves at work on projects, or filming their classmates as part of a prevention project.

*Flexibility and patience.* No youth project operates exactly as it was intended. Teens forget procedures, fool around, and fail to doublecheck things that should be triple-checked. Sundry other maddening slips occur to throw off the best-laid plans. Adult leaders need to expect and tolerate last-minute hitches and adjustments. Flexibility is essential, along with a backup plan.

Other qualities mentioned by project directors as important for the adult leaders are the capacity to feel empathy for the lifestyle and life pressures of

---

[3]Adapted from Alcohol, Drug Abuse, and Mental Health Administration, *Alcohol Prevention Programs,* DHHS Publication No. (ADM) 81-1131 (1981), p. 4.

adolescents, to be open to criticism and new ideas, to care about youngsters, and to want to help.

## Alcohol and Mass Media

Through advertising and the mass media, a climate has developed in our country that supports the idea that chemicals can be used for coping; this, indeed, is one way many drinkers rationalize their use of alcohol. The alcoholic beverage industry would identify alcohol with the attainment of otherwise unattainable dreams and the alteration of the image by which the drinker is perceived by himself/herself and others. Dr. Straus has made some excellent points concerning this issue. He suggests that social drinking as pictured by advertising is associated with being admired or loved (but not with loving), being a winner (but never a loser), being a popular and distinctive person of glow and gusto. Emphasis is on what a person does and how he/she is perceived by others, never on what he/she is.(143) Drinking is depicted over and over again as appropriate to a variety of work and leisure situations. The images of drinking promulgated by the mass media are generally biased in terms of the functions and safety of drinking. In television and movies the public is exposed to countless images of intoxication, the use of alcohol for coping, the casual consumption of huge quantities of alcohol without complications, and the association of heavy drinking with status, prestige, popularity, wealth, success, and sexual fulfillment. The propriety of many types of situational drinking is also reinforced.

Perhaps one of our most effective preventive approaches would be in line with recent recommendations of the National Commission on Marijuana and Drug Abuse. The commission suggested that alcoholic beverage labels should "point out the dangers of excessive use" and that the alcohol industry should "reorient its advertising to avoid making alcohol use attractive to populations especially susceptible to irresponsible use."[4]

Many organizations and public service groups have conducted advertising campaigns on television and radio. These campaigns have not been very successful, however, in providing adequate public education on alcohol use and abuse. One problem with such mass media campaigns is that the media rather than the campaign originators determine what times, how often, and over what period of time program messages are presented.

## Alcohol Education and the Driver

Alcohol education may reasonably take two forms: education for responsible alternatives to drinking and driving, and education for countermeasures against drinking and driving. Education needs to promote other responsible alternatives to drinking and driving while still intoxicated. Education might stress, for example,

---

[4]National Commission on Marijuana and Drug Abuse, *Drug Use in America: Problem in Perspective,* Second Report (1973).

that as an alternative one may consider abstaining on a social occasion if he/she has to drive home from that occasion. It is the host's/hostess's responsibility to provide both alcoholic and nonalcoholic beverages, so the abstainer will surely not have to go "drinkless" at the occasion.

Another alternative is to plan ahead—realize that drinking may be a part of the social occasion, and as such, it may be wise to appoint a nondrinking friend as chauffeur for the evening. If there are no nondrinkers in the company, one might call a cab to escape the danger and risk of driving home. Education might stress the fact that a third alternative is to play the waiting game. One can always wait one hour per average drink before driving to ensure that he/she gets home safely.

In addition, the public needs to be educated about the possible countermeasures that can be taken against drinking and driving. These countermeasures take the form of interventions in the drinking/driving process. Primary intervention is aimed at preventing individuals from combining drinking and driving in the first place. It may be effected by public awareness measures, which in turn may be achieved by media and educational campaigns. Secondary intervention is oriented toward removing the impaired driver from the road before he/she has a collision. This primarily means that there must be a determination of where, how many, and when collisions take place so that adequate and effective police power may be deployed. Tertiary intervention centers on the court action taken after detection, charging, and conviction of those involved in alcohol-related traffic incidents. The major thrust of this aspect of intervention is educative rehabilitation.(59)

## Alcohol Education and the Community

Experts tend to agree that if the incidence of alcoholism in the United States is to be lowered, three types of social change will have to come about: certain characteristics of American drinking practices will need to be modified, tougher laws will need to be enacted and enforced, and the conditions which lead to improved mental health of individuals and families will have to be encouraged.(6)

At the heart of many alcoholism prevention programs today is the recognition that responsible drinking behavior depends largely on knowing how to drink. Many feel that public education campaigns stressing only the dangers of alcoholism are unproductive. As one authority, Dr. Robert Straus of the University of Kentucky, says: "It is as if the driver-education courses in schools would be concerned only with gorier aspects of speeding and reckless driving. This might frighten a few students, but it would not produce many who know how to handle an automobile safely. With the emphasis placed solely on alcoholism, alcohol education might similarly frighten a few students, but it would not produce many who know about drinking, or how to handle alcohol safely."[5]

[5]Robert Straus, ed., "Alcohol and Society," *Psychiatric Annals* 3, no. 10 (Oct. 1973): 95-96.

For those who want to continue responsible drinking or for educators who want to encourage people to drink responsibly, five steps have been outlined to keep drinking habits at a social stage. These steps must be strictly adhered to if alcoholism is to be prevented. They are:

1. You must accept the knowledge that alcoholism is something which could happen to you if you drink.
2. You must decide you wish to take any steps necessary to make sure that this illness does not overtake you.
3. You must adopt a specific policy of absolute moderation with no exceptions if you want to play it safe.
4. You must set an absolute limit on the number of drinks you will take on any drinking occasion.
5. You must establish certain definite nights in each week when you will not drink at all.(64)

Current public education efforts by those who seem to be the most enlightened teachers encourage individuals to assume responsibility for their own drinking behavior. They encourage abstinence for those who choose it but accept the fact that many will choose to drink. Those who drink are encouraged to understand how they and alcohol interact and to behave in a responsible manner when they use alcohol. Responsible drinking means that you never have to feel sorry for what has happened while you were drinking.[6]

Education for prevention and responsible drinking might center on the following four concepts:

1. Make sure that alcohol use improves social relationships, rather than impairing or destroying them.
2. Make sure the use of alcohol is an adjunct to an activity rather than being the primary focus of action.
3. Make sure that alcohol is used carefully in connection with other drugs.
4. Make sure human dignity is served by the use of alcohol.

At this time we should direct our efforts more toward helping young people understand and appreciate themselves and their feelings through development of healthy interpersonal relationships. Teaching people to feel better about themselves and others is a must in our preventive efforts. Alcohol is too often used as a "crutch," an "insulator" or as a "people substitute" for dealing with life.(6)

It is clear, as previously indicated, that we have glamorized the drinking of alcoholic beverages. We must act to de-glamorize it. Dr. Henry Brill has said that

---

[6]Ruth C. Engs, *Responsible Drug and Alcohol Use* (New York: Macmillan Publishing Co., Inc., 1979), p. 000.

"anything that tends to glorify alcohol as an ingredient of a wild, good time, is very bad."[7]

On the possible glamorization of alcohol through education, Dr. Marvin Block, a well-known authority on alcoholism, has stated, "Teaching people to drink properly will not necessarily prevent alcoholism later in life when circumstances change.[8] One of the primary goals of education should be to develop good character and conduct. And, as Dr. Winton Beaven has pointed out, "How to best use the knowledge of science that we have is a moral problem, an ethical problem; so education must not only give us knowledge of the facts, but it must try to get people to act rightly on the basis of the facts. The aim of all education should be to help students develop their own value system and then live by them. If we can succeed in doing this, we can expect to create a whole new generation of people who will begin to find more useful solutions, not only to the problems of alcohol in our society, but in all problems that deal in the moral and ethical realm."[9] It would also seem that, if done properly and truthfully, teaching abstinence could be as important and effective as teaching people how to drink responsibly.

The concept of teaching people to drink responsibly sounds good but probably does little to prevent or solve alcohol problems. There are those who use alcohol to deal with the emotional and social dimensions of their lives because they lack adequate coping skills. This type of person may try to drink in a responsible manner but usually is unable to do so. They only way he/she can control his/her drinking is to abstain completely. A continued attempt to teach him/her to drink "responsibly" may encourage him/her to become alcoholic. There will always be people who are unable, or unwilling, to sustain safe drinking practices regardless of how intense social and other pressures upon them may be.

The concept of educating individuals to drink responsibly or not at all is not new. It is patterned largely on safety concepts applicable to driving and other risky activities. It is inherent in the habits and attitudes of cultural groups which have demonstrated, over many centuries, an ability to use alcoholic beverages with a minimum of danger. Implicit is the idea that young people are rational beings and should be given whatever education possible—in school, in church, and particularly at home—to enable them to understand that it is not essential for them to drink—and that they would probably be better if they did not. But if they do drink, they should know how to do so with maximum safety for themselves and others.

Among the most important principles in alcohol education to be considered are these:

*It is not essential to drink.* An individual—youth or adult—who decides to

[7]Winton Beaven, "Toward Prevention," *Report on Alcohol,* Summer 1973, p. 19.
[8]Marvin A. Block, *Alcoholism: Its Facets and Phases* (New York: John Day Co., 1965), p. 000.
[9]Beaven, "Toward Prevention," p. 20.

abstain from alcohol for moral, medical, economic, or other reasons should not be placed under pressures to drink by other members of society.

*Excessive drinking does not indicate adulthood, virility, or masculinity.* In an adult society, one can no more establish such qualities by the ability to hold a large amount of liquor than by the ability to hold a large amount of dessert.

*Controlled drinking depends on specific physical and psychosocial factors.* These include: (1) early development of healthy attitudes toward drinking, within a stable family environment; (2) prevention of dangerous blood-alcohol levels by restricting alcohol consumption to small amounts, in appropriate dilution, and preferably in combination with food; (3) recognition that drinking is dangerous when used in an effort to solve emotional problems; and (4) universal agreement that intoxication will not be sanctioned by the group. This latter point is particularly important. Being drunk is not funny, and it is not a solution to problems; it is a condition in which a person is out of control and prone to poor coordination and judgment.

*Uncontrolled drinking or alcoholism is an illness.* Children, including the children of alcoholic parents, should be aware that alcoholism is not a perversity, a character defect, or even the direct result of drinking. They should know that an alcoholic, like a victim of diabetes or tuberculosis, is a sick person who can and should be helped.

*"Alcohol education" should not be restricted to "alcoholism education."*

*Alcohol education should focus on the individual and the environment.* Education may take some of the following forms: emphasis on alternative activities (other than drinking) that can be engaged in and alternative beverages that can be used at social gatherings, peer education to promote informed decision-making, mass media messages, compaigns by voluntary organizations, and information on modifications of the drinking setting that can be affected.

Research shows that teenagers follow adult models in their drinking patterns, and the best single indicator of the teenage drinking patterns in any specific community is the adult drinking pattern there. There are certainly exceptions, but if parents drink, there is a high probability that teenagers will drink; similarly, abstinent parents usually produce abstinent children.(6)

One college study found that students who violate a family custom of abstinence or very light drinking are likely to go further in their drinking than students in whose families drinking is acceptable behavior.

A young person's decision to drink or not to drink is usually made on the basis of a complex of forces, including the practices and wishes of his/her parents, the attitudes of his/her church, the influence of his/her peers, how much money he/she has to spend, and how strongly he/she is impelled to assert independence from adult authority.(6)

For both adults and teenagers, drinking patterns vary with sex, socioeconomic level, status, religion, ethnic background, place of residence, and other factors.

# Alcohol and the Environment

Environmental approaches may focus on the setting in which drinking occurs, the conditions under which a person must function when intoxicated, and the cultural mores that influence drinking behavior. Research on preventive measures involving the drinker's surroundings has not been as extensive as work with individuals. Further experimentation is needed to determine how altering the drinking environment affects drinking behavior.

### Modifying Drinking Settings

The physical properties of alcohol and its effect on the body underlie attempts to modify settings in which drinking takes place. Many believe excessive drinking and drunkenness result from hurried or tense situations such as cocktail parties in which alcoholic beverages are liberally available without food or nonalcoholic drinks. Sufficient amounts of food, promotion of nonalcoholic beverages, friendly conversation, and other means of reducing the focus on drinking could control the tendency to drink too much. Several prevention programs, particularly among the college aged, have used this type of modification with some success.

It is part of drinking etiquette for the guest to be able to drink socially without becoming drunk and possibly obnoxious. The following are suggested rules for becoming a better guest:

1. Know your limit.
2. Eat while you drink.
3. Do not drink fast. Sip for enjoyment; do not gulp for effect.
4. Accept a drink only when you really want it.
5. Cultivate taste. Choose quality rather than quantity.
6. Skip a drink now and then.
7. When dining out, if you must drive home, have your drinks with dinner, not afterward.
8. Beware of unfamiliar drinks.
9. Do not drink to relax when what you really need is a change of pace or some sleep.
10. Remember that the purpose of a party is togetherness, not tipsiness.

A host or hostess also has a responsibility to the guests. He or she needs to promote party togetherness while keeping things under control. The following are guidelines for the host or hostess at a gathering where drinks will be served:

*The home setting.* Provide seats for all, plan for people movement, and keep the lights on.

*The bartender.* Choose a bartender of known discretion. The eager volunteer may turn out to be a pusher who uses the role to give every glass an extra "shot."

*Pace the drinks.* Serve drinks at regular, reasonable intervals. The length of the interval will depend on whether the guests are enjoying the company or the drinks more. A drink-an-hour schedule means good company prevails.

*Don't double up.* Many people count and pace their drinks. If you serve doubles, they will be drinking twice as much as they planned. Doubling up is not hospitality; it is rude.

*Don't push drinks.* Let the glass be empty before you offer a refill. And then do not rush, especially if someone comes up empty too fast. When a guest says "no, thanks" to an alcohol drink—do not insist.

*Push the snacks.* Do this while your guests are drinking, not after. This is important because food slows down the rate at which alcohol is absorbed into the bloodstream. It also slows the rate at which people drink.

*Serve nonalcoholic drinks, too.* One out of three adults chooses not to drink at all. Occasional drinkers sometimes prefer not to. Offer a choice of drinks besides alcohol—fruit and vegetable juices, tea, coffee, and soft drinks.

*Offer more than drinks.* When guests focus on the drinks, the party is slipping. Stir up conversation. Share a laugh. Draw out the guest talent. A good host or hostess has more to give than just food and drinks.

*Serving dinner.* If it is a dinner party, serve before it is too late. A cocktail hour is supposed to enhance a fine dinner, not compete with it. After too many drinks, guests may not know what they ate or how it tasted.

*Set drinking limits.* When a guest has had too much to drink, you can politely express your concern for him by offering a substitute drink—coffee, perhaps. This is a gentle way of telling a guest that he has reached the limits you have set for your home.

*Closing the bar.* Decide in advance when you want your party to end. Then give appropriate cues by word and action that it is time to leave. A considerate way to close the drinking phase is to serve a substantial snack. It also provides some nondrinking time before your guests start to drive home.

## Insulating Drinking Behavior

Measures to insulate drinking behavior can be oriented toward physical, cultural, or temporal separation. Physical separation is the most obvious. For example, most states prohibit taverns within a certain distance of schools and churches. Cultural separation includes informal zoning policies that designate certain areas where drinking may occur. Temporal separation refers to measures that allow sufficient time between the drinking occasion and potentially harmful situations. Examples of temporal measures include installing ignition systems in automobiles that require mental alertness to operate, closing bars earlier during the work week, and providing beds for intoxicated guests after a party.

### Changing Reactions to Drinking Behavior

An alternative way of reducing some social problems related to drinking is to react less strongly. In some cases, such as a parent's panic over a drinking episode by a teenage son or daughter, the reaction may be more harmful than the drinking itself. This approach has become possible primarily because the stigma of alcoholism gradually has been reduced. Alcoholics are being encouraged to seek treatment and their families and friends are encouraged to treat drunken behavior as an alcohol, not a moral problem.

### Modifying the Consequences of Drinking

The occurrence and outcome of accidents often could be changed by a variety of environmental modifications. In this way, the consequences of drinking are challenged without changing the drinking. For instance, intoxicated individuals are especially likely to benefit from automobile airbag crash systems, lowered speed limits, fireproof bedding, and from having transportation provided for them or having the need for transportation eliminated.

### Influencing Cultural Mores

One of the most difficult areas for experimentation but one with promise for possible long-range effects is the attempt to modify the cultural significance of drinking. Sanctions on drinking exercise a great influence over the individual drinker and operate to establish a status quo within the community. Thus, introduction of healthy drinking attitudes could go far to influence individual and group drinking patterns and behaviors.(9)

## Alcohol and Social Tolerance

If we are going to make any preventive programs concerning alcohol problems work, it is vital that we understand the following concept, presented by Dr. Seldon D. Bacon: problem drinking and alcoholism will persist as long as and in direct proportion to the weakness, conflict, uncertainty, or avoidance reactions which appear as societal responses. Dr. Bacon suggests that instances of these two factors—people exhibiting the behavior and the time span over which one person will show this behavior—will increase under the following conditions:

1. The level of tolerance for the behavior in the society is undefined, uncertain, irregular, and inconsistent.
2. The labeling of the deviant behavior is uncertain, irregular, and even consciously false.
3. Sanctions are not only uncertain but even recognized sanctions are irregular and inconsistent in application.
4. Major sources of authority in the society, for example, parents, religious

leaders, scientists, statesmen, professionals, educators, etc., are unconcerned or avoid concern.
5. The acting functionaries expected to act in similar problem situations, to help or punish, or to advise or explain, do not act or react in ways appropriate to those roles.

These conditions provide, so to speak, a terrain favorable for the emergence and for the continuation of the deviant behavior. This is a terrain above and beyond any internal susceptibility of the individual for that behavior. To put this in more colloquial terms in relation to drunkenness, if parents and peers and neighbors frequently look the other way or even openly criticize other police and teachers who do try to exert sanctions; if physicians and social workers and personnel officers refuse to recognize or label or pay any attention to repetitive patterns of deviant drinking; and if there is widespread communication about the fun, prestige and social acceptance of such deviant behavior, then drunkenness patterns of repetitive deviant use and alcohol problems will flourish. If, in addition, it is widely known or believed that the law or perhaps religion officially states that "you must not drink" while it is equally widespread knowledge and belief that despite this almost "everybody does," which is the case for many 16-21 year olds in relation to alcohol use in our society, then there may be even more than the favorable terrain for such behavior. There may be positive though perhaps unintentional incitement for such behavior. It may be that this particular condition does not in fact incite behavior but rather molds the form of that behavior, always molding it towards the deviant in terms of time, place, amount, accompanying attitude, etc.[10]

It should be rather obvious that the magnitude of the alcohol problem and its effect on almost every aspect of life in society warrants a major local and national investment in efforts to understand these problems, develop and implement better strategies of preventive intervention, and provide comprehensive treatment for those who are already victims of problem drinking and alcoholism.

And lest we be lulled asleep by any immediate and easy answers, it is necessary to understand that "alcohol problems are caught up in a massive clustering of human pathology in which problems invariably beget problems. Because they do not occur as isolated problems, they are not receptive to intervention aimed simply at altering or preventing self-destruction through drinking."[11] The complexity of alcohol problems themselves, and their relationship to numerous other problems, presents serious dilemmas for those who would develop enlightened social policies and preventive programs dealing with drinking and its consequences.

[10]Seldon D. Bacon, "Drug Abuse and Alcohol Abuse: The Social Problem Perspective," *The Prosecutor* (Jan.–Feb. 1969).

[11]Ray Oakley, *Drugs, Society, and Human Behavior* (St. Louis: C.V. Mosby Co., 1972), p. 126.

## Can Drinking Patterns Change? [12]

Societies can change over time. Drunkenness was a problem among the ancient Hebrews. Yet temperate drinking became the established norm among Jews when their national culture was reformed around 525-350 B.C. Among Jews today, especially the religiously affiliated, drinking is an integral part of numerous religious observations; drinking is moderate and is rarely done for its own sake, but is considered appropriate when coincidental to ceremonies, festivals, celebrations, or meals. Among Italians, wine is viewed as a good, a necessary part of a substantial meal, as well as an accompaniment of celebrations, such as weddings, christenings, and holidays.

Changes in consumption patterns need not take generations. For example, in a recent ten-year period, France was the only major western nation to reduce its per-capita consumption of alcohol, apparently in response to a national campaign calling for moderation in drinking. Similarly, high taxation of distilled spirits in Denmark changed consumption patterns in that country during World War I to such an extent that even today beer is the alcoholic beverage more frequently consumed.

Another illustration derives from a study of adolescents that produced a typology of individuals, among which were two with a particular proneness to deviant alcohol use. Moreover, the categories of individuals responded differently to alternative alcohol education programs. That is, some combinations of educational materials and types produced a lessening of alcohol deviancy while other combinations produced an increase. The implication of this is that it is both necessary and possible to develop special prevention programs for special groups of people.

## A National Drinking Environment

Fully aware of the complexities involved, the NIAAA is beginning the task of creating a new national drinking environment, based on facts and a feeling of responsibility regarding alcoholic beverages. The following guidelines have been proposed:

1. The public should understand the facts about alcohol and its effects on the human body.
2. More people should realize that, among other things, alcohol is an anesthetic drug capable of causing euphoria, sedation, unconsciousness, and death, as well as adverse social effects.
3. The decision to drink or not to drink should be a personal, private decision. However, anyone choosing to drink has a responsibility not to destroy himself/herself or to impair his/her relation with society.

[12]Reprinted from NIAAA, *Alcohol and Health,* Second Special Report to the U.S. Congress from the Secretary of Health, Education, and Welfare, June 1974, p. 198.

4. The improper use of alcohol can be socially, psychologically, and physically harmful.
5. Those who drink should respect the decision of the proportion of the population of this country who choose not to drink.
6. People who serve alcoholic beverages should recognize their responsibility. Bartenders who refuse to sell drinks to an inebriated customer hosts/hostesses who do not push unwanted or "loaded" drinks or guests are acting responsibly and contributing to a healthy drinking environment.
7. Those who drink should not become intoxicated.
8. People must understand that adults are significantly responsible for the drinking habits of teenagers because the example set by adult has a great influence on the subsequent drinking attitudes and practice of young people.
9. The public must realize that the line between alcohol misuse and alcoholism is mostly a matter of degree and consequence and, therefore, there is a direct link between irresponsible attitudes toward drinking and the problem of alcoholism.(6)

In view of these proposed guidelines, the Secretary of Health, Education and Welfare, in the recent Second Special Report to the U.S. Congress on Alcohol and Health, made the following recommendations:

*That the growing store of knowledge about alcohol and alcoholism be made more readily available for use by specialists and the public.* The need to systemize and process the growing worldwide experience, study, and research so that it will be available to scholars, researchers, legislators, educators, administrators, professionals, and all citizens is critical. The further development of the National Clearing House for Alcohol Information in collaboration with appropriate academic and other sources should, therefore, be pursued energetically.

*That educational resources for professionals in schools be expanded and developed.* The rehabilitation of problem drinkers and alcoholic people requires the help of a wide variety of professional and allied personnel with special skills and understanding. Resources for the training and accreditation of such specialized personnel should be identified in model form, and states or regional consortiums should be encouraged to adopt these approaches as appropriate to their own needs. The long-range prevention of alcohol misuse depends in part on the transfer of both knowledge about alcohol and the understanding of its use and non-use to the younger generation. Schools throughout the nation have an appropriate role in this process. Suitable models of alcohol education should be developed by the National Center for Alcohol Education and regional centers. State and local school systems can adapt these models to their curriculums.

*That efforts to decriminalize and provide community care for alcoholism and public intoxication be redoubled.* The uniform alcoholism and intoxication treatment act, recommended to the states by the National

Conference of Commissioners on Uniform State Laws and by the Secretary of Health, Education and Welfare, provides a model for states to decriminalize and establish the legal framework within which to approach alcoholism and public intoxication from a community care standpoint. This section has been recommended by the courts, presidential commissions, and professional organizations. A special grant, in public law 93-282, to states that adopt the legal framework and approach is a fundamental recognition by Congress and the administration of its importance.

*That the new laws protecting the privacy and confidentiality of all citizens with drinking problems be strictly and immediately enforced.* Public law 93-282 amends section 333 of the alcoholism act to provide the first comprehensive approach to the issue of confidentiality and privacy for people with drinking problems.

*That efforts be speeded up to assume quality care for and to reduce the carnage among Spanish-speaking Americans, Native Americans, young Black men and those who commute on the highways.*

*That the values of early identification and treatment programs in business and industry be recognized throughout the country.* The magnitude of the cost to the nation's economy stemming from problem drinking and alcoholism is staggering. It is imperative to encourage the wider establishment in government as well as in private sector of the types of program that, with the cooperation of labor and management, have successfully restored substantial majorities of affected personnel to health and normal function. The economic benefits of effective, early identification and treatment programs demonstrably outweigh the cost, and the human benefits are beyond valuation.

*That quality comprehensive care be extended to alcoholic people through coverage under health and disability benefits and the establishment of standards for care.* Total coverage for the treatment of alcoholism through traditional and other third-party payment plans should continue to be studied. The application of such coverage in both general and special therapeutic settings should be explored, with particular consideration to the continuum of health and human service needs of alcoholic people in the process of recovery and rehabilitation. Standards and certification for such are crucial to insurance coverage and to the quality of care that can be obtained by alcoholic people.

*That new and revised policies and guidelines governing the distribution and sale of alcoholic beverages be developed.* Current laws and regulations need to be re-evaluated to determine whether they are fulfilling their intended purposes. To the extent that they are not, a set of model codes of alcoholic beverage control should be formulated which states and communities may adopt with modifications to suit their own needs.

*That it be recognized that the multiplicity and extent of alcohol-related problems cannot be the exclusive responsibility of the federal government.* We should find ways to strengthen the involvement and the role of private enterprise in reducing the problems of alcohol abuse and alcoholism, enhance the role of voluntary agencies, and encourage support by state and local governments in activities related to the care of the afflicted and in contributing to preventive efforts.

*That efforts be made to intensify the study of the relationship of alcohol use to cancer, heart disease, liver disorders, pregnancy and fetal health, aging, longevity and mortality, brain function, and the addictive process.*

*That a new national consensus concerning what constitutes responsible use and non-use of alcoholic beverages be formulated and articulated.* Current concepts and mores concerning the use and non-use of alcoholic beverages are confused, inconsistent, and sometimes destructive. Knowledge about the use and misuse of alcohol needs to be shared more widely and continually so that citizens, and especially our young people, are given the opportunity to base their decisions to drink or not to drink on the best information that is available. In addition, new and alternative recreational and social settings should be considered in which drinking will be a coincidental function rather than a main reason for frequenting them.(8)

# Summary of Alcohol Problem Prevention

In summary, the following preventive efforts are suggested as realistic, feasible, and necessary:

*Establish legal guidelines concerning control and availability of alcohol, and enforce those guidelines.* The aim should be to protect society from alcoholism and other problems directly attributable to the use and abuse of alcohol. The guidelines should include provisions for care and treatment of the alcoholic, making every attempt to return him/her to society as a useful member.

*Pass legislation against drinking and driving* that is stringent and unvaryingly enforced, as is the case in Europe.

*Stop the mass media advertising campaigns that entice people to use alcohol for unrealistic and unscientific reasons.* We should consider banning all alcoholic beverage advertising. At the very least, where advertising is allowed, warnings about possible consequences should be mandatory on container labels.

*Reduce social stigmas, taboos, and myths about alcoholism to make it easier and less painful for problem drinkers to call for help.* Part of successful alcoholism prevention lies in allowing citizens in distress greater freedom to seek help and in making their problem a legitimate reason for treatment and assitance.

*Provide skilled people and facilities to manage alcohol problems.* Effective treatment of the alcoholic and his "significant others" within their cultural setting is required for reduction of alcoholism.

*Educate doctors, people in helping professions, law enforcement personnel, and, especially, teachers.* They should develop acumen for recognition of potential alcoholism and the role of alcohol in our society as it effects the physical, emotional, social, intellectual, and spiritual dimensions of people. Another "must" for the reduction of alcoholism is early recognition and diagnosis. Individuals with beginning alcohol problems typically show verbal or behavioral symptoms. The task of early case finding must be shared by professionals and lay people.

*Make the public aware of the dangers inherent in the consumption of alcohol.* As the consumption level increases, the incidence of antisocial consequences disruptive to families and society also increases. The concept of abstinence needs to be popularized without militant "prohibitionist" attitudes.

*Develop educational programs in schools that help young people understand alcohol,* its responsible use, and problems of inappropriate use, communicating the idea that alcohol need not and should not be used as a means of self-medication in physical, emotional, or social disturbances.

*Educate the public about alcoholism.* An immediate task is to disseminate well-founded facts, as opposed to myths (similar to the accomplishments in the area of smoking and health education). This should include an understanding that social acceptance of intoxication as a part of drinking behavior contributes to a high incidence of alcoholism. Young people derive their values, attitudes, and practices from adults. If adult attitudes regarding alcohol and alcoholism can be altered, there is hope for diminution of alcoholism and the disruptive consequences of consumption. "It must include the education of a whole generation of young people with values so powerful they will assist in protecting themselves and their families from dependence upon a potentially destructive drug."[13]

*If a traditional family lifestyle has been chosen, encourage family unity in which parents share themselves with their children—not a family life in which people simply coexist.* This should include an understanding of the importance of environmental influences on behavior learned in childhood through the processes of imitation, identification, and role-modeling by parents and other significant persons.

*Establish programs in schools, churches, and in the community that help young people enhance their self-esteem and develop emotional and coping skills that enable them to feel good about themselves and others.*

*Continue research into the nature, cause, treatment, and prevention of alcoholism and alcohol-related problems.*

*Solicit necessary support from private enterprise and national, state, and local governments for these programs.*

The underlying concept and the major objective in the prevention of alcoholism should be promotion of the mental health of individuals within their chosen lifestyle, whether it be family, single-parent, single, or some other lifestyle, so that the individual can safely resolve his/her tensions and anxieties.

# 9

# Laws, Regulations, and Drinking Patterns[1]

"What happened? Did I hit someone?"[1]

Bryan P., 20 years old, asked those questions from his hospital bed Saturday. Police say what happened was that his drunken driving killed a family of six.

P., of Kankakee, said he had been to three or four taverns before the accident Friday evening. Police tests showed he was intoxicated when he crashed into the rear of the car carrying Brenda and Dennis Allen and their four children home to Bradley from a family birthday party.

P. probably wouldn't have been drunk on that Downstate highway if he had been too young to be served in those taverns.

This account of a fatal automobile accident, caused by a youth's drunken driving, appeared in a *Chicago Sun-Times* editorial (April 1979) and reflects at least one aspect of the issue of availability of alcoholic beverages: that is, what is the minimum age at which young people should legally be able to purchase or consume alcoholic beverages?

But—although this topic has received a great deal of public and official attention recently, as states reviewed and often revised their minimum drinking-age laws—this is but one aspect of the overall availability issue. In the foregoing editorial, for instance, one might ask if it would have made a difference in the outcome if:

[1]This chapter is adapted from Shirley Aldoory, "ABC Laws," *Alcohol Health and Research World* (NIAAA), Winter 1979/80, pp. 2-9.

253

1. the youth involved had had less "disposable" pocket money to spend on drinks?
2. the alcoholic beverages had been priced beyond the youth's ability to buy?
3 the bartender at one of the taverns had recognized that the youth was "getting loaded" and had exercised an option not to serve him any more drinks?
4. the taverns had not been so close together? Or one of them had been closed?
5. the ignition design on the youth's car would have prevented start-up when the young man reached the stage of intoxication?
6. or, the young man had better things to do than to get drunk?

# Availability the Pervasive Issue

Control of the availability of alcohol for human consumption has a history as old as the written laws. The famous Code of Hammurabi, formulated some 4,000 years ago, contained four articles on the topic. The usual objective of such control, both in the Old World and in the New, was to prevent fraudulent selling practices, to assure availability, and to secure revenue for the state.

Only recently has one of the principal concerns in alcohol legislation come to be the attempt to control or prevent the occurrence of alcohol-related problems. In North America, especially, this concern has centered upon various aspects or features of control legislation spawned at the local level after the repeal of national prohibition laws. In the United States these features have included: pricing and taxation of alcoholic beverages; minimum age restrictions; the hours and days alcoholic beverage facilities may be open; density formulas for determining the number and type of beverage outlets; licensing regulations; advertising restrictions; local options—that is, the existence of "dry" and "wet" counties and cities; certain "dram shop" acts that prohibit sale of alcoholic beverages to intoxicated persons; restrictions on the kinds of on-premise facilities established and the ways in which they serve their beverages (such as with food only); and restrictions on licenses according to proximity to schools or churches.

One of the most obvious facets of attempted control centers around the "legal drinking age"—the age at which alcohol can legally be purchased. Age requirements vary from state to state: it's legal to purchase alcohol at 18 in some states, but not legal until the age of 21 in many others. Even where the legal drinking age is 21, some states allow the purchase of beer or of beer and wine at the age of 18.

There's some indication, that higher legal drinking ages may reduce the number of accidents among young drivers. In Michigan, the number of alcohol-related accidents among 18- to 20-year-old motorists went from 12,507 in one year to 9,627 the year after the legal drinking age was changed from 18 to 21.[2]

[2] "Drinking Age Law Reduces Accidents, Arrests," *The Bottom Line on Alcohol in Society*, Vol. 4, No. 4 (Fall 1981), p. 23.

While public interest in the features of the alcoholic beverage control (ABC) laws has generally stemmed from either moral or practical concerns, social researchers and those concerned with public health issues have been heavily involved in isolating and studying each aspect of alcohol beverage availability for the particular effect the feature of the law may have on drinking behavior.

## Where Shall We Sell?

The single most frequently employed means for control of availability over the centuries has been regulation of the number of places in which alcoholic beverages may be purchased. Some studies—especially in Canada and Finland—have shown that arrests for drunkenness are higher where there are fewer numbers of outlets. Other studies have shown that consumption, but not inebriety, may increase where control policy has made alcoholic beverages accessible in areas where they were formally illegal. Yet a time-trend analysis of drunkenness arrests in Finland indicated that the trend in inebriety actually closely followed trends in other indicators of alcohol problems. One is led to the view that indicators of inebriety may not be dependent upon outlet frequency, but rather on differences between countries rather than between regions within a country.

Many authors have come to believe that increasing the availability of alcoholic beverages may lead to increases in consumption that may contribute to alcohol problems *other than* public drunkenness—owing to the development of a more permissive attitude toward intoxication.

## Who Shall Sell, And How?

"Many earlier writers (and a few in recent times) considered the facilities and physical features of the American saloon or the English public-house to be among the seducers of the working man to a life of insobriety." Although "'planned alternatives" to drinking remain a part of many prevention programs and have been shown by some advocates to have an effect on drinking behaviors, they have certain limitations.

Nevertheless, the moral and aesthetic sentiments that compelled restrictions on the physical attributes of drinking establishments apparently still guide thinking in the development of local ABC laws in the United States. The "crazy quilt" of liquor control laws, which usually have some meaning for local residents, and usually are aimed at certain kinds of control—such as location of outlet, decor, physical attributes, requirements for food, among many others—certainly may seem erratic to an outside observer, and, in many instances, may inconvenience essentially mobile Americans.

## Cognac and the Corner Drugstore

For instance: an American beginning his vacation in Colorado can buy a bottle of brandy, scotch, wine, or a 6-pack of beer in the corner drugstore, as long as he doesn't try to make his purchases between 2 and 7 a.m. Or, he can have a martini in a hotel lounge, in a club, or in a restaurant with food, if he prefers. Crossing the

Colorado-Kansas border, however, the traveler discovers that his purchases of anything other than beer must be made at licensed liquor stores and he may not buy "liquor by the drink."

In some Oklahoma counties, he cannot buy anything other than 3.2 beer. By the time he reaches Texas, he is anxious to make other purchases, but finds he is unable to buy in "dry" locales, while in some cities he finds he can buy liquor at the same grocery store where he purchases the bread, meat, and cheese for his lunch.

Traveling up the eastern seabroad, he discovers that restaurants in South Carolina will sell him drinks—but in unopened miniatures, while in Virginia, he may purchase a drink of liquor whith his food—as long as the restaurant is "primarily" a food establishment.

A detour through West Virginia places the traveler in the position of being unable to purchase a drink because he is not a member of a "private" club. He heads back toward home through Indiana, where he finds that he is able to purchase a drink of liquor in a restaurant if there are more than 500 residents in the town. Depending upon his state of mind, this traveler may return to Colorado determined never to take another vacation without carrying along his own liquor supply.

Although writers have frequently pointed out the problems with the American experience—such as "gulping" drinks in "dry" areas where drinks may be sold in certain clubs only, or where the "bottle"—alcohol sold in bottles only—rule applies; or driving across state lines to "booze up" because the age limit is lower in a neighboring state; or hoarding alcoholic beverages when going from a "wet" to a "dry" area—there is very little hard data to prove that restrictions controlling the type and makeup of the alcoholic beverage selling establishment have a significant local effect.

## The Saloon Versus the Basement Bar

During the mid-1960s in Victoria, Canada, closing time for public drinking places was extended from 6 until 10 P.M. It was found there was no change in the overall total of personal injury accidents, but it was found that the peak of occurence for such accidents shifted from between 6 and 7 P.M. to between 10 and 11 P.M.

Also, this accident pattern was absent on Sunday, when the outlets were closed. The results of this study indicate that changes in closing hours may have a significant effect upon the pattern of consumption; but that the total consumption, or, at least the frequency with which patrons consume impairing amounts of alcohol may remain unaffected.

Observers note that studies dealing with changes in local alcohol control laws should be considered in the context of the nation as a whole, keeping in mind that usually several changes—not just one—occur simultaneously. Also—and significantly—the importance of public drinking places, at least in North America, has declined since the early 1900s, because of the increased attractiveness of the home as a place in which to drink.

A *Milwaukee Journal* editorial entitled "Papa Didn't Know Best" notes that a father hosting a party for his 17-year-old son was complaining of being fined for serving drinks to minors. The last paragraph says, "Many Wisconsinites argue that the legal drinking age should be raised to 19. But would that have had much effect on the alcohol abuse at the M. party? We doubt it. ...." The article further appeals for the repeal of a "lackadaisical attitude that many adults have about drinking—as it relates to their kids and themselves."

This article clearly points up an area of concern that haunts many of those favoring control legislation as a means for preventing alcohol abuse—that is, how to reach the users in their own homes, where they may privately consume as much alcohol as they are able to buy. Many advocates believe that the shortest distance to the consumers' homes in the purview of control is through the pocketbook.

# The Price of a Drink

A man found guilty of public intoxication appealed the charge on the grounds that he was "afflicted with the disease of chronic alcoholism" and therefore had not appeared drunk in public of his own volition. On a prior appeal, however, the man had appeared sober in court because, as questioning revealed, he admitted having had one drink, but had not had "the price of a second."

This actual court case has been used by some authors to point up the extent to which economic considerations—in addition to others—may influence drinking behaviors. Many advocate such measures as increased prices and taxation of alcoholic beverages as a means for control and prevention of alcohol problems.

The bits of evidence lined up for price control for alcoholic drinks go something like this: Alcoholic drinks appear to behave in the marketplace like other commodities; that is, econometric studies of data for Australia, Canada, Finland, Ireland, Poland, Sweden, and the United States have shown price to be a significant predictor of demand for alcoholic beverages. It is now a well-accepted fact that demand levels and the prevalence of alcohol problems are related; researchers have demonstrated that the death rate from liver cirrhosis varies closely with per-capita sales. A substantial amount of epidemiological data now points to a close association between the rate of occurrence of alcoholism and the level of apparent alcohol consumption. Although some researchers have indicated that demand for alcohol may be more sensitive to changes in income level than in price, a recent review of data demonstrated a significant price effect when income was held constant. Also, study data have shown heavy consumers are responsible for a large part of total alcohol consumption and that such consumers usually purchase the cheaper beverages in each type. Under such circumstances, personal consumer preferences for products are apt to be highly dependent upon the price structure of the pure alcohol contained in the cheapest brands of each type.

Obviously, one of the most serious questions to be raised concerning policy experimentation in legal controls—including pricing and taxation—falls into the realm of ethics and political philosophy: that is, should legal controls be used to protect the public health? In a social atmosphere tending toward greater extension of individual rights, such an approach would be highly unpopular, even if the measure were deemed necessary.

In addition, it is still all too true in the realm of social research that a correlation between factors in a study (such as between price and demand for alcoholic beverages) may not irrevocably mean cause and effect. However, those who believe in a strong effect of price upon drinking behavior say that the evidence is in.

## Beer, the Common Man's Drink

"Getting drunk on beer makes a man vulgar; getting drunk on spirits makes him dangerous; and getting drunk on wine makes him charming."

This old proverb, thought to be of central European origin, expresses the rather widely held belief that alcoholic beverages differ in their effects on behavior, for reasons other than the amount of alcohol involved. This has been the usual justification for an imposition of substantially higher taxes on distilled beverages.

Studies most frequently cited in support of differential taxation have been those of Goldberg and his associates on the relative intoxication potential of beer, wine, and spirits. There are those who point out, however, that the conditions under which these experiments were conducted did not parallel most human drinking practices; for instance, giving subjects undiluted distilled beverages after fasting. On the other hand some studies have compared the effects of beer, wine, and spirits under conditions more closely approximating most drinking situations and found no differences among blood-alcohol curves for the three classes of beverage alcohol.

Other detractions from the belief that beer is a "drink of moderation" include the following: One researcher found a well-known pattern of explosive intoxication associated with the drinking of spirits among Finnish consumers and correlated this with the "anticipation of subjects" as to their expected reactions when drinking spirits; this would introduce a cultural element into the overall reaction scheme. Other researchers have examined blood-alcohol levels of a large sample of drivers and determined that while 58 percent of "control" drivers reported beer as their beverage of choice, 64 percent of labeled "accident" drivers said they usually consumed beer. Cross-national epidemiological studies have failed to find evidence to indict any one class of beverage over another. Actually, the best predictor of the liver cirrhosis death rate is per-capita wine sales, because alcoholics consumed a larger proportion of all wine sold than they did of spirits or beer. The most likely attraction for wine is its relatively low cost. Beer has been implicated in the clinical literature about as frequently as spirits or wine as the consistent factor in a diagnosis of alcoholism.

The conclusion seems inescapable that dependence upon alcohol can be sustained as much with beer or wine as with spirits. Indeed, the beverage preferences of alcoholics seem to reflect the preferences of the populations under study, with a distinct tendency toward cheaper sources of alcohol.

Those who have reviewed the data on studies of beverage preferences indicate that if there is any reason to consider beer differently from wine or spirits, it may be because some researchers have indicated a certain amount of price inelasticity in beer, meaning that if the price increases, consumers will continue to purchase beer in the same amount.

However, such patterns may actually be similar to those experienced in Denmark and Belgium, where an extremely heavy tax was levied on distilled beverages, rendering them inaccessible to much of the population. The lowered consumption rate that this brought about was eventually replaced, however, by increases in the consumption of beer in both countries.

# Effect of Price and Taxation

It should be noted that while the data is perhaps as yet inconclusive concerning the effect pricing and taxation have on drinking behaviors, it is fairly evident that both price and taxation do have some effect—and that they should be considered in any serious discussion of prevention of alcohol problems as a public health concern.

And yet, the federal government also taxes alcoholic beverages by type of product, with distilled spirits taxed at a much higher rate than wine, and beer at a much lower rate than either spirits or wine. The same tax rates have been in effect since 1951 and, given the inflation rate experienced in this country over the last few years, this represents much less than half the absolute dollar amounts originally imposed.

Those who favor economic considerations as possible preventive measures point to the real need for educating the American public to the public health value of such measures, because the experiment with prohibition "did not work." However, as these experts point out, in spite of the adverse consequences of prohibition, during its first few years in Canada, Finland, and the United States, alcohol consumption and alcohol-related problems reached the lowest level achieved in these countries for any period for which there is relevant data.

However, during the latter years of prohibition in the United States when an illegal trade became well established and the speakeasy and clandestine outlets appeared—roughly 1923-1933—consumption increased substantially. Looking at this end of the cycle, the public tends to discount legal or official restraints as having any value in the control of drinking behaviors.

It is this belief that generally pervades the makers of state and country laws for the control of alcoholic beverage consumption in the United States. While temperance may be spelled out clearly as a goal of local enabling acts, researchers have found that the chief aim of legislators and appointed officials who create ABC laws is the "providing of an 'orderly,' 'regulated,' 'gangster-free' alcoholic beverage market."

Thus the presumed costs of official restraints—variously cited as resentment of the system by nonproblem drinkers; increased use of toxic substitutes by at least some heavy users of alcohol; rise of illicit trade with attendant criminality; expense and difficulty of law enforcement; loss of revenue by producers, sellers, and government; loss of respect for the law through widespread evasions; and loss or substantial reduction of personal pleasures and social benefits derived from alcohol use—overshadow and tend to cause complete rejection of legal restraint in any form.

With the possible exception of recent drinking-age legislation, the current trend in North America, and in other parts of the world, appears to be in the direction of liberalizing control laws. There are those who decry this move as possibly quite consequential in the creation of problem drinking habits. But, for the believers in certain consumption theories of control, the problem of proof remains.

## Problems Related to Consumption

In the 1960s, Popham and his colleagues brought the work of French investigator Sully Ledermann to the attention of researchers in North America. Ledermann had indicated that the most important result of his research was "the finding of a 'quasi-mathematical' connection between moderate and heavy consumption" and suggested that this left "little hope for those who want to reduce alcoholism without affecting the (overall) consumption."

This proposed relation between general drinking and drinking by alcoholics in a given population has met with rather consistent opposition, however, both from groups that might be considered to have a vested interest in the sale of alcoholic beverages and from members of the scientifc community.

Part of the reason behind objections to the "single distribution model" of prevention is the presence in North America of two well-developed schools of thought that tend to: (1) set the alcoholic apart from others in the population, in that heavy alcohol consumption by problem drinkers and alcoholics is considered symptomatic of some disorder peculiar to them, and factors that may cause a change in the consumption level of normal drinkers will have little or no effect on pathological drinkers (the "bimodal model"), and (2) view restrictive control measures as fostering an unhealthy ambivalence toward drinking and impeding adoption of healthy drinking styles, such as those found in certain European countries (the "integration model"). Although France was once viewed as a good example for adopting this model of prevention, the high rate of alcoholism among the French is now viewed as a cause for concern for proponents of the integration theory. Proponents of these views, as well as opponents of the single distribution model, are now quite visible in the scientific as well as the professional press.

Propositions that proponents of the single distribution theory believe relevant to prevention are:

1. Change in the average consumption of alcohol in a population is likely to be accompanied by a change in the same direction in the proportion of heavy consumers.
2. Since heavy use of alcohol geneally increased the probability of physical and

social damage, the average consumption should be closely related to the prevalence of such damage in any population.

3. Any measures, such as those regulating the availability of alcohol, which may be expected to affect overall consumption are also likely to affect the prevalence of alcohol problems, and hence should be a central consideration in any program of prevention.

In spite of a growing alcoholism problem and similar increases in alcohol-related concerns, the American states currently have some of the most stringent drinking laws in the modern world. This in itself would seem to cast doubt upon the effectiveness of local control laws—alone—in altering or controlling established drinking habits.

A cursory review of newspaper clippings since the recent minimum drinking-age changes in some states implies a different set of youthful behaviors than had been expected: there appars to be a minimum of deceit regarding age in order to buy alcoholic beverages; so far theres is little clambering across state lines to purchase beverages in an adjoining state with more lenient laws; there has been little stockpiling of beer and other beverages by youth; and—if sample newspaper surveys are to be believed—there is a certain subdued acceptance on the part of the youthful segment of the population affected by the changes. But the drinking in high school parking lots continues.

One reporter was prompted to write, "The grim truth is that the legal age for drinking has very little to do with the availability of alcoholic beverages in and around the high schools of America." Rather, he says, it is the availability of such beverages in the home, it is the amount of money youth has to spend without parents' ever wondering where the money went, it is a general loosening of parental discipline, and perhaps a general slipping away of cultural values.

Other references in the public press have also commented on the role of "regulation of sales and higher prices through taxes" as an option to be considered in the overall prevention of alcohol problems in this country. As Rowan concluded, "There's no clearer gauge of a society's frustration than the extent to which it throws simplistic laws at complex problems."

The recommendations put forth to bring the economic issue into focus within the total picture include developing a taxation policy that maintains a reasonably constant relationship between the price of alcohol and levels of disposable income (income after taxes), a moratorium on further relaxation of alcohol-control measures as well as adoption of a health-oriented policy with respect to such measures, and a public education program designed to increase awareness of the personal hazards of heavy alcohol consumption.

While not all researchers believe that these are the only measures needed to control the increase in alcoholism and alcohol-related problems, almost all now agree that studies are needed concerning the availability of alcoholic beverages and its effect on consumption—especially to ascertain the American experience, since most available documentation is, thus far, based upon research conducted elsewhere.

Many experts now favor the development of a public health model for consumption of alcoholic beverages for this country. Some authorities place the responsibility for initiating such a move at the federal level; some say it should be done by the states. Many agree that it can be a cooperative effort.

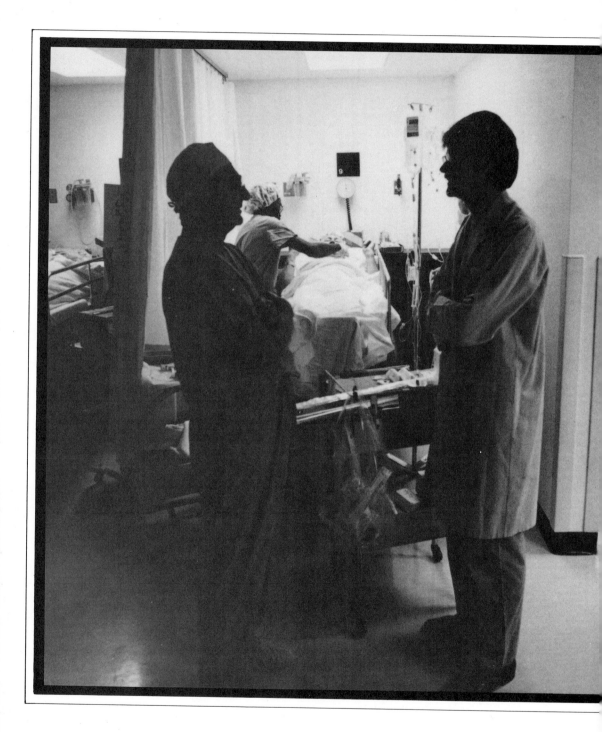

# 10

Alcohol Emergencies

The alcoholic syndrome usually consists of *problem drinking,* during which alcohol is used frequently to relieve tensions or other emotional difficulties, and the stage of *true addiction,* in which abstinence from drinking causes major withdrawal symptoms.[1] The form in which alcohol is ingested is irrelevant; the heavy beer drinker may be as much an alcoholic as the patient who indulges in too much hard liquor. Frequently, alcoholics are dependent on other drugs as well, especially those in the sedative, barbiturate, and tranquilizer categories.

Alcoholic emergencies occur in all social strata. The alcoholic differs in many significant respects from the true social drinker. The alcoholic usually begins drinking early in the day, is more prone to drink alone or secretly, and may periodically go on prolonged binges chracterized by loss of memory ("blackout periods"). Abstinence from alcohol is likely to produce withdrawal symptoms, such as tremulousness, anxiety, or delirium (DTs). As the alcoholic becomes more depedent upon drinking, his/her performance at work and relationships with friends and family are likely to deteriorate. Absences from work, emotional disturbances, and automobile accidents become more frequent.

The alcoholic is more prone to illnesses and injuries.

While it is important to detect evidence of chronic alcoholism or acute

[1]Introductory section adapted from Nancy L. Caroline, *EMT—Advanced,* prepublication edition, Department of Transportation, DOT HS 501207.

intoxication in assessing a patient, it is equally important not to ascribe all signs and symptoms to alcohol until other causes have been ruled out. Thus, the patient found stuporous with alcohol on his/her breath must not be assumed to be simply drunk. His/her stupor may have resulted from anything that causes stupor in the sober individual, including head trauma, hypoglycemia, infection, etc. Furthermore, his/her stupor is no less a threat to life—indeed it may be more so—than in the sober patient. Thus, whatever your suspicions about the patient's alcoholic intake, he/she deserves the same careful assessment and management as any other patient.

Among the syndromes directly related to alcoholism are acute intoxication and alcohol withdrawal syndrome. The signs of *acute intoxication* are similar to those of overdosage with any other central nervous system depressant: drowsiness, disordered speech and gait, and erratic behavior. But beware. This picture may be precisely mimicked by the diabetic patient in insulin shock, so be suspicious and, when in doubt, give sugar. If the patient is not diabetic, no harm will be done, and indeed, many nondiabetic alcoholics have significant hypoglycemia anyway.

Also be alert to the possibility that the patient may have taken a combination of alcohol and sedative drugs. Check the patient's pockets and surroundings for evidence of medications which may significantly complicate this picture. Give the alcoholic in coma emergency care as you would for any other comatose patient. Give attention to the airway, and monitor the patient carefully. In severe cases of acute intoxication, respiratory depression, cardiac arrhythmias, or shock may occur and should be managed as they would be in any other patient.

Alcoholic withdrawal syndrome comprises a wide spectrum of signs and symptoms, ranging from acute anxiety and tremulousness to delirium tremens (DTs). The latter usually occurs between 24 and 72 hours after the patient's last drink but may occur as late as seven to ten days later. DTs are characterized by confusion, tremor, restlessness, and hallucinations, the latter often of a frightening nature (snakes, spiders, rats). DTs should be suspected in any patient with delirium of unknown cause. Reassurance is all that is necessary in the field. *Seizures* are also common to alcoholic withdrawal and tend to occur early in the withdrawal period, usually during the first 24 hours of abstinence.

## Emergency Care of Alcoholic Emergencies

When you encounter an alcohol abuse patient, certain signs indicate that medical attention is needed *immediately.*[2]

1. Signs that the nervous system is depressed—sleepiness, coma, lethargy,

---

[2]List of signs from American Academy of Orthopaedic Surgeons, *Emergency Care and Transportation of the Sick and Injured,* 2nd ed. (Menasha, Wis.: George Banta Company, 1977), p. 294.

decreased response to pain, and so on.
2. Impaired reflexes, coordination, judgment.
3. Tremors (especially if the patient is suffering withdrawal).
4. Extremely low blood pressure.
5. Withdrawal that has become painful.
6. Inappropriate behavior (especially if it is aggressive).
7. Digestive upsets, including gastritis, vomiting, bleeding, and dehydration.
8. Excessively slow or absent breathing.
9. Grand mal seizures.
10. Delirium tremens (terrifying mental confusion, constant tremors, fever, dehydration, rapid heartbeat, and fumbling movements of the hands).
11. Disturbances of vision, mental confusion, and muscular incoordination.
12. Disinterested behavior and loss of memory.
13. Injury to bones and joints that is unexplained and that is in various stages of healing.

Emergency care for patients of alcohol abuse includes the following:[3]

1. Establish and maintain a clear airway. Remove anything from the mouth or throat that might pose a breathing hazard, including false teeth, blood, mucous, or vomitus.
2. Turn the patient's head to the side and downward toward the ground; in case of vomiting, the patient's mouth and throat will drain more easily in this position. Should vomiting occur, hold the patient's tongue forward and down.
3. Monitor the patient's vital signs frequently. In case of respiratory or cardiac complications, treat the life-threatening situations immediately.
4. Speak firmly to the patient. Be understanding and assuring. *Never* ridicule or criticize the patient.
5. If the patient is conscious, offer him/her fluids, preferably juice, by mouth in small amounts.
6. Obtain a brief history so that you know what kind and how much alcohol was consumed. Perform a brief physical assessment to eliminate possibilities of complications or other injuries.
7. Call for emergency medical assistance.

Certain kinds of intoxication call for specialized care in the emergency situation:

1. Uncomplicated intoxication. A patient of uncomplicated intoxication excudes

[3]Guidelines adapted from H.L.P. Resnik, Harvey L. Ruben, and Diane Daskal Ruben, *Emergency Psychiatric Care* (Bowie, Md.: The Charles Press Publishers, Inc., 1975), pp. 64-76.

the odor of alcohol, has an unsteady gait and slurred speech, and is nauseated or vomiting. You should simply assist the patient to his/her home or to a facility where someone can be with him and watch him/her. If in doubt call emergency personnel to transport him/her to the hospital.

2. Intoxication with disorientation. Very young drinkers, elderly drinkers, or drinkers with organic brain damage are extremely susceptible to disorientation resulting from alcohol ingestion. Sometimes disorientation results from taking alcohol in combination with other drugs. Emergency care consists of the following:

   a. Find out exactly what kind of alcohol and drugs, and how much, was ingested.
   b. If the patient is conscious but seems more sedated as time goes by, induce vomiting, if emergency help will not be available for longer than 30 minutes. Collect a sample of the gastric contents, (vomitus) and send with the rescue team.
   c. Assess the patient's vital signs, and support the patient if there is any evidence of life-threatening signs and symptoms.
   d. Never leave the patient alone.

3. Intoxication with assaultive behavior. When you encounter a drinker who is belligerent, aggressive, psychotic, destructive, or paranoid, remember that patients who respond to alcohol with this kind of gross disturbance usually have some underlying problem. Too often, emergency rescuers smell the odor of alcohol, notice the slurred speech, and blame the whole situation on alcohol.

   As the effects of the alcohol wear off, the psychosis (and underlying problem) will surface. If the problem was due to alcohol alone, it will disappear as the alcohol wears off.

   To deal with a disturbed person, follow these guidelines:

   a. Never attempt to handle the patient by yourself.
   b. Approach the patient carefully and slowly. Never touch him/her before you have explained the situation.
   c. Arrange to have the patient immediately transported to a medical facility.

4. Intoxication with depression. Because alcoholics are prone to severe depression, you may occasionally encounter an alcoholic threatening suicide. He/she may be aggressive, verbally abusive, and agitated; he/she may shift quickly from laughter to tears. Deal with the patient in this way:

   a. Convince the patient that he/she needs help.
   b. Stay with him/her at all times; be prepared to physically restrain him/her.
   c. Talk openly and directly to the patient about his/her self-destructive thoughts.
   d. Take all antisuicide preventions.
   e. Arrange to have patient transported to a medical facility.

5. Intoxication with alcoholic stupor. A patient in an alcoholic stupor sits or lies listlessly and sometimes slumps over. He/she breathes deeply and loudly, and

the odor of alcohol is present; his/her face is usually flushed. Although he/she is stuporous, he/she responds to pain stimuli (such as pinching or sticking with a pin) and to very loud talking. Emergency care consists of the following:

   a. Monitor the patient's vital signs and take immediate measures to maintain a clear and adequate airway.

   b. Avoid sedation of any kind.

   c. Call for medical assitance.

6. Intoxication with convulsive seizures. Alcoholics who experience involuntary jerking and twitching of muscles in the arms, legs, hands, feet, or entire body may be suffering from convulsive seizures. Such a patient may drool or bite his/her tongue; his/her eyes may be rolled up. The seizure itself usually lasts thirty to sixty seconds; during that time the patient is unconscious. Immediately following the seizure, the patient falls into a deep sleep.

   Emergency care for a patient with convulsive seizures combined with alcoholism should be:

   a. Protect the patient from hurting himself/herself.

   b. Hold the patient's head in your lap so that he/she will not bang it against the ground.

   c. Call for medical assistance.

7. Intoxication with unconsciousness. Patients who do not respond to loud questioning or to painful stimuli and are breathing irregularly should be cared for in the following way:

   a. Follow the first four steps of basic management for intoxication.

   b. If the patient stops breathing (or if his/her lips and skin become purplish), administer artificial ventilation.

   c. Administer oxygen if available and you know how.

   d. If the patient's heart stops beating, immediately initiate cardiopulmonary measures to resuscitate.

   e. Take supportive measures to prevent or correct shock.

8. Alcohol withdrawal. Patients suffering from alcohol withdrawal will experience seizures during the first three days that their blood level of alcohol decreases. The seizures are accompanied by hyperventilation and extreme sensitivity to light.

   The most serious effects of these seizures are the possibility of falling and incurring a fracture or other injury, and the aspiration of vomitus.

   Care for the patient as you would any other patient with a seizure, and call for medical assistance.

# General Care for a Drug and Alcohol Emergency [4]

Often, you will be unable to tell exactly what the victim has been using. However, there are general guidelines that apply to treatment in all overdose situations.

[4]Final section adapted from Caroline, *EMT Advanced.*

First, do not panic. Squelch your impulses to throw cold water on the victim or to move him/her around. Of course, you should move the victim who is inhaling a harmful substance or is in immediate danger (for instance, a victim who has lost consciousness in a roadway or who is hallucinating in a burning building).

Get medical help quickly. Some drugs bring on life-threatening emergencies (interruption of heartbeat, cessation of breathing, sharp increase in blood pressure, coma, high fever, vomiting while unconscious, or seizures, for example), and medical attention must be given to those symptoms as well as others that could become dangerous if unattended.

Try to determine quickly what happened; try for a quick evaluation. Do not spend a lot of time at this stage finding out what happened, but do ask the victim what was taken; if the victim is unconscious or incoherent, ask friends or family members. Make a quick survey of the victim and the environment; look for empty bottles, syringes, pills, or other drug equipment. Many serious diseases (such as diabetic coma or epilepsy) resemble drug/alcohol overdose; do not make the mistake of assuming that a stuporous, slurry-speeched victim has ingested drugs/alcohol. Never jump to conclusions.

Do not accuse the victim. In many cases, the victim may suffer increased ill effects because of psychological damage incurred during treatment. Be quiet, calm, and gentle; help the victim realize that what is happening is due to ingestion of the drug/alcohol and this phase will pass. A victim who is panicked over a confused mental condition needs reassurance that a drug/alcohol—not mental illness—is causing these symptoms.

Never leave an intoxicated person alone—not even in a jail cell. They should be observed and attended to at all times until the effects of the drug/alcohol have completely worn off.

Provide a reality base for the victim. Tell the person who you are, and what your position is; use the victim's name when addressing him/her. Explain thoroughly that you are there to help. If the victim is responsive, help identify the things around that are familiar: friends, family members, a newspaper, a favorite chair, a television program. Remain calm and self-assured as you help the victim establish a reality base. Anticipate concerns and help solve them. Anticipate the concerns of the victim's family and friends and have answers for their questions if you can. They will want to know what to expect; help them obtain as much information as possible.

Maintain eye contact with the victim. Touch him/her if appropriate; unless a victim is hostile or aggressive, a touch can be reassuring. Maintain a relaxed body posture as you work with the victim; he/she will be able to sense your own anxiety and fear if you tense up.

Encourage the victim to communicate. Communicate directly with the victim; do not communicate though others. Ask clear, simple questions that can be understood by a person in a muddled state; ask your questions slowly, one at a time. If the victim is having trouble thinking or speaking, ask questions that require only a yes or no. Tolerate repetition; do not become impatient if the victim tells you the same thing over and over again. Help the victim gain confidence in you. Listen carefully, in a nonjudgmental way, to what the victim has to say. Respond to feelings; let the victim know that you understand such feelings and that you are not critical. If the victim begins to make progress, identify it and reinforce the progress.

If a victim is aggressive, hostile, violent, or appears to be psychotic, certain tactics should be carefully followed:

1. Call for emergency assistance. If at all possible, keep familiar things with the person—a family member, a friend, a coat, or some other possession.
2. Let the victim sit near the door of the room; do not place any obstacle (or person) between the victim and the door. In other words, do not block the route of escape. A victim who feels trapped in a room and who has no chance of escape will likely become more anxious, which will exaggerate hostility and violence.
3. Never approach a potentially violent victim alone.

# Bibliography

The vast—and growing—body of literature concerning alcohol and its use or abuse includes pamphlets, reports, articles, textbooks and training manuals, and books. A significant number are published by the federal government and by companies and associations concerned with the consequences of alcohol use. The numbered list provided here records not only the resources used directly in the preparation of this volume, but also allied and background materials of interest to students wishing to do further reading and research in given topics.

The many reference numbers in parentheses scattered throughout the text refer the reader to specific sources that provide a starting point for further in-depth research in specific subjects.

Government publications and other items listing no author by name are listed here in alphabetical order under their titles. Many libraries, however, will catalog such items under the name of the issuing agency.

1. *A Chip Off the Old Block: Parents as Models for Their Children's Behavior.* U.S. Department of Health, Education, and Welfare. DHEW Publication No. (ADM) 77-454A, 1977.
2. Ackerman, Robert J. *Children of Alcoholics.* Holmes Beach, Fla.: Learning Publications, 1978.
3. *Alcohol: A Family Affair.* U.S. Department of Health, Education, and Welfare. DHEW Publication No. (ADM) 74-75, 1974.
4. *Alcohol and Alcoholism: A Handbook.* Correctional Association of New York and International Association of Chiefs of Police. New York: The Christopherson Smithers Foundation Inc., 1966.
5. *Alcohol and Alcoholism: Problems, Programs and Progress.* National Institute of Mental Health, National Institute on Alcohol Abuse and Alcoholism. PHS Publication No. (HSM) 72-9127, 1972.
6. *Alcohol and Alcoholism.* U.S. Department of Health, Education, and Welfare, Public Health Service, National Clearinghouse for Mental Health Information, PHS Publication No. 1640.
7. *Alcohol and Health.* National Institute on Alcohol Abuse and Alcoholism. First Special Report on the U.S. Congress on Alcohol and Health from the Secretary of Health, Education, and Welfare. DHEW Publication No. (HSM) 72-9099, 1972.
8. *Alcohol and Health.* National Institute on Alcohol Abuse and Alcoholism. Second Special Report to the U.S. Congress from the Secretary of Health, Education, and Welfare, June 1974.
9. *Alcohol and Health.* National Institute on Alcohol Abuse and Alcoholism. Third Special Report to the U.S. Congress from the Secretary of Health, Education, and Welfare, June 1978.
10. *Alcohol and Health.* National Institute on Alcohol Abuse and Alcoholism. Fourth Special Report to the U.S. Congress from the Secretary of Health and Human Services, January 1981.

11. "Alcohol and Society." Committee on Alcoholism and Drug Dependence. *Journal of the American Medical Association,* May 10, 1971.

12. "Alcohol and the Elderly." *Alcohol Topics in Brief.* National Institute on Alcohol Abuse and Alcoholism, November 1978, pp. 1–3.

13. "Alcohol—Damnation, Disease, Dependence?" *Emergency Medicine,* August 1972, pp. 59-80.

14. "Alcohol Use, Problem Drinking, and Alcoholism." *The Bottom Line on Alcohol in Society* 2 (Fall 1978): 26-31.

15. "Alcoholism: American's Most Destructive Drug Problem." *Medical World News,* February 26, 1971, pp. 43–52.

16. "Alcoholism: New Victims, New Treatment." *Time,* April 22, 1974, pp. 75–81.

17. *All in the Family.* U.S. Jaycees. Tulsa, Okla., 1975.

18. Bacon, Seldon D. "Drug Abuse and Alcohol Abuse: The Social Problem Perspective." *The Prosecutor,* January–February 1969.

19. Bales, R. F. "Cultural Differences in Rate of Alcoholism," in *Drinking and Intoxication,* ed. R. G. McCarthy. New York: New York Free Press, 1959.

20. Beaven, Winton. "Toward Prevention." *Report on Alcohol,* Summer 1973, pp. 3–23.

21. Berger, John, et al. "Explaining the Plain Facts of Alcohol Abuse." *Patient Care,* February 28, 1979, pp. 18–20.

22. Berne, Eric. *Games People Play.* New York: Grove Press, 1967.

23. Block, Marvin A. *Alcoholism: Its Facets and Phases.* New York: John Day Co., 1965.
——. Don't Place Alcohol on a Pedestal." *Journal of the American Medical Association,* May 10, 1976, pp. 2103–2104.

25. ——. "Latest on Overdrinking." *U.S. News and World Report,* June 15, 1964, pp. 50–54.

26. Blum, Eva Maria, and Richard H. Blum. *Alcoholism: Modern Psychological Approaches to Treatment.* San Francisco: Jossey-Bass, 1972.

27. Blum, Richard H., *et al. Society and Drugs.* San Francisco: Jossey-Bass, 1969.

28. Boswell, Bernie, and Sandy Wright. *An Environmental Modification Approach to Counseling in the Treatment of Alcoholism.* Salt Lake City: Environmental Education and Treatment Association, 1973.

29. ——. *Cottage Meeting Program: An Experimental Pilot Program in Alcohol Education.* Salt Lake City: Alcoholism Foundation, 1972.

30. Brecher, Edward M., and Editors of Consumer Reports. *Licit and Illicit Drugs.* Boston: Little, Brown and Co., 1972.

31. Brodie, H. Keith. "The Effects of Ethyl Alcohol in Man," from *Drug Use in America: Problem in Perspective—The Technical Papers of the Report of the National Commission on Marijuana and Drug Abuse.*

32. Cahalan, D. *Problem Drinkers.* San Francisco: Jossey-Bass, 1970.

33. Cahn, Sidney. *The Treatment of Alcoholics.* New York: Oxford University Press, 1970.

34. Calant, H. "The Pharmacology of Alcohol Intoxication." *Quarterly Journal of Studies on Alcohol,* Supplement No. 1, 1961.

35. California Medical Association. "Where We Stand on Drug Abuse." *California Medicine 118 (June 1973): 58–64.*

36. "Can Companies Afford to Help Alcoholic Employees?" *Report on Alcohol* 14 (Summer 1976): 28.

37. Carroll, Charles R. *Alcohol Use, Non-Use and Abuse.* Dubuque, Iowa: William C. Brown Co., 1970.

38. Caviness, Harold. "The Effects of Alcoholism on the Central Nervous System and Personality." *Report on Alcohol,* Winter 1972, 21−31.

39. Chafetz, Morris E. "Alcohol and Alcoholism." *American Scientist 67 (May*−June 1979): 293.

40. Chafetz, Morris E., Howard T. Blane, and Marjorie J. Hill, eds. *Frontiers of Alcoholism.* New York: Science House, 1970.

41. Clarren, Sterling K. "Recognition of Fetal Alcohol Syndrome." *Journal of the American Medical Association,* June 19, 1981, pp. 2436−2439.

42. *Company Controls of Drinking Problems: Studies in Personnel Policy.* Research Report No. 218 from the National Industrial Conference Board, Inc. New York, 1970.

43. "Criteria for the Diagnosis of Alcoholism." Criteria Committee of the National Council on Alcoholism. *American Journal of Psychiatry* 129:2 (August 1972): 127−135.

44. DeFoe, James R., and Warren Breed. "The Mass Media and Alcohol Education: A New Direction." *Journal of Alcohol and Drug Education,* Spring 1980, pp. 48−57.

45. *Developing Community Services for Alcoholics: Some Beginning Principles.* National Institute of Mental Health, National Institute on Alcohol Abuse and Alcoholism. DHEW Publication No. (HSM) 71-9016, 1971.

46. Dirks, Ruth Sanchez. "Reflections on Family Violence." *Alcohol Health and Research World* 1 (Fall 1979): pp. 2−16.

47. Doherty, James. "Disulfiram (Antabuse): Chemical Commitment to Abstinence." *Alcohol Health and Research World,* Spring 1976, p. 7.

48. Downdell, Pamela M. "Alcohol and Pregnancy: A Review of the Literature 1968−1980." *Nursing Times,* October 21, 1981, pp. 1825−1829.

49. "Drinking and Accidents," American Medical Association Department of Transportation, National Institute of Mental Health, National Safety Council, and U.S. Public Health Service. *School Health Review,* April 1970, pp. 33−35.

50. *Drinking and Driving.* American Medical Association, 1971.

51. *Drinking Etiquette.* U.S. Department of Health and Human Services. DHHS Publication No. (ADM) 80-305, 1980.

52. Dunkin, William S. "From the Boiler to the Boardroom—Get Booze Off the Company's Back." *Listen,* n.d., pp. 7−8.

53. Dunn, Robert B., and Allan G. Hedberg. "Treating the Two Faces of Alcoholism." *Modern Medicine,* June 10, 1974, pp. 34−40.

54. Dupont, Robert L. "The Future of Primary Prevention: Parent Power." *Journal of Drug Education* 10, no. 1 (1980): 1−5.

55. *Drug Use in America: Problem in Perspective* (Second Report). National Commission on Marijuana and Drug Abuse, 1973.

56. Edwards, Griffith, and Marcus Grant. *Alcoholism: New Knowledge and New Responses.* London: Croom Helm, 1977.

57. Englebardt, Stanley L. "Are We Teaching Our Kids to Become Alcoholics." *Families,* March 1982, pp. 30−32.

58. Engs, Ruth C. *Responsible Drug and Alcohol Use.* New York: Macmillan Publishing Co., Inc., 1979.

59. Ennis, Pamela, Michael Stern, and Bernard Boyle. "The Drinking/Driving

Dilemma," Private Practioner, April, 1977, n. p., n. d., pp. 64–75.

60. Estes, Nada J., and M. Edith Heinemann. *Alcoholism: Development, Consequences, and Intervention.* St. Louis: C. V. Mosby Company, 1977.

61. *Facts About Alcohol and Alcoholism.* Alcohol, Drug Abuse and Mental Health Administration. DHEW Publication No. (ADM) 80-31, 1980.

62. Faux, Vernelle. "The Dynamics of Alcoholism." *Journal of the Southern Medical Association* 57, no. 8 (August 1964): 914–916.

63. Fort, Joel. *Alcohol, Our Biggest Drug Problem.* Hightstown, N.J.: McGraw-Hill, 1973.

64. Free, James L. *Just One More.* Palo Alto, Cal.: Bull Publishing Co., 1977.

65. Girdano, Dorothy, and Daniel Girdano. *Drugs, A Factual Account.* Menlo Park: Addison-Wesley, 1972.

66. Goodwin, Donald W. "Is Alcoholism Hereditary?" *Archives of General Psychiatry* 25 (December 1971): 545–549.

67. Greenberg, Leon A. *Alcohol Problems Pamphlet No. 4: What the Body Does with Alcohol.* Publications Division, Rutgers Center of Alcohol Studies.

68. Groman, Vida. "Together You Can Make It Work." *Grassroots Education/ Prevention,* January 1982, pp. 1–2.

69. *Guide to Alcohol Programs for Youth.* U.S. Department of Health and Human Services, 1981.

70. Hafen, Brent. *Readings on Drug Use and Abuse.* Provo, Utah: Brigham Young University Press, 1970.

71. Hafen, Brent, and Eugene Faux. *Drug Abuse: Psychology, Sociology, Pharmacology.* Provo, Utah: Brigham Young University Press, 1973.

72. ———. *Self-Destructive Behavior: A National Crisis,* Minneapolis: Burgess Publishing Co., 1972.

73. Hafen, Brent, and Brenda Peterson. *Medicines and Drugs: Problems and Risks, Use and Abuse.* Philadelphia: Lea and Febiger, 1978.

74. Haley, Jay. *Changing Families: A Family Therapy Reader.* New York & London: Grune & Stratton, 1971, p. 127.

75. Hamburg, Marion V. "Education as a Prevention Modality for Alcohol Abuse." *Health Values: Achieving High Level Wellness,* March/April 1980, pp. 75–78.

76. Hamlin, Diane E., *et al.* "Perspectives: Family Violence." *Alcohol Health and Research World* 1 (Fall 1979): 17–22.

77. Hanson, James W., Kenneth L. Gones, and David W. Smith. "Fetal Alcohol Syndrome." *Journal of the American Medical Association* 235 (April 5, 1976): 1460.

78. Hayman, Max. "The Myth of Social Drinking." *The American Journal of Psychiatry* 124 (November 1967): 585–594.

79. *The Health Letter.* Communication Inc. 1, No. 4 (1973). Edited by Lawrence E. Lamb. San Antonio, Texas.

80. Hindman, Margaret. "Child Abuse and Neglect: The Alcohol Connection." *Alcohol Health and Research World,* Spring 1977, pp. 2–7.

81. Hindman, Margaret H. "Family Violence." *Alcohol Health and Research World* 1 (Fall 1979): 2–11.

82. Hecht, Murray. "Children of Alcoholics." *American Journal of Nursing,* October 1973, pp. 1764–1767.

83. Hoff, Ebbe Curtis. *Aspects of Alcoholism.* Philadelphia: J.B. Lippincott Company,

1963.

84. ———. "The Etiology of Alcoholism," *Quarterly Journal of Studies on Alcohol* 57, Supplement No. 1 (1961).

85. Horoshak, Irene. "Teenage Drinking: A Growing Problem or a Problem of Growing?" *RN,* March 1976, p. 67.

86. *How You Think Is How You Drink: Reasons for Drinking.* U.S. Department of Health, Education, and Welfare. DHEW Publication No. (ADM) 77-454A, 1977.

87. Hoyt, Charles N. "Alcoholism, A Review and Overview of the Problem." *The Ohio State Medical Journal,* July 1970, pp. 674–680.

88. Iber, Frank L. "In Alcoholism the Liver Sets the Pace." *Nutrition Today,* January/February 1971, pp. 2–9.

89. *It's Your Life: Personal Standards for Drinking.* U.S. Department of Health, Education, and Welfare. DHEW Publication No. (ADM) 77-454A, 1977.

90. John, Harrison W. "Alcoholism and Criminal Homicide: An Overview." *Alcohol Health and Research World,* Winter 1977/78, pp. 8-13.

91. Johnson, Raymond B., and William M. Lukash. *Medical Complications of Alcohol Abuse.* Chicago: American Medical Association, 1973.

92. Jones, Kenneth L., Louis Shainberg, and Curtis O. Byer. *Drugs and Alcohol,* 2nd ed. San Francisco: Harper and Row, 1973.

93. Keller, John E. *Alcohol. A Family Affair.* Santa Ynez, Cal.: The Kroc Foundation, 1977.

94. Keller, M. "Alcohol and Health and Disease: Some Historical Perspectives." *Annals of the New York Academy of Science* 133 (1966): 820–827.

95. Keller, Mark. "How Alcohol Affects the Body," Pamphlet No. 3 on Alcohol Problems. Rutgers Center of Alcohol Studies, 1965.

96. Kellerman, Joseph L. *Alcoholism: A Merry-Go-Round Named Denial.* Long Grove, Ill.: Kemper Insurance Group, 1970.

97. Kessel, Neil, and Henry Walton. *Alcoholism.* Baltimore: Penguin Books, 1965.

98. Kesselman, Judi R. "How Women Alcoholics Avoid Early Detection." *Practical Psychology for Physicians,* July 1976, p. 21.

99. Kissin, Benjamin, and Henri Begleiter. *The Biology of Alcoholism—Vol. 3:Clinical Pathology.* New York: Plenum Press, 1971.

100. ———. *The Biology of Alcoholism—Vol. 5: Treatment and Rehabilitation of the Chronic Alcoholic.* New York: Plenum Press, 1971.

101. Knott, David H., Mal J. Thomson, and James D. Beard. "The Forgotten Addict." *American Family Physican* 3, no. 6 (June 1970): 92–95.

102. Korcak, Milan. "Alcohol on the Job—What's Being Done." *Addictions* 22 (Winter 1975): 5.

103. Krusich, Walter S. "Alcohol and Health: A Casual or Causal Relationship." *Report: A Quarterly Bulletin Concerned with the Effects of Alcohol Consumption.* American Businessmen's Research Foundation 27, no. 1, Spring 1969.

104. *Lectures and Reports on 1973 Utah School of Alcohol Studies at the University of Utah.* Supplement Manual, 1973.

105. "Liquor May Be Quicker but. . . ." *FDA Consumer,* June 1979, pp. 8–11.

106. Lieber, Charles. "Alcohol and the Liver—A National Problem." *Gastroenterology Medical World News,* 1972, pp. 28–30.

107. ———. "Alcohol and the Liver." *Alcohol Health and Research World,* Spring 1974, pp. 26–28.

108. Mason, M. F., and K. M. Dubowski. "Alcohol, Traffic and Chemical Testing in the U.S.: A Resume and Some Remaining Problems." *Clinical Chemistry* 20, no. 2 (1974): 126–140.

109. Mayer, Jean. "Alcohol as Calories," *Preventive Medicine,* May 1970, pp. 281–282.

110. McCarthy, Raymond G. *Alcohol Education for Classroom and Community.* Heightstown, N.J.: McGraw-Hill, 1964.

111. ———. *Drinking and Intoxication.* College and University Press, 1959. College Park, Maryland.

112. Mendelson, Jack H. "Alcoholism: Some Contemporary Issues and Problems." *American Journal of Psychiatry,* June 1971, pp. 1680–1681.

113. Milgram, Gail Gleason. "Alcoholism in the Family: Implications for the School." *Grassroots Education/Prevention,* January 1982, pp. 3–5.

114. Mirkin, Gabe. "The Dynamics of Drinking." *Family Health,* July/August 1981, pp. 44, 45, 58.

115. Moskow, J. A., R. C. Pennington, and Melvin Knisely. "Alcohol Sludge and Hypoxic Areas of Nervous System, Liver, and Heart." *Microvascular Research* 1 (1968): 174–178.

116. Nicholson, Richard E. "On Hooch and Hazards—Alcoholism and Accidents in Industry." *Occupational Health Nursing* 22 (May 1974): 10–12.

117. Passe, Leslie M. "Commonly Asked Questions About Alcohol and Pregnancy." *Street Pharmacologist* 3 no. 8 (1980): 3–4.

118. Pattison, E. Mansell, Mark B. Sobel, and Linda C. Sobel. *Emerging Concepts of Alcohol Dependence.* New York: Springer Publishing Co., 1977.

119. Pawlak, Vic. "Fetal Alcohol Syndrome: New Developments." *Street Pharmacologist* 3 no. 8 (1980): 1–2.

120. Plaut, Thomas F. A. "Alcohol Problems." A Report to the Nation by the Cooperative Commission on the Study of Alcoholism. New York: Oxford University Press, 1967.

121. Powell, Joan J. "The Tragedy of Fetal Alcohol Syndrome." *RN,* December 1981, pp. 33–35, 92, 94, 96.

122. *Problem Drinking.* Report to the Task Force on Alcohol Problems. National Council of the Churches of Christ in the U.S.A.

123. *Proceedings of the Joint Conference on Alcohol Abuse and Alcoholism.* National Institute of Mental Health, National Institute on Alcohol Abuse and Alcoholism. Publication No. (HSM) 73-9051, 1972.

124. Rada, Richard T. "Alcoholism and Forcible Rape," paper read at the annual meeting of the American Psychiatric Association in Detroit, Mich. 1974.

125. Ray, Oakley. *Drugs, Society and Human Behavior.* St. Louis: C. V. Mosby Co., 1972.

126. Regan, Timothy. "Cardiac Toxicity of Ethyl Alcohol." *Alcohol Health and Research World,* Winter 1973/74, pp. 23–28.

127. *Report on Alcohol.* American Businessmen's Research Foundation, 32, no. 4 (Winter 1974).

128. *Report to the President and Congress on Health Hazards Associated with Alcohol and Methods to Inform the General Public of These Hazards.* U.S. Department of the Treasury and U.S. Department of Health and Human Services, November 1980.

129. "Resources to Help Your Alcoholic Patient." *Drug Therapy,* January 1978, p. 111.

130. Rouse, Kenneth A. "Detour—Alcoholism Ahead." Kemper Insurance Company booklet, 1972.

131. Royce, James E. *Alcohol Problems and Alcoholism: A Comprehensive Survey.* New York: The Free Press, 1981.

132. Rubin, Emmanuel, and Charles S. Lieber. "Alcohol, Alcoholism and Drugs." *Science* 172 (June 11, 1971): 1097, 1102.

133. Sandmaier, Marian. *Alcohol Abuse and Women: A Guide to Getting Help.* National Institute on Alcohol Abuse and Alcoholism, DHS Publication No. (ADM) 80-385, 1980.

134. Satir, Virginia. *Conjoint Family Therapy.* Palo Alto, Cal.: Science & Behavior Books, Inc., 1967.

135. Schmidt, Wolfgang, and Jan D. E. Lint. "The Mortality of Alcoholic People." *Alcohol Health and Research World,* Summer 1973, pp. 16–20.

136. Seixas, Frank A. "Spotting the Female Alcoholic." *The Female Patient,* February 1976, p. 51.

137. Shaywitz, Bennett A. "Fetal Alcohol Syndrome: An Ancient Problem Rediscovered." *Drug Therapy,* January 1978, p. 107.

138. Siegler, Miriam, Humphrey Osmond, and Stephens Newell. "Models of Alcoholism." *Quarterly Journal of Alcohol Studies* 29 (1968): 571–591.

139. Smith, Jackson A. "Psychiatric Treatment of the Alcoholic." *Journal of the American Medical Association* 163 (1957).

140. *Someone Close Drinks Too Much.* Alcohol, Drug Abuse and Mental Health Administration. DHEW Publication No. (ADM) 74-23, 1974.

141. Speck, Ross, and Carolyn Attneave. *Family Networks.* New York: Pantheon Books, 1973.

142. Steiner, Claude. *Games Alcoholics Play: The Analysis of Life Scripts.* New York: Grove Press, 1971.

143. Straus, Robert, ed. "Alcohol and Society." *Psychiatric Annals* 3, no. 10 (October 1973).

144. Streissguth, Ann P. "Maternal Drinking and the Outcome of Pregnancy: Implications for Child Mental Health." *Grassroots,* September 1978 Supplement, p. 30.

145. *Suicide, Homicide, and Alcoholism Among American Indians: Guidelines for Help.* The National Institute of Mental Health, Division of Special Mental Health Programs. DHEW Publication No. (HSM) 73-9124, 1973.

146. *Tailoring Alcoholism Therapy to Client Needs.* U.S. Department of Health and Human Services, 1981.

147. *Task Force Report on Drunkenness.* Task Force on Drunkenness, The President's Commission on Law Enforcement and Administration of Justice, 1967.

148. Teger, A., E. Katkin, and D. Pruitt. "Effects of Alcoholic Beverages and Their Congener Content on Level and Style of Risk Taking." *Journal of Personality and Social Psychology* 11, no. 2 (February 1969): 170–176.

149. Tharp, Roland G., and Ralph J. Wetzel. *Behavior Modification in the Natural Environment.* New York: Academic Press, 1969.

150. *The Community Health Nurse and Alcohol Related Problems.* U.S. Department of Health, Education, and Welfare, 1980.

151. "The Role of Alcohol, Narcotics, Dangerous Drugs in Individual Violence." National Commission on the Causes and Prevention of Violence. *Crimes of Violence* 12 (December 1969).

152. *To Your Health: The Effects of Alcohol on Body Functions.* U.S. Department of Health, Education and Welfare. DHEW Publication No. (ADM) 77-454A, 1977.
153. Toutant, Claire, and Steven Lippmann. "Fetal Alcohol Syndrome." *American Family Physician,* July 1980, pp. 113–117.
154. Trice, Harrison M. *Alcoholism in America.* Hightstown, N.J.: McGraw-Hill, 1966.
155. Victor, Maurice. "Managing Alcoholism." *Drug Therapy,* July 1973, pp. 57–68.
156. Vincent, M. O. "Changing Concepts of Alcoholism." *Report on Alcohol.* Elmhurst, Ill.: American Businessmen's Association, Summer 1974.
157. Voldeng, Karle. *Recovery From Alcoholism.* Chicago: Henry Tegnery Co., 1962.
158. Young, Alex W., Jr. "Cutaneous Stigmata of Alcoholism." *Alcohol Health and World Research,* Summer 1974, p. 24.
159. Wegscheider, Sharon. *Another Chance: Hope and Health for the Alcoholic Family.* Palo Alto, Cal.: Science and Behavior Books, Inc., 1981.
160. Witti, Fritz. "Alcohol and Birth Defects." *FDA Consumer,* May 1973, p. 20.

# Index

sensitivity changes, 85
super-additive (synergistic or potentiating), 63, 85
intolerance to alcohol, drugs producing, 91
marijuana, 91, 96
medical use, drugs in, 83-84
morphine, 91, 93
opiates, 91, 93
prescribed psychoactive drugs and alcohol compared, 3
public misconceptions about alcohol as a drug, 3
response, factors determining
age, 86
body weight and size, 86
health, 87
nutritional state, 87
psychological, 87
sex, 86
stimulants, 89-90, 96
tranquillizers
major, 89
minor, 88-89, 97-98
benzodiazepines, 88, 97
meprobamate, 88, 98

**E**

Education, Alcohol
availability of information, 247
community and, 238-242
dangers, making public aware of, 250
dissemination of well-founded facts, 250
doctors, of, 250
driver and, 237-238
family and, 232-234
helping professions, people in, 250
individual and environment, 241
law enforcement personnel, of 250
schools, need for expansion of educational resources for professions in, 247
skilled people and facilities, providing, 249
teachers, of, 250
Egypt
temperance tract, ancient, 2
Elderly, 171-173
Emergencies, Alcohol
generally, 265-271
emergency care, 266-269

general care, 269-271
Emotional Experience
motivation for drinking, 8-9
Emotions
effects of alcohol on, 46
Enabler (Rescuer), 149, 162, 163
Environment
alcohol and, 242-244
consequences of drinking, modifying, 244
cultural moves, influencing, 244
insulating drinking behavior, 243-244
national drinking environment, proposals for creation of, 246-249
reactions to drinking behavior, changing, 244
settings, modification of drinking, 242-243
Eskimos
effect of metabolism rate on sobering-up, 41
Esophagus
effects of alcohol on, 51
Exercise
effect (lack of) on oxidation of alcohol, 33
Experiential Experience
motivation for drinking, 9-10

**F**

Falls, 72
Family
abuse and alcohol, 75-77
adjustment, 152-153
alcohol education and, 232-234
chances of recovery, 157
child-parent identification pattern, 149
do's and don'ts, 154-156
drinking behavior in, 157-158
effective living skills, chart on, 165
family intervention technique, 158-168
guiding the problem drinker to treatment, 153-154
interpersonal system of treatment for alcoholism, 210-212
learning about problem drinking, 150-152
problem drinking and, 146-168
stages in family's experience with alcoholism
chaos, 162,164
control, 162,164
denial, 162, 164
home treatment, 162, 164
supporting the problem drinker, 156-157

†